THE SOCIOLOGY OF RELIGION

THE SOCIOLOGY
OF RELIGION

Max Weber

Introduction by Talcott Parsons

With a new Foreword by Ann Swidler

BEACON PRESS   BOSTON

Beacon Press
25 Beacon Street
Boston, Massachusetts 02108–2892

Beacon Press books
are published under the auspices of
the Unitarian Universalist Association of Congregations

First published in Germany in 1922 by J. C. B. Mohr (Paul
Siebeck) under the title "Religionssoziologie," from *Wirtschaft
und Gesellschaft*.

Copyright © 1922 by J. C. B. Mohr (Paul Siebeck)

Fourth edition, revised by Johannes Winckelmann,
copyright © 1956 by J. C. B. Mohr (Paul Siebeck)

English translation (from the fourth edition) by Ephraim
Fischoff
copyright © 1963, 1991 by Beacon Press
First published as a Beacon Paperback in 1964
Foreword copyright © 1993 by Beacon Press

99 98 97 96 95   8 7 6 5 4 3 2

Library of Congress Cataloging-in-Publication Data

Weber, Max, 1864–1920.
    [Religionssoziologie. English]
    The sociology of religion / Max Weber; introduction by
Talcott Parsons with a new foreword by Ann Swidler.
      p. cm.
    Includes bibliographical references and index.
    ISBN 0-8070-4205-6
    1. Religion and sociology.   I. Title.
BL60.W43313   1993
306.6—dc20   92–38884
                                         CIP

Contents

The original this-worldly orientation of religiously or magically motivated action by the community. The belief in spirits. The rise of belief in "supernatural" powers. Naturalism and symbolism. The realm of the gods and functional gods. The ancestral cult and the domestic priesthood.

The gods of political associations and of localities. Monotheism and the religion of everyday life. Universalism and monotheism. Coercion of gods, magic, and divine worship. Magicians and priests.

Ethical divinities and gods of legislation. Impersonal powers above the gods. Order as a divine creation. The sociological significance of taboo norms. Totemism. The operation of taboos, community formation, and stereotyping. Magical ethics and religious ethics. The consciousness of sin and the idea of salvation.

Contents

Foreword

by Ann Swidler

Max Weber's *The Sociology of Religion* has provided an inexhaustible resource for students of religion. Major contemporary scholars, such as Robert Bellah and Clifford Geertz, have returned to Weber's work again and again for theoretical inspiration.[1] Others in the social sciences, however, have sometimes neglected *The Sociology of Religion* in attempting to cast Weber as a sociologist of conflict, class, and domination.[2] Yet even for those interested

---

[1] The Weberian influence is particularly evident in Robert N. Bellah, *Tokugawa Religion* (Boston: Beacon Press, 1957) and the generative essay "Religious Evolution" (*American Sociological Review* 29 [June], pp. 358–374), but it can be seen throughout Bellah's work in his concern with how symbolic realities acquire leverage over human action. Clifford Geertz's engagement with Weber pervades his work, but the theoretical links are clearest in *The Religion of Java* (Glencoe, Ill.: Free Press, 1960), which focuses on the relationship between religious ideas and economic action, and in the foundational essay, "Religion as a Cultural System" (pp. 87–125 in *The Interpretation of Cultures* [New York: Basic Books, 1983]) with its emphasis on the problems of suffering and injustice as major sources of religious creativity. Geertz has also returned repeatedly to the problem of rationalization in non-Western religions, as in *Islam Observed* (New Haven: Yale University Press, 1968) and many of the essays in *The Interpretation of Cultures*.

[2] The history of Weber's reception in the United States is a complex one. In brief overview, Weber was introduced to American sociologists by Talcott Parsons and his students as a sociologist of culture, with emphasis on the "idealist" strain in Weber's work. Parsons published his translation of Weber's *The Protestant Ethic and the Spirit of Capitalism* in 1930 (London: George Allen & Unwin) and his interpretation of Weber in *The Structure of Social Action* in 1937 (New York: McGraw-Hill). In 1946, Hans H. Gerth and C. Wright Mills published *From Max Weber* (New York: Oxford University Press), offering a broad selection from Weber's work including essays on

in Weber's political and economic sociologies, *The Sociology of Religion* is the key work that unlocks Weber's larger theoretical achievement. And now, with the resurgence of cultural studies, *The Sociology of Religion* takes on added importance. Sociologists of culture often bemoan the difficulty of simultaneously studying cultural meanings and cultural producers. This book is an unparalleled analysis of how cultural meanings reflect and refract the organizational interests of those who create, maintain, and disseminate culture. It also provides the fullest theory we have of how ideas shape human action.

The Sociology of Religion demonstrates, better than any other of his works, Weber's brilliance as a historical analyst—exemplifying not only the substance but the distinctive method of his historical approach. In *The Sociology of Religion*, the daunting, sometimes cumbersome theoretical apparatus laid out in other portions of Weber's *Economy and Society*—definitions and typologies, lists and explications of concepts—comes to life, revealing the dynamic thrust of his ideas.

Virtually from its first line, *The Sociology of Religion* develops a powerful theory of religious change. Weber's theoretical starting point is deceptively simple: people pursue their interests. But among the weapons people use in their struggles are ideas. Weber's studies of such diverse matters as status-group conflict, types of legitimate domination, and legal codes show how ideas, created to serve group interests, come to define the very world within which interests can be formulated.

Weber begins *The Sociology of Religion* by asking how it is

---

class, domination, and authority. Reinhard Bendix (*Max Weber: An Intellectual Portrait* [Garden City, N.Y.: Doubleday, 1962]) and his students carried on the Weberian project of comparative-historical sociology. Randall Collins, in particular, appropriated Weber as a theorist of social conflict (see *Conflict Sociology* [New York: Academic Press, 1975] and *Weberian Sociological Theory* [New York: Cambridge University Press, 1986] among many other works). Anthony Giddens dealt extensively with Weber's theory of class (*The Class Structure of the Advanced Societies* [New York: Harper and Row, 1973]). The conflict between Parsonian sociology, on the one hand, and Marxist and conflict perspectives, on the other, has cast Weber either as an idealist (based on simplified readings of *The Protestant Ethic*) or as a theorist of conflict and domination. Few commentators, however, have appreciated how centrally Weber's sociology of domination depends on his sociology of ideas.

that religious meanings ever come to matter to human beings, given that pressing material concerns invariably dominate most of life. In Weber's view, the answer is a historical one. Individual men and women, seeking to survive and prosper, originally come to accept help from magicians and others who claim extraordinary powers. For Weber, in direct contrast to Emile Durkheim, magic is the "elementary form" of religion. And magic is practical action aimed at achieving earthly benefits. But when the magician invokes special powers—which Weber terms "charisma"—he accounts for those powers by claiming that spirits or other beings are "concealed 'behind' and responsible for the activity of the charismatically endowed natural objects, artifacts, animals, or persons" (p. 3). Continuing encounters between magicians and their clients lead to a "process of abstraction" in which magicians give symbolic form to their claims to extraordinary powers, finally creating a new realm of experience: "Before, only the things or events that actually exist or take place played a role in life; now certain experiences, of a different order in that they only signify something, also play a role in life. Magic is transformed from a direct manipulation of forces into a symbolic activity" (p. 6).

The common view of Weber as an "idealist" who believes that ideas are the major influence on human action misses what is most original in Weber's work. Weber does not argue that ideas always or necessarily influence action. Instead, he tries to understand *variation* in the influence of ideas on action. Weber builds a powerful theory to explain why some kinds of cultural systems have much more influence on economic and political action than others do. He analyzes the critical historical contingencies that determine whether and how ideas guide action. And at each historical juncture, real human beings, acting on their interests as they understand them, are the focus of Weber's theoretical concern.

One attribute that gives ideas power is comprehensiveness— how much of the world they explain and how little they leave to chance. Weber explores how religious practitioners come to develop comprehensive belief systems. Magicians are solo practitioners vulnerable to day-to-day fluctuations in demand for their services. Through cult associations, however, they elaborate theories of the powers they represent and create an ongoing enterprise with a more regular demand for their services. Priests, in turn, develop conceptions of powerful, universal gods whose adherents are obligated to remain loyal to them and to support their priests. Thus the development of religious imagery is driven by a logic of interests, expressed in and eventually constrained by ideas.

To understand how religious ideas develop, Weber analyzes the typical motives of different religious actors. Laypersons seek promises of immediate relief from suffering and guarantees of ultimate salvation; priests strive for orderly obedience while trying to sublimate lay demands for miraculous cures and sure victories; prophets break through priestly routines to reawaken unfulfilled spiritual needs and restore religious vitality. The interaction of these competing religious interests pushes religions to order, unify, and deepen their religious understandings.

For Weber, interests are always at work in shaping the development of religion. But, as Weber's famous "switchman" metaphor so beautifully articulates, ideas in turn shape what people's interests are: "Not ideas, but material and ideal interests, directly govern men's conduct. Yet very frequently the 'world images' that have been created by 'ideas' have, like switchmen, determined the tracks along which action has been pushed by the dynamic of interest."[3]

WEBER'S HISTORICAL METHOD

Weber's apparently simple model of the relation of ideas and interests is the key to the enormously sophisticated analytic technique that underlies his historical sociology. Weber can sometimes sound like a complex, subtle but relentlessly materialist or reductionist theorist. He suggests, for example, that certain classes and social strata prefer particular religious imageries: peasants, subject to an irrational nature, seldom become carriers of salvation religions; warrior nobilities resist religious demands which interfere with their sense of status honor; urban middle classes develop rational salvation religions which link rewards and merit. The interests of rulers and dominant classes, and even such historical "accidents" as defeats in battle (which led the ancient Jews, for example, to

---

[3] Max Weber, "The Social Psychology of the World Religions," in Gerth and Mills, *From Max Weber*, p. 280.

make a covenant with a foreign god), can have great consequence for the development of religious ideas.

Weber's method of historical analysis employs these disparate causal factors in two distinct ways, which may be thought of as governing different phases of religious development. In the early formative period of a religion's development, diverse interests and historical accidents affect the religion's conception of the divine and its promise of salvation. But, Weber argues, once a religion is sufficiently "rationalized"—that is, systematized and unified—its core religious ideas come to have a logic of their own. Weber's great typologies—inner-worldly versus other-worldly ends of salvation and ascetic versus mystical paths to salvation—operate during the second phase, once a religion's promises have been unified and rationalized into a full religion of salvation.

Once consolidated, religious ideas become a powerful independent influence on further religious development. A god conceived (perhaps under the influence of a warrior caste) as an impersonal determiner of human fates will suggest an image of salvation as "other-worldly" escape from the desires and decay of earthly life. A personal god, adopted to ensure collective success in war, may suggest an "inner-worldly" image of salvation as the reward for those who obey god. Once established, these religious promises are shaped by priests and prophets, rulers, dominant classes, and laities. But now these actors must contend with a particular religious conception of the world. The myriad forces of group interest are still at work, but their causal significance has changed. Now these forces act not directly, but indirectly, to stimulate, impede, or reorient rationalization of the fundamental religious message. Rather than describing a concatenation of discrete causal factors, Weber's approach allows the historical analyst to focus on how the varied forces of group interest bring forth, blunt, or redirect a religion's core message.

Weber was trying to solve the central methodological problem of historical sociology: how to use general causal theory to account for unique historical outcomes. Weber's solution was a brilliant one. He developed broad historical generalizations, like those about the religious affinities of social groups or the typical rationalizing strategies of prophets versus priests. But then, Weber cross-cut his general causal claims with culturally grounded typologies, like those of inner-worldly and other-worldly salvation or the three possible "rational" solutions to the problems of suffering and evil. Rather than seeing history as pure contingency, Weber used "ideal type" delineations of the inner logic of particular meaning systems to anchor and focus his historical analysis. He did not argue that the inner logic of ideas drove history; but he did show that one could better understand the role of such historical factors as rulers' interests, status group conflicts, and popular religious aspirations by examining how they influenced which of several typical paths religious ideas took and how far or fast they moved along that path.

RATIONALITY AND RATIONALIZATION

Rationalization is the central and most enticing, but also most problematic, of Weber's concepts. Weber dealt with rationality in three quite different senses.[4] He was most often concerned with "rationalization," the process of ordering and unifying systems of ideas, which could and did take place in all cultural traditions. People could rationalize magical practices, rituals, and techniques of meditation as well as images of the divine. While the underlying pressure for rationalization derives from tendencies toward order in human thought, Weber was interested in the practical and political circumstances that could advance or retard rationalization. For example, religious specialists tend to rationalize ideas and practices when they are organized in independent religious communities, while the impulse toward rationalization dissipates where religious specialists are dependent on political leaders or fully integrated with the laities they serve.

Rationalization, for Weber, is very different both from practical "rationalism," which is a universal feature of the human quest for pragmatic mastery of the ordinary contingencies of life, and from the unique (and on many counts irrational) culture of Western "rationality," which attempts to order all of life according to a unified set of meanings. In stark contrast to practical rationalism,

---

[4] For a fuller treatment of this argument, see Ann Swidler, "The Concept of Rationality in the Work of Max Weber," *Sociological Inquiry* 43 (Spring 1973), pp. 35–42.

there is nothing natural about Western rationality which indeed involves the repression of many natural human feelings and aspirations, including, in the case of "rational capitalism," the "restraint, or at least the rational tempering," of the human drive toward acquisition.[5]

Although a unique historical trajectory produced modern Western rationality, rationalization occurs throughout human history. It is a powerful source of religious change. Rationalization increases the inner coherence of religious beliefs and thereby creates new, distinctively religious dilemmas. If a religion proclaims that an all-powerful god created and controls the world, the very existence of suffering and evil becomes problematic. Before, believers could come to their priests seeking relief from suffering or promises of a better life in the world to come. But told that a unified power governs the world, they ask why a just god permits evil to flourish. Their unmerited suffering becomes a *religious* problem in the sense that it challenges the fundamental claims of the religious world view. This is the deep significance of religious rationalization in Weber's work. The more rationalized a religious world view, the deeper and more pressing the contradictions it creates, and the stronger the impulse for religious innovation.

If rationalization is the central and the most theoretically troublesome of Weber's concepts, only in *The Sociology of Religion* does the full force of the concept become apparent. For Weber, rationalization gives ideas their power, because rationalization intensifies and deepens the meaning of inherently non-rational, and ultimately *non-rationalizable*, aspects of human experience. Precisely because injustice and evil are incomprehensible in a universe created by an all-powerful, just, and merciful god, they generate continuing religious creativity: the story of Job, the doctrine of "original sin," the debates between Luther and Erasmus over free will, and Calvin's doctrine of predestination are all attempts to answer the intractable problems given force by religious rationalization.

For Weber, the non-rational animates human life, but rationalization focuses and directs the power of the non-rational. We can see

[5] Max Weber, *The Protestant Ethic and the Spirit of Capitalism* (New York: Charles Scribner's Sons, 1958), p. 20.

the importance Weber attributes to the ultimately non-rationalizable aspects of human experience in his remarkable study of Western music. Rationalization of the Western tonal system, Weber argues, left the dominant seventh chord with "irrational properties," which no system of chordal rationalization could overcome. But these "rebels" and the "contradications" they create make possible the beauty of modern music. Weber writes, "Without the tensions motivated by the irrationality of melody, no modern music could exist." It is "an elemental fact of music, that chordal rationalization lives only in continuous tension with melodicism which it can never completely devour." The tension between rationalization and what is non-rationalizable creates the possibility of beauty in music.[6]

It is not only music that flourishes where rationalization meets the irremediably non-rational. For Weber, religious attempts to find coherent terms in which to confront the inherent irrationality of life utimately generate those moments, such as the rise of Calvinism, in which religion can have world-transforming significance. The Calvinist doctrine of predestination (which, along with the doctrine of Karma and Zoroastrian dualism, Weber calls one of only three "rationally satisfactory answers to the questioning for the basis of the incongruity between destiny and merit"[7]) had such powerful effects precisely because it confronted passionate non-rational motives—the believer's quest for knowledge of salvation. Rather than accepting that one's fate as either saved or damned was foreordained and unknowable, Calvinists developed the doctrine of "proof." They were motivated systematically to order every aspect of daily life, and to work in a calling, so that they might see proof of salvation in their conduct.[8] Religion thus affects action most forcefully when the tension between non-rational motives and a powerful rationalizing

[6] Max Weber, *The Rational and Social Foundations of Music* (Carbondale: Southern Illinois University Press, 1958), pp. 6, 10.
[7] Weber, "The Social Psychology of the World Religions," p. 275.
[8] In a famous footnote to *The Protestant Ethic and the Spirit of Capitalism* (p. 232), Weber notes that the doctrine of "proof" is a great testimony to the role of non-rational motives in religious development. "The Calvinistic faith is one of the many examples in the history of religions of the relation between the logical and the psychological consequences for the practical religious attitude to be derived from certain religious ideas. Fatalism is, of course, the only logical consequence of predestination. But on account of the idea of proof the psychological result was precisely the opposite."

impulse is at its height. A fully closed, rational system would be devoid of meaning, while non-rationalized religions have little leverage over human conduct.

Weber's *Sociology of Religion* is a systematic analysis of the historical factors that have sometimes focused the power of the non-rational, concentrating its rays and thus igniting transformations of social action. In our current historical era, when fruitful tension between rationalization and the irreducibly non-rational in human experience is increasingly difficult to maintain, Weber's analytic stance and his moral vision are ever more valuable.

Translator's Preface

Here is presented to the reader of English a unique work (or more correctly a portion of a work, as will be explained presently) by the most eminent sociologist of recent times. Many of Weber's works have become available in English during the generation since Frank H. Knight translated *Wirtschaftsgeschichte* (*General Economic History*) in 1927. That first English translation of a Weber work was followed by Talcott Parsons' translation of Weber's most famous essay, *Die protestantische Ethik und der Geist des Kapitalismus* (*The Protestant Ethic and the Spirit of Capitalism*) in 1930. Since then a large body of Weber's works have been translated into English, including all of the essays or monographs collected in Weber's *Gesammelte Aufsätze zur Religionssoziologie.*[1] But until now there has been no English language version of the important treatise on the sociology of religion entitled *Religionssoziologie* (*The Sociology of Religion*), of mono-

[1] This posthumous collection of Weber's studies of particular religions and sundry problems in comparative religion, entitled "Collected Essays in the Sociology of Religion," has now been translated into English in its entirety. The collection consists of three lengthy volumes in German. Since Parsons' translation of *The Protestant Ethic and the Spirit of Capitalism,* a section of Volume I in the German, the remainder of Volume I has been translated into English: the Weber anthology compiled by Hans H. Gerth and C. Wright Mills, *From Max Weber: Essays in Sociology,* 1946, presented translations of three essays drawn from Volume I, namely: "Die protestantischen Sekten und der Geist des Kapitalismus" ("The Protestant Sects and the Spirit of Capitalism"), "Die Wirtschaftsethik der Weltreligionen" ("The Social Psychology of the World Religions"), and "Zwischenbetrachtung" ("Religious Rejections of the World"); and the remainder of Volume I was translated separately by Hans H. Gerth as "The Religion of China: Confucianism and Taoism," 1951. Volume II, dealing with the religions of India, was translated by Hans H. Gerth and Don Martindale as *The Hindu Social System,* 1950. Volume III was translated by Hans H. Gerth and Don Martindale as *Ancient Judaism,* 1952.

graph length, which forms part of his vast systematization of the social sciences, *Wirtschaft und Gesellschaft* (*Economics and Society*).

Weber not only coined the term "Religionssoziologie" for the social analysis approach to Christian and non-Christian religions, as Joachim Wach pointed out, but also Weber, with his friends Ernst Troeltsch and Werner Sombart, actually created the discipline of the sociology of religion. Of these three founders of the sociology of religion, Weber has received by far the greatest praise for his logic, his systematization, his fabulous erudition, and the brilliance, lucidity, and energy of his thinking. Toward the end of his life, Weber embarked upon the writing of a systematic summary of the sociology of religion, the work here translated into English, not as an independent undertaking but as a part of his massive but never completed *Wirtschaft und Gesellschaft*. The monographic section devoted to the sociology of religion has not previously been translated into English, despite its undeniable importance and stimulus, because of various untoward circumstances.

To a far greater degree than Weber's famous Protestant essay, which experienced peculiar vicissitudes after it left the author's hand, in that its intention has often been misconstrued,[2] his major work *Wirtschaft und Gesellschaft* has been bedeviled by various mischances, even in regard to the very state of the text. Here is a work of great importance and difficulty, left unfinished by the author's sudden death, the initial section of which was prepared for publication years after the main portion of the text, thereby creating certain theoretical problems caused by the juxtaposition of divergent perspectives. Moreover, the text, which was published posthumously by dint of the widow's great drive and dedication, underwent displacements that garbled the intention of the author, as Johannes F. Winckelmann, of whom we shall speak later, has

---

[2] Cf. Ephraim Fischoff, "The Protestant Ethic and the Spirit of Capitalism: The History of a Controversy," *Social Research*. February 1944, Vol. II, pp. 53-77; now in Robert W. Green, ed. *Protestantism and Capitalism: The Weber Thesis* (Problems in European Civilization) Heath, 1959, pp. 107-114. For another interpretation of Weber's intention in his work on the Protestant ethic, see the comments of Hans H. Gerth and C. Wright Mills in *From Max Weber: Essays in Sociology*, p. 447, chap. III, note 20.

now demonstrated on internal and other evidence. Even in Germany the imperfect state of the text and its difficulty have prevented *Wirtschaft und Gesellschaft* from exerting the influence a work of its scope might have been expected to exert—as witness the assertion of Carl Schmitt regarding the total lack of influence among legal scholars of that portion of the grand treatise dealing with the sociology of law. Finally, the fate of Weber's final system of sociology, in regard to English translation, has been less than fortunate because of piecemeal translation. For this great work has been rent into segments[3] and even now, after the appearance of the present volume, some sections of the huge treatise will remain

[3] Four translations of portions of this work have appeared thus far. They are: (1) *From Max Weber: Essays in Sociology,* translated and edited by Hans H. Gerth and C. Wright Mills. Included in this book, together with pieces from other works of Weber, are the following selections from the 1925 edition of *Wirtschaft und Gesellschaft:* in *Max Weber: Essays in Sociology,* chapters VI (pp. 159-179), VII (pp. 180-195), VIII (pp. 196-240), IX (pp. 245-252), and X (pp. 253-266) are based on *Wirtschaft und Gesellschaft,* Part III, chapters 3 (pp. 619-630), 4 (pp. 631-640), 6 (pp. 650-667), 9 (pp. 753-757), and 5 (pp. 642-649), respectively. (2) Talcott Parsons and A. M. Henderson, *Max Weber: The Theory of Social and Economic Organization,* translated by A. M. Henderson and Talcott Parsons, with an introduction and annotations by T. Parsons, 1947, 2nd ed., 1950. This translation is based on Part I of the 1925 edition of *Wirtschaft und Gesellschaft* (pp. 1-180). (3) *Max Weber: On Law and Economy in Society,* translated by Edward Shils and Max Rheinstein; with introduction and notes by Max Rheinstein (20th Century Legal Philosophy Series: Vol. VI), 1954. This translation, also based on the 1925 edition, includes the following segments of *Wirtschaft und Gesellschaft* (the page references to the German text are to the 1956 edition): the fundamental sociological categories, pp. 1-20; selections on the economic system and the normative system, pp. 181-198; and the entire section on the sociology of law, pp. 382-575, but with some excisions. (4) Max Weber, *The Rational and Social Foundations of Music* (*Die rationalen und soziologischen Grundlagen der Musik, Wirtschaft und Gesellschaft,* 2nd ed., pp. 818-869; and 4th edition pp. 877-928), translated and edited by Don Martindale, Johannes Riedel and Gertrude Neuwirth.

It may be apposite to note other works by American scholars containing selections from the corpus of Weberian writings: *Max Weber, On the Methodology of the Social Sciences,* translated and edited by Edward A. Shils and Henry A. Finch, with a foreword by Edward A. Shils, 1949; Reinhold Bendix, *Max Weber, An Intellectual Portrait,* 1960; *The City,* translated and edited by Don Martindale and Gertrude Neuwirth, 1958; and *The Three Types of Legitimate Rule,* translated by H. H. Gerth, 1958, in Berkeley Publications in Society and Institutions, Vol. IV, No. 1 (1958).

untranslated. A detailed analysis of the background and fate of Weber's *magnum opus,* of which the present translation is a segment, self-contained and therefore suitable for separate publication notwithstanding its integral relation to the totality, will be given in Appendix II to this edition. At this point it will suffice to note that many of the aforementioned imperfections in the text of *Wirtschaft und Gesellschaft* have recently been corrected in good measure by the diligent labors of Johannes F. Winckelmann, now the curator of the Max Weber Archiv of the Soziologisches Institut at the University of Munich. Winckelmann's new (fourth) edition of Weber's sociological treatise is the basis of the present translation.

In the new edition of *Wirtschaft und Gesellschaft,* the "Religionssoziologie" section appears toward the end of the first volume, in the second part dealing with economics and social institutions and forces. The monographic chapter on the sociology of religion is preceded by one dealing with types of communital and societal institutions and their relations to the economy, and another expounding ethnic relations and institutions. The opening portion of *Wirtschaft und Gesellschaft* sets forth the basic categories of sociology in chapters entitled: "Fundamental Concepts of Sociology" and "Fundamental Sociological Categories of Economic Activity." This initial segment of *Wirtschaft und Gesellschaft* constitutes an extensive methodological and conceptual analysis of great abstraction and challenge, which is followed by systematic analysis of the major areas of social activity: economic, political, religious, and esthetic. Always present in the analysis is a keen consciousness of the respective methods appropriate to the aims and subjects of the social sciences. The entire *Wirtschaft und Gesellschaft* compressed a vast range of historical and sociological data into a typology, a system of concepts—one which gave and still gives witness to Weber's uncommon range of learning, concern with methodological refinement, and skill in descriptive analysis.

The "Religionssoziologie" chapter bears the subtitle "Typen der religiösen Vergemeinschaftung" ("Types of Religious Association"); this suggests the definition of the situation for Weber as a sociologist, oriented to the social causes and influences as well as the social effects and interrelations of religion upon group life. To some extent this monograph, which abstracts and summarizes a vast range of factual data upon which Weber had been working for almost a generation, presupposes all the material which Weber had been studying since the publication of his first essay in the sociology of religion, *The Protestant Ethic and the Spirit of Capitalism*, the one that brought him international repute and became a stimulus to his comparative studies of culture. Hence in a thorough reading of "Religionssoziologie" one must bear in mind both Weber's earlier descriptive books on the major religions of the world and Weber's other chapters or monographic treatises in *Wirtschaft und Gesellschaft*, especially those concerned with charismatic authority and the forms of domination.[4]

Weber's rich empirical studies of the world's great historical religions were controlled by his focal interest in the religious influences upon modern capitalism and by the far more comprehensive question as to religious influences upon the evolution of occidental rationalism in general. It can be argued that this truly sociological perspective is broader than the reductionist economic focus of Marx's and the reductionist positivistic focus of Comte's studies of history. Even Weber's associates in the founding of German theoretical sociology, Ferdinand Tönnies and Georg Simmel, did not rival Weber for scope of purely sociological perspective. The almost miraculous richness of "Religionssoziologie" could be produced only by Weber's extraordinary combination of erudition in the social sciences, disinterested and impartial observation, and poignant yet scientifically cautious nostalgia toward religious phenomena of the past.

Too often, even generally, the study of religion has fallen into the hands of professional and specialized religionists, who are apt to lack both the scientific detachment and the sociological perspective necessary to the analytical treatment of this human activity. Rare indeed are those religious specialists in the history and phenomenology of religion, such as Franz Overbeck, who have endeavored to penetrate religious phenomenology though remaining religiously detached. On the other hand, the rationalistic, scientistic, materialistic, and even operational biases of many mod-

---

[4] See especially: Max Weber, *The Theory of Social and Economic Organization*, translated by Talcott Parsons, 1947.

ern social scientists insulate them from a subjective appreciation of the formative role of religious phenomena in cultural evolution. But in Weber's treatment of religion we find combined some of the universality of Burckhardt's *Weltgeschichtliche Betrachtungen* (without the vagaries of Spengler and Toynbee); the existential perceptivity required of those coming after Nietzsche, Marx, Dilthey, and Freud; and a superb penchant for the architectonic construction of sociological categories. National and chronological factors as well as personal gifts contributed to Weber's preparedness for the study of religion. His resulting work is unusually stimulating, despite its lacunae and its formal imperfections. The treatments of legal and political sociology, institutional economics, and the sociology of music contained in *Wirtschaft und Gesellschaft* are comparable in insightfulness to the treatment of the sociology of religion here translated, the whole inchoate and sprawling tome constituting the most erudite and penetrating achievement of modern social science.

Weber's "Religionssoziologie," herewith presented in English translation, holds unusual interest for us, notwithstanding its incompleteness, as the final formulation of his sociology of religion. Indeed, the entire fundamental work *Wirtschaft und Gesellschaft* continues to be held in greatest esteem. Throughout, the hand of the master is evident in the ordering of immense masses of scholarly material from various disciplines, according to unique world historical perspectives.

Even in its incomplete state, the massiveness and scope of Weber's posthumous manual of sociology clearly stamp it as a monument of intellectual power. As the unfinished biography of Schleiermacher by Wilhelm Dilthey is possibly one of the greatest German biographies, so this treatise is one of the most comprehensive and powerful works of scholarship in the social sciences. It is certainly the most impressive work of sociology in German during the twentieth century and has few compeers elsewhere. It unites formidable erudition in all the social sciences with theoretical conceptualization of a high order, impressive even among German sociologists, whose metaphysical orientation preordained them for a concern with methodology. Many have referred to it as a scholarly torso of colossal proportions. Thus Karl Jaspers has termed *Wirtschaft und Gesellschaft* "a gigantic work, embracing everything" ("alles umgreifenden Riesenwerk");[5] and Réné König contemporary sociologist, in his biographical summary of Max Weber in *Die Grossen Deutschen* (vol. 4, 1956, p. 414) avers that *Wirtschaft und Gesellschaft* remains the greatest achievement of German sociology. Indeed, Weber's life work of which *Wirtschaft und Gesellschaft* is the supreme literary expression, continues to exercise great influence. His stimulus and power is admitted even by writers who are critical of some of Weber's major positions. Thus Leo Strauss, who has subjected Weber's political theory to strong criticism, says of Weber, "Whatever may have been his errors, he is the greatest social scientist of our century";[6] and another critic of Weber's relativism refers to the "grandeur" of Weber's work, "more sensed than understood." [7]

Serious problems of translation are created by Weber's almost studied disdain of the ordinary proprieties of language (lest verbal facility, which Weber certainly commanded in his lectures, for example, seduce the reader by extra-scientific appeals), by his adoption of neologisms, by his formidable learning (in many languages), by his multiplication of the shadings of meanings (from almost excessive caution and circumspection), by his syntactical idiosyncrasies, and by his nominalistic irony (which manifests itself in strange uses of familiar terms). Hans Gerth, in his preface to *From Max Weber: Essays in Sociology,* has perceptively characterized Weber's style of writing as "Gothic-castle," and "Platonizing." Some of Weber's terms are virtually untranslatable, e.g., *Perhorreszierung, charisma, Berufsekstatiker, Bewährung, gesinnungsethisch sublimiert, Gemeindereligiosität, Heilsmethodik, Gnadenspendung,* and *Wahlkreisgeometrie.* Many translators of Weber's works into English have commented upon the difficulties of his language and style, and have differed in their exact renderings of the same German words (e.g., *Herrschaft* has been rendered by Gerth

[5] In his Max Weber, *Deutches Wesen im politischen Denken im Forschen und Philosophieren,* 1932, p. 79; cf. K. Jaspers, *Gedenkrede,* of July 17, 1920, p. 4; Heinrich Rickert, Preface to *Die Grenzen der naturwissenschaftlichen Begriffsbildung,* 5 ed., 1921, p. xxiv; Marianne Weber, *Max Weber, Ein Lebensbild,* 1926, p. 425.

[6] Leo Strauss, *Natural Right and History,* 1953, p. 36.

[7] Erich Voegelin, *The New Science of Politics,* 1952.

as "authority," by Parsons as "imperative control," and by Rheinstein as "domination"). Even German thinkers interested in understanding and interpreting rather than translating Weber's works,
such as Karl Jaspers, have referred to the idiosyncrasies of Weber's
style and the gap between the acuity of his thought and the un-
studied disorder of his style of expression.[8] In a few cases the
present translation gives Weber's German words and phrases in
parentheses where their translation is particularly ambiguous, but
attempts to limit this practice to a necessary minimum.

In the present translation, the relative claims of style and accuracy have consistently been settled in favor of the latter. Every
effort has been made to reduce the length of paragraphs, which in
some cases run an entire quarto page or more, and even the length
of sentences. Wherever accuracy was not a factor, the relative
claims of Weber's literary pattern and English language accessibility have been settled in favor of the latter. In the interest of clarity
and readability in English, some brief sections have been incorpo-

[8] Jaspers, Karl: *Max Weber, Deutsches Wesen,* especially the following
passage on page 70f: "Weber's depreciation of his role as a savant, as a
sage, appears in his language. At first contact with Weber's text, the
reader is surprised at the contrast between his penetrating thought, his
incisive conceptualization, his careful ratiocination, and his indifference
to his work as expressed in its linguistic form, composition, extent, and
proportion. Weber never worked at his style. He wrote out of intensive
cerebral activity and imaginative power but never polished his material.
Hence the style is frequently colorless, but even at such times there is
something distinctively Weberian present.

As far as content is concerned, his writing contains repetitions and
excursuses with returns to the central concern, and is frequently marked
by not quite necessary enumerations, parentheses, and incidental notions.
It is characteristic that Weber was loath to read his manuscripts or even
his printed pieces . . . He took no pleasure in his work but proceeded
further along the path in which each work was a step.

Yet because Max Weber was exclusively concerned with the substance
itself, rather than with language, he was able without any effort to dis-
close in his language the original source—his genuinely honest sound-
ings of the human spirit in the contemporary world. Because he was form-
less at a time when there was a general striving to blow up puny forms,
he achieved a form of such genuineness that it is the adequate expression
of truly original thought and fulfilled humanity.

In his use of language, as in all else, Max Weber is extravagant, un-
assuming, and open. He gives himself as he really is at the moment in
his objective discipline and in his humanity, without any airs. Hence Max
Weber lies bare before us. He dares to show himself and never clambers
up to any artificial elevation of expression."

rated into shorter chapters, some of the longer chapters have been broken up, some changes have been made in titles and subheadings, and a very few passages have been shifted in sequence within the body of the text—but no attempt whatsoever has been made to re-edit the work. No material has been shifted between text and footnotes; and all of the text is translated here.

After many vicissitudes, then, the last of Weber's long studies dealing with the sociology of religion and culture is to be available to students who can scarcely cope with the "anfractuosities" (to use the term employed by Macaulay in referring to Samuel Johnson) of Weber's intellect and temper when expressed in his native Teutonic idiom. The preparation of this English version owes much to the clerical and editorial assistance rendered by my wife, Marion Judson Fischoff, and Alice M. Childs. From the outset, encouragement and intellectual stimulus were provided by Professor James Luther Adams, to whom a very special debt of gratitude is recorded. Friendly interest also was shown by former directors of the Beacon Press, Melvin Arnold and Thomas A. Bledsoe, and by the present editor Karl Hill. Acknowledgment is also made to Professor Robert Bellah and to Professor Talcott Parsons, whose contribution to the advancement of Weber studies and the development of sociological theory in the United States is incalculable, for their interest in the project and for editorial suggestions on particular points.

Late in life the aged Goethe, in a letter to Carlyle, sonorously described translators as agents of intellectual commerce among the nations. Such a sense of responsibility has animated the present translator in his labor to convey the thought and spirit of an important foreign work. It is hoped that this English version of yet another portion of Weber's mighty opus will increase knowledge of the considerable contributions made by one of the most distinguished savants of the century. Perhaps our admiration for Weber's contribution may stimulate increased application to the enrichment of the fields in which he worked. As Karl Jaspers remarked in a Weber memorial address at Heidelberg, July 17, 1920: "The way to honor a great man is to endeavor to make his labors one's own and develop further the lines of his ideas."

Lynchburg, Virginia   *Ephraim Fischoff*

Introduction

by Talcott Parsons

In the more than forty years since Max Weber's untimely death, recognition of his stature as one of the principal founders of modern social science, in particular modern sociology, has slowly been growing. But the magnitude of his contributions has not yet been fully appreciated; barriers to the understanding of Weber's thought are still presented by technical difficulties and by cultural resistance.

Appreciation of Weber's stature as a sociological theorist has been greatest in the United States, though Americans encounter a formidable barrier in the difference of languages and the extraordinary difficulty of Weber's German. Translations of Weber's works into English have become available piecemeal and without plan, and the technical quality of the translations has often left much to be desired. A further technical difficulty has been provided by the enormous scope of Weber's interests and contributions, a scope which makes formidable the task of critically appraising Weber's various sociological concepts and contributions. Added to these technical difficulties have been problems of understanding and problems of acceptance, which are interesting in themselves from the standpoint of the sociology of knowledge. Cultural resistance to the appreciation of Weber's work has been sufficiently formidable in the United States, but has been the primary cause of an even greater retardation of understanding and appreciation in Continental Europe, particularly in Weber's native Germany.

The most central focus of Weber's thought lay in the field of religion, though the scope of his theoretical work extended to problems of economic organization and process, of political systems, of formal organization, and of law. His original training was in the field of historical jurisprudence, and from that he turned to historical economics. When he turned his studies toward religion, his focus was not upon religion "as such," as the theologian or church historian conceives it, but upon *the relations between* religious ideas and commitments and other aspects of human conduct, especially the economic characteristics of human conduct within a society. Weber's concern with religion was thus focused upon the *sociology* of religion. With Durkheim, who approached religion from a very different point of view, and with such modern anthropologists as Malinowski and Radcliffe-Brown, Weber inaugurated a new phase in the understanding of the relations between religious aspects and other aspects of human behavior.

The Reference Points for Weber's Sociology of Religion in His Work as a Whole. Weber's work in the sociology of religion first came to be known through his essay on the *Protestant Ethic and the Spirit of Capitalism,* which, controversial as it has been, must certainly count as one of the major landmarks of recent Western intellectual history.[1] This essay was at first received as an attempted "complete explanation" of the modern world, and especially as a counterattack against the Marxist assertion of the predominance of "material" interests in the historical process. Only gradually has it become more generally understood that in Weber's broad plan of work the book was intended as no more than an *essay* in historical-sociological interpretation. It was a fragment which provided Weber a point of departure, not a culmination, for his main contributions to the sociology of religion. Now it clearly has attained the status of a classic, but it should be appraised as such within the context of its author's total contribution, not in isolation.

If the *Protestant Ethic* was Weber's point of departure, his immediate scholarly destination was the series of comparative monographs in the sociology of religion of which three were com-

---

[1] As Rostow notes in *The Stages of Economic Growth,* economic historians must now "pay their respects" to the problem of the Protestant ethic, even though as individuals they have no real interest in Weber's problems.

pleted, those of Chinese religion (Confucianism and Taoism), of Indian religion (Hinduism and Buddhism), and of Ancient Judaism. All of these are now available in English translation.[2] This series was left incomplete at Weber's death. He had planned, at the very least, comparable studies of Islam, of Early Christianity and of Mediaeval Catholicism.

In the *Protestant Ethic,* Weber raised a set of theoretical problems in the field of human social action of the very first order of importance. The central problem was whether men's conceptions of the cosmic universe, including those of Divinity and men's religious interests within such a conceptual framework could influence or shape their concrete actions and social relationships, particularly in the very mundane field of economic action. This possibility was entertained seriously, and the question of *how* to conceive the operation of religious ideas became central. In the case of the relation between Protestantism and capitalism, the study of the operation of religious ideas led to questions of historical interpretation. But Weber early became acutely aware, as many participants in the discussion still are not, that the problem of causation involved an *analytical* problem, one of the isolation of variables and the testing of their significance in situations where they could be shown to vary independently of each other. The purely "historical" method, seeking ever more detailed knowledge of the "ideal" and "material" historical antecedents of modern economic organization, is inherently circular. It was only by establishing a methodological equivalent of experimental method, in which it is possible to hold certain factors constant, that even the beginnings of an escape from circularity was possible. Weber doubtless had many other motives for embarking upon a broad comparative study of the relations between religious orientations and social structure. But the decisive motive for his scientific method proceeded from his realization that without comparative evidence he could not hope to progress in the solution of his original central question.

In embarking upon comparative studies, Weber attempted

[2] *The Religion of China,* trans. by Hans H. Gerth, The Free Press, 1951; *Ancient Judaism,* trans. by Hans H. Gerth and Don Martindale, The Free Press, 1952; *The Religion of India,* trans. by Hans H. Gerth and Don Martindale, The Free Press, 1958.

to hold the factor of "economic organization" constant and to treat religious orientation as his independent variable. He sought to equate the "degrees of favorableness" of material factors to the development of capitalism. On the basis of a careful survey he judged this favorableness to be approximately equal in the European, in the Chinese, and in the Indian cases, taking account of the considerable changes within each main civilization over the long periods involved. Given the very critical differences in outcome in the three great civilizations, he then had a *prima facie* case for the importance of the religious movements as *differentiating* factors, not of course as total "explanations" of social developments. Weber repeatedly repudiated any imputation of an intent to "explain" all social developments as emanations and consequences of "idealistic" elements. His general position was as far removed from idealistic "emanationism" as it could possibly be.

Weber's orientation toward analytical methods requiring comparative studies led him to a particularly sharp break with the intellectual traditions in which he had been educated, the historical schools of social study predominant in late 19th century Germany —in Weber's case, historical jurisprudence and economics. These traditions of historical social study had philosophical foundations in German Idealism, which distinguished different or opposed methods as appropriate to the natural sciences and to humanistic studies. These historical traditions rooted in Idealistic conceptions held that studies of human society and culture must be pursued by "ideographic" methods, not by the "nomothetic" methods employed in the natural sciences. Studies of human phenomena should delineate the development or unfolding of unique historical patterns, and attempt to grasp the central meanings of these unique patterns. Since these philosophical and methodological traditions were widely accepted in Weber's intellectual surroundings, it is not surprising that Weber, while publishing the *Protestant Ethic* and deciding to embark upon comparative studies, also published a series of essays[3] sharply attacking the historical methods predominant in social disciplines, especially economics. The general

[3] Collected in his *Gesammelte Aufsätze zur Wissenschaftslehre*, Verlag von J. C. B. Mohr (Paul Siebeck), 1922. Some have been translated in Shils and Finch, *Max Weber's Methodology of Science*, The Free Press, 1949.

purport of these critical essays was Weber's insistence that in studies of society, as much as in the natural sciences, causal explanation depends upon the employment of analytical theory. Causes of human behavior cannot be found and established without the implicit or explicit use of abstract and general concepts and propositions.

But despite Weber's sharp critique of his own intellectual background, he retained and utilized the most important substantive elements of the historicist and Idealist traditions. His conservation of selected historical and Idealist conceptions creates a sharp contrast between his own methodology and the positivistic reductionism then and later so prominent in France, Britain and the United States, of which Behaviorism was an extreme manifestation.

There were two crucial foci of the historical element in Weber's work. The first was his attempt to interpret action by understanding the motives of the actor from a "subjective" point of view, i.e., the investigator attempting to put himself in the actor's place. However, Weber held that this subjective interpretation does not require the complete individualization of interpretations, since there are *typical* patterns of meaning which can be abstracted from the individualized totality. This line of argument, formalized in his well-known concept of the "ideal type," was Weber's main path to the formulation of a general theory which incorporated "subjective" factors, the famous method of *Verstehen*.

The second primary focus of Weber's historicist conceptions, of particular importance in the present context, was his concern with systems of meaning (*Sinnzusammenhänge*) which could be interpreted ("understood," in Weber's special sense) and which, as definitions of situations for the actions of individuals, could be linked with individuals' "interests" (their motives in a psychological sense). Thus Weber initiated a line of theoretical analysis in many respects similar to, though in origin largely independent of, that initiated in the United States by such theorists as G. H. Mead and W. I. Thomas. Weber's "cultural complex of meanings," in one respect a system of "ideas," was also an instrument for the understanding of the action of individuals, and in this respect it was almost identical with Thomas' famous conception of the definition of the situation.

These were Weber's primary points of reference in his attempt to develop at least the beginnings of a technical body of theory in the field of social action (Weber's German technical term was *Handeln*). He was deeply committed to the need for theory. The elements of theory available to him from his intellectual environment were extremely important, yet fragmentary and seriously incomplete. He did much to extend and codify social theory, making various completely original contributions, yet his social theory remained at his death far more a beginning than an end.[4]

Weber approached problems of theory from the standpoint of an intellectual tradition which minimized the potential contribution of theory to social studies. He approached problems of theory cautiously, and primarily when theory was required for his program of empirical research. In the field of the sociology of religion he progressed from empirical studies to the development of theory, a pattern of intellectual movement he had already followed in the fields of economic and political organization. In these latter fields, he had written a considerable number of empirical monographs, especially in economic history broadly conceived,[5] before venturing into theory in the *Protestant Ethic* and in his methodological attacks upon Historicism. Only much later, in *Wirtschaft und Gesellschaft,* did he attempt to codify this material on a theoretical level. Similarly, he first pursued his program of studies in the sociology of religion through monographs. Though he engaged in a number of studies simultaneously during his most fruitful years, from time to time turning from one to another, the broad

[4] The incompleteness of Weber's theory of society will be apparent from what is said here of his theories in the specifically religious field. There has not in recent years, during which perspective on theory has advanced greatly, been published any comprehensive critical treatment of Weber's contributions as a theorist, in the strict sense. Bendix, in his *Max Weber: An Intellectual Portrait,* explicitly decided not to undertake the task of a comprehensive appraisal of Weber as a theorist, preferring for his purposes to concentrate upon Weber's empirical work. The present writer's *The Structure of Social Action,* especially Chapter XVII, may still be the most comprehensive analytical treatment of Weber's accomplishments in theory.

[5] A number of these economic and political monographs have been collected in the volume *Gesammelte Aufsätze zur Sozial-und Wirtschaftsgeschichte.*

orientation of his primary attention was first toward China, then toward India, and then toward Ancient Judaism. Though in these three monographic studies there is much implicit and some explicit theory, a careful and thorough critical analysis would be required to discover the general conceptual scheme Weber was applying here, and indeed there are not only serious gaps but certainly a good many inconsistencies in the implied conceptual scheme.

It was rather later in his program, though before he had reached fifty years of age, that he undertook a systematization which required far more attention to theoretical problems than he had hitherto devoted to them. It was an "external" stimulus upon Weber to which we are indebted for his systematic undertaking. This stimulus was the grandiose plan for a *Grundriss der Sozialoekonomik,* freely translated, a "General Outline of the Social and Economic Sciences," conceived by a group of German social scientists of which Weber was not only a member but clearly a ringleader. It was as part of this ambitious plan that Weber undertook to contribute a *general* survey of the relations between "economy and society" which took the German title of *Wirtschaft und Gesellschaft.* To this we owe the systematic, as distinguished from historical, monograph which is presented in the present volume.

The translator, Dr. Fischoff, has provided a highly illuminating account of the genesis, the general character, and the problems presented by this extraordinary work. It was not only left unfinished at Weber's death, but left in such a state that the editors could not be certain even of the general plan of the work and hence the degree to which it approached completion. The more recent and very careful work of Dr. Winckelmann, which has resulted in the latest and substantially improved German edition, has helped greatly in understanding the problem, as Dr. Fischoff shows.

Wirtschaft und Gesellschaft seems clearly to have been intended originally as a work of codification rather than a work of new empirical research or new theory, but in the hands of Weber it became much more than a codification. It was characteristic of the scope of his knowledge and thinking that several "chapters," pre-eminently the one on the sociology of law[6] and the present one, turned out in fact to be substantial books when nearly completed.[7] It is to this project that we owe Weber's only attempt to present a systematic account, as distinguished from a monographic case study, of his views on the sociology of religion.

In many future English-language bibliographies, there will be references to "Weber, 1962" and many readers will not stop to consider that the English translation is appearing a full half-century after the work was written. In appraising it, it is essential to keep this in mind. Weber was a scholar who avidly assembled and digested any empirical materials available in the relevant literature, within the limits of his considerable command of languages. (He did not command several of the languages most important to the study of comparative religion.) He did his unusually competent best to discover the actual facts and to correctly interpret them, over an enormous range of subject matter. But many of his detailed facts and interpretations cannot be accepted today as reliable, in part because of the very scope of his inquiries and in part because of rapid progress in the sociology of religion since Weber's time. Many of his empirical generalizations, which we may call "middle range theories," are clearly dated. Weber would have altered many of his opinions and generalizations, if he had had access to the subsequent fifty years' anthropological research into primitive religion and historical scholarship relevant to advanced religions. Given Weber's qualities as a scholar, we can be sure that he would have exploited to the limit such opportunities to improve his work.[8]

The general framework within which Weber conceived and treated, in this monograph, the problems of the sociology of reli-

[6] Translated as *Max Weber on Law*, by Rheinstein and Shils, Harvard Univ. Press, 1954.

[7] A number of others like the one on social stratification ("Theory", Chapter IV) are clearly fragments.

[8] As in the field of theory, in this and a number of other more empirical fields, a great service could be done by a careful appraisal of what difference it would make in Weber's interpretations and generalizations on the sociology of religion if account were taken of the materials, both specifically factual and interpretive, which have become available since Weber wrote—and of course the relevance of things available at the time which he may have neglected.

gion is less likely to be dated by the contributions of the intervening half-century than is the case with many matters of specific fact, and of middle-level generalization. *Religion and the Problem of Social Evolution.* Weber's perspective, especially in the sociology of religion, but elsewhere as well was basically evolutionary. This is particularly important in the light of the intellectual history of the period. After a brief and somewhat superficial flirtation of social science with the idea of evolution, under the impact of Darwinism in the biological sciences (the names of Spencer, Ward and Sumner come to mind), there developed among social scientists a sharp reaction against the idea of evolution. The evolutionary conception has made little progress in social science since Weber's time, since much of the work of historians has been particularistic, while for an entire generation most of the comparative research was carried out by anthropologists, whose thought was militantly anti-evolutionary. But it is significant that Weber and his great contemporary Emile Durkheim, the other most important founder of modern sociology, both thought in evolutionary terms.[9]

Weber had to develop a conception of primitive religion, and that is indeed the task to which he addressed himself in the first section of this book. Since Weber's time, anthropological research has enormously enriched our knowledge in this field, though Durkheim's codification and analysis of Australian totemism remains perhaps the most eminent single monographic contribution, because it is both a great monograph and much more than that.[10] But these additions of material do not invalidate the general outline of Weber's view of primitive religion. Indeed, the convergence between Weber's and Durkheim's conceptions of primitive religion, in the absence of any apparent influence of either theorist on the other, is notable.

A first crucial point in Weber's theory is that there is no known human society without something which modern social scientists would classify as religion. Every society possesses some

[9] Cf. Robert N. Bellah, "Durkheim and History," *American Sociological Review*, Vol. 24, p. 447, 1959.

[10] Emile Durkheim, *Les formes élémentaires de la vie religieuse*, 1912, translated as *The Elementary Forms of the Religious Life*, currently published by The Free Press.

conceptions of a supernatural order, of spirits, gods or impersonal forces which are different from and in some sense superior to those forces conceived as governing ordinary "natural" events, and whose nature and activities somehow give meaning to the unusual, the frustrating and the rationally impenetrable aspects of experience. The existence of the supernatural order is taken seriously, in that many concrete events of experience are attributed, in part at least, to its agency, and men devote an important part of their time and resources to regulating their relations with this order as they conceive it.

This view that belief in the supernatural is universal has been completely confirmed by modern anthropology. Religion is as much a human universal as language or an incest taboo, which is to say a kinship system. Any conception of a "natural man" who is not encumbered with such "cultural baggage" belongs to a fictional picture of prehistory, for which there is no solid evidence for the human, socially organized stage. The view that such "baggage" *ought* to be dispensed with and that rational man should "face reality" without any "superstition" is a product of sophisticated culture, in no way true of the original human condition.

Weber combined his view of the ubiquity of conceptions of the supernatural with an insight into the *symbolic character* of the conceptions of supernatural beings and their acts, although Weber did not develop this latter insight as systematically as did Durkheim. Particularly important is Weber's insistence that the conception of a supernatural order does not imply any "transcendental" goals or focus of interest for man. The aid of the supernatural is sought, so far as "primitive man" is concerned, entirely in the interest of mundane, worldly concerns: health, long life, defeat of enemies, good relations with one's own people, and the like. There are important questions about the effect of beliefs in the supernatural upon the priorities and relativities among these various mundane or "common sense" interests, but Weber does not much explore this line of problems, which we would now refer to as the field of value orientations and value integrations.

Weber's discussion of the sociology of religion, from this starting point in the universality of belief in the supernatural, proceeds to a systematic exploration of the directions in which, and the developmental paths by which, "breakthroughs" from the primitive religious state can occur. Comparative and historical evidence for the existence of such breakthroughs is sought. The possibilities are canvassed by searching back and forth between the "material" sphere of the conditions, structure and utilitarian interests of ordinary living, and the "ideal" sphere of the meanings of various conceptions of the supernatural and of other aspects of experience. Essential for the analysis of social process is Weber's emphasis upon *differentiation*, not only between the spheres, but also within each sphere to the extent that situations are differently defined with reference to action. It is methodologically important that Weber's differentiations are predominantly dichotomous; twofold distinctions introduced for the solution of some particular problem. Weber repeatedly abstracts from the total social process some set of two principal alternatives of social structuring, after which his methodological problem is to clarify the differences and relations between these alternatives, as well as to clarify the conditions relevant to tipping the balance in one or the other direction.[11]

The concept of breakthrough is, I think, crucial. At each primary decision point, where Weber makes a primary distinction, the alternative is between a direction which makes for a source of evolutionary change in the "established" order (which Weber tended to conceptualize under the heading of traditionalism), and another direction which tends either to reinforce the established order or at least not to change it drastically. He makes a further distinction between tendencies which do and do not carry the potentiality of firmly organized "viability" under the realistic conditions of social life (in current sociological terminology, the poten-

---

[11] This is most emphatically not to say that Weber was a partisan of the "logic of dichotomies" in either a naive or a rigid sense. Very few writers display such awareness, indeed not only awareness, but enormous knowledge, of the tremendous complexity of the empirical material and the subtleties of transition from one type to another, a circumstance which makes the reading of this material, both in the original and in translation, particularly difficult. But when one comes to try to isolate the main *logical* outline of Weber's analysis, the prominence of the pattern of dichotomization is striking. It seems to us entirely appropriate to a focus on the process of differentiation. It is also notable that this focus is shared by Weber and Durkheim.

tiality of effective institutionalization). Weber's *primary* interest is in religion as a source of the dynamics of social change, not religion as a reinforcement of the stability of societies.[12]

The Primary Components of a Religious System. The first of the theoretical dichotomies which Weber develops is that between the function of the magician and the function of the priest in mediating between humans and the supernatural, a dichotomy which will reappear as the distinction between magic and religion. Weber's distinction is somewhat different from the similar distinc‹ tions made by Durkheim and Malinowski. Weber's distinction is that the magician's function copes with relatively *ad hoc* interests and tensions, while the priestly function is organized into a systematic and stabilized *cult,* which is to a significant extent independent of the *ad hoc* exigencies which impinge upon the ordinary population of the society. Further, magical forces can be "forced" (*gezwungen*) to serve human needs by the magician's correct use of formulae, while religious agents must be "worshipped" or solicited. Religious forces are conceived to have an independent capacity to guide human destiny which the magical forces do not.

The range of different aspects of these problems which Weber reviews is enormous, and many penetrating observations are made along the way, such as that of the special relation between religious precepts and the later development of law in Rome. Through all this, Weber's underlying thesis is the importance of the development of conceptions of the supernatural order, the claims of this supernatural order upon human attention and performance, and the implementation of these claims through agencies which may

[12] It is probably correct to say that this is a primary difference of emphasis between Weber and Durkheim. That Weber focused his structural analysis upon process and change is of current interest, in view of the contemporary allegation that the dominant "structural-functional" trend in sociological theory channels interest toward stability and order, to the neglect of problems of change. Weber and Durkheim are usually considered intellectual ancestors of the "structural-functional" school, and however plausible the accusation against Durkheim of a "static bias" may be—I do not think it can be pressed very far, especially in the light of Bellah's analysis, *op. cit.*—it is almost impossible to make a plausible case for such a bias on Weber's part. Perhaps this allegation of a static bias proceeds from a belief held by the critics that the "real" forces of change cannot be found in the sphere of "ideas" but consist of "material" interests.

attain a sufficient independence from the traditionally established social order to exert leverage upon that social order and change it. Already present in this underlying thesis is Weber's evaluative distinction between what we may call progressive and regressive changes. He holds that those changes, associated at the primitive level with priestly cults, which make for a more stringent and systematic ordering of the patterns of living are more favorable to breakthrough than are those changes which tend toward the indulgence of immediate emotional needs and pressures, which he associates with "orgiastic" components in magic and religion, but which also include needs for security.

Weber moves next, not to the problem of differentiating the roles and interests involved in the distinction between the magical and priestly functions, but to the problem of differentiating between types of normative social order based upon "religious ethics" and upon "taboo." These types represent different levels in the normative control of action, and the former type is associated with priesthood and cult, the latter type with magic. Nevertheless, many elements of taboo are empirically associated with priestly cults. The essential distinction is that taboo is concerned with the prescription and still more the proscription of specific acts, while religious ethics is more concerned to enforce a generalized orientation or pattern of action. The existence and efficacy of a religious ethic is dependent upon a conception of divinity, by no means necessarily monotheistic. According to Weber, divinities are either conceived as entering into quasi-contractual relationships with men, by which the divinities themselves assume obligations, or conceived as promulgating general laws which they expect humans to observe, much as an absolute monarch promulgates positive laws. A religious ethic is conceptualized at a higher level of generality than a system of taboo, and therefore a religious ethic is universalistic, its observance requires a high level of responsibility, and its infractions by men cannot be counteracted directly by magical punishments.

These three distinctions may be considered to formulate the main setting of the problem of religion as a force for dynamic social change, as Weber saw it. His view was that all societies at whatever level of development have had, not only secular or natural, but also supernatural elements of culture. All supernatural components have both magical and religious elements, though in widely varying proportions and relations; all have roles approximating those of magician and priest, though again with varying combinations of the components; and all have in their supernaturally sanctioned normative order elements both of a system of taboo and a system of religious ethics. With those elements and distinctions shared by the religions of all human societies, the problems of the sociology of religion become these: Under what cultural definitions of the religious situation can processes of change and breakthrough take place? Through what agencies and forms of organization can processes of change and breakthrough take place? In what situations are breakthroughs most probable?

The Process of Rationalization. Rationalization is the master conception through which cultures define their religious situation, and through which the sociology of religion must understand such cultural definitions of the situation. Rationalization comprises first the intellectual clarification, specification and systematization of ideas. Ideas are generated by what Weber called the teleological *meanings* of man's conceptions of himself and his place in the universe, conceptions which legitimize man's orientations in and to the world and which give *meaning* to man's various goals. Such ideas imply metaphysical and theological conceptions of cosmic and moral orders, as well as man's position in relation to such wider orders.

Rationalization comprises, second, normative control or sanction. This is so because the teleological reference of the ideas in question implies that human actions are goal-oriented, in means-ends terms. This in turn implies that human actions should be subject to a fundamental "hierarchy of control," and that the higher levels of this hierarchy should lie on the cultural plane. Therefore, all human societies embody references to a normative cultural order which places teleological "demands" upon men. But men's conception of the nature of this normative order is not a constant; rather, there is a differentiated variety of possible normative orders, and even a single society's conceptions of normative order change in the course of history. Weber's primary concern is the exploration of these different possible natures, and the directions these natures may take when attempting to answer by rationalizing the problems of the meaning of life. Weber's "rationalization" is thus intellectual, in that it has special reference to "existential" (though nonempirical) ideas, but is also teleological or normative, in that it places obligations on men with respect to their conduct in this life.

Third, rationalization comprises a conception of motivational commitment. The ideas in question imply, not only social and behavioral patterns, but kinds and levels of motivational commitment required for the implementation of these implied patterns. The motivational commitments include both "belief," in the sense of seriousness of commitment to the cognitive validity of the ideas, and practical commitment, in the sense of readiness to put one's own interests at stake in the service of the ideas. Here the dimension of rationalization concerns in the first instance the systematization of a pattern or program *for life as a whole,* which is given meaning by an existential conception of the universe, and within it the human condition in which this action is to be carried out.

Prophecy, Charisma, and the Process of Breakthrough. It is within this framework that the place of Weber's key concept of *prophecy* is to be understood. The prophet is above all the agent of the process of breakthrough to a higher, in the sense of more rationalized and systematized, cultural order, an order at the level of religious ethics, which in turn has implications for the nature of the society in which it becomes institutionalized. This, of course, is the focus of Weber's much-discussed concept of charisma which, though not originating with him, has become part of the common language of social and cultural discussion mainly through his influence. For Weber the role of the religious prophet was the prototype, though not the only example, of "charismatic leadership."

There are two particularly notable points about the concept of charisma, the significance of which should be assessed in the light of the relation of the concept to the development of *conceptions* of order, i.e., the cognitive aspect of the process of rationalization. The first is the focus on the *individual* person who takes the responsibility for announcing a *break* in the established normative order and declaring this break to be morally *legitimate,* thereby setting himself in significant respects in explicit opposition to the established order.[13] In order to legitimize his sponsorship of such a break the prophet must in turn invoke a source of moral authority, an imperative which leads directly into the problem of the conceptions of meaning and order. The essential question is whether it is in an evolutionary sense a higher order, a question which can only be answered in a comparative and evolutionary perspective.

It may be remarked that this individualistic emphasis in Weber's treatment of the concept of charisma has tended to obscure the fact that he treated it not *only* as a quality of an individual person, but also of a normative *order*. The latter reference, for example, is a necessary basis for making use of the important concepts of lineage-charisma (*Gentilcharisma*) and charisma of office (*Amtscharisma*). In this latter context Weber's concept of charisma is identical with Durkheim's concept of the sacred.[14]

The second notable and closely connected point about the concept of prophecy is Weber's insistence that, in spite of the very close connection between it and cognitive conceptions of order, there is a crucial noncognitive aspect of it, namely that of *commitment* to the break and the order embodied in the break. Prophecy is by no means an intellectual exercise in metaphysical or theological speculation, but very much a case of what Durkheim had in mind when he said of religion, *c'est de la vie sérieuse*. This in turn is associated with the frequent violent emotionalism of prophetic movements, sometimes—as Weber emphasizes—bordering on the pathological.

Weber is very careful to distinguish the prophet from closely similar types, namely the "lawgiver" and the teacher, especially in respect to the rationalization of religious orientations. Prophets

---

[13] The Jews of the time of Christ were pre-eminently a "people of the Book." Hence for Weber a prototypical expression of the prophetic attitude in this respect was the phrase, frequently reiterated in the Gospels, "It is written . . . , but I say unto you . . ." of course something in conflict with what is written.

[14] So prominent indeed is the individualistic aspect of charisma in most of Weber's writings which dealt with it, that it was only in connection with the present book, and then only on a careful second reading, that I was able to see the resemblance of Weber's charisma in its normative social aspect to Durkheim's concept of the collective sacred, which I described in *Structure of Social Action,* Chap. XVII.

may well perform both functions of lawgiver and teacher in addition to their prophecy; Moses and Muhammad are famous examples of the lawgiver, and most certainly were prophets in Weber's sense. But the essential criterion of prophecy for Weber is whether or not the message is a call to break with an established order; he cites the Hindu *guru* as a pre-eminent example of the religious teacher who implements an established order rather than breaking with it.

There is, however, in Weber's discussion, one type of role which involves such a break, but to which he does not apply the conception of prophet, and this is what he calls the "mystagogue," a concept apparently thought of as the religious counterpart of the demagogue. The essential difference from the prophet is that the mystagogue defines his source of legitimation primarily in magical terms, not those of a religious ethic. He is not an agent of rationalization, but of escape from the problems of meaning which exert pressure to rationalize, i.e. to establish new levels of normative order.

Within the category of prophecy, Weber then introduces another of his central dichotomies, namely that between exemplary and ethical prophecy. The exemplary prophet provides a model for a way of life which can be followed by others, embodying in a religious sense what is defined as a higher level of personal virtue. There is, however, no implication that the standards of this pattern or "way" are binding on any social community as such. The ethical prophet, on the other hand, imposes demands on certain categories of men in such a way that not only do they have an opportunity, but it is rather their *duty* to follow his precepts. These precepts in turn are defined, not so much to exhort followers to emulate the prophet's personal example, as they are to exhort them to conform with an impersonally defined normative order. Both the definition of this order and—beyond that—the reasons why acceptance of it is morally obligatory, are incorporated in the prophet's conception of the nature of his mission. This implies a very different conception of their relations to a source of legitimation on the part of the two types of prophet. The exemplary type tends to define himself as a *vessel,* as standing in some personal relation of identification with the divine, whereas the ethical prophet thinks of himself as an *instrument* of a divine will, as having a mission to promulgate an order for others which expresses that will. He himself, however, need not become personally "sanctified."

Hence the cognitive conception of the nature of divinity underlying the two types of prophecy tends to bifurcate. The conception associated with exemplary prophecy is that of an immanent, pantheistic principle of divinity, in which the prophet participates, and offers others who follow his example the opportunity to participate. But the ethical prophet tends to legitimize his teachings by reference to a transcendental conception of divinity, a conception of one or more gods who stand *outside* and above the world in which the human condition is situated, and who "legislate" for it. The religious philosophy of India represents the extreme example in the former direction, that of Judaism, Christianity, and Islam, in the latter.

The next very essential step in Weber's analytical construction is the definition of the religious community (*Gemeinde*). It is characteristic not only of primitive religion, as he sees it, but of many other types, that the organization of religion at the collectivity level is an "aspect" of the organization of the society in other functional respects, notably the political, but also of kinship and the like. There may be specialized roles like those of magician and priest, but they, together with their clientele, do not constitute an organized collectivity structurally differentiated from the rest of the society. Such persons may be "private practitioners" or they may be "functionaries" of a collectivity which is more than a religious one. The type of collectivity in which Weber is here interested is one specifically organized about religious interests as such, which is thereby distinct from other "secular" collectivities in the same society.

There is of course a close connection between the religious community and prophecy in that the type of break with an established order which Weber associates with prophecy favors the definition, both on their own part and of others, of the status of the prophet and his followers as standing in a special position different from that of nonfollowers. Of course the prophet may, like Moses, carry a whole "people" with him—though there may well be important defections—but the case Weber has in mind in his concept of religious community is that of a collectivity with a distinctive religious character, which is not a society, but rather a religiously specialized subgroup within a society, a "sect" or a "church."

Two particularly important problems arise at this point. The first is that of the relation of the religious leadership or specialists, in the first instance prophets, to followers who are not specialists or "virtuosos," but who are "ordinary people" in all senses except that they adhere to the special doctrine or way, or are loyal to the leader. In the religious sense these are the "laity." Weber makes much of the fact that the capacities of different types of religious movement for the effective organization of such a collectivity and in particular of the laity, vary greatly. Very broadly, exemplary prophecy tends to produce "elitist" movements of those who achieve superior religious status, and to leave the others in a status of dubious belongingness, apart from the belongingness they derive from their secular statuses. It is on the basis of ethical prophecy and an order binding on whole categories of persons that anything like a firmly organized "church" can most readily be built up.

The basic duality between magic and ethic, or emotional and rational-social, which characterizes Weber's thought throughout the book, appears in this context as the distinction between the religious community and the "sacralized polity," if we may use that term, namely the politically organized society in which the religious and the secular aspects of organization are not differentiated at the higher collectivity levels—in Western terms, a community which is both "church" and "state" at the same time.

In the entire context of the process of rationalization, Weber emphasizes the importance of the development of a *written* sacred tradition, of sacred books. The timing of its appearance is by no means a function of literacy since, for example, preservation of the oral tradition may be positively promoted in esoteric groups to protect their exclusiveness. This seems to have been the case with the Vedic tradition in India for a long period. Once there are sacred texts, however, these are subject both to continual editing and to complex processes of interpretation and tend to become the focus of specialized intellectual competence and prestige in the religious field and on the cultural level of rationalized systems of religious doctrine. Groups who have a special command of the sacred writings may then attain a special position in the religious system as a whole—the Jewish rabbis of the Talmudic tradition present a particularly salient case.

Written tradition provides a basis for further differentiation of the system precisely because it is a focus of stability which can be made independent of complete traditionalization of the status of concrete groups, notably priestly groups. One of the most important advances from this base, particularly associated with prophecy, is the development of preaching of "the Word" as distinguished from administration of the cult. Preaching, Weber holds, is a function possible only where there are prophetic definitions of the situation, and tends to be particularly prominent where ethical prophecy occurs. Another very important development of further differentiation is concern for the religious state of the individual through the "cure of souls" in various forms: confession, special spiritual exercises, special teaching and the like.

Religion and Social Status. Having thus established his main framework for analyzing the process of cultural breakthrough under religious auspices, Weber turns to consideration of the varieties of types of "soil" in which such movements may or may not be expected to grow. He extensively reviews types of social strata, examined for their sensitivity to possible prophetic, and also mystagogic, appeals, and among these he distinguishes those social strata sensitive to exemplary and to ethical prophecy.[15]

Careful consideration of this remarkable essay—in its extensiveness perhaps better termed a monograph—should end once and for all the allegation among serious scholars that Weber held a naive one-way conception of the development of human societies as the product of "ideas" without due attention to what he himself called the "other side of the causal chain." It may perhaps be called, in present terminology, a study in the sociological determinants of the "propensity to alienation." After all, what he is

---

[15] Chapter VI of this book. In the German this is the section entitled *Stände, Klassen und Religion*. It is the only part of the present book previously, though only briefly, available to English-speaking readers. A translation, by Christine Kayser, has been included in *Theories of Society*, Parsons, Shils, Naegele and Pitts, eds., The Free Press, 1961, Vol. II, Section B, No. 9, pp. 1138-1161.

emphasizing as the decisive aspect of progressive (evolutionary) social change is the condition necessary to bring about what we have been calling a "break" with an established, sociologically speaking an institutionalized, order. In the earlier sections of the book he has been considering the possible nature of "stimuli" to such a break, and now he turns to the factors influencing a probable "response." It seems to be almost a truism that different societies, and different structural elements within each, will have different sensitivities to the same stimulus to break with the established order. This sensitivity is perhaps the same thing as what is now called "alienation." The alienated elements are those which are relatively "available" to be stirred by prophetic movements.

He starts with the two principal bases on which a minimum of alienation is to be expected—in each case reviewing an immense mass of comparative evidence. Those groups most likely to be strongly embedded in "traditionalism"—and here his prototypical case is that of peasants—and those most heavily involved in secular responsibility are least susceptible to prophecy or alienation. In the latter case groups with institutionalized military functions, such as feudal nobilities, figure prominently, but in a somewhat different way the concept is extended to "bureaucracies." In their very different ways, each of these types of group has a very heavy investment in maintaining the established order and "making it work," and, as Weber emphasized, the personal self-respect of the typical member is very much bound up with the completeness of his identification with this order. The case of peasantries is a kind of "base line" which is related to the whole conception of primitive societies. Weber repeatedly dwells on the close connection between peasant status and the prevalence of magical beliefs and practices, the significance of which does not require further comment in the present frame of reference. But the case of the military, extended to that of the politically responsible elements more generally, is one of great interest in the present context.

The case of the politically responsible elements is significant because of the elements of ambivalence and strain involved in their status. On the one hand there is a special "moral complexity" attached to such statuses, not least to the military because of the inherent conflicts implicit in any use of violence in relation to other human beings. Precisely in proportion to the level of development of effective political organization, which by definition is a matter of disposal over resources, pre-eminently human resources whose functions cannot be traditionally ascribed, problems arise not only of realistic capacity to command such resources, but of *rights* to do so. Since, however, human beings, with respect to their own services or their physical possessions, are highly sensitive to the rights to pre-empt their uses, groups in a position of political responsibility are peculiarly sensitive, not only to the amount of power they command, in the strictly "realistic" sense of this term, but to the basis of *legitimation* of the use of this power, which in the longer run is a primary factor in the extent of power itself.

I think I am correct in interpreting Weber's view to be that the "conservative" tendency among groups exercising political responsibility is heavily determined by their need for legitimation essentially because the use of power without regard to legitimation is possible only in the very short run. However, in the nature of the position of such groups, they are responsible for the more immediate consequences of their decisions. Hence, and this is a very crucial proposition, their general tendency is to rely upon *established* sources of legitimation. This is to say, their interest lies in attempting to stabilize, not necessarily their practical decisions, but the basis on which they can count on continuing in power and on relative freedom from the kind of internal opposition which would seriously impair their capacity to act. The principal effect of this combination of factors is to give such groups a primary interest in the stability of their sources of legitimation, precisely as a condition of their freedom to act flexibly in current decision-making.

It may or may not be true that such groups as peasants are any freer from tensions and frustrations than others; Weber, I think, would hesitate to suggest that they were. His point is rather that they are less likely to seek to resolve these tensions through adherence to presumptively new orders than are some others. He felt that they were more prone to magical mechanisms.[16]

[16] This raises the question whether Weber put forward a view which was contrary to the facts in those cases which have happened since he wrote of the roles of the peasantry, different as they were, in the Russian and the Chinese revolutions respectively. The reasons why this is probably not so have to do with the kind of new order which has an ap-

Specifically in contrast to the peasant case, Weber remarks on the regularity with which religious movements have centered in urban populations. Very notably, the early Christians were so definitely urban that the very word for non-Christian, namely pagan, originally meant simply a countryman. This of course is significant in that the major processes of social change tend to center in urban communities; they are in general less traditionalized than the rural communities.

Within urban populations there is a very great variety of social types and, Weber emphasizes, a wide range of religious propensities. Very broadly, he finds little relation between religious propensities and economic statuses as such. Above all, he is concerned to show that prophetic movements have not been primarily movements of economic protest, motivated mainly by the economic interests of the disadvantaged classes. Middle classes of various types and solid handicraft groups have been very prominent. Generally the poorest classes have not. The groups which have taken up such movements have frequently burdened themselves economically rather than improved their lot. This was the subject of an important controversy in Weber's time in Germany because certain socialist writers, notably Karl Kautsky, contended that early Christianity was essentially a proletarian movement of economic protest.

A whole range of "bourgeois" classes, in the more generic sense, constitute a particularly important type of soil for the growth of religious radicalism, if we except the lowest groups and the groups most directly involved with social responsibility, like those financiers of "politically oriented capitalism"—as Weber calls it—who stand in very close association with the more responsible groups. If I may try to state the two most important favoring fac-

peal; Weber would hold, not that peasants are immune to any sort of appeal against currently dominant interests, but rather that they were more immune than others to appeal to the specific kind of moral break with the pattern of the established order which Weber was concerned with. Thus, to put it rather banally, it is easy to mobilize peasant opposition to landowning classes, but not so easy to mobilize them against a system in which landed proprietorship, large or small, is a major organizing principle. This has something to do with the fact that in both cases, after enjoying initial peasant support, the regime has had to resort to drastic reorganization of the agricultural system, in both cases apparently involving drastic conflicts with peasant groups.

tors, the first type seems to be characterized by an occupational involvement which entails some order of relatively generalized rationalization of the pattern of life (*habitus* is Weber's main term). Both artisans and mercantile groups fit in this context, the first on technological grounds, the second on economic. They are identified with elements of order which cannot readily be identified with the traditionalized institutions of a society. The other type are elements which are in a status-position which reduces their level of identification with the established order—thus among artisans Weber particularly notes the apprentice and journeyman categories in connection with the very general institutionalization of "wandering," i.e., of moving from place to place in search of work and experience. The most general theme is dissociation from the firmer types of anchorage in a traditional order.

Weber next turns to a very crucial problem, namely that of the dispositions of groups which have a special involvement in intellectual functions. The importance of the problem of course derives from the fact that rationalization is, in his view, the single most crucial dynamic factor in the process of change and the intellectually cognitive aspect is in turn central to rationalization. The problem concerns the relation of this implicit intellectual dynamism to the other two factors we have stressed, identification with a specifically urgent set of teleological demands on men, and the level of motivational commitment which members of the group in question may be expected to make.

His general view is that even high levels of intellectualism may, in their dynamic implications, be counteracted by sufficiently high levels of identification with an established order. The typical case is priestly intellectualism, which, above all through the rationalization of written sacred traditions, may go very far indeed toward a breakthrough, but still operate as a conservative force. This can be said of Brahmanic intellectualism in India, and to a certain extent, though with important qualifications, of Christian theologians and pre-eminently, in the postexilic period, of the Talmudic scholars of the Jewish Rabbinate. Very generally this is more likely to be true the higher the general social status of the intellectually inclined and trained groups, though, as in the Jewish case, pariah status may also strongly reinforce it.

There is, however, inherent dynamism in the intellectual function as such, so that in spite of such counteracting factors there may still be a radically innovative influence. In this connection Weber makes an extremely important generalization to the effect that the religious intellectualism of "elite" (*vornehm*) groups, where it does become a dynamic force, tends to work in the direction of the immanent conception of divine order, pantheism, and as we shall see presently, of seeking salvation through mystical, contemplative channels. The need for breaking with the established order, the need for "salvation" in the individual case, arises for these groups from *inner* tensions, not the pressures of the external, pre-eminently social situation. Rather than focusing on personal suffering or exposure to evil, this need is concerned with the question of the meaningfulness even of the *best* of fortune in worldly things— Gautama was in this respect the prototypical case. The broad conception is that intellectual breakthrough in this direction offers the opportunity for personal promotion in a scale of standing or prestige above *any* level accessible in worldly terms. Tensions involved in the feeling of meaninglessness can thus be resolved in this direction. Indeed elite intellectualism did play a central part in the development of Indian religious philosophy, and Weber mentions various other cases, notably perhaps that of Gnosticism as a movement primarily among Hellenistic intellectuals, which had it gained ascendancy, would have diverted Christianity very much in the Indian direction.

Parenthetically, it may be remarked that Weber does not say much about science, in this context, though he says a good deal about it in other contexts. Science, of course, is not directly concerned with religious problems. The interesting point, however, is that science in recent times seems to be a pre-eminent case of institutionalizing the dynamism of the process of rationalization, with repercussions throughout the society and culture. Moreover, scientists and the professions using applied science have become among the most important elite elements in modern society, a fact the sociological implications of which would repay a great deal of study.

On grounds such as the above, Weber concludes that in the tradition of ethical prophecy and the attempt at religiously mo-

tivated mastery over the world, a very special type of intellectualism has played a critical part. This is the intellectualism of
relatively nonprivileged groups,[17] who for one reason or another are
somewhat outside the main prestige structure of their societies.
Since peasant groups are almost never bearers of a strongly intellectual tradition, the primary intellectual types are found among
the urban classes which have been mentioned above, especially
craftsmen and various kinds of merchants. Separateness may involve the very special pariah status of the postexilic Jews, organization in sectarian groups, or something short of that in degree of
radical dissociation from the main social structure.

In any case Weber lays particular stress on three historic
cases of such groups. One, of course, was the almost incredible
elaboration of knowledge of the Talmudic law among Jews. To
be sure the rabbis were more or less full-time specialists in such
knowledge, though many of them earned a living in humble occupations. But the ordinary Jew was not too far behind, and
consciously and strenuously emulated rabbinical examples. The
whole Jewish community thus came to be permeated with a
kind of legalistic intellectualism which, however prominent such
features as the search for revenge and utopian chiliasm may
have been, provided a special foundation for many types of later
rationalization.

The second case Weber stresses was a direct beneficiary of
this, namely the intellectualism of early Christian communities,
whose members were on the whole people of very humble (though
urban) social status. An important contingent of them were, however, converted Jews, and the status of the Bible as a whole
meant mainly that the New Testament was added to the Old as an
object of study. There is of course a direct link with preaching in
that along with the development of the monastic orders and of the
sacramental secular priesthood, a major role was played by exposition of the Christian doctrine, and, not least, exhortation to follow
it.

The third case, finally, is that of the Puritans, the earlier generations in the development of ascetic Protestantism. These also,

---

[17] Who may, in current sociological terms, be said to be affected by
situations of "relative deprivation."

though some of their adherents and leaders were English "gentle-men," were by and large not centrally situated in the main prestige-structure. The rank and file were yeomen farmers, craftsmen, small merchants, and the like. The essential point here is their extraor-dinary knowledge of and concern with the details of the Bible, and the utter seriousness with which they took the theological prob-lems which were discussed, leaning on varying interpretations of biblical texts. Almost as much as the Jews they were "people of the Book."

This is but a sample from Weber's exceedingly rich discussion of the complex relations between social status and the propensity for alienation which in turn underlies accessibility to the influence of prophetic types of religious movement. Let me emphasize that Weber's view of this problem is pluralistic. He in no way denies —rather he specifically emphasizes—that there are very impor-tant differential propensities. Thus on the negative side his discus-sions of peasantries and of military elites are cases in point, on the positive certain types of artisan and other "lower-middle-class" groups. But just as important as these concepts of predilection, is his contention that there is *no* simple one-to-one relationship be-tween "group interests" or any other specific status-positions in the concrete social structure, and the probability that a prophetic movement will either arise or take hold. Differential patterning ap-plies, not only to propensities, but also to the *content* of the reli-gious orientation itself, and this can never be treated as a simple reflex of the social position of its proponents (particularly their *Interessenlage*).

Weber's analysis in this section outlines relations of inter-dependence and of independent variability. His most important conclusion is not the high degree to which religious developments are "determined" by their sociological contexts, on both the leader-ship and the followership levels, but the degree to which the social structure leaves a range of flexibility open so that when, for what-ever reasons, a charismatic innovation appears, there is a limited but highly significant range of flexibility which allows the in-novation an opportunity to take hold and eventually become insti-tutionalized.

Radical Solutions of the Problem of Meaning. Having for a

second time expanded his analysis of the background, Weber again turns to the problem of the basic content of religious orientations themselves. Here the question is where a "breakthrough" leads if it is pressed, precisely by intellectual reasoning, to the most radical conclusions. This leads to the problem of theodicy, which in turn is the basis of the doctrines of radical salvation which have shaped the greatest religious movements.

Here Weber employs again the basic dichotomy already outlined, between the conception of an immanent principle of divinity which is part of the world from eternity and to which in some sense man can "adapt" himself and the conception of a transcendental divinity, in principle fundamentally separate from the world, controlling it from above and, in the extreme case, conceived as having created it *ex nihilo*. Again the Brahman of Indian religious philosophy and the Semitic creator god are at the extremes. Weber held that whichever direction the process of rationalization takes, it inevitably leads to monotheism, and if divinities other than the supreme one survive in a religious system, they are conceived as in some sense subordinate to the supreme one. In this connection, he remarks that only Judaism and Islam have been monotheistic in the strictest sense, since the Christian Trinity has at least polytheistic aspects, and of course in Catholicism the angels, Mary, Satan, and even the ordinary saints have often been regarded as quasi-divinities, if not in certain phases and areas full-fledged divinities. In spite of the generality of the monotheistic trend, however, it is one of Weber's important points that the direction of the immanent conception of divinity, however monotheistic at the highest philosophical levels, is much more favorable to the retention and prominence of polytheistic elements in the total system than is the transcendental type.

Against this background Weber then deals with an aspect of the problem of meaning which is particularly important for him, and indeed is one of the main threads of his whole thought: the integrations and discrepancies between expectation systems which are institutionalized in normative orders and the actual experiences people undergo. The interest lies in what the people interpret to be the consequences *for them* and for the aspects of the human condition to which they are attached, of conformity or nonconformity with an established normative order. There are two essential dimensions of this problem. The first concerns the *level* of rationalization, a point which was built into the early distinction between taboo and religious ethic. If there is a low level of rationalization the possibility exists of a piecemeal resolution of the tensions which arise from discrepancies between normative expectations and actual experiences. This indeed comes close to Weber's very conception of magic, as the use of supernatural agency to resolve *ad hoc* elements of tension in life-situations.

The second dimension is that of discrepancy itself and its implications. Here Weber takes the fundamental position that, *regardless of the particular content of the normative order,* a major element of discrepancy is inevitable. And the more highly rationalized an order, the greater the tension, the greater the exposure of major elements of a population to experiences which are frustrating in the very specific sense, not merely that things happen and contravene their "interests," but that things happen which are "meaningless" in the sense that they *ought* not to happen. Here above all lie the problems of suffering and of evil, not merely the existence of phenomena defined in these terms, but also the prevalence of the suffering of those who do not morally deserve to suffer, the prevalence of the exposure to evil of the morally just, who thus are punished rather than rewarded for their pains, and perhaps even worse, the fact that evil consequences often will ensue from the actions of those who exactly follow the precepts of the moral law. A classic expression of the discrepancy is the saying that "the good die young and the wicked flourish as the green bay tree."

Weber postulates a basic "drive" toward meaning and the resolution of these discrepancies on the level of meaning, a drive or tendency which is often held in check by various defensive mechanisms, of which the pre-eminent one here relevant is that of magic. But whatever the situation regarding the effectiveness of this drive, there is a crucial point concerning the *direction* in which this tendency propels the development of culture. This is that the search for grounds of meaning which can resolve the discrepancies must lead to continually more "ultimate" reference points which are progressively further removed from the levels of common sense experience on which the discrepancies originally arise. The "explanations," i.e., solutions to the problems of meaning, must be grounded in increasingly generalized and "fundamental" philosophical conceptions.

Given this movement toward generalized explanations, rationalization can take either of two paths. One, under the assumption of immanence, seeks to ground meaning in progressively greater extension of the time span to which it applies, and in increasingly higher "levels" of participation in the sources of ultimate "satisfaction." This is the path which led in India to the philosophies of *karma* and transmigration and to the drastic "relativizing" of the "good things of this life." The other path, under the assumption of transcendence, grounds meaning in the conception of a creation which is inherently destined—by Divine Will—to bring about a resolution of the discrepancies by creating a world and a human condition which does or will in fact accord with the prescriptions of the normative order, a "Kingdom of God on Earth."

Weber saw these two trends as culminating, at the level of moral philosophy, in the two fully consistent philosophies of moral meaning, or theodicies, which have appeared in religious history. The first of these is the doctrine of *karma,* which postulates a complete closure of the moral system over time spans altogether incommensurable with the human life span, though not strictly speaking eternal. The other consistent theodicy is the Calvinistic conception that ultimate resolution depends upon relations between an absolute, all-powerful God, whose "motives" are in principle inaccessible to finite human understanding, and a Creation, including man, which is absolutely and completely dependent on his Will.[18]

To be sure, these two theodicies resolve the problem of discrepancy by carrying it to a ground where the "moral issue" can no longer be relevant. This seems to be a special case of the general fact that logical systems must always rest on primitive postulates which cannot themselves be "proved." In Christian terms, the at-

---

[18] The Zarathustrian conception of an eternal, in principle completely indecisive, conflict between the "Principles" of "Good" and "Evil" is logically consistent, but not so much a solution as a declaration of the philosophical insolubility of the problem.

tempt at human justification of the Will of God presumes being
above God, subjecting Him to an order which the speaker understands independently of God and God must obey.[19] Similar considerations apply in the case of *karma*.

Radical Salvation and the Orientation of Action. If one
presses the theme of the necessary discrepancy between interests
"in this world" and the nature of an order thought to be intrinsically
capable of providing an answer in terms of truly "ultimate" meaning, the tendency is to widen the gap between the two. Hence, for
those who cannot be satisfied with the "compromises" of worldly
balances, there develops the need for radical solutions on a personal basis. Weber calls this the *need for salvation,* which we may
describe as the need for a basis of personal legitimation which is
in accord with these ultimate standards, themselves conceived as
standing in essential conflict with those of *any* institutionalized
worldly order.

As usual, Weber canvasses an immense range of different
modes and levels of conception of the problem of salvation. All of
them, however, are treated as partial solutions leading up to the
two radical possibilities. In both of them the conception of the
"world" is central; there is no such thing as a problem of salvation
except in relation to the world. The need for salvation, of course,
makes sense only because the interests in the things of the world
are themselves relativized, and hence of inferior value, in some
sense, if not positively "evil." Along these lines then, Weber arrives
at twin conceptions, first of the increased *tension* between worldly
possibilities and the need to satisfy the need for "perfection," and
second, of the *direction* in which resolution of the tension may be
sought.

In Weber's very complex discussion the keynote is the importance of the balance between degrees of radicalism in the conception of the problem of salvation and the various devices by which
radical implications can be mitigated. Among the mitigating devices, a particularly prominent place is occupied by the category already familiar from Weber's discussion of the "magical" solutions,
among which the orgiastic figures prominently, which may be

[19] The Puritan term for this presumption would be Idolatry of the
Flesh.

called a half-way station, the category of ritualized institutional dispensation of salvation. By far the most prominent example of this category is the sacramental system of the Roman Catholic church. In such cases the essential criterion is the provision of opportunity for atomized and piecemeal resolution of the tensions arising from discrepancies. The magical solutions provide a "catharsis," be it periodical or reserved for special occasions, and the sacramental system provides absolution for *particular* sins.

At this point in his study, Weber's crucial problem is the determination of the steps by which men have arrived at consideration of the *total* state of discrepancy, and hence a mode of resolution opening the possibility of a completely generalized solution of the problem, i.e., the problem which in Protestant language is phrased as that of "justification." Stressing the term "systematic" —in accord with the general theme of rationalization—Weber held that there are two and only two basic directions in which this radical solution can be sought, though he was far from holding that the ultimate definition of their bases had been reached in his time.

These two generalized solutions are, stated clearly and simply, resolution of tension by escape from the conflicts of worldly existence, and resolution by active agency attempting to bring the state of the "world" in this sense into accord with the normative requirements of a *radical* religious ethic.

This dichotomy is a truism, in much the sense that the dichotomy between the alternatives of avoidance and approach is a truism in the psychology of behavior. Yet Weber's dichotomy is, in my opinion, very solidly grounded in both historical evidence and general action theory, and is truistic only in the sense in which general action theory is also truistic. Given the other elements of Weber's analysis, his dichotomy between the two ultimate or generalized resolutions of the problem of discrepancies between normative expectations and actual experiences presents an empirically applicable hypothesis, with respect to which the burden of proof rests upon him who would substitute another hypothesis.

Weber then applies this conception of dichotomy to the behavior of individuals, asking what specific *paths* are open to the seeker of radical salvation. The specification of these paths is possible by reference to a polarity of alternatives which is central

in the orientation of all action, namely the polarity between resignedness in a setting of conditions and attempts to master conditions. Both resignedness and mastery are strategies to maintain
or enhance personal dignity within the frame of reference. The
path of mastery Weber calls *asceticism,* that of resignedness—or
"adjustment," if one wishes to use that term—he calls *mysticism.*
Both paths are orientations to the human condition as a whole,
available to societies as well as to individuals.

Whichever path is taken by the seeker after salvation, he may
still choose among various positions relative to the situational
order in which he is placed. On the one hand, he may seek salvation and yet avoid a radical break with the institutional order. He
remains "in the world," even if he breaks with the institutional
order in some subjective way, i.e., he may be—in St. Paul's phrase
—"in the world but not of it." On the other hand, he may minimize
contacts with the established world by becoming a solitary anchorite or by joining with others in some segregated community
(the monastic solution). Weber thus derives four types of solution
and of individual path, by cross-tabulating the distinction between
asceticism and mysticism with the distinction between other-
worldly and inner-worldly positions.

Weber's primary concern is with the bases on which religious
orientations can exert *leverage* toward evolutionary social change,
and here is perhaps the most important single place in his analysis where this problem is brought to a head. It is his clear view
that only one of the four types does in fact provide powerful
leverage, but that it is in the long run a more powerful factor
than any elements of economic or political interest in the usual
senses. The type in question is of course *inner-worldly asceticism.*
Let us elucidate its character by contrast with each of the other
three types.

The two other-worldly types are in the nature of the case unfavorable to this leverage. The basis of legitimation is for all four
types "religious" in a sense involving high tension vis-à-vis
"worldly" interests, but for the two otherworldly types the direction of endeavor is in addition *away from* any concern with the
state of the world, except to the extent that it threatens to interfere with the religious interests of the individual himself. The other-

worldly mystic seeks to avoid subjective "desire" because of its interference with the pursuit of salvation, which is defined as involving dissociation from the world and total loss of interest in its concerns. The other-worldly ascetic on the other hand seeks, phrased in Christian terms, "mastery" over the flesh, the capacity to control worldly motivation, but in the interest of "devotional" goals rather than worldly ones.

In inner-worldly mysticism, there is no attempt to escape involvement in worldly status, but while living in and participating in the world the mystic nevertheless seeks to deprive worldly interests, including concern for the "welfare" of others, of any positive meaning or significance. (The mystic gives meaning to the "welfare" of himself and of others only in the sense that the achievement of complete indifference *is* the inner welfare, and should perhaps be achieved equally by all.)

The inner-worldly ascetic, on the other hand, seeks mastery over the worldly component of his individual personality, and seeks in principle to extend this mastery to *all* aspects of the human condition. His goal is to attain mastery over the human condition as a whole. Weber saw this most significant alternative as rooted in the great transcendental-monotheistic tradition of the Semitic world in Judaism, Christianity, and Islam, and standing in the sharpest contrast with the immanent-pantheistic traditions of India. The extreme types saw their fullest realization in ascetic Protestantism on the one hand, early Buddhism on the other. The former was the purest inner-worldly asceticism, the latter the purest other-worldly mysticism.

Of particular importance in historical development was the fact that the ascetic point of view was inherently more favorable to firm collectivity formation than the mystical, which tended to a very special religious "individualism." Thus, the early Christian church was a firm and specifically differentiated religious collectivity or *Gemeinde* of which no comparable case existed on an oriental religious basis. When other-worldly asceticism developed on a Christian basis, it led to far firmer collectivity organization in the monastic orders than was the case, for example, in Buddhist monasticism. Indeed the orders provided prototypes for Christian secular society, a pattern which finally emerged most fully in ascetic Protestantism, where "every man became a monk" but lived out his "monastic" commitments in secular callings in this world.

Broadly, Weber regarded both Judaism and Islam as "inhibited" stages in the development of innerworldly asceticism, inhibited especially at the social level, above all because they remained bound by ascription, one to a traditionally defined ethnic, the other to a political community which must be "carried along" as a whole to realize the conception of a Kingdom of God on Earth. The modern way of phrasing it is that neither ever achieved the fundamental differentiation between "church" and "state." Catholic Christianity, on the other hand, was another type of way station because its sacramental system stood between the spiritual and the worldly involvements of the individual in such a way as to atomize his moral obligations as an instrument of the divine will. As Weber repeatedly says, it was possible to gain absolution for particular sins, one by one. There was hence no basic focusing of responsibility for the *total* pattern of life.

On the oriental side, Hinduism has been a kind of Indian Catholicism. It mitigated the severity of the pure Buddhist-type doctrine by supplementing it with a social sacramentalism, namely the ritual significance of caste observances, which made the spiritual fate of the individual dependent on what, in Weber's specific sense, were predominantly magical factors. Of course similar tendencies developed within the Buddhist tradition itself, notably in the *Mahayana* branch.

Though he says relatively little about them in this book, Weber seems to have regarded Confucianism and Greek "humanism" as less radical, in some sense less "religious," versions of the two basic tendencies which dominated his analysis. Confucianism was, on the background of a relatively nonrationalized culture, the institutionalization of a religious ethic of specifically *social* responsibility; it was specifically hostile to any doctrine of radical salvation. Its main cultural background was, furthermore, immanent rather than transcendent. Within its special framework it was, in Weber's classic phrase, a "rational doctrine of adaptation *to* the world," not one of "rational mastery *over* the world," which designation he reserved for ascetic Protestantism. A major indication of this, to Weber, was the failure of rationalism within the Confucian tradition to combat the magical elements of the tradition *in principle,* rather than to relativize them by declaring them to be beneath the concern of the "superior man."

The Greek, or more broadly the classical Mediterranean case, is least systematically dealt with by Weber here, though there are many more or less scattered observations about it. I believe that he viewed it as broadly parallel to the Confucian. Both, on their respective bases, represented a first main level of breakthrough of the process of rationalization, in the Confucian case that of a sacralized conception of social order, in the Greek of a cultural order, of a "rational law of nature." "Magical" elements, such as the Homeric pantheon, were fully subordinated in relation to rational laws of nature, but there was no "radical breakthrough" to the idea of an order so drastically different from the human and "natural" that there must emerge a religious ethic demanding a pattern of life drastically different in quality from even the best patterns of life in the established order.

The above is an outline of the main structure of Weber's analysis of the problem of radical salvation, the paths to it, and the implications of such commitments for orientation to "the world." This outline fails to do justice to the immense richness of Weber's discussions of the many nuances of transition and the complex compromise formations. The historical-comparative justification of Weber's main conceptual framework will doubtless long be a subject of fundamental controversy. It seems fair to say that probably no modern scholar has put forward a framework of such scope and conceptual clarity for the ordering of this central aspect of cultural and sociological analysis.

There is an important sense in which this section is the culmination of Weber's construction of a complex analytical scheme in the religious field. But since he has been dealing again here with the principal patterns of orientation themselves, he still has the task of tracing their application to the realistic conditions of implementation, i.e., of institutionalization, and along the way the kinds of conflict which are encountered by social groups whose members have become committed to these radical religious positions.

Types of Religious Ethics in Relation to the World. It goes without saying that any religious movement organized about a conception of radical salvation in the nature of the case stands in a state of high tension in its relations to an institutionalized worldly order. Weber's concern is to analyze some of the main foci of this tension and the ways in which the movement, particularly after its initial phases, can cope with them.

His main point of reference is the proposition that such movements generate an ethic of brotherly love certainly between their members, and very generally "spilling over" to other categories, in the extreme case to all mankind or even all living things. The Christian injunction to "love the Lord thy God with all thy heart, and love thy neighbor as thyself" is prototypical, and by no means confined to one religious tradition.

If it is a religion of radical salvation its reference points for brotherly love as well as for love of God are in some sense extraworldly, though not necessarily otherworldly in the sense of the foregoing discussion. Using a term which Weber did not, they may be said to be "undifferentiated" with reference to the exigencies of social organization in the world. Every attitude and act toward one's "neighbor" should be a full expression of religiously motivated love and should be unaffected by "practical" considerations. The result is an extreme instance of what Weber called a *Gesinnungsethik,* an ethic of moral sentiment rather than of responsibility for consequences. The essential question is whether such an ethic is inherently utopian in the sense that acting fully and directly in accord with its mandate is not compatible with the necessary conditions of the functioning of concrete human societies.

Weber's answer to this, as to so many questions, is far from simple. It depends on at least three considerations: the other components of the pattern of religious orientation itself, the way it is "spelled out" in application to social conditions, and the kind of society in question, since this is far from being a constant. The tension is likely to be least in very simple societies, and in specially segregated religious communities, whether they be monastic orders or such segregated communities as the Hutterites and many other sectarian groups have formed.

A second basic difference is generated by the two main directions in which salvation may be sought. The mystical direction is connected with a tendency to declare the structure of worldly society itself to be irrelevant to true religious interests, and any concern with it to be inherently distracting from the important things. This has dual consequences. It conduces to the maximal extension of the sentiments of solidarity on the level of sentiment as such. It is probably no accident that it is on a Brahman–Hindu–Buddhist background that the radical doctrine of *ahimsa*—the prohibition of killing of any living thing, except plants of course—has arisen, and that vegetarianism is very much a virtue among high caste Hindus. The other consequence, however, is reluctance to accept any realistic conditions of implementing the ethic of brotherly love. Thus, as Weber several times emphasizes, under the strict rules of early Buddhist monasticism there was an absolute prohibition of work of any kind—unless devotions be called work—and the monk could only eat by the charity of laymen, interpreted in a very strict sense. Ideally he could not even solicit gifts of food—he could not in our sense "beg"—but was dependent on the layman's purely spontaneous recognition of his need. This is perhaps as far as the maxim "take no thought for the morrow" has ever been carried in an institution. It is hard to see how a total society could be organized on this basis and indeed, it is one of Weber's major points that this life was in principle accessible only to members of an elite.

Generally speaking the ascetic path to salvation has had a very different emphasis. It may even be said that sheer "mortification of the flesh" on an individual basis is a kind of "work" in that it is oriented to coping with the nature of worldly motives. Weber then lays great stress on the place occupied by work, i.e. "useful" work in a worldly sense, such as growing crops in the Benedictine Rule, as an ascetic exercise. This he regarded as a case in point of the general orientation to mastery—one does not "master" a situation without reference to criteria of effectiveness in dealing with concrete conditions. Weber held that the ascetic path is inherently more likely to produce ways of dealing with realistic exigencies of human relationships than is the mystical.

Weber then reviews some of the main aspects of social organization, especially the economic aspect, from the point of view of this problem. As just noted, for the mystical tradition even the level of simple utilitarian physical production was highly problematical, but this was not so for the ascetic tradition except at the otherworldly extremes which may be said to have involved "mystical" motives. After all, as Weber repeatedly emphasized, most of the early Christians were artisans, and while they regarded the higher order of Roman society as evil, they did not so regard their simple fields of work. Questions arise, however, with advance from the simpler level of technology to the level of complex economics, involving markets and monetary exchange. Here the directness of mutual helpfulness in the simpler exchanges evaporates, and by entrusting interests to the market, one simply does not know in advance what the morally significant consequences of an act may be.[20]

The particular question to which Weber pays the most attention in this area is that of the taking of interest. In the predominantly mystical tradition it could never become a salient problem—almost by definition it belonged on the lower level from which the religious elite must disengage themselves. In the West, however, it has been a particularly central focus of problems of economic ethics. In earlier phases, taking interest has, Weber says, always been regarded as incompatible with the ethic of brotherly love. In the Western world its gradual acceptance took place only through stages involving very severe struggles. Various problems were involved such as Aristotle's famous doctrine of the "sterility" of money, the special role of the Jews and their "double ethic" in this respect, and various others. He was also particularly con-

[20] Thus, for example, Menno Simons, the founder of the Mennonite sect, in no way disapproved the simpler concerns with worldly welfare, e.g. health, preservation of life, even comfort. The economic problem for him was the possibility that a producer who entrusted his product to the market could not guarantee the moral quality of the use to which a consumer, unknown to him, might put it. Hence he forbade all involvement where such risks might be involved. It is relatively difficult, on a Christian background, to use food unethically, hence agriculture, even in a market context, is a relatively approved occupation for Mennonites. The automobile is quite another matter. This has posed a much more serious moral problem, on which apparently there has been some "give" in recent times. The even more strictly sectarian Hutterites seem still to maintain a nearly absolute prohibition of its use.

cerned with the history of the attitudes of the Catholic Church in this matter, the eventual upshot of which was recognition of the positive functional significance of interest-taking finance in even a "Christian society." But the Church had so involved itself in the other point of view that it could not simply "repeal" the prohibition of usury, and had to let the prohibition become a dead letter.

Weber is careful to emphasize that the usury question, and back of it the more general question of the financial aspect of capitalism, is not for him the major issue with respect to the problem of the relation of the Protestant ethic to modern economic development. Rather, the major issue is the moral legitimation of productivity and the channelling of the needs of individuals for justification in the religious sense in this direction, which is the decisive point, in this context, about ascetic Protestantism. For Weber, the "typical" capitalist was not the socially elite banker, but the middle class industrial entrepreneur.

Weber reviews extensively the ethical dilemmas posed to a religious ethic by the problems of political power, especially the role of physical force in politics. From the point of view of the pure ethic of brotherly love, the use of force is perhaps the prototypical evil. Yet violence is historically intertwined in the most complex ways with the processes of the extension of order in human societies. There have here, as well as in the economic field, been deep tensions over the status of religious groups in relation to the exigencies of the world.

In the process of its institutionalization Christianity gave religious sanction to political authority in secular society, a process which occurred in two main steps. The first step was the "constantinian," which involved not only the conversion of a Roman emperor to Christianity, but equally the recognition by the Church, for the successors of Constantine, that an emperor could be a Christian. Later, on the basis of a much sharper *differentiation* between church and state, this sanction of political authority was symbolized by the coronation of an emperor, Charlemagne, by the Pope, an emperor whose obligation to defend his realm by military means was obviously taken for granted. The dilemmas of the use of force, and more generally of coercion by legitimate authority ultimately religiously legitimated authority—are, Weber held, inescapable. Only the main ascetic trend could develop a positive religious basis of such legitimation.

The fields of economic and political interests duly differentiated from each other, not fused as is done by Marxists, are the prototypical ones involved in the adjustment of a radical religious ethic to the exigencies of the world. In addition to these, Weber also discusses the tensions arising over the erotic sphere, and over that of art, thus manifesting an important sensitivity to problems on the one hand of the relation of the personality of the individual to its organic base, on the other hand to problems of the cultural system other than problems in the religious aspect as such. His interest in the non-religious aspects of culture is rounded out by various discussions in his work of the relation of religion to concern with science.

Weber concludes his discussion of orientations to the world, and indeed the book as a whole, with a brief and, the German editors tell us, incomplete discussion of the relevance of these problems to that of "capitalism." He makes clear that the essential point for him is not the relation between religion and capitalism in the most general formal sense of orientation to monetary profit-making. Again and again in his work he emphasizes that capitalism in this generic sense has occurred wherever the monetary mechanism itself has been developed. There are many subvarieties.

His principal interest, therefore, is not in capitalism in general but in a very special variety of it, which Weber called "rational bourgeois capitalism." This may be defined broadly as the maximization of the conception of rational effectiveness and efficiency in the organization of economic production in a market-oriented system. It includes not only profit-making, but bureaucratic organization in the interest of productivity, and various other things.

In the half-century since Weber wrote it has become increasingly clear that his main interest and focus was modern industrial society *as a whole,* not its "capitalistic" subvariety. The problem of the specific role of markets is not the essential problem from Weber's point of view, but one particularly important sub-problem of the more general complex with which he was concerned. More than any other single writer in the background of our own generation, Weber gave us the primary reference points for analyzing the broad *common* patterns of modern social, political, and economic development.

As I have suggested a number of times, Weber's was the type of mind which, in an often baffling way, combined enormous sensitivity to the most complex detail with certain not only very broad, but very precisely conceived main lines of analysis. I have thought that this introduction could be most useful by attempting to highlight the main logical and substantive structures of Weber's sociology of religion, since the reader will be immersed in the detail by the mere fact of reading, and Weber does not succinctly sum up this analytical component as a whole at any point in his exposition in this book or elsewhere.

To sum up our own perspective: This book is clearly the strategically central part of a generally evolutionary view of the development of human society. It is the one in which Weber attributes prime causal significance to the factor of "religious orientation" as an initiating factor and as a differentiating factor in the process. This factor is, however, nowhere treated as automatically unfolding or "actualizing itself" except through highly complex processes of interaction with other factors and independent. The outcomes are always resultant from and attributable to such interaction, never to any one factor alone. Weber clearly insisted on the independent significance of the ideas which originated as solutions of the problems of meaning, independent significance of the "religious interests" which operate within this framework. But at the same time he made as great a single contribution to the understanding of the role of "material" factors in the process of social development as did any scholar, at least up to his time—including, it seems to me, Karl Marx.

Within this analytical framework, Weber in turn treated the development of the modern Western world, and particularly the sector of it influenced by ascetic Protestantism, as standing in the vanguard of the most important general evolutionary trend. He sees its place as having been decisively influenced by its religious background—with all the appropriate qualifications—by comparison with the other great cultural traditions. The decisive significance in the turbulent contemporary world of economic development at the industrial levels and indeed of the more modern levels of political organization, cannot be understood apart from this broader evolutionary context. As Weber insisted again and again, the problem of accounting for the origination of a pattern of cultural and social organization is fundamentally different from the problem of accounting for its diffusion from examples already established. That modern industrial society has become the primary model for the world as a whole can scarcely be doubted.

It is to be hoped that the publication of this work in English will contribute materially to a higher level of understanding of these problems of what has been happening to the human condition in the mid-twentieth century. Weber would have been the very last to claim anything like definitiveness for his own work. It seems unlikely, however, that a better assessment can be arrived at without a very thorough coming to terms with the nature and implications of Weber's work. The volume here presented is probably, for historical evaluation, the most important single segment of his work.

In spite of the soundness and scope of Weber's theoretical framework for the sociology of religion, the present day usefulness of that theoretical framework is at least partially limited by three considerations. First, the application of the framework to concrete problems requires such flexibility and such a fund of knowledge as Weber possessed. Second, the religious phenomena themselves have changed, especially in the United States, since Weber formulated his framework and his hypotheses. Third, sociological theory has in some respects advanced beyond Weber's theoretical framework. After discussing these limitations, I shall return to the basic thesis of this introduction, the enduring greatness of Weber's theoretical framework for the sociology of religion.

Weber's enormous historical erudition, as well as his high level of empirical insight and judgment, served to cover over whatever theoretical deficiencies were inherent in his conceptual framework. There is a brilliant *ad hocness* to Weber's analysis, particularly when he deals with problems of transition. Whether the problems involve a transition between types, without reference to genetic relatedness, or involve a transition in the developmental process from one phase or stage to another, such problems of transition bring to prominent attention both the difficulties inherent in Weber's conceptual framework and the brilliance with which Weber found *ad hoc* solutions to each such difficulty. But Weber's scheme itself, when applied by scholars of lesser genius than Weber, can hardly yield comparable results. This may be a principal reason why there has been relatively little cumulative development of Weber's sociological contributions. But we shall also see that sociology has developed newer and possibly better theoretical methods for dealing with the cultural phenomena which Weber treated under the concepts of "prophetic break" and "motivation."

In the fifty years since Weber wrote, much has happened in the religious situation of Christendom, and perhaps especially in the religious situation of the United States. The three dominant "faiths" of American society have come to be integrated into a single socio-religious system, a development which even in the late nineteenth century seemed highly unlikely. This system has evolved under the "historical leadership of American liberal Protestantism," but has very much involved and modified all three major faiths. For instance, the pariah status of the Jewish faith, on which Weber laid great stress, has been modified, not only through greater "toleration" of Jews by Gentiles, but also by a new level of Jewish acceptance of the *legitimacy* of the outside order in which Jews come into contact with Gentiles, especially the occupational system. For all Jews except the most rigidly orthodox, a religiously sanctioned life is no longer confined to the internal life of the Jewish community. The position of the Roman Catholic community in the United States is undergoing similar modifications, of which visible indices can be found in the broad Protestant acceptance of a Roman Catholic president, and the American Catholic hierarchy's failure to repudiate that president's expressed position on the separation between Church and State. These changes have occurred by a developmental restructuring, without a prophetic break with the established order. The basic value-pattern common to all three faiths has been at least partially institutionalized at a higher level of generality, and the "privitization" of religion through denominational pluralism has been extended from the Protestant group to the whole range of faiths.[21]

Such developments in the religious situation were only beginning in Weber's time, and it would be a great deal to demand of his writings that they predict the present phase. However, the fact that the present phase was highly unlikely from Weber's point of view may be a valid index of the theoretical difficulties inherent in his position.

Weber's mode of thinking was dominated by the concept of the ideal type, which he applied to both cultural content and individual motives. He was quite right to insist, against a background of idealistic historicism, that explanatory concepts be applicable to the understandable motives of individuals. And when we consider how often the "methodological individualism" of English-speaking social scientists has led them to biopsychological reductionism, we can see that Weber was indeed right to insist that the inclusion of cultural content is indispensable to the analysis of orientations to the great problems of meaning. But it is now possible to go somewhat beyond the concept of the ideal type, by making a more sophisticated and thorough use of the concept of system.

Weber, as many "culture and personality" theorists have done since his time, tended to treat "typical" motives—which for him always involved cultural "definitions of the situation"—as rigidly unchangeable entities. Thus, he used ideal types to "atomize" his material into rigid units which could only be combined and recombined in a "mechanistic" way or absorbed into higher-order "patterns." His own theoretical method suffers to some extent from the "trait atomism" of the intellectual tradition from which he came and against which he partially revolted, and his method even resembles the process of rationalization which he traces in religious phenomena. He frequently atomizes traits, and when

---

[21] The first writer to express a clear conception of this new American religious pattern, to my knowledge, was Will Herberg in his *Protestant, Catholic, Jew*, first edition 1951, second and extended edition 1960. I have dealt with some phases of the new pattern in "Some Comments on the Pattern of Religious Organization in the United States," *Daedalus*, Summer, 1959, reprinted as Chapter 10 of my volume of essays, *Structure and Process in Modern Societies*, 1960.

this proves unsatisfactory, postulates unduly rigid higher-order cultural configurations.[22]

This tendency to atomize traits instead of interrelating them within systems appears in Weber's treatments of what we now term personality, society, and culture. Surprisingly, it is most evident in his treatment of society, even though he is thought of in the first instance as a sociologist. Though he was well versed in economic theory and contributed some of the most penetrating comments about markets that were made in his time, it is still true that his analysis of modern capitalism stressed an overly rigid typological formula of the harnessing of "bureaucratic" organization to an orientation to profit. On the one hand, he did not sufficiently analyze the articulation of these "bureaucratic" organizational units with each other.[23] On the other hand, he treated the organizational units themselves too narrowly, not taking sufficient account of the range of variation of both organizational types and the role structures within them. Most conspicuously, he failed to sufficiently recognize or analyze the roles of applied science and scientific research itself when harnessed within "bureaucratic" organizations. Less obviously, but of comparable importance, he did not adequately delineate the subtle transitions between orientation to profit-making, orientation within various "fiduciary" organizations, and orientation within public organizations. His neglect of these transitions in orientation led him to postulate a sharper dichotomy between "capitalistic" and "socialistic" forms of economic organization—as distinguished from forms of economic ideology—than the facts and trends of development warranted. The same typological rigidity makes its appearance in Weber's sociology of religion.

The theoretical difficulties caused by typological rigidity and trait atomism, covered over in many instances by Weber's enormous erudition, insight and *ad hoc* resourcefulness, come to the

[22] The present writer has commented upon the atomism of ideal types in *The Structure of Social Action*, Chap. XVII, and on a more advanced basis in the Introduction to Weber's *Theory of Social and Economic Organization*, 1947.

[23] Consider the fruitfulness of Durkheim's analysis of the role of institutionalization of contract in the articulation and interrelation of organizational units.

surface at two main points: his analyses of the prophetic *break* and of "motivation." We have seen in our review of the religious situation in the United States how gradual, cumulative, and inter-related changes can be; yet Weber seemed unable to conceive that major evolutionary steps could take place by gradual process. Such prophetic breaks as he describes have probably occurred, but he seems to have a theoretical bias toward highlighting them, to the neglect of the possibility of more gradual and cumulative processes of change. In treating phenomena of "motivation," he displays a similar theoretical bias toward hypostatizing rigid types of "motives," imputed to both individuals and classes of individuals, and paralleling the "ideal types" which are his primary units of analysis. He even reifies the famous "profit motive," though less so than has been common in the utilitarian tradition of analysis. In the field of the sociology of religion, he reifies such motives as the "need for salvation," and tends to dissociate such motives from other and more ordinary motives present at the level of individual personality. Motives are related to cultural "ideal types" in a morphological framework rather than related to other motives in the system of personality and other processes in the systems of society and culture.

Weber's scheme, in the sociology of religion and generally, constituted a great advance in its time, has provided a foundation for further progress in sociology, and remains relevant at its broadest morphological levels. Though Weber's conceptual scheme is certainly far from complete or definitive, it seems unlikely that the broadest outline of the evolutionary pattern of the development of religious orientations, including the conception of the two basic directions of rationalization in the field of meaning, will be radically invalidated.

Difficulties seem to become more prominent as attention is focused on problems of transition, whether it be transition between types, without reference to genetic relatedness, or transition in the developmental process from one phase or stage to the next. As Weber deals with such problems there seems to be a certain *ad hocness* when, so to speak, theoretical deficiencies are covered over by his enormous historical erudition and excellent level of empirical insight and judgment. The suggestion is, however, that in the hands of a scholar of lesser genius than Weber, it would be very difficult to get comparable results through the use of his scheme. This may well be one principal reason for the relatively small cumulative outcome of Weber's work.

There are, perhaps, two main points at which a theoretical difficulty comes to the surface in spite of Weber's *ad hoc* resourcefulness. One of these has just been suggested, namely, his particularly sharp emphasis on the importance of the prophetic *break*. Essentially, it is as if he could not conceive of major evolutionary steps by gradual process. This is not at all to deny that such breaks have occurred and have been of decisive importance, but only to suggest that there is a theoretical bias in favor of highlighting them and, conversely, neglecting the possibilities of more gradual cumulative processes of change.

The second point concerns his treatment of motivation. Very broadly it may be said that he is under a theoretical pressure to hypostatize types of motives, imputed to individuals and classes, which match the ideal types which are his primary units of analysis. He is even, I think, guilty of too great a reification of the famous "profit motive," though, of course, far less so than has been usual in the Western utilitarian tradition. The same tendency appears in the religious field, perhaps most conspicuously in such conceptions as the "need for salvation" and the degree to which Weber tends to dissociate it at the personality level from the other, more ordinary motives of individuals.

The main point is that Weber's atomism of types introduces into his analysis a rigidity which tends to suppress notice of the ranges of variation between the components included in the types. I have suggested that this typological rigidity becomes evident at two main points in Weber's analysis. First, it suppresses notice of independent variables which may account for more gradual, cumulative socio-cultural changes; and hence it leads Weber to feel that there must be abrupt shifts from one type to another. Second, typological rigidity appears in his analysis of motivation, suppressing the flexibility of transition from one motive to another, and thus tending to tie motivational categories to types of concrete social action, thereby unduly "psychologizing" the interpretation of concrete social actions in the context of analysis of the social system.

These last criticisms are not intended to derogate in any way the importance of Weber's contribution in this field, which is a permanent contribution. Indeed, if the hindsight of fifty years' development of theory in the field were not able to uncover important theoretical difficulties in such a body of thought as Weber's sociology of religion, rather than merely trivial errors of fact, this would be a sad commentary upon the progress of social science, which has in fact been real progress.

It is my view that this book is *the* most crucial contribution of our century to the comparative and evolutionary understanding of the relations between religion and society, and even of society and culture generally. But it, like any great contribution to science, is both a synthesis and a point of departure for another set of steps in the unending series of steps which constitutes the process of the improvement of knowledge.

THE SOCIOLOGY OF RELIGION

I. The Rise of Religions

To define "religion," to say what it *is*, is not possible at the start of a presentation such as this. Definition can be attempted, if at all, only at the conclusion of the study. The essence of religion is not even our concern, as we make it our task to study the conditions and effects of a particular type of social behavior.

The external courses of religious behavior are so diverse that an understanding of this behavior can only be achieved from the viewpoint of the subjective experiences, ideas, and purposes of the individuals concerned—in short, from the viewpoint of the religious behavior's "meaning" (*Sinn*).

The most elementary forms of behavior motivated by religious or magical factors are oriented to *this* world. "That it may go well with thee . . . and that thou mayest prolong thy days upon the earth" (Deut. 4:40) expresses the reason for the performance of actions enjoined by religion or magic. Even human sacrifices, uncommon among urban peoples, were performed in the Phoenician maritime cities without any otherworldly expectations whatsoever. Furthermore, religiously or magically motivated behavior is relatively rational behavior, especially in its earliest manifestations. It follows rules of experience, though it is not necessarily action in accordance with a means-end schema. Rubbing will elicit sparks from pieces of wood, and in like fashion the simulative actions of a magician will evoke rain from the heavens. The sparks resulting from twirling the wooden sticks are as much a "magical" effect as the rain evoked by the manipulations of the rainmaker. Thus, religious or magical behavior or thinking must not be set apart from the range of everyday purposive conduct, particularly since even the ends of the religious and magical actions are predominantly economic.

1

Only we, judging from the standpoint of our modern views of nature, can distinguish objectively in such behavior those attributions of causality which are "correct" from those which are "fallacious," and then designate the fallacious attributions of causality as irrational, and the corresponding acts as "magic." Quite a different distinction will be made by the person performing the magical act, who will instead distinguish between the greater or lesser ordinariness of the phenomena in question. For example, not every stone can serve as a fetish, a source of magical power. Nor does every person have the capacity to achieve the ecstatic states which are viewed, in accordance with primitive experience, as the preconditions for producing certain effects in meteorology, healing, divination, and telepathy. It is primarily, though not exclusively, these extraordinary powers that have been designated by such special terms as "mana," "orenda," and the Iranian "maga" (the term from which our word "magic" is derived). We shall henceforth employ the term "charisma" for such extraordinary powers.

Charisma may be either of two types. Where this appellation is fully merited, charisma is a gift that inheres in an object or person simply by virtue of natural endowment. Such primary charisma cannot be acquired by any means. But charisma of the other type may be produced artificially in an object or person through some extraordinary means. Even then, it is assumed that charismatic powers can be developed only in people or objects in which the germ already existed but would have remained dormant unless evoked by some ascetic or other regimen. Thus, even at the earliest stage of religious evolution there are already present *in nuce* all forms of the doctrine of religious grace, from that of *gratia infusa* to the most rigorous tenet of salvation by good works. The strongly naturalistic orientation (lately termed "pre-animistic") of the earliest religious phenomena is still a feature of folk religion. To this day, no decision of church councils, differentiating the "worship" of God from the "adoration" of the icons of saints, and defining the icons as mere instruments of devotion, has succeeded in deterring a south European peasant from spitting on the statue of a saint when he holds it responsible that a favor he sought did not materialize, even though the customary procedures were performed.

A process of abstraction, which only appears to be simple, has usually already been carried out in the most primitive instances of religious behavior which we examine. Already crystallized is the notion that certain beings are concealed "behind" and responsible for the activity of the charismatically endowed natural objects, artifacts, animals, or persons. This is the belief in spirits. At the outset, "spirit" is neither soul, demon, nor god, but something indeterminate, material yet invisible, nonpersonal and yet somehow endowed with volition. By entering into a concrete object, spirit endows the latter with its distinctive power. The spirit may depart from its host or vessel, leaving the latter inoperative and causing the magician's charisma to fail. In other cases, the spirit may diminish into nothingness, or it may enter into another person or thing.

That any particular economic conditions are prerequisites for the emergence of a belief in spirits does not appear to be demonstrable. But belief in spirits, like all abstraction, is most advanced in those societies within which certain persons possess charismatic magical powers that inhere only in those with special qualifications. Indeed it is this circumstance that lays the foundation for the oldest of all "vocations," that of the professional necromancer. In contrast to the ordinary layman, the magician is the person who is permanently endowed with charisma. Furthermore, he has taken a lease on, or has at least made a unique object of his cultivation, the distinctive subjective condition that notably represents or mediates charisma, namely ecstasy. For the layman, this psychological state is accessible only in occasional actions. Unlike the merely rational practice of wizardry, ecstasy occurs in a social form, the orgy, which is the primordial form of communal religious association. But the orgy is an occasional activity, whereas the enterprise of the magician is continuous and he is indispensable for its operation.

Because of the routine demands of living, the layman may experience ecstasy only occasionally, as intoxication. To induce ecstasy, he may employ any type of alcoholic beverage, tobacco, or similar narcotics—and especially music—all of which originally served orgiastic purposes. In addition to the rational manipulation of spirits in accordance with economic interests, the manner in which ecstasy was employed constituted another important concern of the magician's art, which, naturally enough, developed almost everywhere into a secret lore. On the basis of the magician's experience with the conditions of orgies, and in all likelihood under the influence of his professional practice, there evolved the concept of "soul" as a separate entity present in, behind or near natural objects, even as the human body contains something that leaves it in dream, syncope, ecstasy, or death.

This is not the place to treat extensively the diversity of possible relationships between a spiritual being and the object behind which it lurks and with which it is somehow connected. These spirits or souls may "dwell" more or less continuously and exclusively near or within a concrete object or process. But on the other hand, they may somehow "possess" types of events, things, or categories, the behavior and efficacy of which they will decisively determine. These and similar views are animistic. The spirits may temporarily incorporate themselves into things, plants, animals, or people; this is a further stage of abstraction, achieved only gradually.

At the highest stage of abstraction, which is scarcely ever maintained consistently, spirits may be regarded as invisible essences that follow their own laws, and are merely "symbolized by" concrete objects. In between these extremes of naturalism and abstraction there are many transitions and combinations. Yet even at the first stage of the simpler forms of abstraction, there is present in principle the notion of "supersensual" forces that may intervene in the destiny of people in the same way that a man may influence the course of the world about him.

At these earlier stages, not even the gods and demons are yet personal or enduring, and indeed they do not even have names of their own. A god may be thought of as a power controlling the course of one particular event (Usener's *Augenblicksgötter*), to whom no one gives a second thought until the event in question is repeated. On the other hand, a god may be the power which somehow emanates from a great hero after his death. Either personification or depersonalization may be a later development. Then, too, we find gods without any personal name, who are designated only by the name of the process they control. At a later time, when the semantics of this designation is no longer understood, the designation of this process may take on the character of a proper name for the god. Conversely, the proper names of powerful chieftains or prophets have become the designations of divine powers, a procedure there employed in reverse by myth to derive the right to transform purely divine appellations into personal names of deified heroes. Whether a given conception of a deity becomes enduring and therefore always to be approached by magical or symbolic means, depends upon many different circumstances. The most important of these is whether and in what manner the clientele of a magician or the personal following of a secular chieftain accept the god in question on the basis of their own personal experiences.

Here we may simply note that the result of this process is the rise on the one hand of the idea of the "soul," and on the other of ideas of "gods," "demons," and "supernatural" powers, the ordering of whose relations to men constitutes the realm of religious behavior. At the outset, the soul is neither a personal nor yet an impersonal entity. It is frequently identified—in a naturalistic fashion—with something that disappears after death, e.g., with the breath or with the beat of the heart in which it resides and by the ingestion of which one may acquire the courage of his dead adversary. Far more important is the fact that the soul is frequently viewed as a heterogeneous entity. Thus, the soul that leaves man during dreams is distinguished from the soul that leaves him in ecstasy—when his heart beats in his throat and his breath fails, and from the soul that inhabits his shadow. Different yet is the soul that, after death, clings to the corpse or stays near it as long as something is left of it, and that continues to exert influence at the site of the person's former residence, observing with envy and anger how the heirs are relishing what had belonged to it in its life. Still another soul is that which appears to the descendants in dreams or visions, threatening or counseling, or that which enters into some animal or into another person—especially a newborn baby— bringing blessing or curse, as the case may be. The conception of the "soul" as an independent entity set over against the "body" is by no means universally accepted, even in the religions of salvation. Indeed, some of these religions, such as Buddhism, specifically reject this notion.

What is primarily distinctive in this whole development is not the personality, impersonality or superpersonality of these supernatural powers, but the fact that new experiences now play a role in life. Before, only the things or events that actually exist or take place played a role in life; now certain experiences, of a different order in that they only signify something, also play a role in life. Magic is transformed from a direct manipulation of forces into a symbolic activity.

A notion that the soul of the dead must be rendered innocuous developed, beyond the direct and animal-like fear of the physical corpse (a fear manifested even by animals), which direct fear often determined burial postures and procedures, e.g., the squatting and upright postures, cremation, etc. After the development of ideas of the soul, the body had to be removed or restrained in the grave, provided with a tolerable existence, and prevented from becoming envious of the possessions enjoyed by the living; or its good will had to be secured in other ways, if the survivors were to live in peace. Of the various magical practices relating to the disposal of the dead, the notion with the most enduring economic consequences is that the corpse must be accompanied to the grave by all its personal belongings. This notion was gradually attenuated to the requirement that the goods of the deceased must not be touched for at least a brief period after his death, and frequently the requirement that the survivors must not even enjoy their own possessions lest they arouse the envy of the dead. The funerary prescriptions of the Chinese still fully retain this view, with consequences that are equally irrational in both the economic and the political spheres. One of the interdictions during the mourning period related to the occupancy of a benefice or inheritance; since the usufruct thereof constituted a possession, it had to be avoided.

Various consequences of significance to magical art emerged from the development of a realm of souls, demons, and gods. These beings cannot be grasped or perceived in any concrete sense but manifest a type of transcendental being which normally is accessible only through the mediation of symbols and significances, and which consequently is represented as shadowy and even unreal. Since it is assumed that behind real things and events there is something else, distinctive and spiritual, of which real events are only the symptoms or indeed the symbols, an effort must be made to influence, not the concrete things, but the spiritual powers that express themselves through concrete things. This is done through actions that address themselves to a spirit or soul, hence done by instrumentalities that "mean" something, i.e., symbols. Thereafter, naturalism may be swept away by a flood of symbolic actions. The occurrence of this displacement of naturalism depends upon the success with which the professional masters of the symbolism use their status of power within the community to impart vigor and intellectual elaboration to their beliefs. The displacement of naturalism will also depend upon the significance of magic for the distinctive character of the economy and upon the power of the organization the necromancers succeed in creating.

The proliferation of symbolic acts and their supplanting of the original naturalism will have far-reaching consequences. Thus, if the dead person is accessible only through symbolic actions, and indeed if the god expresses himself only through symbols, then the corpse may be satisfied with symbols instead of real things. As a result, actual sacrifices may be replaced by shewbreads and puppet-like representations of the surviving wives and servants of the deceased. It is of interest that the oldest paper money was used to pay, not the living, but the dead. A similar substitution occurred in the relationship of men to gods and demons. More and more, things and events assumed significances other than the real potencies that actually or presumably inhered in them, and efforts were made to achieve real effects by means of various symbolically significant actions.

Every purely magical act that had proved successful in a naturalistic sense was of course repeated in the form once established as effective. This principle extended to the entire domain of symbolic significances, since the slightest deviation from the ostensibly successful method might render the procedure inefficacious Thus, all areas of human activity were drawn into this circle of magical symbolism. For this reason the greatest conflicts between purely dogmatic views, even within rationalistic religions, may be tolerated more easily than innovations in symbolism, which threaten the magical efficacy of action or even—and this is a new concept supervening upon symbolism—arouse the anger of a god or an ancestral spirit. Thus, the question whether a cross should be made with two or three bars was a basic reason for the schism of the Russian church as late as the seventeenth century. Again, the fear of giving serious affront to two dozen saints by omitting the days sacred to them from the calendar year has hindered the reception of the Georgian calendar in Russia up to this time.* Among the magicians of India, faulty singing during ritual dances was immediately punished by the death of the guilty singer, to remove the evil magic or to avert the anger of the god.

The religious stereotyping of pictorial artifacts, the oldest form of stylization, was directly determined by magical conceptions and indirectly determined by the fact that these artifacts came to be produced professionally for their magical significance. This stylizing tended alone to automatically favor the production of art objects based upon design rather than upon representative reproduction of natural objects. The significance of the religious factor in art is exemplified in Egypt, where the devaluation of the traditional religion by the monotheistic campaign of Amenhotep IV (Ikhnaton) immediately stimulated naturalism. Other examples of the religious stylization of art may be found in the magical uses of alphabetical symbols; the developments of mimicry and dance as homeopathic, apotropaic, exorcistic, or magically coercive symbolisms; and the stereotyping of admissible musical scales, or at least admissible musical keynotes (*raga* in India), in contrast to grace notes. Another manifestation is found in the widespread substitutions of therapies based upon exorcism or upon symbolic homeopathy for the previous empirical methods of medical treatment, which were frequently considerably developed but still seemed only a cure of the symptoms, from the point of view of symbolism and the animistic doctrine of possession by spirits. From the standpoint of animistic symbolism's own basic assumptions its therapeutic methods might be regarded as rational, but they bear the same relation to empirical therapy as astrology, which grew from the same roots, bears to empirical computation of the calendar.

These and related phenomena had incalculable significance for the substantive evolution of culture, though we cannot go into

* [This was written prior to 1914. German editor's note.]

any additional details here. The first and fundamental effect of religious views upon the conduct of life and therefore upon economic activity was generally stereotyping. The alteration of any practice which is somehow executed under the protection of supernatural forces may affect the interests of spirits and gods. To the natural uncertainties and resistances of every innovator, religion thus adds powerful impediments of its own. The sacred is the uniquely unalterable.

Transitions from pre-animistic naturalism to symbolism were altogether variable as regards specific details. When the primitive tears out the heart of a slain foe, or wrenches the sexual organs from the body of his victim, or extracts the brain from the skull and then mounts the skull in his home or esteems it as the most precious of bridal presents, or eats parts of the bodies of slain foes or the bodies of especially powerful animals—he really believes that he is coming into possession, in a naturalistic fashion, of the various powers attributed to these physical organs. The war dance is in the first instance the product of a mixture of fury and fear before the battle, and it directly produces a heroic frenzy; to this extent it too is naturalistic rather than symbolic. But insofar as the war dance, in the pattern of manipulations by sympathetic magic, mimetically anticipates victory and seeks to insure it by magical means, insofar as animals and men are slaughtered in fixed rites, and insofar as the gods and spirits of the tribe are summoned to participate in the ceremonial repast, the transition to symbolism is at hand. Finally, there is involved in the passage to symbolism the tendency for the participants in the consumption of the sacrificial animal to regard themselves as having a distinctively close kin relationship to one another because the soul of this animal has entered into them.

The term "mythological thinking" has been applied to the pattern of thought which is the basis of the fully developed circle of symbolic concepts, and considerable attention has been given to the clarification of its distinctive character. We cannot occupy ourselves with these problems here, and only one generally important aspect of this type of thinking is of concern to us: the significance of analogy, especially in its most effective form, the comparison. Simile has exerted a lasting influence upon, indeed has controlled, not only the forms of religious expression but also juristic thinking in the treatment of precedents, even when purely empirical techniques of legal thinking had already been developed. The syllogistic construction of concepts through rational subsumption emerged from the comparative process only gradually. Analogical thinking originated in the region of magic, which is based completely upon analogy, rationalized into symbolism.

Gods were not originally represented in human form. To be sure they came to possess the form of enduring beings, which is absolutely essential for them, only after the suppression of the purely naturalistic view still evident in the Vedas (e.g., that actual fire is a god, or is at least the body of a concrete god of fire) in favor of the view that a god, forever identical with himself, possesses all individual fires, controls them, or somehow incorporates them all within himself. This abstract conception becomes really secure only through the continuing activity of a "cult" dedicated to one and the same god—through the god's connection with a continuing association of men, a community for which he has special significance as the enduring god. We shall presently consider this process further. Once this perseveration of the forms of the gods has been secured, the intellectual activity of those concerned in a professional way with such problems may be devoted to the systematic organization of these complexes of ideas.

The gods frequently constituted an unordered miscellany of accidental entities, held together fortuitously by the cult, and this condition was by no means confined to periods of meager social development. Thus, even the gods of the Vedas did not form an ordered commonwealth of gods. But there is generally a tendency for a pantheon to evolve, once systematic thinking concerning religious practice has taken place and a certain (though quite variable) level of rationalization of life generally has been attained, resulting in certain characteristic demands with regard to the responsibilities of the various gods. This entails, on the one hand, the specialization and the fixed characterization of particular gods and, on the other, the allocation to them of constant attributes and differentiated responsibilities. Yet the increasing anthropomorphic personification of the gods is in no way identical with or parallel to the increasing firmness of their respective jurisdictions. Frequently the opposite is true. Thus, the scope of the Roman *numina* is incomparably more fixed and unequivocal than that of the Hellenistic gods. On the other hand, the anthropomorphization and plastic representation of the latter as real personalities went very much further than in the authentic religion of the Romans.

Sociologically, the most important basis for this development is to be found in the fact that the genuine Roman view concerning the general nature of the supernatural tended to retain the pattern of a national religion appropriate to a peasantry and a landed gentry. On the other hand, Greek religion inclined to reflect the general structure of a regional and knightly culture, such as that of the Homeric age with its heroic gods. The partial reception of these conceptions and their indirect influence on Roman soil changed little of the national religion, many of these conceptions attaining only an esthetic existence there. On the other hand, the primary characteristics of the Roman tradition were conserved virtually unchanged in ritual practices. In contrast to the Greek way, the Roman attitude remained permanently adverse to religions of the orgiastic or mystery type. Quite naturally, the capacity of magical powers to develop differentiated forms is much less elastic than the "jurisdiction" of a god conceived as a person. Roman religion remained *religio* (whether the word be derived etymologically from *religare* or from *relegere*); it denoted a tie with tested cultic formulae and a concern for spirits (*numina*) of all types which are active everywhere.

The authentic Roman religion contained, besides the trend toward formalism which resulted from the factors just mentioned, another important characteristic trait that stands in contrast with Greek culture, namely a conception of the impersonal as having an inner relationship to the objectively rational. The *religio* of the Roman surrounded his entire daily life and his every act with the casuistry of a sacred law, a casuistry which temporally and quantitatively occupied his attention quite as much as the attention of the Jews and Hindus was occupied by their ritual laws, quite as much as the attention of the Chinese was occupied by the sacred laws of Taoism. The Roman priestly lists (*indigitamenta*) contained an almost infinite number of gods, particularized and specialized. Every act and indeed every specific element of an act stood under the influence of special *numina*. It was therefore the part of discretion for one engaged in an important activity to invoke and honor, besides the *dii certi* to whom tradition had already assigned a fixed responsibility and influence, various ambiguous gods (*incerti*) whose jurisdiction was uncertain and indeed whose sex, effectiveness, and possibly even existence were dubious. As many as a dozen of the *dii certi* might be involved in the various activities connected with the acquisition of a field. While the Romans tended to regard the *ekstasis* (Latin: *superstitio*) of the Greeks as a mental alienation (*abalienatio mentis*) that was socially reprehensible, the casuistry of Roman *religio* (and of the Etruscan, which went even further) appeared to the Greek as slave-like dread (*deisidämonie*). The Roman interest in keeping the *numina* satisfied had the effect of producing a conceptual analysis of all individual actions into their components, each being assigned to the jurisdiction of a particular *numen* whose special protection it enjoyed.

Although analogous phenomena occurred in India and elsewhere, the listed number of spirits (*numina*) to be derived and formally listed (*indigitieren*) on the basis of purely conceptual analysis, and hence intellectual abstraction, was nowhere as large as among the Romans, for among them was the focus of ritual practice thoroughly concentrated upon this procedure. The characteristic distinction of the Roman way of life which resulted from this abstraction (and this provides an obvious contrast to the influence of Jewish and Asiatic rituals upon their respective cultures) was its ceaseless cultivation of a practical, rational casuistry of sacred law. Another consequence was the development of a sort of advisory sacred jurisprudence and the tendency to treat these matters to a certain extent as lawyer's problems. In this way, sacred law became the mother of rational juristic thinking. This essentially religious characteristic of Roman culture is still evident in the histories of Livy. In contrast to the practical orientation of the Jewish tradition, the Roman emphasis was always on the demonstration of the "correctness" of any given institutional innovation, from the point of view of sacred and national law. The Roman was centrally concerned with questions of legal etiquette, not questions of sin, punishment, penitence, and salvation. However, both traditions contained within themselves the tendency to produce an ever widening rationalization of the worship of the god, as well as of the god concept itself.

For our purposes here, the examination of particular varieties of gods and demons would be of only slight interest, although gods and demons, like vocabularies of languages, have been directly influenced primarily by the economic situations and the historic destinies of different peoples. Since these developments are concealed from us by the mists of time, it is frequently no longer possible to determine why some particular type of deity achieved superiority over others. A certain god may have achieved eminence because he was originally a natural object of importance for economic life; such was the case with gods derived from the stellar bodies. Or he may have originated from some organic process which the gods and demons possess or influence, evoke or impede: disease, death, birth, fire, drought, rainstorm, and harvest failure. The outstanding economic importance of certain events may enable a particular god to achieve primacy within the pantheon, as for example the primacy of the god of heaven. He may be conceived of primarily as the master of light and warmth, but among groups that raise cattle he is most frequently conceived of as the lord of reproduction.

That the worship of chthonic deities such as "Mother Earth" generally presupposes a relative importance of agriculture is fairly obvious, but such parallelism is not always direct. Nor can it be maintained that the heavenly gods, as representatives of a hero's paradise beyond the earth, have everywhere been noble gods rather than chthonic deities of the peasantry. Even less can it be maintained that the development of "Mother Earth" as a goddess parallels the development of matriarchal clan organization. Nevertheless, the chthonic deities who controlled the harvest have customarily borne a more local and popular character than the other gods. In any case, the inferiority of earth divinities to celestial personal gods who reside in the clouds or on the mountains is frequently determined by the development of a feudal culture, and there is a tendency to permit originally tellurian deities to take their place among the gods who are resident in the skies. Conversely, the chthonic deities frequently combine two functions in primarily agrarian cultures: they control the harvest, thus granting wealth, and they are also the masters of the dead who have been laid to rest in the earth. This explains why frequently, as in the Eleusinian mysteries, these two most important practical interests, namely earthly riches and fate in the hereafter, depend upon them. On the other hand, the heavenly gods are the lords of the stars in their courses. The fixed laws by which the celestial bodies are obviously regulated favor a development whereby the rulers of the celestial bodies become masters of everything that has or ought to have fixed laws, particularly of judicial decisions and morality.

Both the increasing objective significance of typical components and types of conduct and subjective reflection about them lead to objective specialization among the gods. This may be of a rather abstract type, as in the case of the gods of "incitation" (*Antreibens*) and many similar gods in India. Or it may lead to qualitative specialization according to particular lines of activity, e.g., praying, fishing, or plowing. The classic paradigm of this fairly abstract form of deity-formation is the highest conception of the ancient Hindu pantheon, Brahma, as the lord of prayer. Just as the Brahmin priests monopolized the power of effective prayer, i.e., of the effective magical coercion of the gods, so did a god in turn now monopolize the disposition of this capacity, thereby controlling what is of primary importance in all religious behavior; as a result, he finally came to be the supreme god, if not the only one. In Rome, Janus, as the god of the correct "beginning" who disposes of everything, achieved more unpretentiously a position of relatively universal importance.

Yet there is no communal activity, as there is no individual action, without its special god. Indeed, if an association is to be permanently guaranteed, it must have such a god. Whenever a grouping does not appear to be the personal following of a single master who forcefully controls it, but rather appears as a genuine group, it has need of a special god of its own. This is already true of such primitive groups as the household and the sib, in which the primary bond is the relationship to the spirits of ancestors, actual or imaginary. To these there are later added the *numina* and the gods of the hearth and the hearth fire. The importance attributed by the group to its cult, which is performed by the head of the house or *gens,* is quite variable and depends on the structure and practical importance of the family. A high degree of development in the domestic cult of ancestors generally runs parallel to a patriarchal structure of the household, since only in a patriarchal structure is the home of central importance, even for the men. But as the example of Israel demonstrates, the connection between these factors is not a simple one, for the gods of other social groupings, especially those of a religious or political type, may by reason of their priests effectively suppress or entirely destroy the domestic cult and the priestly functioning of the family head.

But where the power and significance of the ancestral gods remain unimpaired, they naturally form an extremely strong personal bond, which exercises a profound influence on the family and the *gens,* unifying the members firmly into a strongly cohesive group. This cohesive force also exerts a strong influence on the internal economic relationships of the domestic communities. It effectively determines and stamps all the legal relationships of the family, the legitimacy of the wife and heirs, and the relation of sons to their father and of brothers to one another. From the viewpoint of the family and clan, the religious reprehensibility of marital infidelity is that it may bring about a situation where a stranger, i.e., one not related by blood, might offer sacrifice to the ancestors of the clan which would tend to arouse their indignation against the blood relatives. For the gods and *numina* of a strictly personal association will spurn sacrifices brought by one lacking authorization. Strict observance of the principle of agnate relationship, wherever it is found, certainly is closely connected with this, as are all questions relating to the legitimation of the head of the household for his functioning as priest.

Similar sacral motivations have influenced the testamentary rights of succession of the eldest son, either as sole or preferred heir, though military and economic factors have also been involved in this matter. Furthermore, it is largely to this religious motivation that the Asiatic (Chinese and Japanese) family and clan, and that of Rome in the Occident, owe the maintenance of the patriarchal structure of their economy throughout all changes in economic conditions. Wherever such a religious bond of the domestic community exists, only two possible types of more inclusive associations, especially of the political variety, may emerge. One of these is the religiously dedicated confederation of actual or imaginary clans. The other is the patrimonial rule of a royal joint household over comparable joint households of the subjects, constructed on the attenuated pattern of a patrimonial domestic economy. Wherever the patrimonial rule of the royal household developed, the ancestors and personal gods, the *numina* and *genii,* of the most powerful household took their place beside the domestic gods belonging to subject households and thus lent a religious sanction to the position of the ruler. This was the case in the Far East, as in China, where the emperor as high priest monopolized the cult of the supreme spirits of nature. The sacred role of the *genius* of the Roman ruler (*princeps*), which resulted in the universal reception of the person of the emperor into the lay cult, was calculated to produce similar results.

Where the development was in the direction of a religiously buttressed confederation, there developed a special god of the political organization as such, as was the case with Yahweh. That he was a God of the federation—which according to tradition was an alliance between the Jews and the Midianites—led to a fateful consequence. His relation to the people of Israel, who had accepted him under oath, together with the political confederation and the sacred order of their social relationships, took the form of a covenant (*berith*), a contractual relationship imposed by Yahweh and accepted submissively by Israel. From this, various ritual, canonical, and ethical obligations which were binding upon the human partner were presumed to flow. But it was also deemed appropriate for the human partner, through certain forms enjoined as proper when approaching an omnipotent god, to remind the divine partner of obligations on his part. This is the primary root of what is most distinctive in Israelite religion: the trait of mutual promise which despite various analogues is found nowhere else in such intensity.

On the other hand, it is a universal phenomenon that the formation of a political association entails subordination to a tribal god. In the Mediterranean area synoecism was a reorganization, if not necessarily a new creation, of a cultic community under a civic deity. The classical bearer of the important phenomenon of a political local god was of course the *polis,* yet it was by no means the only one. On the contrary, every permanent political association had a special god who guaranteed the success of the political action of the group. When fully developed, this god was altogether exclusive with respect to outsiders, and in principle he accepted offerings and prayers only from the members of his group, or at least he was expected to act in this fashion. But since one could not be certain of this, disclosure of the method of effectively influencing the god was usually prohibited strictly. The stranger was thus not only a political, but also a religious alien. Even when the god of another society had the same name and attributes as that of one's own polity, he was still considered to be different. Thus the Juno of the Vejienti is not that of the Romans, just as for the Neapolitan the Madonna of each chapel is different from the others; he may adore the one and berate or dishonor the other if she helps his competitors. An effort may be made to render the god disloyal to one's adversaries by promising him, for example, welcome and adoration in the new territory if only he will abandon the foes of the group in question (*evocare deos*). This invocation to the gods of a rival tribe to reject their group in behalf of another was practiced by Camillus before Veji. The gods of one group might be stolen or otherwise acquired by another group, but this does not always accrue to the benefit of the latter, as in the case of the ark of the Israelites which brought plagues upon the Philistine conquerors.

In general, political and military conquest also entailed the victory of the stronger god over the weaker god of the vanquished group. Of course not every god of a collective group was a local god, spatially anchored to the group's administrative center. The *lares* of the Roman family changed their venue as the family moved; the God of Israel was represented, in the narrative of the wandering in the wilderness, as journeying with and before his people. Yet, in contradiction to this account, Yahweh was also represented—and this is his decisive hallmark—as a God from afar, a God of the nations who resided on Sinai, and who approached in the storm with his heavenly hosts (*zebaoth*) only when the military need of his people required his presence and participation. It has been assumed correctly that this particular quality of "effective influence from afar," which resulted from the reception of a foreign god by Israel, was a factor in the evolution of the concept of Yahweh as a universal and omnipotent God. Yet the fact that a god was regarded as a local deity, or that he sometimes demanded of his followers exclusive "monolatry" did not lead to monotheism, but rather, tended to strengthen religious particularism. Conversely, the development of local gods resulted in an uncommon strengthening of political particularism.

This was true even of the *polis,* which was as exclusive of other communities as one church is toward another, and which was absolutely opposed to the formation of a unified priesthood overarching the various groupings. In marked contrast to our state, which is conceived as an institution, the *polis,* as a result of this political particularism, remained essentially a *personal* association of cultic confrères of the civic god. The *polis* was further organized internally into a personal cultic association of tribal, clan, and domestic gods, who were exclusive of one another with respect to their individual cults. Moreover, the *polis* was also exclusive of all those who, within its own boundaries, stood apart from the particular cults of clans and households. Thus in Athens, a man who had no household god (*Zeus herkeios*) could not hold office, as was the case in Rome with anyone who did not belong to the "society of the *patres.*" The special plebeian official (*tribunus plebis*) was covered only by a human oath (*sacro sanctus*); he had no auspices, and hence no *legitimes imperium,* but only a *potestas.*

The local geographical connection of the group god reached its maximum development where the very locale of a particular society came to be regarded as specifically sacred to the god. This was increasingly the case of Palestine with regard to Yahweh, with the result that the tradition depicted him as a god who, living far off but desiring to participate in his cultic association and to honor it, required cartloads of Palestinian soil to be brought to him.

The rise of genuinely local gods is associated not only with permanent settlement, but also with certain other conditions that mark the local association as an agency of political significance. Normally, the god of a locality and his cultic association reach fullest development on the foundation of the state as a separate political association with corporate rights, independent of the court and the person of the ruler. Consequently, such a full development of the local god is not found in India, eastern Asia, or Iran, and occurred only in limited measure in northern Europe, in the form of the tribal god. On the other hand, outside the sphere of judicial civic organization, this development occurred in Egypt, even at the stage of zoolatric religion, for the purpose of apportioning districts. From the city-states, the local deities spread to confederacies such as those of the Israelites and Aetolians, which were oriented to their model. From the viewpoint of the history of ideas, the concept of the association as the local carrier of the cult is an intermediate link between a completely patrimonial view of political communal behavior and a purely objective approach to a purposive association and institution, roughly comparable to the idea of the modern "local corporate organization" (*Gebietskörperschafts-Idee*).

Not only political societies but also occupational and vocational associations have their special deities or saints. These were still entirely absent in the Vedic pantheon, which was a reflection of that particular level of economic development. On the other hand, the creation of the ancient Egyptian god of scribes indicates a rise of bureaucratization, just as the presence all over the globe of special gods and saints for merchants and various types of crafts reflects increasing occupational differentiation. Again, that the Chinese army in the nineteenth century carried through the canonization of its war god signifies that the military was regarded as a special vocation among others. This is in contrast to the conception of the war gods of the ancient Mediterranean littoral and of the Medes, who were always great national gods.

II. Gods, Magicians, and Priests

Just as the forms of the gods vary, depending on natural and social conditions, so too there are variations in the potential of a god to achieve primacy in the pantheon, or to monopolize divinity. Only Judaism and Islam are strictly monotheistic in their essence. The Hindu and Christian forms of the sole or supreme deity are theological concealments of the fact that an important and unique religious interest, namely in salvation through the incarnation of a divinity, stands in the way of strict monotheism. The path to monotheism has been traversed with varying degrees of consistency, but nowhere was the existence of spirits and demons permanently eliminated. Even in the Reformation spirits and demons were simply subordinated unconditionally to the one god, at least in theory.

The decisive consideration was and remains: who is deemed to exert the stronger influence on the individual in his everyday life, the theoretically supreme god or the lower spirits and demons? If the spirits, then the religion of everyday life is decisively determined by them, regardless of the official god-concept of the ostensibly rationalized religion. Where a political god of a locality developed, it was natural enough that he frequently achieved primacy. Whenever a plurality of settled communities with established local gods expanded the area of their political association through conquest, the usual result was that various local gods of the newly amalgamated communities were thereupon welded into a religious totality. Within this amalgamated totality, the empirical and functional specializations of the gods, whether original or subsequently determined by new experiences concerning the special spheres of the gods' influences, would reappear in a division of labor, with varying degrees of clarity.

The local deities of the most important political and religious centers (and hence of the rulers and priests in these centers), e.g., Marduk of Babel or Amon of Thebes, advanced to the rank of the highest gods, only to disappear again with the eventual destruction or removal of the residence, as happened in the case of Assur after the fall of the Assyrian empire. Once a political association as such has come to be regarded as a society under the tutelage of a particular deity, it would seem to be unprotected until the gods of the individual members were also incorporated, amalgamated, and even adopted locally in a sort of synoecism. This practice, so common in antiquity, was re-enacted when the great sacred relics of the provincial cathedrals were transferred to the capital of the unified Russian empire.

The possible combinations of the various principles involved in the construction of a pantheon or in the achievement of a position of primacy by one or another god are almost infinite in number. Indeed, the jurisdictions of the divine figures are as fluid as those of the officials of patrimonial regimes. Moreover, the differentiation between jurisdictions of the various gods is intersected by the practice of religious attachment or courtesy to a particular god who is especially cultivated or directly invoked and who is treated as functionally universal. Thus all possible functions are attributed to the universal god, even functions which have been assigned previously to other deities. This is the "henotheism" which Max Müller erroneously assumed to constitute a special stage of evolution. In the attainment of primacy by a particular god, purely rational factors have often played an important concomitant role. Wherever a considerable measure of constancy in regard to certain prescriptions became clearly evident—most often in the case of stereotyped and fixed religious rites—and where this was recognized by rationalized religious thought, then those deities that evinced the greatest regularity in their behavior, namely the gods of heaven and the stars, had a chance to achieve primacy.

Yet in the routinized religion of everyday life (*Alltagsreligiosität*), only a comparatively minor role was played by those gods who, because they exerted a major influence upon universal natural phenomena, were interpreted by metaphysical speculation as very important and occasionally even as world creators. The reason for this is that these natural phenomena vary but little in their course, and hence it is not necessary to resort in everyday religious practice to the devices of sorcerers and priests in order to influence them. A particular god might be of decisive importance for the entire religion of a people (e.g., Osiris in Egypt) if he met a pressing religious need, in this case a soteriological one; but even so, he might not achieve primacy in the pantheon. The process of rationalization (*ratio*) favored the primacy of universal gods; and every consistent crystallization of a pantheon followed systematic rational principles to some degree, since it was always influenced by professional sacerdotal rationalism or by the rational striving for order on the part of secular individuals. Above all, it is the aforementioned relationship of the rational regularity of the stars in their heavenly courses, as regulated by divine order, to the inviolable sacred social order in terrestrial affairs, that makes the universal gods the responsible guardians of both these phenomena. Upon these gods depend both rational economic practice and the secure, regulated hegemony of sacred norms in the social community. The priests are the primary protagonists and representatives of these sacred norms. Hence the competition of the stellar deities Varuna and Mithra, the guardians of the sacred order, with the storm god Indra, a formidable warrior and the slayer of the dragon, was a reflection of the conflict between the priesthood, striving for a firm regulation and control of life, and the powerful warlike nobility. Among this warrior class, the appropriate reaction to supernatural powers was to believe in a heroic god avid for martial exploits as well as in the disorderly irrationality of fate and adventuresomeness. We shall find this same contrast significant in many other contexts.

The ascension of celestial or astral gods in the pantheon is advanced by a priesthood's propagation of systematized sacred ordinances, as in India, Iran, or Babylonia, and is assisted by a rationalized system of regulated subordination of subjects to their overlords, such as we find in the bureaucratic states of China and Babylonia. In Babylonia, religion plainly evolved toward a belief in the dominion of the stars, particularly the planets, over all things, from the days of the week to the fate of the individual in the afterworld. Development in this direction culminates in astrological fatalism. But this development is actually a product of later sacerdotal lore, and it is still unknown to the national religion of the politically independent state. A god may dominate a pantheon without being an international or universal deity, a transnational god of the entire world. But his dominance of a pantheon usually suggests that he is on his way to becoming that.

As reflection concerning the gods deepened, it was increasingly felt that the existence and nature of the deity must be established unequivocally and that the god should be "universal" in this sense of unequivocal. Among the Greeks, philosophers interpreted whatever gods were found elsewhere as equivalent to and so identical with the deities of the moderately organized Greek pantheon. This tendency toward universalization grew with the increasing predominance of the primary god of the pantheon, that is, as he assumed more of a "monotheistic" character. The growth of a world empire in China, the extension of the power of the Brahmin caste throughout all the varied political formations in India, and the development of the Persian and Roman empires favored the rise of both universalism and monotheism, though not always in the same measure and with quite different degrees of success.

The growth of empire (or other comparable social processes that tend in the same direction) has by no means been the sole or indispensable lever for the accomplishment of this development. In the Yahweh cult, a case of fundamental importance in the history of religion, there evolved at least an approach to universalistic monotheism, namely monolatry, as a result of a concrete historic event—the formation of a confederacy. In this case, universalism was a product of international politics, of which the pragmatic interpreters were the prophetic protagonists of the cult of Yahweh and the ethics enjoined by him. As a consequence of their preaching, the deeds of other nations that were profoundly affecting Israel's vital interests also came to be regarded as wrought by Yahweh. At this point one can see clearly the distinctively and eminently *historical* character of the theorizing of the Hebrew prophets, which stands in sharp contrast to the speculations concerning nature characteristic of the priesthoods of India and Babylonia. Equally striking is the ineluctable obligation resulting from Yahweh's promises: the necessity of interpreting the entire history of the Hebrew nation as consisting of the deeds of Yahweh, and hence as constituting a pattern of world history. In view of the many dire threats to the people's survival, its history appeared contradictory to the divine promises, as well as inextricably intertwined with the destinies of other nations. Thus, the ancient warrior god of the confederacy, who had become the local god of the city of Jerusalem, took on the prophetic and universalistic traits of transcendently sacred omnipotence and inscrutability.

In Egypt, the monotheistic, and hence necessarily universalistic, transition of Amenhotep IV (Ikhnaton) to the solar cult resulted from an entirely different situation. One factor was again the extensive rationalism of the priesthood, and in all likelihood of the laity as well, which was of a purely naturalistic character, in marked contrast to Israelite prophecy. Another factor was the practical need of a monarch at the head of a bureaucratic totalitarian state to break the power of the priests by eliminating the multiplicity of sacerdotal gods, and to restore the ancient power of the deified Pharaoh by elevating the monarch to the position of supreme solar priest. On the other hand, the universalistic monotheism of Christianity and Islam must be regarded as derivative of Judaism, while the relative monotheism of Zoroastrianism was in all likelihood determined at least in part by Near Eastern rather than intra-Iranian influences. All of these monotheisms were critically influenced by the distinctive character of "ethical" prophecy, rather than by the "exemplary" type—a distinction to be expounded later. All other relatively monotheistic and universalistic developments are the products of the philosophical speculations of priests and laymen. They achieved practical religious importance only when they became associated with the quest for salvation. We shall return to this matter later.

Almost everywhere a beginning was made toward some form of consistent monotheism, but practical impediments thwarted this development in the workaday mass religion (*Alltagsreligion*), with the exceptions of Judaism, Islam, and Protestant Christianity. There are different reasons for the failure of a consistent monotheism to develop in different cultures, but the main reason was generally the pressure of the powerful material and ideological interests vested in the priests, who resided in the cultic centers and regulated the cults of the particular gods. Still another impediment to the development of monotheism was the religious need of the laity for an accessible and tangible familiar religious object which could be brought into relationship with concrete life situations or with definite groups of people to the exclusion of outsiders, an object which would above all be accessible to magical influences. The security provided by a tested magical manipulation is far more reassuring than the experience of worshipping a god who—precisely because he is omnipotent—is not subject to magical influence. The crystallization of developed conceptions of supernatural forces as gods, even as a single transcendent god, by no means automatically eliminated the ancient magical notions, not even in Christianity. It did produce, however, the possibility of a dual relationship between men and the supernatural. This must now be discussed.

A power conceived by analogy to living persons may be coerced into the service of man, just as the naturalistic power of a spirit could be coerced. Whoever possesses the requisite charisma for employing the proper means is stronger even than the god, whom he can compel to do his will. In these cases, religious behavior is not worship of the god but rather coercion of the god, and invocation is not prayer but rather the exercise of magical formulae. Such is one ineradicable basis of popular religion, particularly in India. Indeed, such coercive religion is universally diffused, and even the Catholic priest continues to practice something of this magical power in executing the miracle of the mass and in exercising the power of the keys. By and large this is the original, though not exclusive, origin of the orgiastic and mimetic components of the religious cult—especially of song, dance, drama, and the typical fixed formulae of prayer.

The process of anthropomorphization may take the form of attributing to the gods the human behavior patterns appropriate to a mighty terrestrial potentate, whose freely disposed favor can be obtained by entreaty, gifts, service, tributes, cajolery, and bribes. On the other hand, his favor may be earned as a consequence of the devotee's own faithfulness and good conduct in conformity with the divine will. In these ways, the gods are conceived by analogy to earthly rulers: mighty beings whose power differs only in degree, at least at first. As gods of this type evolve, worship of divinity comes to be regarded as a necessity.

The two characteristic elements of "divine worship," prayer and sacrifice, have their origin in magic. In prayer, the boundary between magical formula and supplication remains fluid. The technically rationalized enterprise of prayer (in the form of prayer wheels and similar devices, or of prayer strips hung in the wind or attached to icons of gods or saints, or of carefully measured wreaths of roses—virtually all of which are products of the methodical compulsion of the gods by the Hindus) everywhere stands far closer to magic than to entreaty. Individual prayer as real supplication is found in religions that are otherwise undifferentiated, but in most cases such prayer has a purely business-like, rationalized form that sets forth the achievements of the supplicant in behalf of the god and then claims adequate recompense therefor.

Sacrifice, at its first appearance, is a magical instrumentality that in part stands at the immediate service of the coercion of the gods. For the gods also need the soma juice of the sorcerer-priests, the substance which engenders their ecstasy and enables them to perform their deeds. This is the ancient notion of the Aryans as to why it is possible to coerce the gods by sacrifice. It may even be held that a pact can be concluded with the gods which imposes obligations on both parties; this was the fateful conception of the Israelites in particular. Still another view of sacrifice holds that it is a means of deflecting, through magical media, the wrath of the god upon another object, a scapegoat or above all a human sacrifice.

But another motive for sacrifice may be of greater importance, and it is probably older too: the sacrifice, especially of animals, is intended as a *communio,* a ceremony of eating together which serves to produce a fraternal community between the sacrificers and the god. This represents a transformation in the significance of the even older notion that to rend and consume a strong (and later a sacred) animal enables the eaters to absorb its potencies. Some such older magical meaning—and there are various other possibilities—may still provide the act of sacrifice with its essential form, even after genuine cultic views have come to exert considerable influence. Indeed, such a magical significance may even regain dominance over the cultic meaning. The sacrificial rituals of the Brahmanas, and even of the Atharva Veda, were almost purely sorcery, in contrast to the cultic sacrifices of the ancient Nordics. On the other hand, there are many departures from magic, as when sacrifices are interpreted as tribute. First fruits may be sacrificed in order that the god may not deprive man of the enjoyment of the remaining fruits; and sacrifice is often interpreted as a self-imposed punishment or sacrificial sin-offering that averts the wrath of the gods before it falls upon the sacrificer. To be sure, this does not yet involve any awareness of sin, and it initially takes place in a mood of cool and calculated trading, as for example in India.

An increasing predominance of non-magical motives is later brought about by the growing recognition of the power of a god and of his character as a personal overlord. The god becomes a great lord who may fail on occasion, and whom one cannot approach with devices of magical compulsion, but only with entreaties and gifts. But if these motives add anything new to mere wizardry, it is initially something as sober and rational as the motivation of magic itself. The pervasive and central theme is: *do ut des*. This aspect clings to the routine and the mass religious behavior of all peoples at all times and in all religions. The normal situation is that the burden of all prayers, even in the most otherworldly religions, is the aversion of the external evils of this world and the inducement of the external advantages of this world.

Every aspect of religious phenomena that points beyond evils and advantages in this world is the work of a special evolutionary process, one characterized by distinctively dual aspects. On the one hand, there is an ever-broadening rational systematization of the god concept and of the thinking concerning the possible relationships of man to the divine. On the other hand, there ensues a characteristic recession of the original, practical and calculating rationalism. As such primitive rationalism recedes, the significance of distinctively religious behavior is sought less and less in the purely external advantages of everyday economic success. Thus, the goal of religious behavior is successively "irrationalized" until finally otherworldly non-economic goals come to represent what is distinctive in religious behavior. But the extra-economic evolution just described requires as one of its prerequisites the existence of specific personal carriers of the otherworldly goals.

The relationships of men to supernatural forces which take the forms of prayer, sacrifice and worship may be termed "cult" and "religion," as distinguished from "sorcery," which is magical coercion. Correspondingly, those beings that are worshipped and entreated religiously may be termed "gods," in contrast to "demons," which are magically coerced and charmed. There may be no instance in which it is possible to apply this differentiation absolutely, since the cults we have just called "religious" practically everywhere contain numerous magical components. The historical development of the aforementioned differentiation frequently came about in a very simple fashion when a secular or priestly power suppressed a cult in favor of a new religion, with the older gods continuing to live on as demons.

The sociological aspect of this differentiation is the rise of the "priesthood" as something distinct from "practitioners of magic." Applied to reality, this contrast is fluid, as are all sociological phenomena. Even the theoretical differentiae of these types are not unequivocally determinable. Following the distinction between "cult" and "sorcery," one may contrast those professional functionaries who influence the gods by means of worship with those magicians who coerce demons by magical means; but in many great religions, including Christianity, the concept of the priest includes such a magical qualification.

Or the term "priest" may be applied to the functionaries of a regularly organized and permanent enterprise concerned with influencing the gods, in contrast with the individual and occasional efforts of magicians. Even this contrast is bridged over by a sliding scale of transitions, but as a pure type the priesthood is unequivocal and can be said to be characterized by the presence of certain fixed cultic centers associated with some actual cultic apparatus.

Or it may be thought that what is decisive for the concept of priesthood is that the functionaries, regardless of whether their office is hereditary or personal, be actively associated with some type of social organization, of which they are employees or organs operating in the interests of the organization's members, in contrast with magicians, who are self-employed. Yet even this distinction, which is clear enough conceptually, is fluid in actuality. The sorcerer is not infrequently a member of an organized guild, and is occasionally the member of a hereditary caste which may hold a monopoly of magic within the particular community. Even the Catholic priest is not always the occupant of an official post. In Rome he is occasionally a poor mendicant who lives a hand-to-mouth existence from the proceeds of single masses, the acquisition of which he solicits.

Yet another distinguishing quality of the priest, it is asserted, is his professional equipment of special knowledge, fixed doctrine, and vocational qualifications, which brings him into contrast with sorcerers, prophets, and other types of religious functionaries who exert their influence by virtue of personal gifts (charisma) made manifest in miracle and revelation. But this again is no simple and absolute distinction, since the sorcerer may sometimes be very learned, while deep learning need not always characterize working priests. Rather, the distinction between priest and magician must be established qualitatively with reference to the different nature of the learning in the two cases. As a matter of fact we must later, in our exposition of the forms of domination, distinguish the rational training and discipline of priests from the different preparation of charismatic magicians. The latter preparation proceeds in part as an "awakening education" using irrational means and aiming at rebirth, and proceeds in part as a training in purely empirical lore. But in this case also, the two contrasted types flow into one another.

"Doctrine" has already been advanced as one of the fundamental traits of the priesthood. We may assume that the outstanding marks of doctrine are the development of a rational system of religious concepts and (what is of the utmost importance for us here) the development of a systematic and distinctively religious ethic based upon a consistent and stable doctrine which purports to be a "revelation." An example is found in Islam, which contrasted its scriptural religion with simple paganism. But this description of priesthood and this assumption about the nature of doctrine would exclude from the concept of priesthood the Japanese Shinto priests and such functionaries as the mighty hier-

ocrats of the Phoenicians. The adoption of such an assumption
would have the effect of making the decisive characteristic of the
priesthood a function which, while admittedly important, is not
universal.

It is more correct for our purpose, in order to do justice to
the diverse and mixed manifestations of this phenomenon, to set
up as the crucial feature of the priesthood the specialization of a
particular group of persons in the continuous operation of a cultic
enterprise, permanently associated with particular norms, places
and times, and related to specific social groups. There can be
no priesthood without a cult, although there may well be a cult
without a specialized priesthood. The latter was the case in China,
where state officials and the heads of households exclusively conducted the services of the official gods and the ancestral spirits.
On the other hand, both novitiate and doctrine are to be found
among typical, pure magicians, as in the brotherhood of the
Hametze among the Indians, and elsewhere in the world. These
magicians may wield considerable power, and their essentially
magical celebrations may play a central role in the life of their
people. Yet they lack a continuously operative cult, and so the
term "priests" cannot be applied to them.

A rationalization of metaphysical views and a specifically religious ethic are usually missing in the case of a cult without priests,
as in the case of a magician without a cult. The full development
of both a metaphysical rationalization and a religious ethic requires an independent and professionally trained priesthood, permanently occupied with the cult and with the practical problems
involved in the cure of souls. Consequently, ethics developed into
something quite different from a metaphysically rationalized religion in classic Chinese thought, which lacked an independent
priesthood; and this also happened with the ethics of ancient Buddhism, which lacked both cult and priesthood.

Moreover, as we shall later explicate, the rationalization of
religious life was fragmentary or entirely missing wherever the
priesthood failed to achieve independent class status, as in classical antiquity. Wherever a class of primitive magicians and sacred
musicians did rationalize magic, but failed to develop a genuinely
sacerdotal occupational pattern (as was the case with the Brahmins

in India), the priesthood developed in a rather strange way. Not every genuine priesthood developed the distinguishing features of a rational metaphysic and a religious ethic. Such developments generally (though there were exceptions) presupposed the operation of one or both of two forces outside the priesthood: prophets, the bearers of metaphysical or religious-ethical revelation, and the laity, the non-priestly devotees of the cult.

Before we examine the manner in which these factors outside the priesthood influenced religion sufficiently to enable it to transcend the stages of magic, which are rather similar the world over, we must discuss some typical trends of religious evolution which are set in motion by the existence of vested interests of a priesthood in a cult.

III. The Idea of God,
Religious Ethics, and Taboo

Whether one should try to influence a particular god or demon by coercion or by entreaty is a very simple question, and the answer is whatever method has proved successful. As the magician must keep up his charisma, so too the god must continually demonstrate his prowess. Should the effort to influence a god prove to be permanently inefficacious, then it is concluded that either the god is impotent or the correct procedure of influencing him is unknown, and he is abandoned. In China, to this day, a few striking successes suffice to enable a god to acquire prestige and power (*shen ling*), thereby winning a sizeable circle of devotees. The emperor, as the representative of his subjects vis-à-vis the heavens, provides the gods with titles and other distinctions whenever they have proven their capacity. Yet a few striking disappointments subsequently will suffice to empty a temple forever. Indeed Isaiah's steadfast prophecy that, all appearances to the contrary notwithstanding, God would not permit Jerusalem to fall into the hands of the Assyrian hordes, if only the Judean king remained firm, actually came to fulfillment by historical accident, thereby creating a permanent, unshakeable foundation for the subsequent position of this god and prophets.

Something of this kind occurred in respect to the pre-animistic fetish and charisma of those possessing magical endowment. In the event of failure, the magician ultimately paid with his life. On the other hand, priests have enjoyed the contrasting advantage of being able to deflect the blame for failure away from themselves and onto their god. Yet even the priests' prestige is in danger of falling with that of their gods. However, priests may find ways of interpreting failures in such a manner that the responsibility falls, not upon the god or themselves, but upon the behavior of the god's worshippers. There might even arise from such interpretation the idea of worshipping god, as distinct from coercing him. The problem of why god has not hearkened to his devotees might then be explained by stating that they had not honored their god sufficiently, that they had not satisfied his desires for sacrificial blood or soma juice, or finally that they neglected him in favor of other gods. Even renewed and increased worship of the god is of no avail in some situations, and since the gods of the adversaries remain more powerful, the end of his reputation is at hand. In such cases, there may be a defection to the stronger gods, although there still remain methods of explaining the wayward conduct of the old god in such a way that his prestige might not dwindle and might even be enhanced. Such methods may even be improvised by priests, under certain circumstances. This was proved possible by the priests of Yahweh, whose attachment to his people became, for reasons to be expounded later, ever stronger as Israel became increasingly enmeshed in the toils of tragedy. But for this to happen, a new series of divine attributes must evolve.

The qualitative superiority of anthropomorphically conceived gods and demons over man himself is at first only relative. Their passions and their lusts for pleasure are believed to be unlimited, as those of strong men. But they are neither omniscient nor omnipotent (obviously not many could possess these attributes), nor necessarily eternal (the gods of Babylon and of the Germans were not). However, they often have the ability to secure their glamorous existence by means of magical food and drink which they have reserved for themselves, much as human lives may be prolonged by the magical potions of the medical man. The only qualitative differentiation that is made between these anthropomorphic gods and demons is that between powers useful to man and those harmful to man. Naturally, the powers useful to him are usually considered the good and high gods, who are to be worshipped, while the powers harmful to him are usually the lower demons, frequently endowed with incredible guile or limitless spite,, who are not to be worshipped but magically exorcised.

Yet the differentiation did not always take place along this particular line, and certainly not always in the direction of degrading the masters of the noxious forces into demons. The measure of cultic worship that gods receive does not depend upon their goodness, nor even upon their cosmic importance. Indeed, some very great and good gods of the sky frequently lack cults, not because they are too remote from man, but because their influence seems equable, and by its very regularity appears to be so secure that no special intervention is required. On the other hand, powers of clearly diabolical character, such as Rudra, the Hindu god of pestilence, are not always weaker than the good gods, but may actually be endowed with a tremendous power potential.

In addition to the important qualitative differentiation between the good and diabolical forces, which assumed considerable importance in certain cases, there might develop within the pantheon gods of a distinctively ethical character. The possibility that a god may possess ethical qualities is by no means confined to monotheism. Indeed, this possibility exists at various stages in the formation of a pantheon; but it is at the level of monotheism that this development has particularly far-reaching consequences. A specialized functional god of legislation and a god who controls the oracle will naturally be found very frequently among the ethical divinities.

The art of "divining" at first grows out of the belief in spirits that function in accordance with certain principles of order, as do living creatures. Once knowing how the spirits operate, one can predict their behavior from symptoms or omens that make it possible to surmise their intentions, on the basis of previous experience. Where one builds houses, graves and roads, and when one undertakes economic and political activities is decided by reference to that which experience has established as the favorable place or time. Wherever a social group, as for example the so-called priests of Taoism in China, makes its living from the practice of the diviner's art, its doctrine (*feng shui*) may achieve ineradicable power. When this happens, all efforts at economic rationalization founder against the opposition of the spirits. Thus, no location for a railroad or factory could be suggested without creating some conflict with them. Chinese capitalism was able to cope with this factor only after it had reached its fullest power. As late as the Russo-Japanese War, the army of Japan seems to have missed several favorable opportunities because the diviners had declared them to be of ill omen. On the other hand, Pausanias had already adroitly manipulated the omens, favorable and otherwise, at Plataea, to make them fit the requirements of military strategy. Whenever the political power appropriated judicial or legislative functions (e.g., transforming into a mandatory verdict an arbitrator's indecisive judgment terminating a clan feud, or transforming into an orderly procedure the primordial lynch justice practiced by a threatened social group in cases of religious or political malfeasance), the particular solution was almost always mediated by a divine revelation (a judgment of god). Wherever a class of diviners succeeded in appropriating the preparation and interpretation of the oracles or the divine judgments, they frequently achieved a position of enduring dominance.

Quite in keeping with the realities of actual life, the guardian of the legal order was nowhere necessarily the strongest god: neither Varuna in India nor Maat in Egypt, much less Lykos in Attica, Dike, Themis or even Apollo. What alone characterized these deities was their ethical qualification, which corresponded to the notion that the oracle or divine judgment was revealed everywhere in the same manner. It was not because he was a deity that the ethical god was the guardian of morality and the legal order, for the anthropomorphic gods originally had but little to do with ethics, in fact less than human beings. Rather, the reason for such a god's ethical pre-eminence was that he had taken this particular type of behavior under his aegis.

Increased ethical demands were made upon the gods by men, parallel with four developments. First, the increasing quality and power of orderly legislation within large and pacified political groupings, and hence increasing claims upon legislation. Second, the increasing scope of a rational comprehension of an external, enduring, and orderly cosmos. (The cause of this is to be sought in the meteorological orientation of economic activity.) Third, the increasing regulation of ever new types of human relationships by conventional rules, and the increasing dependence of men upon the observance of these rules in their interactions with each other.

Fourth, the growth in social and economic importance of the reliability of the given word—whether of friends, vassals, officials, partners in an exchange transaction, debtors, or whomever else.

What is basically involved in these four developments is the increased importance of an ethical attachment of individuals to a cosmos of obligations, making it possible to calculate what the conduct of a given person may be. This has the greatest significance.

Even the gods to whom one turns for protection are henceforth regarded as either subject to some social and moral order or as the creators of such an order, which they made the specific content of their divine will. In the first case, a superordinate and impersonal power makes its appearance behind the gods, controlling them from within and measuring the value of their deeds. Of course this supra-divine power may take many different forms. It appears first as "fate." Among the Greeks fate (*moira*) is an irrational and, above all, ethically neutral predestination of the fundamental aspects of every man's destiny. The predetermination is elastic within certain limits, but flagrant interferences with predestined fate by wicked maneuvers may imperil even the greatest of the gods (*hypermoron*). This provides one explanation for the failure of so many prayers. This kind of predestinarian view is very congenial to the normal psychological attitude of a military caste, which is particularly unreceptive to the rationalistic belief in an ethically concerned, yet impartial, wise and kindly "providence." In this we glimpse once again the deep sociological distance separating a warrior class from every kind of religious or purely ethical rationalism. We have already made brief reference to this cleavage, and we shall have occasion to observe it in many other contexts.

Of quite different aspect is the impersonal power of bureaucratic or theocratic strata, e.g., the Chinese bureaucracy or the Hindu Brahmins. Theirs is the providential power of the harmonious and rational order of the world, which may in any given case incline to either a cosmic or an ethical and social format, although as a rule both aspects are involved. In Confucianism as in Taoism, this order, to which even the gods are subject, has both a cosmic and a characteristic ethical-rational character; it is an impersonal, providential force that guarantees the regularity and felicitous order of world history. This is the view of a rationalistic bureaucracy. Even more strongly ethical is the Hindu *rita,* the impersonal power of the fixed order of religious ceremonial and the fixed order of the cosmos, and hence of human activity in general. This is the conception of power held by the Vedic priesthood, which practiced an essentially empirical art of influencing the god, more by coercion than by worship. The later Hindu notion of a supradivine and cosmic all-unity, superordinate to the gods and alone independent of the senseless change and transitoriness of the entire phenomenal world—this conception was entertained only by speculative intellectuals who were indifferent to worldly concerns.

Even when the order of nature and of the social relationships which are normally considered parallel to it, especially law, are not regarded as superordinate to the gods, but rather as their creations (later we shall inquire under what circumstances this occurs), it is naturally postulated that god will protect against injury the order he has created. The intellectual implementation of this postulate has far-reaching consequences for religious behavior and for the general attitude toward the god. It stimulated the development of a religious ethic, as well as the differentiation of demands made upon man by god from demands made upon man by nature, which latter so often proved to be inadequate. Hitherto, there had been two primordial methods of influencing supernatural powers. One was to subject them to human purposes by means of magic. The other was to win them over by making oneself agreeable to them, not by the exercise of any ethical virtue, but by gratifying their egotistic wishes. To these methods was now added obedience to the religious law as the distinctive way to win the god's favor.

To be sure, religious ethics do not really begin with this view. On the contrary, there was already another and highly influential system of religious ethics deriving from purely magical norms of conduct, the infraction of which was regarded as a religious abomination. Wherever there exists a developed belief in spirits, it is held that extraordinary occurrences in life, and sometimes even routine life processes, are generated by the entrance into a person of a particular spirit, e.g., in sickness, at birth, at puberty, or at menstruation. This spirit may be regarded as either sacred or unclean; this is variable and often the product of accident, but the practical effect is the same. In either case one must avoid irritating the spirit, lest it enter into the officious intruder himself, or by some magical means harm him or any other persons whom it might possess. As a result, the individual in question will be shunned physically and socially and must avoid contact with others and sometimes even with his body. In some instances, e.g., Polynesian charismatic princes, such a person must be carefully fed lest he magically contaminate his own food.

Naturally, once this set of notions has developed, various objects or persons may be endowed with the quality of taboo by means of magical manipulations invoked by persons possessing magical charisma; thereupon, contact with the new possessor of taboo will work evil magic, for his taboo may be transmitted. This charismatic power to transfer taboo underwent considerable systematic development, especially in Indonesia and the South Sea area. Numerous economic and social interests stood under the sanctions of taboos. Among them were the following: the conservation of forests and wild life (after the pattern of the prohibited forests of early medieval kings); the protection of scarce commodities against uneconomic consumption, during periods of economic difficulty; the provision of protection for private property, especially for the property of privileged priests or aristocrats; the safeguarding of common war booty against individual plundering (as by Joshua in the case of Achan); and the sexual and personal separation of the classes in the interest of maintaining purity of blood or class prestige. This first and most general instance of the direct harnessing of religion to extra-religious purposes also reveals the idiosyncratic autonomy of the religious domain, in the somewhat incredible irrationality of its painfully onerous norms, which applied even to the beneficiaries of the taboos.

The rationalization of taboos leads ultimately to a system of norms according to which certain actions are permanently construed as religious abominations subject to sanctions, and occasionally even entailing the death of the malefactor in order to prevent evil sorcery from overtaking the entire group because of the transgression of the guilty individual. In this manner there arises an ethical system, the ultimate warrant of which is taboo. This system comprises dietary restrictions, the proscription of work on taboo or "unlucky" days (the Sabbath was originally a taboo day of this type), and certain prohibitions against marriage to specified individuals, especially within the circle of one's blood relations. The usual process here is that something which has become customary, whether on rational grounds or otherwise, e.g., experiences relative to illness and other effects of evil sorcery, comes to be regarded as sacred.

In some fashion not clearly understood, there developed for certain classes a characteristic association between specific norms having the quality of taboo and various important indwelling spirits inhabiting particular objects or animals. Egypt provides the most striking example of how the incarnation of spirits as sacred animals may give rise to cultic centers of local political associations. Such sacred animals, as well as other objects and artifacts, may also become the foci of other social groupings, which may be either organic or artificially created in any particular case.

The most widespread of the social institutions which developed in this fashion is that known as totemism, which is a specific relationship of an object, usually a natural object and in the purest manifestations of totemism an animal, with a particular social group. For the latter, the totemic animal is a symbol of kinship; and originally the animal symbolized the common possession by the group of the spirit of the animal, after it had been consumed by the entire group. There are, of course, variations in the scope of this fraternalism, just as there are variations in the nature of the relationship of the members to the totemic object. In the fully developed type of totemism, the brotherliness of the group comprises all the fraternal responsibilities of an exogamous clan, while the kinship notion involves a prohibition of slaying and consuming the totemic animal, except at the cultic meals of the group. These developments culminate in a series of quasi-cultic obligations following from the common, though not universal, belief that the group is descended from the totem animal.

The controversy concerning the development of these widely diffused totemic brotherhoods is still unresolved. For us it will suffice to say that the totems are the functional counterparts in animism of the gods found in cultic associations. As previously mentioned, such gods generally allied themselves with all sorts of social groups, since the non-empirical thinking of the cults required for its continuance a purely artificial, concrete, and purposive organization of fraternization based on personal and religious motivations. For this reason the regulation of sexual behavior, which the clans undertook to effect, especially attracted religious sanctions having the nature of taboo, which are best provided by totemism. But this system was not limited to the purposes of sexual regulation, nor was it confined to the clan, and it certainly did not necessarily arise first in this context. Rather, it is a widely diffused method of placing fraternal groupings under magical sanctions. The belief in the universality of totemism, and certainly the belief in the derivation of virtually all social groups and all religions from totemism, constitutes a tremendous exaggeration that has been rejected completely by now. Yet totemism has frequently been very influential in producing a division of labor between the sexes which is guaranteed and enforced by magical motivations. Then too, totemism has frequently played a very important role in the development and regulation of barter as a regular intra-group phenomenon (as contrasted with trade outside the limits of the group).

Taboos, especially the dietary restrictions based on magic, show us a new source of the institution of commensality, which has such far-reaching importance. We have already noted one source of this institution, namely the domestic community of the family. Another aspect is the restriction of commensality to comrades having equal magical qualifications, which is a consequence of the doctrine of impurity by taboo. These two facets of commensality may enter into competition or even conflict. For example, when a woman is descended from another clan than that of her husband, there are frequently restrictions upon her sitting at the same table with him, and in some cases she is even prohibited from seeing him eat. Nor is commensality permitted to the king who is hedged in by taboos, or to members of privileged status groups such as castes or religious communities, both of which are also under taboo. Furthermore, highly privileged castes must be shielded from the glances of "unclean" strangers during cultic repasts or even everyday meals. Conversely, the provision of commensality is frequently a method of producing religious fellowship, which may on occasion lead to political and ethnic alliances. Thus, the first great turning point in the history of Christianity was the communal feast arranged at Antioch between Peter and the uncircumcised proselytes, to which Paul, in his polemic against Peter, attributed such decisive importance.

On the other hand, norms of taboo may give rise to extraordinarily severe impediments to the development of communal barter and other types of social intercourse. The absolute impurity of those outside one's own religion, as taught by the Shiite sect of Islam, has created in its adherents crucial impediments to intercourse with others, even in recent times, though recourse has been made to fictions of all sorts to ease the situation. The caste taboos of the Hindus restricted intercourse among people far more forcefully than the *feng shui* system of spirit beliefs interfered with trade in China. Of course, even in these matters there are natural limits to the power of religion in respect to the elementary needs of life. Thus, according to the Hindu caste taboo, "The hand of the artisan is always clean." Also clean are mines, workshops, and whatever merchandise is available for sale in stores, as well as whatever articles of food have been touched by a mendicant student (an ascetic disciple of the Brahmins). The only Hindu caste taboo that was apt to be violated in any considerable measure was the taboo on sexual relationships between castes, under the pressure of the wealthy classes' interest in polygamy. To some extent, it was permissible to take girls of lower castes as concubines. The caste system of labor in India, like the *feng shui* system in China, was slowly but surely rendered illusory wherever railroad transportation developed.

In theory, these taboo restrictions of caste need not have rendered capitalism impossible. Yet it is perfectly obvious that economic rationalization would never have arisen originally where taboo had achieved such massive power. Despite all efforts to reduce caste segregation, certain psychological resistances based on the caste system remained operative, preventing artisans of different crafts from working together in the same factory. The caste system tends to perpetuate a specialization of labor of the handicraft type, if not by positive prescription then as a consequence of its general spirit and presuppositions. The net effect of the religious sanction of caste upon the spirit of economic activity is diametrically opposite to that of rationalism. In the caste system particular crafts, insofar as they are the indicia of different castes, are assigned a religious sanction and the character of a sacred vocation. Even the most despised of Hindu castes, not excluding that of thieves, regards its own enterprise as ordained by particular gods or by a specific volition of a god, assigned to its members as their special mission in life; and each caste nourishes its feeling of worth by its technically expert execution of its assigned vocation.

But this vocational ethic of a caste system is—at least as far as the crafts are concerned—notably traditionalistic, rather than rational. It finds its fulfillment and confirmation in the absolutely qualitative perfection of the product fashioned by the craft. Very alien to its mode of thinking is the possibility of rationalizing the method of production, which is basic to all modern rational technology, or the possibility of systematically organizing a commercial enterprise along the lines of a rational business economy, which is the foundation of modern capitalism. One must go to the ethics of ascetic Protestantism to find any ethical sanction for economic rationalism and for the entrepreneur. Caste ethics glorifies the spirit of craftsmanship and enjoins pride, not in economic earnings measured by money, nor in the miracle of rational technology as exemplified in the rational use of labor, but rather in the personal virtuosity of the producer as manifested in the beauty and worth of the product appropriate to his particular caste.

Finally, we must note, however briefly, that what was decisive for the Hindu caste system in particular was its connection with a belief in transmigration, and especially its connection with the tenet that any possible improvement in one's chances in subsequent incarnations depended on the faithful execution in the present lifetime of the vocation assigned him by virtue of his caste status. Any effort to emerge from one's caste, and especially to intrude into the sphere of activities appropriate to other and higher castes, was expected to result in evil magic and entailed the likelihood of unfavorable incarnation hereafter. This explains why, according to numerous observations on affairs in India, it is precisely the lowest classes, who would naturally be most desirous of improving their status in subsequent incarnations, that cling most steadfastly to their caste obligations, never thinking of toppling the caste system through social revolutions or reforms. Among the Hindus, the Biblical emphasis echoed in Luther's injunction, "Remain steadfast in your vocation," was elevated into a cardinal religious obligation and was fortified by powerful religious sanctions.

Whenever the belief in spirits became rationalized into belief in gods, that is, whenever the coercion of spirits gave way to the coercion or worship of the gods who are served by a cult, the magical ethic of the spirit belief underwent a transformation too. This reorientation developed through the notion that whoever flouted divinely appointed norms would be overtaken by the ethical displeasure of the god who had these norms under his special care. This made possible the assumption that when enemies conquered or other calamities befell one's group, the cause was not the weakness of the god but rather his anger against his followers, caused by his displeasure at their transgression against the laws under his guardianship. Hence, the sins of the group were to blame if some unfavorable development overtook it; the god might well be using the misfortune to express his desire to chastise and educate his favorite people. Thus, the prophets of Israel were always able to point out to their people misdeeds in their own generation or in their ancestors', to which God had reacted with almost inexhaustible wrath, as evidenced by the fact that he permitted his own people to become subject to another people that did not worship him at all.

This idea, diffused in all conceivable manifestations wherever the god concept has taken on universalistic lines, forms a religious ethic out of the magical prescriptions which operate only with the notion of evil magic. Henceforth, transgression against the will of god is an ethical sin which burdens the conscience, quite apart from its direct results. Evils befalling the individual are divinely appointed temptations and the consequences of sin, from which the individual hopes to be freed by "piety" (behavior acceptable to god) which will bring the individual salvation. In the Old Testament, the idea of "salvation," pregnant with consequences, still has the elementary rational meaning of liberation from concrete ills.

In its early stages, the religious ethic consistently shares another characteristic with magical worship, in that it is frequently composed of a complex of heterogeneous prescriptions and prohibitions, derived from the most diverse motives and occasions. Within this complex there is little differentiation between important and unimportant requirements; any infraction of the ethic constitutes sin. Later, a systematization of these ethical concepts may ensue, which leads from the rational wish to insure personal external pleasures for oneself by performing acts pleasing to the god, to a view of sin as the unified power of the anti-divine (diabolical) into whose grasp man may fall. The good is then envisaged as an integral capacity for an attitude of holiness, and for consistent behavior derived from such an attitude. During this process of transformation, there also develops a hope for salvation as an irrational yearning to be able to be good for its own sake, or in order to gain the beneficent awareness of such virtuousness.

An almost infinite series of the most diverse conceptions, crossed again and again by purely magical notions, leads to the sublimation of piety as the enduring basis of a specific pattern of life, by virtue of the continuous motivation it engenders. Of course such a sublimation is extremely rare and is attained in its full purity only intermittently by routine religion. The conceptions of sin and piety as integral powers, envisaged as rather like material substances, still remained within the circle of magical notions. At this stage, the nature of the "good" or "evil" of the acting person is construed after the fashion of a poison, a healing antidote, or a bodily temperature. Thus in India *tapas,* the power of the sacred which a man achieved by asceticism and contained within his body, originally denoted the heat engendered in fowls during their mating season. It is the same power that is generated by the creator of the world at the cosmogony, that is produced by the magician during his sacred hysteria, that is induced by mortifications, and that leads to supernatural powers.

It is a long way from the notion that the person who acts with goodness has received into himself a special soul of divine provenience, to the various forms of inward possession of the divine to be described later So too, it is a far cry from the conception of sin as a poison in the body of the malefactor, which must be treated by magical means, to the conception of an evil demon which enters into possession of him, and on to the culminating conception of the diabolical power of the radical evil, with which the evildoer must struggle lest he succumb to its dangerous power.

By no means every ethic traversed the entire length of the road culminating in these conceptions. Thus, the ethics of Confucianism lack the concept of radical evil, and in general lack the concept of any integral diabolical power of sin. Nor was this notion contained in the ethics of Greece or Rome. In both those cases, there was lacking not only an independently organized priesthood, but also prophecy, that historical phenomenon which normally, though not necessarily always, produced a centralization of ethics under the aegis of religious salvation. In India, prophecy was not absent, but as will be expounded later, it had a very special character and a very highly sublimated ethic of salvation.

Prophets and priests are the twin bearers of the systematization and rationalization of religious ethics. But there is a third significant factor of importance in determining the evolution of religious ethics: the laity, whom prophets and priests seek to influence in an ethical direction. We must now devote a brief examination to the collaboration and interaction of these three factors.

IV. The Prophet

What is a prophet, from the perspective of sociology?

We shall forego here any consideration of the general question regarding the "bringer of salvation" (*Heilbringer*) as raised by Breysig. Not every anthropomorphic god is a deified bringer of salvation, whether external or internal salvation. And certainly not every provider of salvation became a god or even a savior, although such phenomena were widespread.

We shall understand "prophet" to mean a purely individual bearer of charisma, who by virtue of his mission proclaims a religious doctrine or divine commandment. No radical distinction will be drawn between a "renewer of religion" who preaches an older revelation, actual or supposititious, and a "founder of religion" who claims to bring completely new deliverances. The two types merge into one another. In any case, the formation of a new religious community need not be the result of doctrinal preaching by prophets, since it may be produced by the activities of non-prophetic reformers. Nor shall we be concerned in this context with the question whether the followers of a prophet are more attracted to his person, as in the cases of Zoroaster, Jesus, and Muhammad, or to his doctrine, as in the cases of Buddha and the prophets of Israel.

For our purposes here, the personal call is the decisive element distinguishing the prophet from the priest. The latter lays claim to authority by virtue of his service in a sacred tradition, while the prophet's claim is based on personal revelation and charisma. It is no accident that almost no prophets have emerged from the priestly class. As a rule, the Indian teachers of salvation were not Brahmins, nor were the Israelite prophets priests. Zoroaster's case is exceptional in that there exists a possibility that he may have descended from the hieratic nobility. The priest, in clear contrast, dispenses salvation by virtue of his office. Even in cases in which personal charisma may be involved, it is the hierarchical office that confers legitimate authority upon the priest as a member of a corporate enterprise of salvation.

But the prophet, like the magician, exerts his power simply by virtue of his personal gifts. Unlike the magician, however, the prophet claims definite revelations, and the core of his mission is doctrine or commandment, not magic. Outwardly, at least, the distinction is fluid, for the magician is frequently a knowledgeable expert in divination, and sometimes in this alone. At this stage, revelation functions continuously as oracle or dream interpretation. Without prior consultation with the magician, no innovations in communal relations could be adopted in primitive times. To this day, in certain parts of Australia, it is the dream revelations of magicians that are set before the councils of clan heads for adoption, and it is a mark of secularization that this practice is receding.

On the other hand, it was only under very unusual circumstances that a prophet succeeded in establishing his authority without charismatic authentication, which in practice meant magic. At least the bearers of new doctrine practically always needed such validation. It must not be forgotten for an instant that the entire basis of Jesus' own legitimation, as well as his claim that he and only he knew the Father and that the way to God led through faith in him alone, was the magical charisma he felt within himself. It was doubtless this consciousness of power, more than anything else, that enabled him to traverse the road of the prophets. During the apostolic period of early Christianity and thereafter the figure of the wandering prophet was a constant phenomenon. There was always required of such prophets a proof of their possession of particular gifts of the spirit, of special magical or ecstatic abilities.

Prophets very often practiced divination as well as magical healing and counseling. This was true, for example, of the prophets (*nabi, nebim*) so frequently mentioned in the Old Testament, especially in the prophetic books and Chronicles. But what distinguishes the prophet, in the sense that we are employing the term, from the types just described is an economic factor, i.e., that his prophecy is unremunerated. Thus, Amos indignantly rejected the appellation of *nabi*. This criterion of gratuitous service also distinguishes the prophet from the priest. The typical prophet propagates ideas for their own sake and not for fees, at least in any obvious or regulated form. The provisions enjoining the non-remunerative character of prophetic propaganda have taken various forms. Thus developed the carefully cultivated postulate that the apostle, prophet, or teacher of ancient Christianity must not professionalize his religious proclamations. Also, limitations were set upon the length of the time he could enjoy the hospitality of his friends. The Christian prophet was enjoined to live by the labor of his own hands or, as among the Buddhists, only from alms which he had not specifically solicited. These injunctions were repeatedly emphasized in the Pauline epistles, and in another form, in the Buddhist monastic regulations. The dictum "whosoever will not work, shall not eat" applied to missionaries, and it constitutes one of the chief mysteries of the success of prophetic propaganda itself.

The period of the older Israelitic prophecy at about the time of Elijah was an epoch of strong prophetic propaganda throughout the Near East and Greece. It is likely that prophecy in all its forms arose, especially in the Near East, in connection with the growth of great world empires in Asia, and the resumption and intensification of international commerce after a long interruption. At that time Greece was exposed to the invasion of the Thracian cult of Dionysos, as well as to the most diverse types of prophecies. In addition to the semiprophetic social reformers, certain purely religious movements now broke into the magical and cultic lore of the Homeric priests. Emotional cults, emotional prophecy based on "speaking with tongues," and highly valued intoxicating ecstasy vied with the evolving theological rationalism (Hesiod); the incipient cosmogonic and philosophic speculation was intersected by philosophical mystery doctrines and salvation religions. The growth of these emotional cults paralleled both overseas colonization and, above all, the formation of cities and the transformation of the *polis* which resulted from the development of a citizen army.

It is not necessary to detail here these developments of the eighth and seventh centuries, so brilliantly analyzed by Rohde, some of which reached into the sixth and even the fifth century.

They were contemporary with Jewish, Persian, and Hindu prophetic movements, and probably also with the achievements of Chinese ethics in the pre-Confucian period, although we have only scant knowledge of the latter. These Greek "prophets" differed widely among themselves in regard to the economic criterion of professionalism, and in regard to the possession of a "doctrine." The Greeks also made a distinction between professional teaching and unremunerated propagandizing of ideas, as we see from the example of Socrates. In Greece, furthermore, there existed a clear differentiation between the only real congregational type of religion, namely Orphism with its doctrine of salvation, and every other type of prophecy and technique of salvation, especially those of the mysteries. The basis of this distinction was the presence in Orphism of a genuine doctrine of salvation.

Our primary task is to differentiate the various types of prophets from the sundry purveyors of salvation, religious or otherwise. Even in historical times the transition from the prophet to the legislator is fluid, if one understands the latter to mean a personage who in any given case has been assigned the responsibility of codifying a law systematically or of reconstituting it, as was the case notably with the Greek *aisymnete* (e.g., Solon, Charondas, etc.). In no case did such a legislator or his labor fail to receive divine approval, at least subsequently.

A legislator is quite different from the Italian *podesta,* who is summoned from outside the group, not for the purpose of creating a new social order, but to provide a detached, impartial arbitrator, especially for cases in which the adversaries are of the same social status. On the other hand, legislators were generally, though not always, called to their office when social tensions were in evidence. This was apt to occur with special frequency in the one situation which commonly provided the earliest stimulus to a planned social policy. One of the conditions fostering the need for a new planned policy was the economic development of a warrior class as a result of growing monetary wealth and the debt enslavement of another stratum; an additional factor was the dissatisfaction arising from the unrealized political aspirations of a rising commercial class which, having acquired wealth through economic activity, was now challenging the old warrior nobility. It was the function of the *aisymnete* to resolve the conflicts between classes and to produce a new sacred law of eternal validity, for which he had to secure divine approbation.

It is very likely that Moses was a historical figure, in which case he would be classified functionally as an *aisymnete*. For the prescriptions of the oldest sacred legislation of the Hebrews presuppose a money economy and hence sharp conflicts of class interests, whether impending or already existing, within the confederacy. It was Moses' great achievement to find a compromise solution of, or prophylactic for, these class conflicts (e.g., the *seisachthie* of the year of release) and to organize the Israelite confederacy by means of an integral national god. In essence, his work stands midway between the functioning of an ancient *aisymnete* and that of Muhammad. The reception of the law formulated by Moses stimulated a period of expansion of the newly unified people in much the same way that the leveling of classes stimulated expansion in so many other cases, particularly in Athens and Rome. The scriptural dictum that "after Moses there arose not in Israel any prophet like unto him" means that the Jews never had another *aisymnete*.

Not only were none of the prophets *aisymnetes* in this sense, but in general what normally passes for prophecy does not belong to this category. To be sure, even the later prophets of Israel were concerned with social reform. They hurled their "woe be unto you" against those who oppressed and enslaved the poor, those who joined field to field, and those who deflected justice by bribes. These were the typical actions leading to class stratification everywhere in the ancient world, and were everywhere intensified by the development of the city-state (*polis*). Jerusalem too had been organized into a city-state by the time of these later prophets. A distinctive concern with social reform is characteristic of Israelite prophets. This concern is all the more notable, because such a trait is lacking in Hindu prophecy of the same period, although the conditions in India at the time of the Buddha have been described as relatively similar to those in Greece during the sixth century.

An explanation for Hebrew prophecy's unique concern for social reform is to be sought in religious grounds, which we shall set forth subsequently. But it must not be forgotten that in the motivation of the Israelite prophets these social reforms were only means to an end. Their primary concern was with foreign politics, chiefly because it constituted the theater of their god's activity. The Israelite prophets were concerned with social and other types of injustice as a violation of the Mosaic code primarily in order to explain god's wrath, and not in order to institute a program of social reform. It is noteworthy that the real theoretician of social reform, Ezekiel, was a priestly theorist who can scarcely be categorized as a prophet at all. Finally, Jesus was not at all interested in social reform as such.

Zoroaster shared with his cattle-raising people a hatred of the despoiling nomads, but the heart of his message was essentially religious. His central concerns were his faith in his own divine mission and his struggle against the magical cult of ecstasy. A similar primary focus upon religion appeared very clearly in the case of Muhammad, whose program of social action, which Umar carried through consistently, was oriented almost entirely to the goal of the psychological preparation of the faithful for battle in order to maintain a maximum number of warriors for the faith.

It is characteristic of the prophets that they do not receive their mission from any human agency, but seize it, as it were. To be sure, usurpation also characterized the assumption of power by tyrants in the Greek *polis*. These Greek tyrants remind one of the legal *aisymnetes* in their general functioning, and they frequently pursued their own characteristic religious policies, e.g., supporting the emotional cult of Dionysos, which was popular with the masses rather than with the nobility. But the aforementioned assumption of power by the prophets came about as a consequence of divine revelation, essentially for religious purposes. Furthermore, their characteristic religious message and their struggle against ecstatic cults tended to move in an opposite direction from that taken by the typical religious policy of the Greek tyrants. The religion of Muhammad, which is fundamentally political in its orientation, and his position in Medina, which was in between that of an Italian *podesta* and that of Calvin at Geneva, grew primarily out of his purely prophetic mission. A merchant, he was first a leader of pietistic conventicles in Mecca, until he realized more and more clearly that the organization of the interests of warrior clans in the acquisition of booty was the external basis provided for his missionizing.

On the other hand, there are various transitional phases linking the prophet to the teacher of ethics, especially the teacher of social ethics. Such a teacher, full of a new or recovered understanding of ancient wisdom, gathers disciples about him, counsels private individuals in personal matters and nobles in questions relating to public affairs, and purports to mold ethical ways of life, with the ultimate goal of influencing the crystallization of ethical regulations. The bond between the teacher of religious or philosophical wisdom and his disciple is uncommonly strong and is regulated in an authoritarian fashion, particularly in the sacred laws of Asia. Everywhere the disciple-master relationship is classified among those involving reverence. Generally, the doctrine of magic, like that of heroism, is so regulated that the novice is assigned to a particularly experienced master or is required to seek him out. This is comparable to the relationship in German fraternities, in which the junior member (the *Leibbursche*) is attached by a kind of personal piety to the senior member (the *Leibfuchs*), who watches over his training. All the Greek poetry of pederasty derives from such a relationship of respect, and similar phenomena are to be found among Buddhists and Confucianists, indeed in all monastic education.

The most complete expression of this disciple-master relationship is to be found in the position of the *guru* in Hindu sacred law. Every young man belonging to polite society was unconditionally required to devote himself for many years to the instruction and direction of life provided by such a Brahminic teacher. The obligation of obedience to the *guru*, who had absolute power over his charges, a relationship comparable to that of the occidental *famulus* to his *magister*, took precedence over loyalty to family, even as the position of the court Brahmin (*purohita*) was officially regulated so as to raise his position far above that of the most powerful father confessor in the Occident. Yet the *guru* is, after all, only a teacher who transmits acquired, not revealed, knowledge, and this by virtue of a commission and not on his own authority.

The philosophical ethicist and the social reformer are not prophets in our sense of the word, no matter how closely they may seem to resemble prophets. Actually, the oldest Greek sages, who

like Empedocles are wreathed in legend, and other Greek sages
such as Pythagoras stand closer to the prophets. They have left at
least some legacy of a distinctive doctrine of salvation and conduct
of life, and they laid some claim to the status of savior. Such intellectual teachers of salvation have parallels in India, but the Greek
teachers fell far short of the Hindu teachers in consistently focusing
both life and doctrine on salvation.

Even less can the founders and heads of actual "schools of
philosophy" be regarded as prophets in our sense, no matter how
closely they may approach this category in some respects. From
Confucius, in whose temple even the emperor made obeisance,
graded transitions lead to Plato. But both of them were simply
academic teaching philosophers, who differed chiefly in that Confucius was centrally concerned and Plato only occasionally concerned to influence princes in the direction of particular social
reforms.

What primarily differentiates such figures from the prophets
is their lack of that vital emotional preaching which is distinctive of
prophecy, regardless of whether this is disseminated by the spoken
word, the pamphlet, or any other type of literary composition (e.g.,
the *suras* of Muhammad). The enterprise of the prophet is closer
to that of the popular orator (*demagogue*) or political publicist
than to that of the teacher. On the other hand, the activity of a
Socrates, who also felt himself opposed to the professional teaching
enterprise of the Sophists, must be distinguished in theory from the
activities of a prophet, by the absence of a directly revealed religious mission in the case of Socrates. Socrates' daemon (*dai-
monion*) reacted only to concrete situations, and then only to dis-
suade and admonish. For Socrates, this was the outer limit of his
ethical and strongly utilitarian rationalism, which occupied for
him the position that magical divination assumed for Confucius.
For this reason, Socrates' daemon cannot be compared at all to
the conscience of a genuine religious ethic; much less can it be
regarded as the instrument of prophecy.

Such a divergence from the characteristic traits of the Hebrew
prophets holds true of all philosophers and their schools as they
were known in China, India, ancient Hellas, and in the medieval
period among Jews, Arabs, and Christians alike. All such philoso-

phies had the same sociological form. But philosophic teaching, as in the case of the Cynics, might take the form of an exemplary prophecy of salvation (in the sense presently to be explained) by virtue of practicing the pattern of life achieved and propagated by a particular school. These prophets and their schools might, as in the case of the Cynics, who protested against the sacramental grace of the mysteries, show certain outer and inner affinities to Hindu and Oriental ascetic sects. But the prophet, in our special sense, is never to be found where the proclamation of a religious truth of salvation through personal revelation is lacking. In our view, this qualification must be regarded as the decisive hallmark of prophecy.

Finally, the Hindu reformers of religion such as Shankara and Ramanuja and their occidental counterparts like Luther, Zwingli, Calvin, and Wesley are to be distinguished from the category of prophets by virtue of the fact that they do not claim to be offering a substantively new revelation or to be speaking in the name of a special divine injunction. This is what characterized the founder of the Mormon church, who resembled, even in matters of detail, Muhammad and above all the Jewish prophets. The prophetic type is also manifest in Montanus and Novitianus, and in such figures as Mani and Manus, whose message had a more rational doctrinal content than did that of George Fox, a prophet type with emotional nuances.

When we have separated out from the category of prophet all the aforementioned types, which sometimes abut very closely, various others still remain. The first is that of the mystagogue. He performs sacraments, i.e., magical actions that contain the boons of salvation. Throughout the entire world there have been saviors of this type whose difference from the average magician is only one of degree, the extent of which is determined by the formation of a special congregation around him. Very frequently dynasties of mystagogues developed on the basis of a sacramental charisma which was regarded as hereditary. These dynasties maintained their prestige for centuries, investing their disciples with great authority and thus developing a kind of hierarchical position. This was especially true in India, where the title of *guru* was also used to designate distributors of salvation and their plenipotentiaries. It was likewise the case in China, where the hierarch of the Taoists and the heads of certain secret sects played just such hereditary roles. Finally, one type of exemplary prophet to be discussed presently was also generally transformed into a mystagogue in the second generation.

The mystagogues were also very widely distributed throughout the Near East, and they entered Greece in the prophetic age to which reference was made earlier. Yet the far more ancient noble families, who were the hereditary incumbents of the Eleusinian mysteries, also represented at least another marginal manifestation of the simple hereditary priestly families. Ethical doctrine was lacking in the mystagogue, who distributed magical salvation, or at least doctrine played only a very subordinate role in his work. Instead, his primary gift was hereditarily transmitted magical art Moreover, he normally made a living from his art, for which there was a great demand. Consequently we must exclude him too from the conception of prophet, even though he sometimes revealed new ways of salvation.

Thus, there remain only two kinds of prophets in our sense, one represented most clearly by the Buddha, the other with especial clarity by Zoroaster and Muhammad. The prophet may be primarily, as in the cases just noted, an instrument for the proclamation of a god and his will, be this a concrete command or an abstract norm. Preaching as one who has received a commission from god, he demands obedience as an ethical duty. This type we shall term the "ethical prophet." On the other hand, the prophet may be an exemplary man who, by his personal example, demonstrates to others the way to religious salvation, as in the case of the Buddha. The preaching of this type of prophet says nothing about a divine mission or an ethical duty of obedience, but rather directs itself to the self-interest of those who crave salvation, recommending to them the same path as he himself traversed. Our designation for this second type of prophecy is "exemplary."

The exemplary type is particularly characteristic of prophecy in India, although there have been a few manifestations of it in China (e.g., Lao Tzu) and the Near East. On the other hand, the ethical type is confined to the Near East, regardless of racial differences there. For neither the Vedas nor the classical books of the

Chinese—the oldest portions of which in both cases consist of songs of praise and thanksgiving by sacred singers, and of magical rites and ceremonies—makes it appear at all probable that prophecy of the ethical type, such as developed in the Near East or Iran, could ever have arisen in India or China. The decisive reason for this is the absence of a personal, transcendental, and ethical god. In India this concept was found only in a sacramental and magical form, and then only in the later and popular faiths. But in the religions of those social classes within which the decisive prophetic conceptions of Mahavira and Buddha were developed, ethical prophecy appeared only intermittently and was constantly subjected to reinterpretations in the direction of pantheism. In China the notion of ethical prophecy was altogether lacking in the ethics of the class that exercised the greatest influence in the society. To what degree this may presumably be associated with the intellectual distinctiveness of such classes, which was of course determined by various social factors, will be discussed later.

As far as purely religious factors are concerned, it was decisive for both India and China that the conception of a rationally regulated world had its point of origin in the ceremonial order of sacrifices, on the unalterable sequence of which everything depended. In this regard, crucial importance was attached to the indispensable regularity of meteorological processes, which were thought of in animistic terms. What was involved here was the normal activity or inactivity of the spirits and demons. According to both classical and heterodox Chinese views, these processes were held to be insured by the ethically proper conduct of government, that followed the correct path of virtue, the Tao; without this everything would fail, even according to Vedic doctrine. Thus, in India and China, rita and Tao respectively represented similar superdivine, impersonal forces.

On the other hand, the personal, transcendental and ethical god is a Near-Eastern concept. It corresponds so closely to that of an all-powerful mundane king with his rational bureaucratic regime that a causal connection can scarcely be overlooked. Throughout the world the magician is in the first instance a rainmaker, for the harvest depends on timely and sufficient rain, though not in excessive quantity. Until the present time the pontifical Chinese emperor has remained a rainmaker, for in northern China, at least, the uncertainty of the weather renders dubious the operation of irrigation procedures, no matter how extensive they are. Of greater significance was the construction of dams and internal canals, which became the real source of the imperial bureaucracy. The emperor sought to avert meteorological disturbances through sacrifices, public atonement, and various virtuous practices, e.g., the termination of abuses in the administration, or the organization of a raid on unpunished malefactors. For it was always assumed that the reason for the excitation of the spirits and the disturbances of the cosmic order had to be sought either in the personal derelictions of the monarch or in some manifestation of social disorganization. Again, rain was one of the rewards promised by Yahweh to his devotees, who were at that time primarily agriculturalists, as is clearly apparent in the older portions of the tradition. God promised neither too scanty rain nor yet excessive precipitation or deluge.

But throughout Mesopotamia and Arabia, however, it was not rain that was the creator of the harvest, but artificial irrigation alone. In Mesopotamia, irrigation was the sole source of the absolute power of the monarch, who derived his income by compelling his conquered subjects to build canals and cities adjoining them, just as the regulation of the Nile was the source of the Egyptian monarch's strength. In the desert and semiarid regions of the Near East this control of irrigation waters was indeed one source of the conception of a god who had created the earth and man out of nothing and not merely fashioned them, as was believed elsewhere. A riparian economy of this kind actually did produce a harvest out of nothing, from the desert sands. The monarch even created law by legislation and rationalization, a development the world experienced for the first time in Mesopotamia. It seems quite reasonable, therefore, that as a result of such experiences the ordering of the world should be conceived as the law of a freely acting, transcendental and personal god.

Another, and negative, factor accounting for the development in the Near East of a world order that reflected the operation of a personal god was the relative absence of those distinctive classes who were the bearers of the Hindu and Chinese ethics, and who created the godless religious ethics found in those countries. But even in Egypt, where originally Pharaoh himself was a god, the attempt of Ikhnaton to produce an astral monotheism foundered because of the power of the priesthood, which had by then systematized popular animism and become invincible. In Mesopotamia the development of monotheism and demagogic prophecy was opposed by the ancient pantheon, which was politically organized and had been systematized by the priests, and was further opposed and limited by the rigid development of the state.

The kingdom of the Pharaohs and of Mesopotamia made an even more powerful impression upon the Israelites than the great Persian monarch, the *basileus kat exochen,* made upon the Greeks (the strong impact of Cyrus upon the Greeks is mirrored in the eulogistic account of him formulated in the pedagogical treatise, the *Cyropaidia,* despite the defeat of this monarch). The Israelites had gained their freedom from the "house of bondage" of the earthly Pharaoh only because a divine king had come to their assistance. Indeed, their subsequent establishment of a worldly monarchy was expressly declared to be a declension from Yahweh, the real ruler of the people. Hebrew prophecy was completely oriented to a relationship with the great political powers of the time, the great kings, who as the rods of God's wrath first destroy Israel and then, as a consequence of divine intervention, permit Israelites to return from the Exile to their own land. In the case of Zoroaster too it can be asserted that the range of his vision was also oriented to the views of the civilized lands of the West.

Thus, the distinctive character of the earliest prophecy, in both its dualistic and monotheistic forms, seems to have been determined decisively—aside from the operation of certain other concrete historical influences—by the pressure of relatively contiguous great centers of rigid social organization upon less developed neighboring peoples. The latter tended to see in their own continuous peril from the pitiless bellicosity of terrible nations the anger and grace of a heavenly king.

Regardless of whether a particular religious prophet is predominantly of the ethical or predominantly of the exemplary type, prophetic revelation involves for both the prophet himself and for his followers—and this is the element common to both varieties—

a unified view of the world derived from a consciously integrated and meaningful attitude toward life. To the prophet, both the life of man and the world, both social and cosmic events, have a certain systematic and coherent meaning. To this meaning the conduct of mankind must be oriented if it is to bring salvation, for only in relation to this meaning does life obtain a unified and significant pattern. Now the structure of this meaning may take varied forms, and it may weld together into a unity motives that are logically quite heterogeneous. The whole conception is dominated, not by logical consistency, but by practical valuations. Yet it always denotes, regardless of any variations in scope and in measure of success, an effort to systematize all the manifestations of life; that is, to organize practical behavior into a direction of life, regardless of the form it may assume in any individual case. Moreover, it always contains the important religious conception of the world as a cosmos which is challenged to produce somehow a "meaningful," ordered totality, the particular manifestations of which are to be measured and evaluated according to this requirement.

The conflict between empirical reality and this conception of the world as a meaningful totality, which is based on a religious postulate, produces the strongest tensions in man's inner life as well as in his external relationship to the world. To be sure, this problem is by no means dealt with by prophecy alone. Both priestly wisdom and all completely nonsacerdotal philosophy, the intellectualist as well as the popular varieties, are somehow concerned with it. The ultimate question of all metaphysics has always been something like this: if the world as a whole and life in particular were to have a meaning, what might it be, and how would the world have to look in order to correspond to it? The religious problem-complex of prophets and priests is the womb from which non-sacerdotal philosophy emanated, wherever it developed. Subsequently, nonsacerdotal philosophy was bound to take issue with the antecedent thought of the religious functionaries; and the struggle between them provided one of the very important components of religious evolution. Hence, we must now examine more closely the mutual relationships of priests, prophets, and non-priests.

V. The Religious Congregation, Preaching, and Pastoral Care

If his prophecy is successful, the prophet succeeds in winning permanent helpers. These may be apostles (as Bartholomaeus translates the term of the Gathas), disciples (Old Testament and Hindu), comrades (Hindu and Islamic), or followers (Isaiah and the New Testament). In all cases they are personal devotees of the prophet, in contrast to priests and soothsayers who are organized into guilds or official hierarchies. We shall devote additional consideration to this relationship in our analysis of the forms of domination. Moreover, in addition to these permanent helpers, who are active co-workers with the prophet in his mission and who generally also possess some special charismatic qualifications, there is a circle of followers comprising those who support him with lodging, money, and services and who expect to obtain their salvation through his mission. These may, on occasion, group themselves into a congregation for a particular temporary activity or on a continuous basis.

A "community" or "congregation" in the specifically religious sense (for this term is also employed to denote an association of neighboring groups which may have originated for economic or for fiscal or other political purposes) does not arise solely in connection with prophecy in the particular sense used here. Nor does it arise in connection with every type of prophecy. Primarily, a religious community arises in connection with a prophetic movement as a result of routinization (*Veralltäglichung*), i.e., as a result of the process whereby either the prophet himself or his disciples secure the permanence of his preaching and the congregation's distribution of grace, hence insuring the economic existence of the enterprise and those who man it, and thereby monopolizing as well the privileges reserved for those charged with religious functions.

It follows from this primacy of routinization in the formation of religious congregations that congregations may also be formed around mystagogues and priests of nonprophetic religions. For the mystagogue, indeed, the presence of a congregation is a normal phenomenon. The magician, in contrast, exercises his craft independently or, if a member of a guild, serves a particular neighborhood or political group, not a specific religious congregation. The congregations of the mystagogues, like those of the Eleusinian practitioners of mysteries, generally remained associations that were open to the outer world and fluid in form. Whoever was desirous of salvation would enter into a relationship, generally temporary, with the mystagogue and his assistants. The Eleusinian mysteries, for example, always remained a regional community, independent of particular localities.

The situation was quite different in the case of exemplary prophets who unconditionally demonstrated the way of salvation by their personal example, as did, for example, the mendicant monks of Mahavira and the Buddha, who belonged to a narrower exemplary community. Within this narrower community the disciples, who might still have been personally associated with the prophet, would exert particular authority. Outside of the exemplary community, however, there were pious devotees (e.g., the *Upasakas* of India) who did not go the whole way of salvation for themselves, but sought to achieve a relative optimum of salvation by demonstrating their devotion to the exemplary saint. These devotees tended to lack altogether any fixed status in the religious community, as was originally the case with the Buddhist *Upasakas*. Or even might they be organized into some special group with fixed rules and obligations. This regularly happened when priests, priestlike counselors, or mystagogues like the Buddhist *bonzes,* who were entrusted with particular responsibilities, were separated out from the exemplary community. This had not been the case in the earliest stages of Buddhism, but the prevailing Buddhist practice was the free organization of devotees into occasional religious communities, which the majority of mystagogues and exemplary prophets shared with the temple priesthoods of particular deities from the organized pantheon. The economic existence of these congregations was secured by endowments and maintained by sacrificial offerings and other gifts provided by persons with religious needs.

At this stage there was still no trace of a permanent congregation of laymen. Our present conceptions of membership in a religious denomination are not applicable to the situation of that period. As yet the individual was a devotee of a god, approximately in the sense than an Italian is a devotee of a particular saint. There is an almost ineradicable vulgar error that the majority or even all of the Chinese are to be regarded as Buddhists in religion. The source of this misconception is the fact that many Chinese have been brought up in the Confucian ethic (which alone enjoys official approbation) yet still consult Taoist divining priests before building a house, and that Chinese will mourn deceased relatives according to the Confucian rule while also arranging for Buddhist masses to be performed in their memory. Apart from those who participate in the cult of a god on a continuous basis and ultimately form a narrow circle having a permanent interest in it, all that we have at this stage are occasional laymen or, if one is permitted to use metaphorically a modern political designation, "independent voters."

Naturally, this condition does not satisfy the interests of those who man the cult, if only because of purely economic considerations. Consequently, in this kind of situation they endeavor to create a congregation whereby the personal following of the cult will assume the form of a permanent organization and become a community with fixed rights and duties. Such a transformation of a personal following into a permanent congregation is the normal process by which the doctrine of the prophets enters into everyday life, as the function of a permanent institution. The disciples or apostles of the prophets thereupon become mystagogues, teachers, priests or pastors (or a combination of them all), serving an organization dedicated to exclusively religious purposes, namely a congregation of laymen.

But the same result can be reached from other starting points. We have seen that the priests, whose function evolved from that of magicians to that of generic priesthood, were either scions of landed priestly families, domestic court priests of landed magnates or noblemen, or trained priests of a sacrificial cult who had become organized into a separate class. Individuals or groups applied to these priests for assistance as the need arose, but normally they were engaged in any occupation not deemed dishonorable to their status group. One other possibility is that priests might become attached to particular organizations, vocational or otherwise, and especially those in the service of a political association. But in all these cases there is no actual congregation which is separate from all other associations.

Such a congregation may arise when a clan of sacrificing priests succeeds in organizing the particular followers of their god into an exclusive association. Another and more usual way for a religious community to arise is as a consequence of the destruction of a political association, wherever the religious adherents of the tribal god and his priests continue as a religious congregation. The first of these types is to be found in India and the Near East, in numerous intermediate gradations associated with the transition of mystagogic and exemplary prophecy or of religious reform movements into a permanent organization of congregations. Many small Hindu denominations developed as a result of such processes.

By contrast, the transition from a priesthood serving a political association into a religious congregation was associated primarily with the rise of the great world empires of the Near East, especially Persia. Political associations were annihilated and the population disarmed; their priesthoods, however, were assigned certain political powers and were rendered secure in their positions. This was done because the religious congregation was regarded as a valuable instrument for pacifying the conquered, just as the coercive community resulting from the neighborhood association was found to be useful for the protection of financial interests. Thus, by virtue of decrees promulgated by the Persian kings from Cyrus to Artaxerxes, Judaism evolved into a religious community under royal protection, with a theocratic center in Jerusalem. It was probably the Persian victory that brought similar chances and opportunities to the Delphic Apollo and to the priestly class servicing other gods, and possibly also to the Orphic prophets. In Egypt, after the decline of political independence, the national priesthood built a sort of "church" organization, apparently the first of its kind, with synods. On the other hand, religious congregations in

India arose in the more limited sense as exemplary congregations. There, the integral status of the Brahmin estate, as well as the regulations of asceticism, survived the multiplicity of ephemeral political structures, and as a consequence, the various systems of ethical salvation transcended all political boundaries. In Iran, the Zoroastrian priests succeeded during the course of the centuries in propagandizing a closed religious organization which under the Sassanides became a political "denomination." (The Achaemenides, as their documents demonstrate, were not Zoroastrians, but rather, followers of Mazda.)

The relationships between political authority and religious community, from which the concept of religious denomination (*Konfession*) derived, belong in the analysis of domination (*Herrschaft*). At this point it suffices to note that congregational religion is a phenomenon of diverse manifestations and great fluidity. Here we desire to consider its status only where the laity has been organized into a continuous pattern of communal behavior, in which it actively participates in some manner. Where one finds a tiny island of administrative concern which delimits the prerogatives of priests, this is a parish, but not yet a congregational community. But even the concept of a parish, as a grouping different from the secular, political, or economic community, is missing in the religions of China and ancient India. Again, the Greek and other ancient phratries and similar cultic communities were not parishes, but political or other types of associations whose collective actions stood under the guardianship of some god. As for the parish of ancient Buddhism, moreover, this was only a district in which temporarily resident mendicant monks were required to participate in the semimonthly convocations.

In medieval Christianity in the Occident, in post-Reformation Lutheranism and Anglicanism, and in both Christianity and Islam in the Near East, the parish was essentially a passive ecclesiastical association and the jurisdictional district of a priest. In these religions the laymen generally lacked completely the character of a congregation. To be sure, small vestiges of community rights have been retained in certain oriental churches and have also been found in Occidental Catholicism and Lutheranism. On the other hand, ancient Buddhist monasticism, like the warrior class of ancient Islam, Judaism, and ancient Christianity, had religious communities with an entirely different principle of social organization. Without going into any details, it will suffice to say that it was far more rigid. Furthermore, a certain actual influence of the laity may be combined with the absence of a rigidly regulated local congregational organization. An example of this would be Islam, where the laity wields considerable power, particularly in the Shiite sect, even though this is not legally secure; the Shah never appointed priests without being certain of the consent of the local laity.

On the other hand, it is the distinctive characteristic of every sect, in the technical sense of the term (a subject we shall consider later), that it is based on a restricted association of individual local congregations. From this principle, which is represented in Protestantism by the Baptists and Independents, and later by the Congregationalists, a gradual transition leads to the typical organization of the Reformed Church. Even when the latter has actually become a universal organization, it nevertheless makes membership conditional upon a quasi-contractual entry into some particular congregation. We shall return later to some of the problems which arise from these diversities. At the moment, we are particularly interested in just one consequence of the development of genuine congregational religion, which has very important results.

With the development of a congregation, the relationship between priesthood and laity within the community is of crucial significance for the practical effect of the religion. As the organization assumes the specific character of a congregation, the very powerful position of the priest is increasingly confronted with the necessity of keeping in mind the needs of the laity, in the interest of maintaining and enlarging the membership of the community. Actually, every type of priesthood is to some extent in a similar position. In order to maintain its own status, the priesthood must frequently meet the needs of the laity in a very considerable measure. The three forces operative within the laity with which the priesthood must come to grips are: (a) prophecy, (b) the traditionalism of the laity, and (c) lay intellectualism. In contrast to these forces, another decisive factor at work here derives from the necessities and tendencies of the priestly enterprise as such. A few words need to be said about this last factor in its relation to those mentioned earlier.

As a rule, the ethical and exemplary prophet is himself a layman, and his power position depends on his lay followers. Every prophecy by its very nature devalues the magical elements of the priestly enterprise, but in very different degrees. The Buddha and others like him, as well as the prophets of Israel, rejected and denounced adherence to knowledgeable magicians and soothsayers, and indeed they scorned all magic as inherently useless. Salvation could be achieved only by a distinctively religious and meaningful relationship to the eternal. Among the Buddhists it was regarded as a mortal sin to boast vainly of magical capacities; yet the existence of the latter among the unfaithful was never denied by the prophets of either India or Israel, nor denied by the Christian apostles or the ancient Christian tradition as such. All ethical prophets, by virtue of their rejection of magic, were necessarily skeptical of the priestly enterprise, though in varying degrees and fashions. The god of the Israelite prophets desired not burnt offerings, but obedience to his commandments. The Buddhist would have nothing to do with Vedic knowledge and ritual in his quest for salvation; and the sacrifice of soma so esteemed by priests was represented in the oldest *Gathas* as an abomination to *Ahura-mazda*.

Thus, tensions between the prophets and their lay followers on the one hand, and between the prophets and the representatives of the priestly tradition on the other existed everywhere. To what degree the prophet would succeed in fulfilling his mission, or would become a martyr, depended on the outcome of the struggle for power, which in some instances, e.g., in Israel, was determined by the international situation. Apart from his own family, Zoroaster depended on the clans of the nobles and princes for support in his struggle against the nameless counter-prophets; this was also the case in India and with Muhammad. On the other hand, the Israelite prophets depended on the support of the urban and rural middle class. All of them, however, made use of the prestige which their prophetic charisma, as opposed to the charisma held by technicians of the routine cults, had gained for them among the laity. The sacredness of a new revelation opposed that of tradition; and depending on the success of the propaganda by each side, the priesthood might compromise with the new policy, surpass its doctrine, or conquer it, unless it were subjugated itself. In every case, however, the priesthood had to assume the obligation of codifying either the victorious new doctrine or the old doctrine which had maintained itself despite an attack by the prophets. The priesthood had to delimit what must and must not be regarded as sacred and had to infuse its views into the religion of the laity, if it was to secure its own position. Such a development might have causes other than an effort by hostile prophets to imperil the position of the priesthood, as for example in India, where this took place very early. The simple interest of the priesthood in securing its own position against possible attack, and the necessity of insuring the traditional practice against the scepticism of the laity might produce similar results. Wherever this development took place it produced two phenomena, viz., canonical writings and dogmas, both of which might be of very different scope, particularly the latter. Canonical scriptures contain the revelations and traditions themselves, whereas dogmas are priestly interpretations of their meaning.

The collection of the prophetic religious revelations or, in the other case, of the traditionally transmitted sacred lore, may take place in the form of oral tradition. Throughout many centuries the sacred knowledge of the Brahmins was transmitted orally, and setting it down in writing was actually prohibited. This of course left a permanent mark on the literary form of this knowledge and also accounts for the not inconsiderable discrepancies in the texts of individual schools (*Shakhas*), the reason being that this knowledge was meant to be possessed only by qualified persons, namely the twice-born. To transmit such knowledge to anyone who had not experienced the second birth or who was excluded by virtue of his caste position (*Shudra*) was a heinous sin. Understandably, all magical lore originally has this character of secret knowledge, to protect the professional interest of the guild. But there are also aspects of this magical knowledge which everywhere become the material for the systematic instruction of other members of the group. At the root of the oldest and most universally diffused magical system of education is the animistic assumption that just as the magician himself requires rebirth and the possession of a new soul for his art, so heroism rests on a charisma which must be aroused, tested, and controlled in the hero by magical manipulations. In this way, therefore, the warrior is reborn into heroism. Charismatic education in this sense, with its novitiates, trials of strength, tortures, gradations of holiness and honor, initiation of youths, and preparation for battle is an almost universal institution of all societies which have experienced warfare.

When the guild of magicians finally develops into the priesthood, this extremely important function of educating the laity does not cease, and the priesthood always concerns itself with maintaining this function. More and more, secret lore recedes and the priestly doctrine becomes a scripturally established tradition which the priesthood interprets by means of dogmas. Such a scriptural tradition subsequently becomes the basis of every system of religion, not only for the professional members of the priestly class, but also for the laity, indeed especially for the laity.

Most, though not all, canonical sacred collections became officially closed against secular or religiously undesirable additions as a consequence of a struggle between various competing groups and prophecies for the control of the community. Wherever such a struggle failed to occur or wherever it did not threaten the content of the tradition, the formal canonization of the scriptures took place very slowly. The canon of the Jewish scriptures was not fixed until the year 90 A.D., shortly after the destruction of the theocratic state, when it was fixed by the synod of Jamnia as a dam against apostolic prophecies, and even then the canon was closed only in principle. In the case of the Vedas the scriptural canon was established in opposition to intellectual heterodoxy. The Christian canon was formalized because of the threat to the piety of the lower middle classes from the intellectual salvation doctrine of the Gnostics. On the other hand, the soteriology of the intellectual classes of ancient Buddhism was crystallized in the Pali canon as a result of the danger posed by the missionizing popular salvation religion of the *Mahayana*. The classical writings of Confucianism, like the priestly code of Ezra, were imposed by political force. But they did not on that account take on the quality of authentic sacredness, which is always the result of priestly activity. Indeed, the aforementioned legislation of Ezra received this accolade only later. Only the Quran underwent immediate editing, by command of the Caliph, and became sacred at once, because the semi-literate Muhammad held that the existence of a holy book automatically carries with it the mark of prestige for a religion. This view of prestige was related to widely diffused notions concerning the taboo quality and the magical significance of scriptural documents. Long before the establishment of the biblical canon, it was held that to touch the Pentateuch and the authentic prophetic writings "rendered the hands unclean."

The details of this process and the scope of the writings that were taken into the canonical sacred scriptures do not concern us here and can only be touched upon. It was due to the magical status of sacred bards that there were admitted into the Vedas not only the heroic epics but also sarcastic poems about the intoxicated Indra, as well as other poetry of every conceivable content. Similarly, a love poem and various personal details involved with the prophetic utterances were received into the Old Testament canon. Finally, the New Testament included a purely personal letter of Paul, and the Quran found room in a number of *suras* for records of the most personal kind of family vexations in the life of its prophet.

The closing of the canon was generally accounted for by the theory that only a certain epoch in the past history of the religion had been blessed with prophetic charisma. According to the theory of the rabbis, this was the period from Moses to Alexander, while from the Roman Catholic point of view the period was the Apostolic Age. On the whole, these theories correctly express recognition of the contrast between prophetic and priestly systematization. Prophets systematized religion with a view to simplifying the relationship of man to the world, by reference to an ultimate and integrated value position. On the other hand, priests systematized the content of prophecy or of the sacred traditions by supplying them with a casuistical, rationalistic framework of analysis, and by adapting them to the customs of life and thought of their own class and of the laity whom they controlled.

The development of priestly education from the most ancient charismatic stage to the period of literary education has considerable practical importance in the evolution of a faith into a scriptural religion, either in the complete sense of an attachment to a canon regarded as sacred or in the more moderate sense of the authoritativeness of a scripturally fixed sacred norm, as in the case of the Egyptian Book of the Dead. As literacy becomes more important for the conduct of purely secular affairs, which therefore assume the character of bureaucratic administration and proceed according to regulations and documents, education passes from the hands of secular officials and intellectuals into those of literate priests. The latter, for their part, occupy offices the functions of which involve the use of writing, as in the chancelleries of the Middle Ages. To what degree one or the other of these processes takes place depends also, apart from the degree to which the administration has become bureaucratized, on the degree to which other classes, principally the warrior nobles, have developed their own system of education and have taken it into their own hands. Later on we must discuss the bifurcation of educational systems which may result from this process. We must also consider the total suppression or nondevelopment of a purely priestly system of education which may result from the weakness of the priests or from the absence of either prophecy or scriptural religion.

The establishment of a religious congregational community provides the strongest stimulus, though not the only one, for the development of even the substantive content of the priestly doctrine, since the existence of a religious congregation creates the specific importance of dogmas. Once a religious community has become established it feels a need to set itself apart from alien competing doctrines and to maintain its superiority in propaganda, all of which tends to the emphasis upon differential doctrines. To be sure, this process of differentiation may be considerably strengthened by nonreligious motivations. For example, Charlemagne insisted, in the interests of the Frankish church, on the doctrine of *filioque,* which created one of the differences between the oriental and occidental Christian churches. Moreover his rejection of the canon and its artistic embellishments had political grounds, being directed against the supremacy of the Byzantine church. Adherence to completely incomprehensible dogmas, like the espousal of the Monophysite doctrine by great masses of people in the Orient and in Egypt, was the expression of an anti-imperial and anti-Hellenic separatist nationalism. Similarly, the monophysitic Coptic church later preferred the Arabs to the Romans as overlords. Such trends occurred frequently.

But the struggles of priests against indifference, which they profoundly hated, and against the danger that the zeal of the membership would stagnate generally played the greatest role in pushing distinctive criteria and differential doctrines to the foreground. Another factor was emphasis on the importance of membership in a particular denomination and the priests' desire to make difficult the transference of membership to another denomination. A model for the distinctive sign of religious membership was provided by the tattoo markings of fellow members of a totemistic or warrior clan, which had a magical basis. Closest to totemic tattoo, at least externally, was the differential body painting of the Hindu sects. But the Jewish retention of circumcision and of the Sabbath taboo was also intended, as is repeatedly indicated in the Old Testament, to effect separation from other nations, and it indeed produced such an effect to an extraordinary degree. A sharp differentiation of Christianity from Judaism was produced by the Christian choice of the day of the sun god as a day of rest, although this choice might possibly be accounted for by the Christian reception of the soteriological mythos of mystagogic Near Eastern salvation doctrines of solar religion. Muhammad's choice of Friday for weekly religious services was probably motivated primarily by his desire to segregate his followers from the Jews, after his missionary effort among them had failed. But his absolute prohibition of wine had too many analogies with comparable ancient and contemporary phenomena, e.g., among the Rechabites and Nazirites, to have been determined necessarily by his desire to erect a dam against Christian priests, who are under the obligation to take wine (at Holy Communion).

Differential dogmas have consistently possessed a much more practical and ethical character in India, corresponding to the ethical character of exemplary prophecy. The notorious ten points which produced the great schism of Buddhism at the Council of

Vesali involved mere questions of monastic regulations, including many public details which were emphasized only for the purpose of establishing the separation of the *Mahayana* organization.

Asiatic religions, on the other hand, knew practically nothing of dogma as an instrumentality of differentiation. To be sure, the Buddha enunciated his fourfold truth concerning the great illusions as the basis for the practical salvation doctrine of the noble eight-fold path. But the comprehension of those truths for the sake of their practical consequences, and not as dogma in the occidental sense, is the goal of the work of salvation. This is also the case with the majority of ancient Hindu prophecies.

In the Christian community one of the very first binding dogmas, characteristically, was God's creation of the world out of nothing, and consequently the establishment of a transcendental god in contradistinction to the gnostic speculation of the intellectuals. In India, on the other hand, cosmological and other metaphysical speculations remained the concern of philosophical schools, which were always permitted a very wide range of latitude in regard to orthodoxy, though not without some limitations. In China the Confucian ethic completely rejected all ties to metaphysical dogma, if only for the reason that magic and belief in spirits had to remain untouched in the interest of maintaining the cult of ancestors, which was the foundation of all obedience, both patrimonial and bureaucratic (as expressly stated in the tradition).

Even within ethical prophecy and the congregational religion it produced, there was a wide diversity in the scope of proliferation of genuine dogmas. Ancient Islam contented itself with confessions of loyalty to god and to the prophet, together with a few practical and ritual primary commandments, as the basis of membership. But dogmatic distinctions, both practical and theoretical, became more comprehensive as priests, community teachers, and even the community itself became bearers of the religion. This holds for the later Zoroastrians, Jews, and Christians. But genuinely dogmatic controversy could arise in ancient Israel or Islam only in exceptional cases, since both these religions were characterized by a simplicity of doctrinal theology. In both religions the main area of dispute centered about the doctrine of grace, though there were subsidiary disputes about practical or ethical problems and about ritual and legal questions. This is even truer of Zoroastrianism.

Only among the Christians did there develop a comprehensive, binding and systematically rationalized dogmatics of a theoretical type concerning cosmological matters, the soteriological *mythos* (Christology), and priestly authority (the sacraments). This Christian dogmatics developed first in the Hellenistic portion of the Roman empire, but in the Middle Ages the major elaborations occurred in the Occident. In general, theological development was far stronger in the occidental than in the oriental churches, but in both regions the maximum development of theology occurred wherever a powerful organization of priests possessed the greatest measure of independence from political authorities.

This Christian preoccupation with the formulation of dogmas was in antiquity particularly influenced by the distinctive character of the intellectual classes, which was a product of Greek education; by the special metaphysical presuppositions and tensions produced by the cult of Christ; and by the necessity of taking issue with the educated classes who had remained outside the Christian community. However, the same social situation determined the ancient Christian church's hostility to pure intellectualism (which stands in such contrast to the position taken by the Asiatic religions). Early Christianity was a congregational religion comprising primarily lower-middle-class laymen, who looked with considerable suspicion upon pure intellectualism, a phenomenon which had to be given considerable attention by the bishops. In the Orient, non-Hellenic Greek lower-middle classes increasingly supplied Christianity with monks, especially after the destruction of the Greek system of education in the Orient, and this development brought to an end the rational construction of dogma there.

The development of dogma in Christianity was further influenced by the distinctively hierarchical organizational form of the Christian religious communities. In ancient Buddhism, the complete and purposeful absence of all hierarchical organization necessarily rendered impossible any consensus concerning rational dogmatics, such as was produced in Christianity, even assuming that a salvation doctrine would have needed any such dogmatic consensus. Christianity found it necessary to postulate some power able to make decisions concerning the orthodoxy of doctrines, in order to protect the unity of the community against the activity of priests and against the competing lay rationalism which had been aroused by ecclesiastical education. The result of a long process of evolution, the details of which cannot be expounded here, was that the Roman church produced the infallible doctrinal office of bishops, in the hope that God would not permit the congregation of the world capital to fall into error. Only in this case do we find a consistent doctrinal solution, which assumes the inspiration of the incumbent of the doctrinal office whenever a decision has to be rendered concerning doctrine.

On the other hand, Islam and the oriental churches, for various reasons to be explained below, retained as their basis for determining the validity of dogmatic truths the practice of depending on the consensus of the official bearers of the ecclesiastical teaching organization, who were primarily theologians or priests as the case might be. Islam arrived at this position by holding fast to the assurance of its prophet that god would never permit the congregation of the faithful to fall into error. On the other hand, the oriental churches followed in this regard the model of the earliest practice of the Christian church. The net effect of this was to preclude any possibility of the proliferation of dogma in these religious traditions. Again, the Dalai Lama has power to formulate doctrine, in keeping with the magical and ritualistic character of his religion. Among the Hindus the power of excommunication entrusted to the *gurus* was largely employed for political reasons and only rarely for the punishment of dogmatic deviations.

The work of the priests in systematizing the sacred doctrines was constantly nourished by the new material that was turned up in their professional practice, so different from the practice of magicians. In the ethical type of congregational religion something altogether new and different in kind from magical assistance evolved, namely preaching and rational pastoral care.

Preaching, which in the true sense of the word is collective instruction concerning religious and ethical matters, is normally something uniquely associated with prophecy and prophetic religion. Indeed, wherever it arises apart from these, it is an imitation of them. But as a rule, preaching declines in importance whenever a revealed religion has been transformed into a priestly enterprise by routinization, and the importance of preaching stands in inverse proportion to the magical components of a religion. Buddhism originally consisted entirely of preaching, so far as the laity was concerned. In Christianity the importance of preaching has been proportional to the elimination of the more magical and sacramental components of the religion. Consequently, preaching achieves the greatest significance in Protestantism, in which the concept of the priest has been supplanted altogether by that of the preacher.

Pastoral care, the religious cultivation of the individual, is also in its rationalized and systematized form a product of prophetically revealed religion. It has its source in the oracle and in consultations with the diviner or necromancer. The diviner is consulted when sickness or other blows of fate have led to the suspicion that some magical transgression is responsible, making it necessary to ascertain the means by which the aggrieved spirit, demon, or god may be pacified. This is also the source of the confessional, which originally had no connection with ethical influences on life. The connection between confession and ethical conduct was first effected by ethical religion, particularly by prophecy. Pastoral care may later assume diverse forms. To the extent that it is a charismatic distribution of grace it stands in a close inner relationship to magical manipulations. But the care of souls may also involve the instruction of individuals regarding concrete religious obligations whenever certain doubts have arisen. Finally, pastoral care may in some sense stand midway between charismatic distribution of grace and instruction, entailing the distribution of personal religious consolation in times of inner or external distress.

Preaching and pastoral care differ widely in the strength of their practical influence on the conduct of life. Preaching unfolds its power most strongly in periods of prophetic excitation. In the treadmill of daily living it declines sharply to an almost complete lack of influence upon the conduct of life, for the very reason that the charisma of speech is an individual matter.

Pastoral care in all its forms is the priests' real instrument of power, particularly over the workaday world, and it influences the conduct of life most powerfully when religion has achieved an ethical character. In fact, the power of ethical religion over the masses parallels the development of pastoral care. Wherever the power of an ethical religion is intact, the pastor will be consulted in all the situations of life by both private individuals and the functionaries of groups, just as the professional divining priest would be consulted in the magical religions, e.g., the religion of China. Among these religious functionaries whose pastoral care has influenced the everyday life of the laity and the behavior of political officials in an enduring and often decisive manner have been the counseling rabbis of Judaism, the father confessors of Catholicism, the pietistic pastors of souls in Protestantism, the directors of souls in Counter Reformation Catholicism, the Brahminic *purohitas* at the court, the *gurus* and *gosains* in Hinduism, and the *muftis* and dervish *shaykhs* in Islam.

As for the conduct of the individual's private life, the greatest influence of pastoral care was exerted when the priesthood combined ethical casuistry with a rationalized system of ecclesiastical penances. This was accomplished in a remarkably skillful way by the occidental church, which was schooled in the casuistry of Roman law. It is primarily these practical responsibilities of preaching and pastoral care which stimulated the labors of the priesthood in systematizing the casuistical treatment of ethical commandments and religious truths, and indeed first compelled them to take an attitude toward the numerous problems which had not been settled in the revelation itself. Consequently, it is these same practical responsibilities of preaching and pastoral care which brought in their wake the substantive routinization of prophetic demands into specific prescriptions of a casuistical, and hence more rational, character, in contrast to the prophetic ethics. But at the same time this development resulted in the loss of that unity which the prophet had introduced into the ethics—the derivation of a standard of life out of a distinctive "meaningful" relationship to one's god, such as he himself had possessed and by means of which he assayed not the external appearance of a single act, but rather its meaningful significance for the total relationship to the god. As for priestly practice, it required both positive injunctions and a casuistry for the laity. For this reason the preoccupation of religion with inwardness had necessarily to undergo a recession.

It is evident that the positive, substantive injunctions of the prophetic ethic and the casuistical transformation thereof by the priests ultimately derived their material from problems which the folkways, conventions, and factual needs of the laity brought to the priests for disposition in their pastoral office. Hence, the more a priesthood aimed to regulate the behavior pattern of the laity in accordance with the will of the god, and especially to aggrandize its status and income by so doing, the more it had to compromise with the traditional views of the laity in formulating patterns of doctrine and behavior. This was particularly the case when no great prophetic preaching had developed which might have wrenched the faith of the masses from its bondage to traditions based upon magic.

As the masses increasingly became the object of the priests' influence and the foundation of their power, the priestly labors of systematization concerned themselves more and more with the most traditional, and hence magical, forms of religious notions and practices. Thus, as the Egyptian priesthood pressed towards greater power, the animistic cult of animals was increasingly pushed into the center of religious interest. It is certainly a fact that the systematic intellectual training of the priests had grown by comparison with earlier times. And so too in India, there was an increased systematization of the cult after the displacement by the Brahmins of the *hotar,* the sacred charismatic singers, from first place in the sacrificial ceremonial. The Atharva Veda is much younger than the Rig Veda as a literary product, and the Brahmanas are much younger still. Yet the systematized religious material in the Atharva Veda is of much older provenience than the rituals of the noble Vedic cults and the other components of the older Vedas; indeed, the Atharva Veda is a purely magical ritual (to a far greater degree than the older Vedas). The process of popularization and transformation into magic of religion which had been systematized by the priests continued even further in the Brahmanas. The older Vedic cults are indeed, as Oldenberg has emphasized, cults of the possessing classes, whereas the magical ritual had been the possession of the entire group since ancient times.

A similar process appears to have taken place in regard to prophecy. In comparison with the superior intellectual contemplativeness of ancient Buddhism, which had achieved the highest peaks of sublimity, the *Mahayana* religion was essentially a popularization that increasingly tended to approach pure wizardry or sacramental ritualism. A similar fate overtook the doctrines of Zoroaster, Lao Tzu, and the Hindu religious reformers, and to some extent the doctrines of Muhammad as well, when the respective faiths of these founders became religions of laymen. Thus, the *Zend Avesta* sanctioned the cult of haoma, although it had been expressly and strongly combated by Zoroaster, eliminating merely a few of the bacchantic elements which he had denounced with special fervor. Hinduism constantly betrayed a growing tendency to slide over into magic, or in any case into a semimagical sacramental soteriology. The propaganda of Islam in Africa rested primarily on a massive foundation of magic, by means of which it has continued to outbid other competing faiths, despite the rejection of magic by earliest Islam.

This process, which is interpreted as a decline or petrifaction of prophecy, is practically unavoidable. The prophet himself is normally a righteous lay preacher of sovereign independence whose aim is to supplant the traditional ritualistic religious grace of the ecclesiastical type by organizing life on the basis of ultimate ethical principles. The laity's acceptance of the prophet, however, is generally based on the fact that he possesses a certain charisma. This usually means that he is a magician, in fact much greater and more powerful than other magicians, and indeed that he possesses unsurpassed power over demons and even over death itself. It usually means that he has the power to raise the dead, and possibly that he himself may rise from the grave. In short, he is able to do things which other magicians are unable to accomplish. It does not matter that the prophet attempts to deny such imputed powers, for after his death this development proceeds without and beyond him. If he is to continue to live on in some manner among large numbers of the laity, he must himself become the object of a cult, which means he must become the incarnation of a god. If this does not happen, the needs of the laity will at least insure that the form of the prophet's teaching which is most appropriate for them will survive by a process of selection.

Thus, these two types of influences, viz., the power of prophetic charisma and the enduring habits of the masses, influence the work of the priests in their systematization, though they tend to oppose one another at many points. But even apart from the fact that prophets practically always come out of lay groups or find their support in them, the laity is not composed of exclusively traditionalistic forces. The rationalism of lay circles is another social force with which the priesthood must take issue. Different social classes may be the bearers of this lay rationalism.

VI. Castes, Estates, Classes, and Religion

The lot of peasants is so strongly tied to nature, so dependent on organic processes and natural events, and economically so little oriented to rational systematization that in general the peasantry will become a carrier of religion only when it is threatened by enslavement or proletarization, either by domestic forces (financial, agrarian, or seignorial) or by some external political power.

Ancient Israelite religious history already manifested both major threats to the peasant class: first, pressures from foreign powers that threatened enslavement, and second, opposition between peasants and domestic land owners (who in antiquity resided in the cities). The oldest documents, particularly the *Song of Deborah,* reveal the typical essential elements of the struggle of a peasant confederacy, involving associative processes comparable to those of the Aetolians, Samnites, and Swiss. Another point of similarity with the Swiss situation is that Palestine possessed the geographical character of a land bridge, being situated on a great trade route which spanned the terrain from Egypt to the Euphrates. This facilitated culture contacts, and accordingly, Palestine produced a money economy fairly early. The Israelite confederacy directed its efforts against both the Philistines and the Canaanite land magnates who dwelt in the cities. These latter were knights who fought with iron chariots, "warriors trained from their very youth," as Goliath was described, who sought to enslave and render tributary the peasantry of the mountain slopes through which flowed milk and honey.

It was a most significant constellation of historical factors that this struggle, as well as the unification of the tribes and the expansion of the Mosaic period, was constantly renewed under the leadership of the Yahweh religion's saviors ("messiahs," from *mashiah,* which means "the anointed one"—like Gideon and like others termed "judges"). Because of this distinctive leadership, a religious concern that far transcended the level of the usual agrarian cults entered very early into the ancient religion of the Palestinian peasantry. But not until the city of Jerusalem had been conquered did the cult of Yahweh, with its Mosaic social legislation, become a genuinely ethical religion. Indeed, as the social admonitions of the prophets demonstrate, even here this took place partly under the influence of agrarian social reform movements directed against the urban land magnates and financial nabobs, and by reference to the social prescriptions of the Mosaic law regarding the equalization of classes.

But prophetic religion has by no means been the product of agrarian influences alone. A typically plebeian urban destiny was one of the primary dynamic factors in the social reform doctrine of the first and only theologian of official Greek literature, Hesiod. The more agrarian the essential social pattern of a culture, e.g., Rome, India, or Egypt, the more likely it is that the agrarian element of the population will fall into a pattern of traditionalism and that religion, at least that of the masses, will lack ethical rationalization. Thus, in the later development of Judaism and Christianity, the peasants never appeared as the carriers of rational ethical movements. This statement is completely true of Judaism, while in Christianity the participation of the peasantry in rational ethical movements took place only in exceptional cases and then in a communist, revolutionary form. The puritanical sect of the Donatists in Roman Africa, the Roman province of greatest land accumulation, appears to have been very popular among the peasantry, but this was the sole example of peasant concern for a rational ethical movement in antiquity. The Taborites, who were partially derived from peasant groups, the German peasant protagonists of "divine right" in peasant wars, the English radical communist farmers, and above all the Russian peasant sectarians—all these have points of contact with agrarian communism by virtue of their more or less explicit development of institutionalized communal ownership of land. All these groups felt themselves threatened by proletarization, and they turned against the official church in the first instance because it was the recipient of tithes and served as a bulwark of the financial and landed magnates. The association of the aforementioned peasant groups with religious demands was possible only on the basis of an already existing ethical religion which contained specific prophecies or promises that might suggest and justify a revolutionary "law of nature." More will be said about this in another context.

Hence, manifestations of a close relationship between peasant religion and agrarian reform movements did not occur in Asia, where the combination of religious prophecy with revolutionary currents, e.g., as in China, took a different direction altogether, and did not assume the form of a real peasant movement. Only rarely does the peasant class serve as the carrier of any other sort of religion than their original magic.

Yet the prophecy of Zoroaster apparently appealed to the (relative) rationalism of peasants who, having learned to work in an orderly fashion and to raise cattle, were struggling against the orgiastic religion of the false prophets, which entailed the torture of animals. This, like the cult of intoxication which Moses combated, was presumably associated with the bacchantic rending of live animals. In the religion of the Parsees, only the cultivated soil was regarded as pure from the magical point of view, and therefore only agriculture was absolutely pleasing to god. Consequently, even after the pattern of the religion established by the original prophecy had undergone considerable transformation as a result of its adaptation to the needs of everyday life, it retained a distinctive agrarian pattern, and consequently a characteristically anti-urban tendency in its doctrines of social ethics. But to the degree that the Zoroastrian prophecy set in motion certain economic interests of its own, these tendencies were originally more the concern of noblemen and landed magnates interested in the welfare of their peasantry than the ideas of peasants themselves. As a general rule the peasantry remained primarily involved with weather magic and animistic magic or ritualism; insofar as it developed any ethical religion, the focus was on a purely formalistic ethic of *do ut des* in relation to both god and priests.

That the peasant has become the distinctive prototype of the pious man who is pleasing to god is a thoroughly modern phenomenon, with the exception of Zoroastrianism and a few scattered examples of opposition to urban culture and disorganization on the part of literati representing patriarchal and feudalistic elements, or conversely, of intellectuals imbued with *Weltschmerz*. None of the more important religions of Eastern Asia had any such notion about the religious merit of the peasant. Indeed, in the religions of India, and most consistently in the salvation religion of Buddhism the peasant is religiously suspect or actually proscribed because of *ahimsa,* the absolute prohibition against taking the life of any living thing.

The Israelite religion of preprophetic times was still very much a religion of peasants. On the other hand, in exilic times the glorification of agriculture as pleasing to God was largely the expression of opposition to urban development felt by literary or patriarchal groups. The actual religion had rather a different appearance, even at that time and later on in the period of the Pharisees it was completely different in this regard. To the congregational piety of the *chaberim* the "rustic" was virtually identical with the "godless," the rural dweller being politically and religiously a Jew of the second class. For according to the Jewish ritual law, it was virtually impossible for a peasant to live a pious life, just as in Buddhism and Hinduism. The practical consequences of postexilic theology, and even more so of the Talmudic theology, made it extremely difficult for a Jew to practice agriculture. Even now, the Zionist colonization of Palestine has met with an absolute impediment in the form of the sabbatical year, a product of the theologians of later Judaism. To overcome this difficulty, the eastern European rabbis, in contrast to the more doctrinaire leaders of German Jewish orthodoxy, have had to construe a special dispensation based on the notion that such colonizing is especially pleasing to God.

In early Christianity, it will be recalled, the rustic was simply regarded as the heathen (*paganus*). Even the official doctrine of medieval churches, as formulated by Thomas Aquinas, treated the peasant essentially as a Christian of lower rank, and at best accorded him very little esteem. The religious glorification of the peasant and the belief in the special worth of his piety is the result of a very modern development. It was characteristic of Lutheranism in particular—in rather strongly marked contrast to Calvinism and to most of the other Protestant sects—as well as of modern Russian religion, which manifest Slavophile influences. These are ecclesiastical communities which, by virtue of their type or organization, are very closely tied to the authoritarian interests of princes and noblemen upon whom they are dependent. In modern Lutheranism (for this was not the position of Luther himself) the dominant interest is the struggle against the rationalism of the intellectuals, and against political liberalism. In the ideology of the Slavophile religious peasant, the primary concern was the struggle against capitalism and modern socialism. Finally, the glorification of the Russian sectarians by the *Narodniki* combined an anti-rationalist protest against intellectualism with the revolt of a proletarized class of farmers against a bureaucratic church that was serving the interests of the ruling classes, thereby surrounding both components of the social struggle with a religious aura. Thus, what was involved in all cases was very largely a reaction against the development of modern rationalism, of which the cities were regarded as the carriers.

In striking contrast to all this is the fact that it was the city which, in earlier times, was regarded as the site of piety. As late as the seventeenth century, Baxter saw in the relationships of the weavers of Kidderminster to the metropolis of London (made possible by the development of domestic industry) a definite enhancement of the weavers' piety. Actually, early Christianity was an urban religion, and as Harnack decisively demonstrated, its importance in any particular city was in direct proportion to the size of the urban community. In the Middle Ages too, fidelity to the church, as well as sectarian movements in religion, characteristically developed in the cities. It is highly unlikely that an organized congregational religion, such as early Christianity became, could have developed as it did apart from the community life of a city (notably in the sense found in the Occident). For early Christianity presupposed as already extant certain conceptions, viz., the transcendence of taboo barriers between clans, the concept of office, and the concept of the community as an institution,

(*Anstalt*) an organized corporate entity serving specific realistic functions. To be sure, Christianity, on its part, strengthened these conceptions, and greatly facilitated the renewed reception of them by the growing European cities during the Middle Ages. But actually these notions reached their fullest development exclusively within the Mediterranean culture, particularly in Greek and then definitely in Roman urban law. What is more, the specific qualities of Christianity as an ethical religion of salvation and as personal piety found their real nurture in the urban environment; and it is there that they constantly set in motion new stimuli in contrast to the ritualistic, magical or formalistic re-interpretation favored by the dominant feudal powers.

As a rule, the class of warrior nobles, and indeed feudal powers generally, have not readily become the carriers of a rational religious ethic. The life pattern of a warrior has very little affinity with the notion of a beneficent providence, or with the systematic ethical demands of a transcendental god. Concepts like sin, salvation, and religious humility have not only seemed remote from all elite political classes, particularly the warrior nobles, but have indeed appeared reprehensible to its sense of honor. To accept a religion that works with such conceptions and to genuflect before the prophet or priest would appear plebeian and dishonorable to any martial hero or noble person, e.g., the Roman nobility of the age of Tacitus, or the Confucian mandarins. It is an everyday psychological event for the warrior to face death and the irrationalities of human destiny. Indeed, the chances and adventures of mundane existence fill his life to such an extent that he does not require of his religion (and accepts only reluctantly) anything beyond protection against evil magic or such ceremonial rites as are congruent with his caste, such as priestly prayers for victory or for a blissful death leading directly into the hero's heaven.

As has already been mentioned in another connection, the educated Greek always remained a warrior, at least in theory. The simple animistic belief in spirits which left vague the qualities of existence after death and finally dropped the entire question (though remaining certain that the most miserable status here on earth was preferable to ruling over Hades), remained the normal faith of the Greeks until the time of the complete destruction of their political autonomy. The only develoments beyond this were the mystery religions, which provided means for ritualistic improvement of the human condition in this world and in the next. The only radical departure from this position was the Orphic congregational religion, with its doctrine of metempsychosis.

Periods of strong prophetic or reformist religious agitation have frequently pulled the nobility in particular into the path of prophetic ethical religion, because this type of religion breaks through all classes and estates, and because the nobility has generally been the first carrier of lay education. But presently the routinization of prophetic religion had the effect of eliminating the nobility from the circle of groups characterized by religious enthusiasm. This is already evident at the time of the religious wars in France in the conflicts of the Huguenot synods with a leader like Condé over ethical questions. Ultimately, the Scotch nobility, like the British and the French, was completely extruded from the Calvinist religion in which it, or at least some of its groups, had originally played a considerable role.

As a rule, prophetic religion is naturally compatible with the class feeling of the nobility when it directs its promises to the warrior in the cause of religion. This conception assumes the exclusiveness of a universal god and the moral depravity of unbelievers who are his adversaries and whose untroubled existence arouses his righteous indignation. Hence, such a notion is absent in the Occident of ancient times, as well as in all Asiatic religion until Zoroaster. Indeed, even in Parsism a direct connection between religious promises and war against religious infidelity is still lacking. It was Islam that first produced this conjunction of ideas.

The precursor and model for this was the promise of the Hebrew god to his people, as understood and reinterpreted by Muhammad after he had changed from a pietistic leader of a conventicle in Mecca to the *podesta* of Jathrib-Medina, and after he had finally been rejected as a prophet by the Jews. The ancient wars of the Israelite confederacy, waged under the leadership of various saviors operating under the authority of Yahweh, were regarded by the tradition as holy wars. This concept of a holy war, i.e., a war in the name of god, for the special purpose of avenging a sacrilege, which entailed putting the enemy under the ban and destroying him and all his belongings completely, is not unknown in antiquity, particularly among the Greeks. But what was distinctive of the Hebraic concept is that the people of Yahweh, as his special community, demonstrated and exemplified their god's prestige against their foes. Consequently, when Yahweh became a universal god, Hebrew prophecy and the religion of the Psalmists created a new religious interpretation. The possession of the Promised Land, previously foretold, was supplanted by the farther reaching promise of the elevation of Israel, as the people of Yahweh, above other nations. In the future all nations would be compelled to serve Yahweh and to lie at the feet of Israel.

On this model Muhammad constructed the commandment of the holy war involving the subjugation of the unbelievers to political authority and economic domination of the faithful. If the infidels were members of "religions of the book," their extermination was not enjoined; indeed, their survival was considered desirable because of the financial contribution they could make. It was a Christian war of religion that first was waged under the Augustinian formula *coge intrare,* by the terms of which unbelievers or heretics had only the choice between conversion and extirpation. It will be recalled that Pope Urban lost no time in emphasizing to the crusaders the necessity for territorial expansion in order to acquire new benefices for posterity. To an even greater degree than the Crusades, religious war for the Muslims was essentially an enterprise directed towards the acquisition of large holdings of real estate, because it was primarily oriented to feudal interest in land. In Turkish law the religious war is still an important qualification for preferential status in the distribution of *sipahi* prebendaries. Apart from the anticipated master status that results from victory in a religious war, even in Islam the religious promises associated with the propaganda for war—particularly the promise of an Islamic paradise for those killed in such a war—should not be construed as promises of salvation in the genuine sense of this term, just as Valhalla for Scandinavian warriors, or the paradise reserved for heroes who fall in religious battles as promised to the Hindu *kshatriya,* or to the warrior hero who has become sated with life once he has seen his grandson, or indeed any other hero heaven are not equivalent to salvation. Moreover, those religious elements of ancient Islam which had the character of an ethical religion of salvation largely receded into the background as long as Islam remained essentially a martial religion.

So, too, the religion of the medieval Christian order of celibate knights, particularly the Templars, which was first called into being during the Crusades against Islam and which corresponded to the Islamic warrior orders, had in general only a formal relation to salvation religion. This was also true of the faith of the Hindu Sikhs, which, arising out of a combination of Islamic ideas and Hinduism, was at first strongly pacifist. Persecution drove the Sikhs to the ideal of uncompromising religious warfare. Another instance of the relative meagerness of the relationship of a martial faith to salvation religion is that of the warlike Japanese monks of Buddhism, who for a temporary period maintained a position of political importance. Indeed, even the formal orthodoxy of all these warrior religionists was often of dubious genuineness.

Although a warrior caste having the form of knighthood practically always had a thoroughly negative attitude toward salvation and congregational religion, the relationship is somewhat different in "standing" professional armies, i.e., those having an essentially bureaucratic organization and "officers." The Chinese army plainly had a specialized god as did any other occupation, a hero who had undergone canonization by the state. Then, too, the passionate participation of the Byzantine army in behalf of the iconoclast, was not a result of puritanical principles, but simply the position consciously adopted under the influence of Islam by the recruiting districts for the army. But in the Roman army of the period of the principate, from the time of the second century, the congregational religion of Mithra, which was a competitor of Christianity and held forth certain promises concerning the world to come, played a considerable role, together with certain other preferred cults which do not interest us at this point.

Mithraism was especially important (though not exclusively so) among the centurions, that is the subaltern officers who had a claim upon governmental subsidy. The genuinely ethical requirements of the Mithraistic mysteries were, however, very modest and of a general nature only. Mithraism was essentially a ritualistic religion of purity; in sharp contrast to Christianity, it was entirely masculine, excluding women completely. In general, it was a religion of salvation, and, as already noted, one of the most masculine, with a hierarchical gradation of sacred ceremonies and religious ranks. Again in contrast to Christianity, it did not prohibit participation in other cults and mysteries, which was not an infrequent occurrence. Mithraism therefore came under the protection of the emperors from the time of Commodus, who first went through the initiation ceremonies (just as the kings of Prussia were members of fraternal orders), until its last enthusiastic protagonist, Julian. Apart from promises of a mundane nature which, to be sure, were in this case as in all other religions linked with predictions regarding the world beyond, the chief attraction of this cult for army officers was undoubtedly the essentially magical and sacramental character of its distribution of grace and the possibility of hierarchical advancement in the mystery ceremonies.

It is likely that similar factors recommended the cult to nonmilitary officials, for it was also very popular among them. Certainly, among government officials there have been found other incipient tendencies towards distinctively salvation type religions. One example of this may be seen in the pietistic German officials, a reflection of the fact that middle-class ascetic piety in Germany, exemplifying a characteristically civic pattern of life, found its representation only among the class of officials, and not among the middle class of entrepreneurs. Another instance of the tendency of some government officials to favor the salvation type of religion appeared occasionally among certain really pious Prussian generals of the eighteenth and nineteenth centuries. But as a rule, this is not the attitude to religion of a dominant bureaucracy, which is always the carrier of a comprehensive sober rationalism and, at the same time, of the ideal of a disciplined "order" and security as absolute standards of value. The bureaucratic class is usually characterized by a profound disesteem of all irrational religion, combined, however, with a recognition of the usefulness of this type of religion as a device for controlling the people. In antiquity this attitude was held by the Roman officials while today it is shared by both the civilian and military bureaucracy.[1]

[1] I have had the following experience. At the first appearance of Mr. V. Egidy (First Lieutenant, retired) the Officers' Clubs entertained

The distinctive attitude of a bureaucracy to religious matters has been classically formulated in Confucianism. Its hallmark is an absolute lack of feeling of a need for salvation or for any transcendental anchorage for ethics. In its place resides what is substantively an opportunistic and utilitarian (though aesthetically attractive) doctrine of conventions appropriate to a bureaucratic caste. Other factors in the bureaucratic attitude toward religion include the elimination of all those emotional and irrational manifestations of personal religion which go beyond the traditional belief in spirits, and the maintenance of the ancestral cult and of filial piety as the universal basis for social subordination. Still another ingredient of bureaucratic religions is a certain distance from the spirits, the magical manipulation of which is scorned by the enlightened official (but in which the superstitious one may participate, as is the case with spiritualism among us today). Yet both types of bureaucratic officials will, with contemptuous indifference, permit such spiritualistic activity to flourish as the religion of the masses (*Volksreligiosität*). Insofar as this popular religion comes to expression in recognized state rites, the official continues to respect them, outwardly at least, as a conventional obligation appropriate to his status. The continuous retention of magic, especially of the ancestral cult, as the guarantee of social obedience, enabled the Chinese bureaucracy to completely suppress all independent ecclesiastical development and all congregational religion. As for the European bureaucracy, although it generally shared such subjective disesteem for any serious concern with religion, it found itself compelled to pay more official respect to the existing churches in the interest of control over the masses.

If certain fairly uniform tendencies are normally apparent, in spite of all differences in the religious attitude of the nobility and bureaucracy, the classes with the maximum social privilege, the real "middle" classes evince striking contrasts. Moreover, this is

---

the expectation, inasmuch as the right of such criticism of orthodoxy was obviously open to any comrade, that His Majesty would seize the initiative in demanding that the old fairy tales, which no honest fellow could manage to believe, would not be served up at the military services any longer. But, naturally enough, when no such thing happened it was readily recognized that the church doctrine, just as it was, constituted the best fodder for the recruits.

something quite apart from the rather sharp differences of status which these classes manifest within themselves. Thus, in some instances, merchants may be members of the most highly privileged class, as in the case of the ancient urban patriciate, while in others they may be pariahs, like impecunious wandering peddlers. Again, they may be possessed of considerable social privilege, though occupying a lower social status than the nobility or officialdom; or they may be without privilege, or indeed disprivileged, yet actually exerting great social power. Examples of the latter would be the Roman knights, the Hellenic *metoikoi,* the medieval tailors and other merchant groups, the financiers and great merchant princes of Babylonia, the Chinese and Hindu traders, and finally the bourgeoisie of the modern period.

Apart from these differences of social position, the attitude of the commercial patriciate toward religion shows characteristic contrasts in all periods of history. In the nature of the case, the strongly mundane orientation of their life precludes their having much inclination for prophetic or ethical religion. The activity of the great merchants of antiquity and medieval times represented a distinctive kind of specifically occasional and unprofessional acquisition of money, e.g., by providing capital for traveling traders who required it. Originally rural dwellers possessing landed estates, these merchants became, in historical times, an urbanized nobility which had grown rich from such occasional trade. On the other hand, they might have started as tradesmen who having acquired landed property were seeking to climb into the families of the nobility. To the category of the commercial patriciate there were added, as the financing of public enterprises developed, the representatives of finance whose primary business was to meet the financial needs of the state by supplying necessary material and governmental credit, together with the financiers of colonial capitalism, an enterprise that has existed in all periods of history. None of these classes has ever been the primary carrier of an ethical or salvation religion. At any rate, the more privileged the position of the commercial class, the less it has evinced any inclination to develop an other-worldly religion.

The religion of the noble plutocratic class in the Phoenician trading cities was entirely this-worldly in orientation and, so far as is known, entirely non-prophetic. Yet the intensity of their religious mood and their fear of the gods, who were envisaged as possessing very somber traits, were very impressive. On the other hand, the warlike maritime nobility of ancient Greece, which was partly piratical and partly commercial, has left behind in the *Odyssey* a religious document congruent with its own interests, which betrays a striking lack of respect for the gods. The god of wealth in Chinese Taoism, who is universally respected by merchants, shows no ethical traits; he is of a purely magical character. So, too, the cult of the Greek god of wealth, Pluto, which has primarily an agrarian character, comprised a part of the Eleusinian mysteries which set up no ethical demands apart from ritual purity and freedom from blood guilt. Augustus, in a characteristic political maneuver, sought to turn the class of freedmen, with their strong capital resources, into special carriers of the cult of Caesar by creating the honorific Augustan status. But this class showed no distinctive religious tendencies otherwise.

In India, that section of the commercial class which followed the Hindu religion, particularly all the banking groups, which derived from the ancient classes of state capitalist financiers and large-scale traders, belonged for the most part to the sect of the *Vallabhacharis*. These were adherents of the Vishnu priesthood of Gokulastha Gosain, as reformed by Vallabha Svami. They followed a form of erotically tinged worship of Krishna and Radha in which the cultic meal in honor of their savior was transformed into a kind of elegant repast. In medieval Europe, the great business organizations of the Guelph cities, like the Arte de Calimala, were of course papist in their politics, but very often they virtually annulled the ecclesiastical prohibition against usury by fairly mechanical devices which not infrequently created an effect of mockery. In Protestant Holland, the great and distinguished lords of trade, being Arminians in religion, were characteristically oriented to *Realpolitik,* and became the chief foes of Calvinist ethical rigor. Everywhere, skepticism or indifference to religion are and have been the widely diffused attitudes of large-scale traders and financiers.

But as against these easily understandable phenomena, the acquisition of new capital or, more correctly, capital continuously and rationally employed in a productive enterprise for the acquisition of profit, especially in industry (which is the characteristically modern employment of capital) has in the past been combined frequently and in a striking manner with a rational, ethical congregational religion among the classes in question. In the business life of India there was even a (geographical) differentiation between the Parsees and the Jain sect. The former, adherents of the religion of Zoroaster, retained their ethical rigorism, particularly its unconditional injunction regarding truthfulness, even after modernization had caused a reinterpretation of the ritualistic commandments of purity as hygienic prescriptions. The economic morality of the Parsees originally recognized only agriculture as acceptable to God, and abominated all urban acquisitive pursuits. On the other hand, the sect of the Jains, the most ascetic of the religions of India, along with the aforementioned Vallabhacharis represented a salvation doctrine that was constituted as congregational religion, despite the anti-rational character of the cults. It is difficult to prove that the Islamic commercial religion of traders was particularly widespread among the dervishes, but it is not unlikely. As for Judaism, the ethical rational religion of the Jewish community was already in antiquity largely a religion of traders or financiers.

To a lesser but still notable degree, the religion of the medieval Christian community, particularly of the sectarian type or of the heretical circles was, if not a religion appropriate to traders, nonetheless a middle-class religion, and that in direct proportion to its ethical rationalism. The closest connection between ethical religion and rational economic development—particularly capitalism—was effected by all the forms of ascetic Protestantism and sectarianism in both Western and Eastern Europe, viz., Zwinglians, Calvinists, Reformed Baptists, Mennonites, Quakers, Methodists, and Pietists (both of the Reformed and, to a lesser degree, Lutheran varieties); as well as by Russian schismatic, heretical, and rational pietistic sects, especially the Stundists and Skoptzi, though in very different forms. Indeed, generally speaking, the inclination to join an ethical, rational, congregational religion becomes more strongly marked the farther away one gets from those social classes which have been the carriers of the type of capitalism which is primarily political in orientation. Since the time of Hammurabi this situation has existed wherever there has been tax farming, the profitable provision of the state's political needs, war, piracy, large-scale usury, and colonization. The tendency toward affiliation with an ethical, rational, congregational religion is more apt to be found the closer one gets to those classes which have been the carriers of modern rational productive economic activity, i.e., those classes with middle-class economic characteristics, in the sense to be expounded later.

Obviously, the mere existence of capitalism of some sort is not sufficient, by any means, to produce a uniform ethic, not to speak of an ethical congregational religion. Indeed, it does not automatically produce any uniform consequences. For the time being, no analysis will be made of the kind of causal relationship subsisting between a rational religious ethic and a particular type of commercial rationalism, where such a connection exists at all. At this point, we desire only to establish the existence of an affinity between economic rationalism and certain types of rigoristic ethical religion, to be discussed later. This affinity comes to light only occasionally outside the Occident, which is the distinctive seat of economic rationalism. In the West, this phenomenon is very clear and its manifestations are the more impressive as we approach the classical bearers of economic rationalism.

VII. Religion of Non-Privileged Classes

When we move away from the classes characterized by a high degree of social and economic privilege, we encounter an apparent increase in the diversity of religious attitudes.

Within the lower middle class, and particularly among the artisans, the greatest contrasts have existed side by side. These have included caste taboos and magical or mystagogic religions of both the sacramental and orgiastic types in India, animism in China, dervish religion in Islam, and the pneumatic-enthusiastic congregational religion of early Christianity, practiced particularly in the eastern half of the Roman Empire. Still other modes of religious expression among the lower middle class and artisan groups are the *deisidaemonie* and the orgiastic worship of Dionysos in ancient Greece, Pharisaic fidelity to the law in ancient urban Judaism, an essentially idolatrous Christianity, as well as all sorts of sectarian faiths in the Middle Ages, and various types of Protestantism in early modern times. These diverse phenomena obviously present the greatest possible contrasts to one another.

From the time of its inception, ancient Christianity was characteristically a religion of artisans. Its savior was a semi-rural artisan, and his missionaries were wandering apprentices, the greatest of them a wandering tent maker, so alien to the land that in his epistles he actually employs in a reverse sense a metaphor relating to the process of grafting. The earliest communities of original Christianity were, as we have already seen, strongly urban throughout ancient times, and their adherents were recruited primarily from artisans, both slave and free. Moreover, in the Middle Ages the lower middle class remained the most pious, if not always the most orthodox, stratum of society. But in Christianity as in other religions, widely different currents found a warm reception simultaneously within the lower middle class. Thus, there were the ancient pneumatic prophecies which cast out demons, the unconditionally orthodox (institutionally ecclesiastical) religiosity of the Middle Ages, and the monasticism of the mendicant type. In addition, there were certain types of medieval sectarian religiosity such as that of the *Humiliati,* who were long suspected of heterodoxy, there were Baptist movements of all kinds, and there was the piety of the various Reformed churches, including the Lutheran.

This is indeed a highly checkered diversification, which at least proves that a uniform determinism of religion by economic forces never existed among the artisan class. Yet there is apparent in these lower middle classes, in contrast to the peasantry, a definite tendency towards congregational religion, towards religion of salvation, and finally towards rational ethical religion. But this contrast between the middle class and the peasantry is far from implying any uniform determinism. The absence of uniform determinism appears very clearly in the fact that the rural flatlands of Friesland provided the first localities for the popular dissemination of the Baptist congregational religion in its fullest form, while it was the city of Münster which became a primary site for the expression of its social revolutionary form.

In the Occident particularly, the congregational type of religion has been intimately connected with the urban middle classes of both the upper and lower levels. This was a natural consequence of the relative recession in the importance of blood groupings, particularly of the clan, within the occidental city.* The urban dweller finds a substitute for blood groupings in both occupational organizations, which in the Occident as everywhere had a cultic significance, although no longer associated with taboos, and in freely created religious associations. But these religious relationships were not determined exclusively by the distinctive economic patterns of urban life. On the contrary, the causation might go the other way, as is readily apparent. Thus, in China the great importance of the ancestral cult and clan exogamy resulted in keeping the individual city dweller in a close relationship with

* [*Cf.* Max Weber, *Wirtschaft und Gesellschaft,* 4th ed., ch. IX, Section 8 on "Non-Legitimate Domination" (A Typology of Cities). German editor's note.]

his clan and native village. In India the religious caste taboo rendered difficult the rise, or limited the importance, of any soteriological congregational religion in quasi-urban settlements, as well as in the country. We have seen that in both India and China these factors hindered the city from developing in the direction of a community much more than they hindered the village.

Yet it is still true in theory that the middle class, by virtue of its distinctive pattern of economic life, inclines in the direction of a rational ethical religion, wherever conditions are present for the emergence of a rational ethical religion. When one compares the life of a lower-middle-class person, particularly the urban artisan or the small trader, with the life of the peasant, it is clear that middle-class life has far less connection with nature. Consequently, dependence on magic for influencing the irrational forces of nature cannot play the same role for the urban dweller as for the farmer. At the same time, it is clear that the economic foundation of the urban man's life has a far more rational essential character, viz., calculability and capacity for purposive manipulation. Furthermore, the artisan and in certain circumstances even the merchant lead economic existences which influence them to entertain the view that honesty is the best policy, that faithful work and the performance of obligations will find their reward and are "deserving" of their just compensation. For these reasons, small traders and artisans are disposed to accept a rational world view incorporating an ethic of compensation. We shall see presently that this is the normal trend of thinking among all non-privileged classes. The peasants, on the other hand, are much more remote from this notion of compensation and do not acquire it until the magic in which they are immersed has been eliminated by other forces. By contrast, the artisan is very frequently active in effecting the elimination of this very process of magic. It follows that the belief in ethical compensation is even more alien to warriors and to financial magnates who have economic interests in war and in the political manifestations of power. These groups are the least accessible to the ethical and rational elements in any religion.

The artisan is deeply immersed in magical encumbrances in the early stages of occupational differentiation. Every specialized art that is uncommon and not widely disseminated is regarded as a magical charisma, either personal or, more generally, hereditary, the acquisition and maintenance of which is guaranteed by magical means. Other elements of this early belief are that the bearers of this charisma are set off by taboos, occasionally of a totemic nature, from the community of ordinary people (peasants), and frequently that they are to be excluded from the ownership of land. One final element of this early belief in the magical charisma of every specialized art must be mentioned here. Wherever crafts had remained in the hands of ancient groups possessing raw materials, who had first offered their arts as intruders in the community and later offered their craftsmanship as individual strangers settled within the community, the belief in the magical nature of special arts condemned such groups to pariah status and stereotyped with magic their manipulations and their technology. But wherever this magical frame of reference has once been broken through (this happens most readily in newly settled cities), the effect of the transformation may be that the artisan will learn to think about his labor and the small trader will learn to think about his enterprise much more rationally than any peasant thinks. The craftsman in particular will have time and opportunity for reflection during his work, in many instances. Consequently, the workers in occupations which are primarily of the indoor variety, e.g., in textile mills in our climate, are strongly infused with sectarian or religious trends. This is true to some extent even for the workers in modern factories with mechanized weaving, but very much more true for the workers at the looms in the textile mills of the past.

Wherever the attachment to purely magical or ritualistic views has been broken by prophets or reformers, there has frequently been a tendency for artisans, craftsmen and middle-class people to incline toward a rather primitively rationalistic ethical and religious view of life. Furthermore, their very occupational specialization makes them the bearers of an integrated pattern of life of a distinctive kind. Yet there is certainly no uniform determination of religion by these general conditions in the life of artisans and middle-class groups. Thus the small business men of China, though thoroughly calculating, are not the carriers of a rational religion, nor, so far as we know, are the Chinese artisans. They follow the Buddhist doctrine of *karma,* as well as magical notions. What is primary in their case is the absence of an ethically rationalized religion, and indeed this appears to have influenced the limited rationalism of their technology. This strikes us again and again. The mere existence of artisans and middle-class people has never sufficed to generate an ethical religion, even of the most general type. We have seen an example of this in India, where the caste taboo and the belief in metempsychosis influenced and stereotyped the ethics of the artisan class. Only a congregational religion, especially one of the rational and ethical type, could conceivably win followers easily, particularly among the urban lower middle classes, and then, given certain circumstances, exert a lasting influence on the pattern of life of these classes. This is what actually happened.

Finally, the classes of the greatest economic disability, such as slaves and free day laborers, have hitherto never been the bearers of a distinctive type of religion. In the ancient Christian communities the slaves belonged to the lower middle classes in the cities. The Hellenistic slaves and the retinue of Narcissus mentioned in the Epistle to the Romans (presumably those freed by the famous imperial decree) were either relatively well-placed and independent domestic officials or service personnel belonging to very wealthy men. But in the majority of instances they were independent craftsmen who paid tribute to their master and hoped to save enough from their earnings to effect their liberation, which was the case throughout antiquity and in Russia in the nineteenth century. In other cases they were well-situated slaves of the state.

The religion of Mithra also included among its adherents numerous representatives of this group, according to the inscriptions. The Delphic Apollo (and presumably many another god) apparently functioned as a savings bank for slaves, that was desirable because of its sacred inviolability, so that the slaves might buy their freedom from their masters by the use of these savings. According to the promising hypothesis of Deissmann, this was the pattern in Paul's mind for the redemption of Christians through the blood of their savior, that they might be freed from slavery to sin and to the law. If this be true (and of course the Old Testament terms for redemption, *gaal* and *pada,* must also be regarded as a possible source of the Christian concepts), it shows how much the missionizing effort of earliest Christianity counted upon the aspiring unfree middle-class group which followed an economically rational pattern of life. On the other hand, the "talking inventory" of the ancient plantation, the lowest stratum of the slave class, was not the bearer of any congregational religion, or for that matter a fertile site for any sort of religious mission.

Handicraft apprentices have at all times tended to share the characteristic religion of the lower middle classes, since they are normally distinguished from the independent lower middle classes only by the factor of *Karenzzeit* (the time during which a person employed at some manufactory is pledged to refrain from entering any rival establishment in that locality). The apprentice group also tended to evince a conspicuous inclination toward various forms of unofficial religion of the sect type, which found particularly fertile soil among the lower occupational strata of the city, in view of their workaday struggles with everyday needs, the fluctuations in the price of their daily bread, their quest for jobs, and their dependence on fraternal assistance. Furthermore, the class of small artisans and craft apprentices was generally represented in the numerous secret or half-tolerated communities of "poor folk" that espoused congregational religions which were by turn revolutionary, pacifistic-communistic and ethical-rational, chiefly for the technical reason that wandering handicraft apprentices are the available missionaries of every mass congregational religion. This process is illustrated in the extraordinarily rapid expansion of Christianity across the tremendous area from the Orient to Rome in just a few decades.

Insofar as the modern proletariat has a distinctive religious position, it is characterized by indifference to or rejection of religions common to large groups of the modern bourgeoisie. For the modern proletariat, the sense of dependence on one's own achievements is supplanted by a consciousness of dependence on purely societal factors, economic conjunctures, and power relationships guaranteed by law. Any thought of dependence upon the course of natural or meteorological processes, or upon anything that might be regarded as subject to the influence of magic or providence, has been completely eliminated, as Sombart has already demonstrated in fine fashion. Therefore, the rationalism of the proletariat, like that of the bourgeoisie of developed capitalism when it has come into the full possession of economic power, of which indeed the proletariat's rationalism is a complementary phenomenon, cannot in the nature of the case easily possess a religious character and certainly cannot easily generate a religion. Hence, in the sphere of proletarian rationalism, religion is generally supplanted by other ideological surrogates.

The lowest and the most economically unstable strata of the proletariat, for whom rational conceptions are the least congenial, and also the proletaroid or permanently impoverished lower middle-class groups who are in constant danger of sinking into the proletarian class, are nevertheless readily susceptible to being influenced by religious missionary enterprise. But this religious propaganda has in such cases a distinctively magical form or, where real magic has been eliminated, it has certain characteristics which are substitutes for the magical-orgiastic supervention of grace. Examples of these are the soteriological orgies of the Methodist type, such as are engaged in by the Salvation Army. Undoubtedly, it is far easier for emotional rather than rational elements of a religious ethic to flourish in such circumstances. In any case, ethical religion scarcely ever arises primarily in this group.

Only in a limited sense is there a distinctive class religion of disprivileged social groups. Inasmuch as the *substantive* demands for social and political reform in any religion are based on god's will, we shall have to devote a brief discussion to this problem when we discuss ethics and natural law. But insofar as our concern is with the character of the religion as such, it is immediately evident that a need for salvation in the widest sense of the term has as one of its foci, but not the exclusive or primary one, as we shall see later, disprivileged classes. Turning to the "sated" and privileged strata, the need for salvation is remote and alien to warriors, bureaucrats, and the plutocracy.

A religion of salvation may very well have its origin within socially privileged groups. For the charisma of the prophet is not confined to membership in any particular class; and furthermore, it is normally associated with a certain minimum of intellectual cultivation. Proof for both of these assertions is readily available in the various characteristic prophecies of intellectuals. But as a rule, the aforementioned relationship between salvation religion and privileged classes changes its character as soon as the religion has reached lay groups who are not particularly or professionally concerned with the cultivation of intellectualism, and certainly changes its character after it has reached into the disprivileged social strata to whom intellectualism is both economically and socially inaccessible. One characteristic element of this transformation, a product of the inevitable accommodation to the needs of the masses, may be formulated generally as the emergence of a personal, divine or human-divine savior as the bearer of salvation, with the additional consequence that the religious relationship to this personage becomes the precondition of salvation.

We have already seen that one form of the adaptation of religion to the needs of the masses is the transformation of cultic religion into mere wizardry. A second typical form of adaptation is the shift into savior religion, which is naturally related to the aforementioned change into magic by the most numerous transitional stages. The lower the social class, the more radical are the forms assumed by the need for a savior, once this need has emerged. Hinduism provides an example of this in the *Kartabhajas,* a Vishnuite sect that, in common with many salvation sects, took most seriously the transcendence of the caste taboo. Members of this sect arranged for a limited commensality of their members on private as well as on cultic occasions. Essentially a sect of lower strata people, yet they earned the anthropolatric veneration of their hereditary *guru* to such a point that the cult became extremely exclusive. Similar phenomena can be found elsewhere among religions which recruited followers from the lower social classes or at least were influenced by them. The transfer of salvation doctrines to the masses practically always results in the emergence of a savior, or at least in an increase of emphasis upon the concept of a savior. One instance of this is the substitution for the Buddha ideal, viz., the ideal of exemplary intellectualist salvation into *Nirvana* by the ideal of a Bodhisattva, i.e., a savior who has descended upon earth and has foregone his own entrance into *Nirvana* for the sake of saving his fellow men. Another example is the rise in Hindu folk religion, particularly in Vishnuism, of salvation grace mediated by an incarnate god, and the victory of this soteriology and its magical sacramental grace over both the elite salvation of the Buddhists and the ritualism associated with Vedic education. There are other manifestations of this process, somewhat different in form, in various religions.

The religious need of the middle and lower bourgeoisie expresses itself less in the form of heroic myths than in rather more sentimental legend, which has a tendency toward inwardness and edification. This corresponds to the peaceableness and the greater emphasis upon domestic and family life of the middle classes, in contrast to the ruling strata. This middle-class transformation of religion in the direction of domesticity is illustrated by the emergence of the god-suffused *bhakti* piety in all Hindu cults, both in the creation of the Bodhisattva figure as well as in the cults of Krishna; and by the popularity of the edifying myths of the child Dionysos, Osiris, the Christ child, and their numerous parallels. The emergence of the middle class and the influence of mendicant monks who as a group exerted decisive power over the character of religion resulted in the supplanting of the aristocratic *theotokos* of Nicolo Pisano's imperialistic art by his son's genre depiction of the holy family, and in the parallel transformation of the Krishna child into the darling of popular art in India.

The soteriological myth with its god who has assumed human form or its savior who has been deified is, like magic, a characteristic concept of popular religion, and hence one that has arisen quite spontaneously in very different places. On the other hand, the notion of an impersonal and ethical cosmic order that transcends the deity and the ideal of an exemplary type of salvation are intellectualistic conceptions which are definitely alien to the masses and possible only for a laity that has been educated along rational and ethical lines. The same holds true for the development of a concept of an absolutely transcendent god. With the exception of Judaism and Protestantism, all religions and religious ethics have had to reintroduce cults of saints, heroes or functional gods in order to accommodate themselves to the needs of the masses. Thus, Confucianism permitted such cults, in the form of the Taoist pantheon, to continue their existence by its side. Similarly, as popularized Buddhism spread to many lands, it allowed the various gods of these lands to live on as recipients of the Buddhist cult, subordinated to the Buddha. Finally, Islam and Catholicism were compelled to accept local, functional, and occupational gods as saints, the veneration of which constituted the real religion of the masses in everyday life.

The religion of the disprivileged classes, in contrast to the aristocratic cults of the martial nobles, is characterized by a tendency to allot equality to women. There is a great diversity in the scope of the religious participation permitted to women, but the greater or lesser, active or passive participation (or exclusion) of women from the religious cults is everywhere a function of the degree of the group's relative pacification or militarization (present or past). But the presence of priestesses, the prestige of female soothsayers or witches, and the most extreme devotion to individual women, to whom supernatural powers and charisma may be attributed, does not by any means imply that women have equal privileges in the cult. Conversely, equalization of the sexes in principle, i.e., in relationship to god, as it is found in Christianity and Judaism and, less consistently, in Islam and official Buddhism, may coexist with the most complete monopolization by men of the priestly functions, of law, and of the right to active participation in community affairs; men only are admitted to special professional training or assumed to possess the necessary qualifications. This was the actual situation in the religions to which reference has just been made.

The great receptivity of women to all religious prophecy except that which is exclusively military or political in orientation comes to very clear expression in the completely unconstrained relationships with women maintained by practically all prophets, the Buddha as well as Christ and Pythagoras. But only in very rare cases does this practice continue beyond the first stage of a religious community's formation, when the pneumatic manifestations of charisma are valued as hallmarks of specifically religious exaltation. Thereafter, as routinization and regimentation of community relationships set in, a reaction takes place against pneumatic manifestations among women, which come to be regarded as dishonorable and morbid. In Christianity this appears already with Paul.

It is certainly true that every political and military type of prophecy is directed exclusively to men. Indeed, the cult of a warlike spirit is frequently put into the direct service of controlling and lawfully plundering the households of women by the male inhabitants of the warrior house, who are organized into a sort of club; this happens among the Duk-duk in the Indian archipelago and elsewhere in many similar periodic epiphanies of a heroic *numen*. Wherever an ascetic training of warriors involving the rebirth of the hero is or has been dominant, woman is regarded as lacking a higher heroic soul and is consequently assigned a secondary religious status. This obtains in most aristocratic or distinctively militaristic cultic communities.

Women are completely excluded from the official Chinese cults as well as from those of the Romans and Brahmins; nor is the religion of the Buddhist intellectuals feministic. Indeed, even Christian synods as late as the period of the Merovingians expressed doubts regarding the equality of the souls of women. On the other hand, in the Orient the characteristic cults of Hinduism and one segment of the Buddhist-Taoist sects in China, and in the Occident notably pristine Christianity but also later spiritualist and pacifist sects of Eastern and Western Europe, derived a great deal of their missionizing power from the circumstance that they attracted women and gave them equal status. In Greece, too, the cult of Dionysos at its first appearance gave to the women who participated in its orgies an unparalleled degree of emancipation from conventions. This freedom subsequently became more and more stylized and regulated, both artistically and ceremonially; its scope was thereby limited, particularly to the processions and other festive activities of the various cults. Ultimately, therefore, this freedom lost all practical importance.

What gave Christianity its extraordinary superiority, as it conducted its missionary enterprises among the lower middle classes, over its most important competitor, the religion of Mithra, was that this extremely masculine cult excluded women. The result during a period of universal peace was that the adherents of Mithra had to seek out for their women a substitute in other mysteries, e.g., those of Cybele. This had the effect of destroying, even within single families, the unity and universality of the Mithraic religious community, thereby providing a striking contrast to Christianity. A similar result was to be noted in all the genuinely intellectualist cults of the Gnostic, Manichean, and comparable types, though this need not necessarily have been the case in theory.

It is by no means true that all religions teaching brotherly love and love for one's enemy achieved power through the influence of women or through the feminist character of the religion; this has certainly not been true for the Indian religion of *ahimsa*. The influence of women only tended to intensify those aspects of the religion that were emotional or hysterical. Such was the case in India. But it is certainly not a matter of indifference that salvation religions tended to glorify the non-military and even anti-military virtues, which must have been quite close to the interests of disprivileged classes and of women.

The specific importance of salvation religion for politically and economically disprivileged social groups, in contrast to privileged groups, may be viewed from an even more comprehensive perspective. In our subsequent discussion of castes and classes we shall have a good deal to say about the sense of honor or superiority characteristic of the non-priestly classes that claimed the highest social privileges, particularly the nobility. Their sense of self-esteem rests on their awareness that the perfection of their life pattern is an expression of their underived, ultimate, and qualitatively distinctive *being;* indeed, it is in the very nature of the case that this should be the basis of the elite's feeling of worth. On the other hand, the sense of honor of disprivileged classes rests on some concealed promise for the future which implies the assignment of some function, mission, or vocation to them. What they cannot claim to *be,* they replace by the worth of that which they will one day *become,* to which they will be called in some future life here or hereafter; or replace, very often concomitantly with the motivation just discussed, by their sense of what they signify and achieve in the world as seen from the point of view of providence. Their hunger for a worthiness that has not fallen to their lot, they and the world being what it is, produces this conception from which is derived the rationalistic idea of a providence, a significance in the eyes of some divine authority possessing a scale of values different from the one operating in the world of man.

This psychological condition, when turned outward toward the other social classes, produces certain characteristic contrasts in what religion must provide for the various social strata. Since every need for salvation is an expression of some distress, social or economic oppression is an effective source of salvation beliefs, though by no means the exclusive source. Other things being equal, classes with high social and economic privilege will scarcely be prone to evolve the idea of salvation. Rather, they assign to religion the primary function of legitimizing their own life pattern and situation in the world. This universal phenomenon is rooted in certain basic psychological patterns. When a man who is happy compares his position with that of one who is unhappy, he is not content with the fact of his happiness, but desires something more, namely the right to this happiness, the consciousness that he has earned his good fortune, in contrast to the unfortunate one who must equally have earned his misfortune. Our everyday experience proves that there exists just such a psychological need for reassurance as to the legitimacy or deservedness of one's happiness, whether this involves political success, superior economic status, bodily health, success in the game of love, or anything else. What the privileged classes require of religion, if anything at all, is this psychological reassurance of legitimacy.

To be sure, not every class with high privilege feels this need in the same degree. It is noteworthy that martial heroes in particular tend to regard the gods as beings to whom envy is not unknown. Solon shared with ancient Jewish wisdom the same belief in the danger of high position. The hero maintains his superior position in spite of the gods and not because of them, and indeed he often does this against their wishes. Such an attitude is evinced in the Homeric and some of the Hindu epics, in contrast to the bureaucratic chronicles of China and the priestly chronicles of Israel, which express a far stronger concern for the legitimacy of happiness as the deity's reward for some virtuous human action pleasing to him.

On the other hand, one finds almost universally that unhappiness is brought into relation with the wrath or envy of either demons or gods. Practically every popular religion, including the ancient Hebrew, and particularly the modern Chinese, regards physical infirmity as a sign of magico-ritual or ethical sinfulness on the part of the unfortunate one, or (as in Judaism) of his ancestors. Accordingly, in these traditions a person visited by adversity is prohibited from appearing at the communal sacrifices of the political association because he is freighted with the wrath of the deity and must not enter in the circle of fortunate ones who are pleasing to him. In practically every ethical religion found among privileged classes and the priests who serve them, the privileged or disprivileged social position of the individual is regarded as somehow merited from the religious point of view. What varies is only the form by which good fortune is legitimized.

Correspondingly different is the situation of the disprivileged. Their particular need is for release from suffering. They do not always experience this need for salvation in a religious form, as shown by the example of the modern proletariat. Furthermore, their need for religious salvation, where it exists, may assume diverse forms. Most important, it may be conjoined with a need for just compensation, envisaged in various ways but always involving reward for one's own good deeds and punishment for the unrighteousness of others. This hope for and expectation of just compensation, a fairly calculating attitude, is, next to magic (indeed, not unconnected with it), the most widely diffused form of mass religion all over the world. Even religious prophecies, which rejected the more mechanical forms of this belief, tended as they underwent popularization and routinization to slip back into these expectations of compensation. The type and scope of these hopes for compensation and salvation varied greatly depending on the expectations aroused by the religious promises, especially when these hopes were projected from the earthly existence of the individual into a future life.

Judaism, in both its exilic and post-exilic forms, provides a particularly important illustration of the significance of the content of religious promises. Since the Exile, as a matter of actual fact, and formally since the destruction of the Temple, the Jews became a pariah people in the particular sense presently to be defined. (The sense in which the Jews are a "pariah" people has as little to do with the particular situation of the pariah caste in India as, for example, the concept of *"qadi* justice" (*Kadi-Justiz,* patriarchal justice) has to do with the actual legal principles whereby the *qadi* renders legal decisions.) In our usage, "pariah people" denotes a distinctive hereditary social group lacking autonomous political organization and characterized by prohibitions against commensality and intermarriage originally founded upon magical, tabooistic, and ritual injunctions. Two additional traits of a pariah people are political and social disprivilege and a far-reaching distinctiveness in economic functioning. To be sure, the pariah people of India, the disprivileged and occupationally specialized Hindu castes, resemble the Jews in these respects, since their pariah status also involves segregation from the outer world as a result of taboos, hereditary religious obligations in the conduct of life, and the association of salvation hopes with their pariah status. These Hindu castes and Judaism show the same characteristic effects of a pariah religion: the more depressed the position in which the members of the pariah people found themselves, the more closely did the religion cause them to cling to one another and to their pariah position and the more powerful became the salvation hopes which were connected with the divinely ordained fulfillment of their religious obligations. As we have already mentioned, the lowest Hindu classes in particular clung to their caste duties with the greatest tenacity as a prerequisite for their rebirth into a better position.

The tie between Yahweh and his people became the more indissoluble as murderous humiliation and persecution pressed down upon the Jews. In obvious contrast to the oriental Christians, who under the Umayyads streamed into the privileged religion of Islam in such numbers that the political authorities had to make conversion difficult for them in the interests of the privileged classes, all the frequent mass conversions of the Jews by force, which might have obtained for them the privileges of the ruling classes, remained ineffectual. For both the Jews and the Hindu castes, the only means for the attainment of salvation was to fulfill the special religious commandments enjoined upon the pariah people, from which none might withdraw himself without incurring the fear of evil magic or endangering the chances of rebirth for himself or his descendants. The difference between Judaism and Hindu caste religion is based on the type of salvation hopes entertained. From the fulfillment of the religious obligations incumbent upon him the Hindu expected an improvement in his personal chances of rebirth, i.e., the ascent or reincarnation of his soul into a higher caste. On the other hand, the Jew expected the participation of his descendants in a messianic kingdom which would redeem the entire pariah community from its inferior position and in fact raise it to a position of mastery in the world. For surely Yahweh, by his promise that all the nations of the world would borrow from the Jews but that they would borrow from none, had meant more than that the Jews would become moneylenders in the ghetto. The Jews believed that Yahweh instead intended to place them in the typical situation of citizens of a powerful city-state in antiquity, who held as debtors and debt-slaves the inhabitants of nearby subject villages and towns. The Jews wrought on behalf of his actual descendants, who, on the animistic interpretation, would constitute his earthly immortality. The Hindu also worked for a human being of the future, to whom he was bound by a relationship only if the assumptions of the animistic doctrine of transmigration were accepted, i.e., his future incarnation. The Hindu's conception left unchanged for all time the caste stratification obtaining in this world and the position of his own caste within it; indeed, he sought to fit the future state of his own individual soul into this very gradation of ranks. In striking contrast, the Jew anticipated his own personal salvation through a revolution of the existing social stratification to the advantage of his pariah people; his people had been chosen and called by God, not to a pariah position but to one of prestige.

The factor of resentment (*ressentiment*) thus achieved importance in the Jewish ethical salvation religion, although it had been completely lacking in all magical and caste religions. Resentment is a concomitant of that particular religious ethic of the disprivileged which, in the sense expounded by Nietzsche and in direct inversion of the ancient belief, teaches that the unequal distribution of mundane goods is caused by the sinfulness and the illegality of the privileged, and that sooner or later God's wrath will overtake them. In this theodicy of the disprivileged, the moralistic quest serves as a device for compensating a conscious or unconscious desire for vengeance. This is connected in its origin with the faith in compensation, since once a religious conception of compensation has arisen, suffering may take on the quality of the religiously meritorious, in view of the belief that it brings in its wake great hopes of future compensation.

The development of a religious conception of resentment may be supported by ascetic doctrines on the one hand, or by characteristic neurotic predispositions on the other. However, the religion of suffering acquires the specific character of *ressentiment* only under special circumstances. *Ressentiment* is not found among the Hindus and Buddhists, for whom personal suffering is individually merited. But the situation is quite different among the Jews.

The religion of the Psalms is full of the need for vengeance, and the same motif occurs in the priestly reworkings of ancient Israelite traditions. The majority of the Psalms are quite obviously replete with the moralistic legitimation and satisfaction of an open and hardly concealed need for vengeance on the part of a pariah people. (Some of these passages are admittedly later interpolations into earlier compositions, in which this sentiment was not originally present.) In the Psalms the quest for vengeance may take the form of remonstrating with God because misfortune has overtaken the righteous individual, notwithstanding his obedience to God's commandments, whereas the godless conduct of the heathen, despite their mockery of God's predictions, commandments and authority, has brought them happiness and left them proud. The same quest for vengeance may express itself as a humble confession of one's own sinfulness, accompanied by a prayer to God to desist from his anger at long last and to turn his grace once again toward the people who ultimately are uniquely his own. In both modes of expression, the hope is entertained that ultimately the wrath of God will finally have been appeased and will turn itself to punishing the godless foes in double measure, making of them at some future day the footstool of Israel, just as the priestly historiography had assigned the Canaanite enemies to a similar fate. It was also hoped that this exalted condition would endure so long as Israel did not arouse God's anger by disobedience, thereby meriting subjugation at the hands of the heathen. It may be true, as modern commentators would have it, that some of these Psalms express the personal indignation of pious Pharisees over their persecution at the hands of Alexander Janneus. Nevertheless, a distinctive selection and preservation is evident; and in any case, other Psalms are quite obviously reactions to the distinctive pariah status of the Jews as a people.

In no other religion in the world do we find a universal deity possessing the unparalleled desire for vengeance manifested by Yahweh. Indeed, an almost unfailing index of the historical value of the data provided by the priestly reworking of history is that the event in question, as for example the battle of Megiddo, does not fit into this theodicy of compensation and vengeance. Thus, the Jewish religion became notably a religion of retribution. The virtues enjoined by God are practiced for the sake of the hoped for compensation. Moreover, this was originally a collective hope that the people as a whole would live to see the day of restoration, and that only in this way would the individual be able to regain his own worth. There developed concomitantly, intermingled with the aforementioned collective theodicy, an individual theodicy of personal destiny which had previously been taken for granted. The problems of individual destiny are explored in the Book of Job, which was produced by quite different circles, i.e., the upper classes, and which culminates in a renunciation of any solution of the problem and a submission to the absolute sovereignty of God over his creatures. This submission was the precursor of the doctrine of predestination in Puritanism. The notion of predestination was bound to arise when the emotional dynamics of divinely ordained eternal punishment in hell was added to the complex of ideas just discussed, involving compensation and the absolute sovereignty of God. But the belief in predestination did not arise among the Hebrews of that time. Among them, the conclusion of the Book of Job remained almost completely misunderstood in the sense intended by its author, mainly, as is well known, because of the unshakeable strength of the doctrine of collective compensation in the Jewish religion.

In the mind of the pious Jew the moralism of the law was inevitably combined with the aforementioned hope for revenge, which suffused practically all the exilic and postexilic sacred scriptures. Moreover, through two and a half millenniums this hope appeared in virtually every divine service of the Jewish people, characterized by a firm grip upon two indestructible claims— religiously sanctified segregation from the other peoples of the world, and divine promises relating to this world. From such a compensatory hope the Jews were bound to derive new strength, consciously or unconsciously. Yet as the Messiah delayed his arrival, this hope receded in the religious thinking of the intellectual class, in favor of the value of an inner awareness of God or a mildly emotional trust in God's goodness as such, combined with a readiness for peace with all the world. This happened especially in periods during which the social condition of a community condemned to complete political isolation was tolerable. On the other hand, in epochs characterized by persecutions like the period of the Crusades, the hope for retribution flamed up anew, either with a penetrating but vain cry to God for revenge, or with a prayer that the soul of the Jew might become as dust before the enemy who had cursed him. In the latter case there was no recourse to evil words or deeds, but only a silent waiting for the fulfillment of God's commandments and the cultivation of the heart so that it would remain open to God. To interpret *ressentiment* as the decisive element in Judaism would be an incredible aberration, in view of the many significant historical changes which Judaism has undergone. Nevertheless, we must not underestimate the influence of *ressentiment* upon even the basic characteristics of the Jewish religion. When one compares Judaism with other salvation religions, one finds that in Judaism the doctrine of religious resentment has an idiosyncratic quality and plays a unique role not found among the disprivileged classes of any other religion.

A theodicy of disprivilege, in some form, is a component of every salvation religion which draws its adherents primarily from the disprivileged classes. Wherever a developing priestly ethic met a theodicy of disprivilege halfway, the theodicy became a component of congregational religion, as happened with the pious Hindu and with the Asiatic Buddhist. That these religions lack virtually any kind of social-revolutionary ethics can be explained by reference to their theodicy of rebirth, according to which the caste system itself is eternal and absolutely just. The virtues or sins of a former life determine birth into a particular caste, and one's behavior in the present life determines one's chances of improvement in the next rebirth. Those living under this theodicy experienced no trace of the conflict experienced by the Jews between the social claims based on God's promises and the actual conditions of dishonor under which they lived. This conflict precluded any possibility of finding ease in this life for the Jews, who lived in continuous tension with their actual social position and in perpetually fruitless expectation and hope. The Jews' theodicy of disprivilege was greeted by the pitiless mockery of the godless heathen, but for the Jews the theodicy had the consequence of transforming religious criticism of the godless heathen into ever-watchful concern over their own fidelity to the law. This preoccupation was frequently tinged with bitterness and threatened by secret self-criticism.

The Jew was naturally prone, as a result of his lifelong schooling, to casuistical meditation upon the religious obligations of his fellow Jews, on whose punctilious observance of religious law the whole people ultimately depended for Yahweh's favor. There appeared that peculiar mixture of elements characteristic of post-exilic times which expressed despair at finding any meaning in this world of vanity, submission to the chastisement of God, anxiety lest one sin against God through pride, and finally a fear-ridden punctiliousness in ritual and morals. All these conflicts forced upon the Jew a desperate struggle, no longer for the respect of others, but for self-respect and a sense of personal worth. The struggle for a sense of personal worth must have become precarious again and again, threatening to wreck the whole meaning of the individual's pattern of life, though ultimately the fulfillment of God's promise was the only criterion of one's value before God at any given time.

Success in his occupation actually became the tangible proof of God's personal favor, for the Jew living in the ghetto. But the conception of self-fulfillment (*Bewaehrung*) in a calling (*Beruf*) pleasing to god, in the sense of inner-worldly asceticism (*inner-weltliche Askese*), is not applicable to the Jew. God's blessing was far less strongly anchored in a systematic, rational, methodical pattern of life (the only possible source of the *certitudo salutis*) for the Jew than for the Puritan. Just as the Jewish sexual ethic remained naturalistic and anti-ascetic, so also did the economic ethic of ancient Judaism remain strongly traditionalistic in its basic tenets. It was characterized by a frank respect for wealth, which is of course missing in any system of asceticism. In addition, the entire system of outward piety had a ritualistic foundation among the Jews, and what is more, it was considerably interfused with the distinctive emotional mood of a religion of belief. We must note that the traditionalistic precepts of the Jewish economic ethics naturally applied in their full scope only to one's fellow religionists, not to outsiders, which was the case in every ancient ethical system. All in all, then, the belief in Yahweh's promises actually produced within the realm of Judaism itself a strong component of the morality of *ressentiment*.

It would be erroneous to portray the need for salvation, theodicy, or congregational religion as something that developed only among disprivileged social classes or as a product of resentment, and hence merely as the outcome of a "slave revolt in morality." This would not even be true of ancient Christianity, although it directed its promises most emphatically to the poor in spirit and in worldly goods. What results must follow from the devaluation and transcendence of the ritual laws (which had been purposefully directed to segregating the Jews from the outer world) and from the consequent dissolution of the connection between religion and the castelike position of the faithful as a pariah people, can be readily observed in the immediate consequences of Jesus' prophecy. To be sure, this is not to forget that the Christian message contained very definite elements of a compensatory doctrine, in the sense of the future equalization of human fates (most clearly expressed in the legend of Lazarus), and of God's responsibility for vengeance. Moreover, the Christian preaching also interpreted the Kingdom of God as an earthly kingdom, a realm set apart originally or particularly for Jews who had believed in the true God from ancient times. Yet the new religious proclamations of early Christianity eliminated precisely the characteristic and penetrating feeling of resentment of a pariah people.

Not even Jesus' own warnings, according to the tradition, of the dangers presented by wealth to the attainment of salvation were motivated by asceticism. Certainly the motivation of his preaching against wealth was not resentment, for the tradition has preserved many evidences of Jesus' intercourse, not only with publicans (who in the Palestine of that period were mostly small moneylenders), but also with many wealthy people of the upper class. Furthermore, resentment cannot be regarded as the primary motivation of Jesus' doctrines regarding wealth, in view of the Gospels' impressive indifference to mundane affairs, an indifference based upon the importance attributed to eschatological expectations. To be sure, the rich young man was bidden to unconditionally take his leave of the world if he desired to be a perfect disciple. But it is stated that for God all things are possible, even the salvation of the wealthy. The rich man who is unable to decide to part with his wealth may nonetheless achieve salvation, despite the difficulties in the way. There were no "proletarian instincts" in the doctrine and teaching of Jesus, the prophet of acosmistic love. He brought to the poor in spirit and to the good people of this world the happy tidings of the immediate coming of the Kingdom of God and of freedom from the domination of evil spirits. Similarly, any proletarian denunciation of wealth would have been equally alien to the Buddha, for whom the absolute precondition of salvation was unconditional withdrawal from the world.

The limited occurrence of the factor of *ressentiment* and the dubiousness of applying the conceptual schema of "repression" almost universally appear most clearly when the Nietzschean schema is applied erroneously to the altogether inappropriate example of Buddhism. Buddhism constitutes the most radical antithesis to every type of *ressentiment* morality. Buddhism clearly arose as the salvation doctrine of an intellectual class, originally recruited almost entirely from the privileged castes, especially the warrior caste, which proudly and aristocratically rejected the illusions of life, both here and hereafter. Buddhism may be compared in social provenience to the salvation doctrines of the Greeks, particularly the Neo-Platonic, Manichean, and Gnostic manifestations, even though they are radically different in content. The Buddhist *bhikshu* does not begrudge the entire world, even a rebirth into paradise, to the person who does not desire *Nirvana*.

Precisely this example of Buddhism demonstrates that the need for salvation and ethical religion has yet another source besides the social condition of the disprivileged and the rationalism of the middle classes, which are products of their practical way of life. This additional factor is intellectualism as such, more particularly the metaphysical needs of the human mind as it is driven to reflect on ethical and religious questions, driven not by material need but by an inner compulsion to understand the world as a meaningful cosmos and to take up a position toward it.

VIII. Intellectualism, Intellectuals, and the History of Religion

The destiny of religions has been influenced in a most comprehensive way by intellectualism and its various relationships to the priesthood and political authorities. These relationships were in turn influenced by the provenience of the class which happened to be the most important carrier of the particular intellectualism. At first the priesthood itself was the most important carrier of intellectualism, particularly wherever sacred scriptures existed, which would make it necessary for the priesthood to become a literary guild engaged in interpreting the scriptures and teaching their content, meaning, and proper application. But no such development took place in the religions of the ancient city-states, and notably not among the Phoenicians, Greeks, or Romans; nor was this phenomenon present in the ethics of China. In these instances the development of all metaphysical and ethical thought fell into the hands of non-priests, as did the development of theology, which developed to only a very limited extent, e.g., in Hesiod.

By contrast, the development of intellectualism by the priesthood, was true to the highest degree in India, in Egypt, in Babylonia, in Zoroastrianism, in Islam, and in ancient and medieval Christianity. So far as theology is concerned, the development of intellectualism by the priesthood has also taken place in modern Christianity. In the religions of Egypt, in Zoroastrianism, in some phases of ancient Christianity, and in Brahmanism during the age of the Vedas (i.e., before the rise of lay asceticism and the philosophy of the Upanishads) the priesthood succeeded in largely monopolizing the development of religious metaphysics and ethics. Such a priestly monopoly was also present in Judaism and Islam. But in Judaism it was strongly reduced by the strong impact of lay prophecy, and in Islam the very impressive power of the priesthood was limited by the challenge of Sufi speculation. In all the branches of Buddhism and Islam, as well as in ancient and medieval Christianity, it was the monks or groups oriented to monasticism who, besides the priests or in their stead, concerned themselves with and wrote in all the areas of theological and ethical thought, as well as in metaphysics and considerable segments of science. In addition, they also occupied themselves with the production of artistic literature. In India the inclusion of epic, lyrical and satirical poetry in the Vedas, and in Israel the introduction of erotic poetry into the Bible, was due to the fact that poets belonged to groups important to the religious cult. This circumstance also accounts for the psychological proximity of mystical and spiritual emotion to poetic afflatus, and for the role of the mystic in the poetry of both the Orient and the Occident.

But here we are concerned, not with literary production, but rather the determination of the religion itself by the particular character of the intellectual classes who exerted a decisive influence upon it. The intellectual influence upon religion of the priesthood, even where it was the chief carrier of literature, was of quite varied scope, depending on which non-priestly classes opposed the priesthood and on the power position of the priesthood itself. The specifically ecclesiastical influence reached its strongest expression in late Zoroastrianism and in the religions of Egypt and Babylonia. Although Judaism of the Deuteronomic and exilic periods was prophetic in essence, the priesthood exerted a marked formative influence upon the developing religion. In later Judaism, however, it was not the priest but the rabbi who exercised the decisive influence. Christianity was decisively influenced by the priesthood and by monasticism in its first period and in the late Middle Ages, and then again in the period of the Counter Reformation. On the other hand, pastoral influences were dominant in Lutheranism and early Calvinism. Hinduism was formed and influenced to an extraordinary degree by the Brahmins, at least in its institutional and social components. This applies particularly to the caste system that arose wherever the Brahmins arrived, the social hierarchy of which was ultimately determined by the rank the Brahmins assigned to each particular caste. Buddhism in all its varieties, but particularly Lamaism, has been thoroughly influenced by monasticism, which has to a lesser degree influenced large groups in oriental Christianity.

Here we are particularly concerned with the relationship to the priesthood of the non-ecclesiastical lay intelligentsia other than the monks, and in addition, with the relation of the intellectual classes to the religious enterprise and their position within the religious community. We must at this point establish as a fact of fundamental importance that all the great religious doctrines of Asia are creations of intellectuals. The salvation doctrines of Buddhism and Jainism, as well as all related doctrines, were carried by an intellectual elite that had undergone training in the Vedas. This training, though not always of a strictly academic nature, was appropriate to the education of Hindu aristocrats, particularly members of the Kshatriya class of noble warriors, who stood in opposition to the Brahmins. In China the carriers of Confucianism, beginning with the founder himself and including Lao Tzu, who is officially regarded as the initiator of Taoism, were either officials who had received a classical literary education or philosophers with corresponding training.

The religions of China and India display counterparts of practically all the theoretical variants of Greek philosophy, though frequently in modified form. Confucianism, as the official ethic of China, was entirely borne by a group of aspirants to official positions who had received a classical literary education, whereas Taoism became a popular enterprise of practical magic. The great reforms of Hinduism were accomplished by aristocratic intellectuals who had received a Brahminic education, although subsequently the organization of communities frequently fell into the hands of members of lower castes. This process of reform in India took another direction from that of the Reformation in Northern Europe, although the Reformation was also led by educated men who had received professional clerical training, as well as from that of the Catholic Counter Reformation, which at first found its chief support from Jesuits trained in dialectic, like Salmeron and Laynez. The course of the reform movement in India differed also from the reconstruction of Islamic doctrine by al-Ghazzali, which combined mysticism and orthodoxy, with leadership remaining partly in the hands of the official hierarchy and partly in the hands of a newly developed official aristocracy of men with theological training. So too, Manicheanism and Gnosticism, the salvation religions of the Near East, are both specifically religions of intellectuals. This is true of their founders, their chief carriers, and the character of their salvation doctrines as well.

In all these cases, in spite of various differences among the religions in question, the intellectual classes were relatively high in the social scale and possessed philosophical training that corresponded to that of the Greek schools of philosophy or to the most learned types of monastic or secular humanistic training of the late medieval period. These groups were the bearers of the ethic or the salvation doctrine in each of these cases. Thus intellectual classes might, within a given religious situation, constitute an academic enterprise comparable to that of the Platonic academy and the related schools of philosophy in Greece. In that case the intellectual classes, like those in Greece, would take no official position regarding existing religious practice. They often ignored or philosophically reinterpreted the existing religious practice rather than directly withdrawing themselves from it. On their part, the official representatives of the cult, like the state officials charged with responsibility for a cult in China or the Brahmins in India, tended to treat the doctrine of the intellectuals as either orthodox or heterodox, the latter in the cases of the materialist doctrines of China and the dualist Sankhya philosophy of India. We cannot enter into any additional details here regarding these movements, which have a primarily academic orientation and are only indirectly related to practical religion. Our chief interest is rather in those other movements, previously mentioned, which are particularly concerned with the creation of a religious ethic. Our best examples in classical antiquity are the Pythagoreans and Neo-Platonists. These movements of intellectuals have uniformly arisen among socially privileged classes or been led or decisively influenced by men from the elite group.

A salvation religion developed by socially privileged groups within a nation normally has the best chance of becoming permanent when demilitarization has set in and when the nation has lost either the possibility of political activity or the interest in it. Consequently, salvation religions usually emerge when the ruling classes, noble or middle class, have lost their political power to a bureaucratic, militaristic imperial state. The withdrawal of the ruling classes from politics, for whatever reason, also favors the development of a salvation religion. In such a case, the ruling classes come to consider their intellectual training in its ultimate intellectual and psychological consequences far more important for them than their practical participation in the external affairs of the mundane world. This does not mean that the salvation religions arise only at such times. On the contrary, the intellectual conceptions in question may sometimes arise without the stimulus of such anterior conditions, as a result of unprejudiced reflection in periods of dynamic political or social change. But in that case such modes of thought tend to lead a kind of underground existence, normally becoming dominant only when the intellectual class has undergone a process of depoliticization.

Confucianism, the ethic of a powerful officialdom, rejected all doctrines of salvation. On the other hand, Jainism and Buddhism, which provide radical antitheses to Confucianist accommodation to the world, were tangible expressions of an intellectualist attitude that was utterly anti-political, pacifistic, and world-rejecting. We do not know, however, whether the sometimes considerable following of these two religions in India was increased by the events of the times, which tended to reduce the preoccupation of these people with political matters. The pluralism of tiny states headed by minor Hindu princes at the time of Alexander, states lacking any sort of political dynamic which nevertheless combated the impressive unity of Brahmanism (which was gradually forging to the front everywhere in India), was in itself enough to induce those groups of the nobility who had undergone intellectual training to seek fulfillment of their interests outside of politics. Therefore the scripturally enjoined world-renunciation of the Brahmin (as a *vanaprastha*—forest dweller— who forgoes his portion in old age) and the popular veneration accorded to him resulted in the evolution of non-Brahminic ascetics (*shramanas*). It is possible of course that the actual development went in the other direction, so that the recommendation of world-renunciation to the Brahmin who "has seen the son of his son" is the earlier of the two phenomena, and a borrowing. In any case, the *shramanas*, as the possessors of ascetic charisma, soon outsripped the official priesthood in popular esteem. This form of monastic apoliticism had been endemic among the elite of India since very early times, i.e., long before apolitical philosophical salvation doctrines arose.

The Near Eastern salvation religions, whether of a mystagogic or prophetic type, as well as the oriental and Hellenistic salvation doctrines, whether of a more religious type or a more philosophical type of which lay intellectuals were the protagonists, were, insofar as they included the socially privileged classes at all, virtually without exception the consequence of the educated classes' enforced or voluntary loss of political influence and participation. In Babylonia the turn to salvation religion, intersected by components whose provenience was outside Babylonia, appeared first in Mandaeism, the religion of intellectuals in the Near East. This took place first through participation in the cult of Mithra and the cults of other saviors, and then through participation in the cults of Gnosticism and Manicheism, after all political interest had died off in the educated class. In Greece there had always been salvation religion among the intellectual classes, even before the Pythagorean sect arose, but it did not dominate groups with decisive political power. The success of philosophical salvation doctrines and the propaganda of salvation cults among the lay elite during late Hellenic and Roman times parallels these groups' final turning aside from political participation. Indeed, the somewhat verbose "religious" interests of our German intellectuals of the present time are intimately connected with political frustrations that are responsible for their political indifference.

Quests for salvation which arise among classes of high social privilege are generally characterized by a disposition toward an "illumination" mysticism, presently to be analyzed, which is associated with a distinctively intellectual qualification for salvation. This brings about a strong devaluation of the natural, sensual, and physical, as constituting, according to their psychological experience, a temptation to deviate from their distinctive way of salvation. The exaggeration and impressive refinement of sexuality, along with the simultaneous suppression of normal sexuality in favor of substitute abreactions, were determined by the life patterns of those who might be termed nothing if not intellectuals; and these exaggerations and suppressions of sexuality occasionally played a role for which modern psychopathology has not yet formulated uniformly applicable rules. These phenomena are strongly reminiscent of certain phenomena, especially in the Gnostic mysteries, which clearly appear to have been sublimated masturbatory surrogates for the orgies of the peasantry. These purely psychological preconditions of the process whereby religion is irrationalized are intersected by the natural rationalistic need to conceive the world as a meaningful cosmos. Some typical outcomes are the Hindu doctrine of *karma* (of which more will be said presently) and its Buddhistic variant; the Book of Job among the Hebrews, which presumably derived from aristocratic intellectual groups; and the comparable elements in Egyptian literature, in Gnostic speculation, and in Manichean dualism.

Once a religion has become a mass religion, the development of a salvation doctrine and its ethic by intellectual circles usually results in either esotericism or a kind of aristocratic class ethic adjusted to the needs of the intellectually trained groups within the popularized official religion. Meanwhile, the religion has become transformed into a doctrine of a popular magical savior, thereby meeting the needs of the non-intellectual masses. Thus in China, alongside the Confucianist class ethic of the bureaucracy, who were completely uninterested in salvation, Taoist magic and Buddhist sacramental and ritual grace survived in a petrified form as the faith of the folk, though such beliefs were despised by those who had received a classical education. Similarly, the Buddhist salvation ethic of the monastic groups lived on alongside the magic and idolatry of the laity, the continued existence of tabooistic magic, and the new development of a savior religion within Hinduism. In Gnosticism and its related cults the intellectualist religion took the form of mystagogy, with a hierarchy of sanctifications which the unilluminated were excluded from attaining.

The salvation sought by the intellectual is always based on inner need, and hence it is at once more remote from life, more theoretical and more systematic than salvation from external distress, the quest for which is characteristic of nonprivileged classes. The intellectual seeks in various ways, the casuistry of which extends into infinity, to endow his life with a pervasive meaning, and thus to find unity with himself, with his fellow men, and with the cosmos. It is the intellectual who transforms the concept of the world into the problem of meaning. As intellectualism suppresses belief in magic, the world's processes become disenchanted, lose their magical significance, and henceforth simply "are" and "happen" but no longer signify anything. As a consequence, there is a growing demand that the world and the total pattern of life be subject to an order that is significant and meaningful.

The conflict of this requirement of meaningfulness with the empirical realities of the world and its institutions, and with the possibilities of conducting one's life in the empirical world, are responsible for the intellectual's characteristic flights from the world. This may be an escape into absolute loneliness, or in its more modern form, e.g., in the case of Rousseau, to a nature unspoiled by human institutions. Again, it may be a world-fleeing romanticism like the flight to the people, untouched by social conventions, characteristic of the Russian *Narodnitschestvo*. It may be more contemplative, or more actively ascetic; it may primarily seek individual salvation or collective revolutionary transformation of the world in the direction of a more ethical status. All these doctrines are equally appropriate to apolitical intellectualism and may appear as religious doctrines of salvation, as on occasion they have actually appeared. The distinctive world-fleeing character of intellectualist religion also has one of its roots here.

Yet the philosophical intellectualism of those classes that are usually well provided for socially and economically (particularly apolitical nobles or coupon-clippers, officials, and incumbents of benefices whether of churches, monastic establishments, institutions of higher learning, or the like) is by no means the only kind of intellectualism, and frequently it is not the most important kind of intellectualism for the development of religion. For there is also a proletarian intellectualism that is everywhere connected with aristocratic intellectualism by gradual transitional forms and differs from it only in the character of its distinctive attitude. Members of this class include people at the edge of the minimum standard of living; small officials and incumbents of prebends, who generally are equipped with what is regarded as an inferior education; scribes, who were not members of privileged classes in periods when writing was a special vocation; elementary school teachers of all sorts; wandering poets; narrators; reciters; and practitioners of similar free proletarian callings. Above all, we must include in this category the self-taught intelligentsia of the disprivileged classes, of whom the classic examples are the Russian proletarian peasant intelligentsia in Eastern Europe, and the socialist-anarchist proletarian intelligentsia in the West. To this general category there might also be added groups of a far different background, such as the Dutch peasantry of the first half of the nineteenth century, who had an impressive knowledge of the Bible, the lower middle-class Puritans of seventeenth-century England, and handicraft apprentices, who are almost universally characterized by notable religious interests. Above all, there must be included the classical manifestations of the Jewish laity, including the Pharisees, the Chassidim, and the mass of pious Jews who daily studied the law.

It may be noted that pariah intellectualism, appearing among all proletarian incumbents of small prebends, the Russian peasantry, and the more or less itinerant folk, derives its intensity from the fact that the groups which are at the lower end of or altogether outside of the social hierarchy stand to a certain extent on the point of Archimedes in relation to social conventions, both in respect to the external order and in respect to common opinions. Since these groups are not bound by the social conventions, they are capable of an original attitude toward the meaning of the cosmos; and since they are not impeded by any material considerations, they are capable of intense ethical and religious emotion. Insofar as they belonged to the middle classes, like the religiously self-taught lower-middle-class groups, their religious needs tended to assume either an ethically rigorous or an occult form. On the other hand, the intellectualism of craft apprentices stands midway between the privileged and proletarian manifestations of intellectualism, and is significant because of its contribution to the preparation of the itinerant journeyman for missionizing.

In Eastern Asia and India, so far as is known, pariah intellectualism is practically non-existent, as is intellectualism of the lower middle classes. This is because the middle classes there lack the communal feeling of an urban citizenry, which is a necessity for middle-class intellectualism. They also lack the emancipation from magic which is a precondition for both middle class and pariah intellectualism. Indeed, even those of the Indian *Gathas* that have arisen from the religion of the lower castes derive principally from the Brahmins. In China as well, there is no independent, unofficial intellectualism apart from the Confucian education. Confucianism is *the* ethic of the aristocratic man (i.e., the "gentleman," as Dvorak has correctly translated the term). Confucianism is quite explicitly the ethic of a particular social class, or more correctly, a systematization of rules of etiquette appropriate to an elite class the members of which have undergone literary training. The situation was not different in the ancient Levant and Egypt, so far as is known. There the intellectualism of the scribes, insofar as it led to ethical and religious reflection, belonged entirely to the type of intellectualism which is sometimes apolitical and always aristocratic and anti-plebian.

In ancient Israel, the author of the Book of Job assumed that upper-class groups are among the carriers of religious intellectualism. The Book of Proverbs and related works show traces in their very form of having been touched by the internationalization of the educated and apolitical higher classes resulting from their mutual contact with each other after Alexander's arrival in the East. Some of the dicta in Proverbs are directly attributed to a non-Jewish king, and in general the literature stamped with the name of "Solomon" betrays marks of an international culture. Ben Sira's emphatic stress upon the wisdom of the fathers in opposition to Hellenization already demonstrates that there was a trend in this direction. Moreover, as Bossuet correctly pointed out, the "scriptural scholar" of that time who was learned in the law was, according to the *Book of Ben Sira,* a widely traveled and cultivated gentleman. There is throughout this book, as Meinhold has emphasized, a clearly expressed anti-plebeian line, quite comparable to that found among the Greeks: How can the peasant, the smith, or the potter have wisdom, which only leisure for reflection and dedication to study can produce? Ezra is designated as the "first of the learned in the law," yet the influential position of the ideologists or monks with a dominant religious interest who had swarmed about the prophets, and without whom the imposition of the Book of Deuteronomy would never have taken place, was far older. We should note the decisive power of those learned in the law (almost equivalent to the Islamic *mufti*). These Jewish interpreters of the divine commands, knowledgeable in Hebrew, lived much later than Ezra, the official creator of the theocracy, who had received his powers from the Persian emperor.

The social position of the scribes nevertheless underwent changes. At the time of the Maccabean commonwealth, piety, which was in essence a rather sober wisdom of life, as illustrated by the doctrine of Xenophilia, was regarded as identical with education. Education (*musar, paideia*) was considered the key to virtue and regarded as teachable, in the same sense as among the Greeks. Yet the pious intellectuals of even that period, like the majority of the Psalmists, felt themselves to be in sharp opposition to the wealthy and proud, among whom fidelity to the law was uncommon, even though these intellectuals were of the same social class as the wealthy and proud. On the other hand, the schools of scriptural scholars of the Herodian period, whose frustration and psychological tension grew in the face of the obvious inevitability of subjugation to a foreign power, produced a proletarian class of interpreters of the law. These served as pastoral counselors, preachers and teachers in the synagogues, and their representatives also sat in the Sanhedrin. They influenced decisively the popular piety of those members of the Jewish community who were rigidly faithful to the law in the sense of the *Perushim*. In the Talmudic period, this functional activity developed into the rabbinate, a profession of congregational functionaries. Through the rabbinate there now ensued, in contrast to what had gone before, a tremendous expansion of lower-middle-class and pariah intellectualism, such as we do not find among any other people. Philo already regarded "general public schools" for the diffusion of literacy and of systematic education in casuistical thinking as the hallmark of the Jews. The influence of the rabbis first supplanted, among middle-class urban Jews, the activity of the prophets by the cult of fidelity to the law and study of the sacred scriptures of the law.

This Jewish class of popular intellectuals, the rabbis, entirely remote from any connection with mystery religions, unquestionably occupied a lower social position than the class of philosophers and mystagogues in Hellenistic societies of the Near East. But an intellectualism was undoubtedly already diffused throughout the various social classes of the Hellenistic Orient in pre-Christian times, and in fact produced in the various mysteries and cults of salvation, by allegory and speculation, dogmas similar to those generated by the Orphics, who generally belonged to the middle classes. These mysteries and soteriological speculations were certainly well known to a scriptural scholar like Paul, who rejected them vigorously. It will be recalled that the cult of Mithra was widely diffused in Cilicia during the time of Pompey as a religion of pirates, though the epigraphic evidences of this at Tarsus were not produced until after the establishment of Christianity. It is quite likely that salvation hopes of different kinds and origins existed side by side in Judaism for a long period, especially in the provinces. Otherwise, it would have been impossible for Judaism to produce, in addition to the idea of a future monarch of the Jewish people restored to power, the idea that another king of the poor folk would enter Jerusalem upon a donkey; and indeed it would have been difficult for the Jews to evolve their idea of the "son of man," an obvious linguistic product of Semitic grammar.

All in all, lay intellectualism is involved in every complex soteriology which develops abstractions and opens up cosmic perspectives, going far beyond mythologies oriented to the mere processes of nature or to the simple prediction of the appearance at some future time of a good king who is already waiting somewhere in concealment. The Jewish class of scriptural scholars learned in the law and the class of lower-middle-class intellectuals trained by those scholars extended from Judaism into early Christianity. Paul, apparently an artisan like many of the late Jewish scriptural scholars (in sharp contrast to the intellectuals of the period of Ben Sira, who produced anti-plebeian wisdom doctrines), is an outstanding representative of this class in early Christianity, though of course other traits are also to be found in Paul. His *gnosis*, though very remote from that conceived by the speculative intellectuals of the Hellenistic Orient, could later provide many points of support for the Marcionite movement. Intellectualism rooted in a sense of pride that only those chosen by god understand the parables of the master was also strongly marked in Paul, who boasted that his true knowledge was "to the Jews a stumbling block and to the Greeks foolishness." Paul's doctrine of the dualism of flesh and spirit has some relationship to the attitudes toward sensuality typical of intellectualist salvation doctrines, though Paul's doctrine is rooted in other conceptions. A somewhat superficial acquaintance with Hellenistic philosophy is apparent in his thought. Above all, Paul's conversion was not merely a vision, in the sense of hallucinatory perception. Rather, his conversion was also recognition of the profound inner relationship between the personal fate of the resurrected founder of Christianity and the cultic ideologies of the general oriental savior doctrines and conceptions of salvation (with which Paul was well acquainted), in which latter no place was provided for the promises of Jewish prophecy.

The argumentation of Paul's Epistles represents the highest type of dialectic found among intellectuals of the lower middle classes. Paul assumes a remarkable degree of direct "logical imagination" on the part of the groups he is addressing in such compositions as the Epistle to the Romans. Nothing is more certain than that it was not Paul's doctrine of justification which was really taken over by Christianity, but rather his conception of the relationship between spirit and the community and his conception of the manner in which spirit is accommodated to the facts of the everyday world. The fierce anger directed against him by the Jews of the Diaspora, for whom his dialectical method must have appeared as a misuse of education, only shows how thoroughly just such a method corresponded to the mental attitude of the lower-middle-class intellectual. This dialectical intellectualism was utilized by the charismatic teachers in pristine Christian communities as late as the *Didache;* and Harnack found a specimen of their hermeneutic in the Epistle to the Hebrews. But this intellectualism disappeared with the slow growth of the bishops' and presbyters' monopoly of the spiritual leadership of the community. In replacement of such dialectical intellectuals and teachers came first the intellectualist apologists, than the patristic church fathers and dogmatists, who were almost all clerics though they were also products of Greek education, and then the emperors, who had a dilettante interest in theology. The culmination of this development was the emergence into power in the East, after victory in the iconoclastic struggle, of monks recruited from the lowest non-Greek social groups. Thenceforth it became impossible to eliminate from the oriental church the type of formalistic dialectic common to all these circles and associated with a semi-intellectualistic, semi-primitive, and magical ideal of self-deification.

Yet one factor was decisive for the fate of ancient Christianity. From its inception Christianity was a salvation doctrine in respect to its genesis, its typical carriers, and what is crucial here, the content of its religious pattern of life. From its very beginning, Christianity, notwithstanding the many similarities of its soteriological myth to the general Near Eastern pattern of such myths, from which it borrowed elements that it changed, took a position against intellectualism with the greatest possible awareness and consistency. Nor does it argue against the anti-intellectualism of Christianity that Paul took over the hermeneutical methodology of the scribes. Primitive Christianity took stands against both the ritualistic and legalistic scholarship of Judaism and the soteriology of the Gnostic intellectual aristocrats, and it most strongly repudiated ancient philosophy.

The distinctive characteristics of Christianity were its rejection of the Gnostic denigration of believers and its affirmation that the exemplary Christians were those endowed with *pneuma,* the poor in spirit, rather than the scholars. Christianity also taught that the way to salvation is not derived from academic education in the law, from wisdom about the cosmic or psychological grounds of life and suffering, from knowledge of the conditions of life within the world, from knowledge of the mysterious significance of sacramental rites, or from knowledge of the future destiny of the soul in the other world. To these hallmarks of Christianity must be added the fact that a considerable portion of the inner history of the early church, including the formulation of dogma, represented the struggle of Christianity against intellectualism in all its forms.

If one wishes to characterize succinctly, in a formula so to speak, the types representative of the various classes that were the primary carriers or propagators of the so-called world religions, they would be the following: In Confucianism, the world-organizing bureaucrat; in Hinduism, the world-ordering magician; in Buddhism, the mendicant monk wandering through the world; in Islam, the warrior seeking to conquer the world; in Judaism, the wandering trader; and in Christianity, the itinerant journeyman. To be sure, all these types must not be taken as exponents of their own occupational or material class interests, but rather as the ideological carriers of the kind of ethical or salvation doctrine which most readily conformed to their social position.

As for Islam, its distinctive religiosity experienced an infusion of intellectualism, apart from the official schools of law and theology and the temporary efflorescence of scientific interests, only after its penetration by Sufism; its orientation was not along intellectual lines. Indeed, tendencies toward rationalism were completely lacking in the popular dervish faith. In Islam only a few heterodox sects, which possessed considerable influence at certain times, displayed a distinctly intellectualistic character. Otherwise Islam, like medieval Christianity, produced in its universities tendencies towards scholasticism.

It is impossible to expatiate here on the relationships of intellectualism to religion in medieval Christianity. In any case this religion, at least as far as its sociologically significant effects are concerned, was not specifically oriented to intellectual elements. The strong influence of monastic rationalism upon the substantive content of the culture may be clarified only by a comparison of occidental monasticism with that of the Near East and Asia, of which a brief sketch will be given later. The peculiar nature of occidental monasticism determined the distinctive cultural influence of the church in the West. During the medieval period, occidental Christianity did not have a religious lay intellectualism of any appreciable extent, whether of a middle-class or of a pariah character, although some religious lay intellectualism was occasionally found among the sects. On the other hand, the role of the elite educated classes in the development of the church was not a minor one. The imperialist educated groups of the Carolingian, Ottonic, and Salic periods worked along the lines of an imperial and theocratic cultural organization, just as the Ossipians had done. Above all, the Gregorian reform movement and the struggle for power on the part of the papacy were carried forward by the ideology of an elite intellectual class that entered into a united front with the rising bourgeoisie against the feudal powers. With the increasing dissemination of university education and with the struggle of the papacy to monopolize, for the sake of fiscal administration or simple patronage, the appointment of incumbents to benefices which provided the economic support for this educated class, the ever-growing class of these incumbents of office joined together in what was at first an essentially economic and nationalistic interest in monopoly. Then, following the schism, these intellectuals turned against the papacy ideologically, becoming the carriers of the conciliary reform movement and later of Humanism.

The sociology of the Humanists, particularly the transformation of a feudal and clerical education into a courtly culture based on the largesse of patrons, is not without interest, but we are unable to linger over it at this point. The ambivalent attitude of the Humanists toward the Reformation was primarily caused by ideological factors. Humanists did not place themselves in the service of building the churches of either the Reformation or the Counter Reformation, but they played an extremely important, though not decisive, role in organizing church schools and in developing doctrine. But insofar as they became the carriers of particular religions (actually a whole series of particular types of faith), they remained without permanent influence. In keeping with their entire pattern of life, these Humanist groups of the classically educated were altogether antipathetic to the masses and to the religious sects. They remained alien to the turmoil and particularly to the demagogy of priests and preachers, and they remained fairly thoroughly Erastian or irenic in temper, for which reasons they were condemned to suffer progressive loss of influence.

In addition to clever scepticism and rationalistic enlightenment, the Humanists displayed a tender religion of emotion, particularly in the Anglican group; an earnest and frequently ascetic moralism, as in the circle of Port Royal; and an individualistic mysticism, as in Germany during the first period and in Italy. But struggles involving realistic power and economic interests had to be waged, if not by outright violence, then at least with the means of demagogy, to which these Humanist groups were not equal. It is obvious that at least those churches desiring to win the participation of the ruling classes and particularly of the universities needed classically trained theological polemicists as well as preachers with classical training. Within Lutheranism, as a result of its alliance with the power of the nobility, the combination of education and religious activity rapidly devolved exclusively upon professional theologians.

Hudibras still mocked the Puritan groups for their ostensible philosophical erudition, but what gave the Puritans, and above all the Baptist sects, their insuperable power of resistance was not the intellectualism of the elite but rather the intellectualism of the plebeian and occasionally even the pariah classes, for Baptist Protestantism was in its first period a movement carried by wandering craftsmen or apostles. There was no distinctive intellectual class with a characteristic life pattern among these Protestant sects, but after the close of a brief period of missionary activity by their wandering preachers, it was the middle class that became suffused with their intellectualism. The unparalleled diffusion of knowledge about the Bible and interest in extremely abstruse and ethereal dogmatic controversies which was characteristic of the Puritans of the seventeenth century, even among peasant groups, created a popular religious intellectualism never found since, and comparable only to that found in late Judaism and to the religious mass intellectualism of the Pauline missionary communities. In contrast to the situations in Holland, parts of Scotland, and the American colonies, this popular religious intellectualism soon dwindled in England at least, after the sources of power and the various opportunities for mastering them had been investigated and determined in the religious wars. But since that time a distinctive Anglo-Saxon elite intellectualism has crystallized, marked by a traditional deference toward an enlightened type of religion, of varying degrees of mildness but never anti-clerical. But this is not the place for urther discussion of this point. Since the aforementioned evolution of religious attitudes has been determined by the traditional attitudes and the moralistic interests of the politically powerful middle class, and thus by a religious intellectualism, it provides the sharpest contrast to the evolution in Latin countries of either radical antipathy to the church, which is essentially the product of an elite courtly education, or of absolute indifference to the church.

Both Humanism and mass intellectualism, which are equally anti-metaphysical, provide contrasts to the German brand of apolitical, yet not anti-political, education of the elite, the metaphysical aspect of which is only very little concerned with specifically religious needs, least of all with any quest for salvation. On the other hand, the plebeian and pariah intellectualism of Germany increasingly took a definitely radical, anti-religious turn, like that in the Latin nations. This became particularly plain in the rise of the economic, eschatological faith of socialism. In this, German intellectualism differed from that of the Anglo-Saxon areas, in which the most serious forms of religion ever since Puritan times have had the character of sects, not of authoritarian institutions.

Only those anti-religious sects which were able, at least temporarily, to carry a quasi-religious belief in the socialist eschatology exercised control over a stratum of declassed intellectuals. This particular academic element receded to the extent that those with economic interests took the representation of these interests into their own hands. The further recession of this academic element was brought about by the inevitable disillusionment with an almost superstitious veneration of science, as the possible creator or at least prophet of social evolution, in the sense of a salvation from the class struggle, either violent or pacific. So, too, it came about that the only remaining type of socialism equivalent to a religious faith, namely syndicalism, easily slipped into the position of a romantic game played by groups devoid of economic power.

The last great movement of intellectuals which, though not sustained by a uniform faith, yet possessed enough common elements of faith in fundamentals to simulate the character of a religion, was that of the Russian revolutionary intelligentsia. In this movement, upper-class, academic and noble intellectuals stood side by side with those of plebeian status. The entire movement was carried forward by a proletarian class of minor officials, highly cultivated in their sociological thinking and their universal cultural interests (this was especially true of the administrative body, the so-called "third element," consisting of journalists, secondary school teachers, and revolutionary apostles), and by a peasant group of intellectuals springing out of Russian social movements. In the eighteen-seventies, this movement culminated in an appeal to a theory of natural rights, oriented primarily toward agricultural communism, the so-called *Narodnitschestvo*. In the nineties, this movement entered into a sharp conflict with Marxist dogma, but it also underwent various amalgamations, primarily with Slavophile romantic religiosity and with other vague religious emotionalisms of one sort or another. Under the influence of Dostoievsky and Tolstoy, an ascetic and acosmistic patterning of personal life was created among some relatively large groups of these Russian intellectuals. We shall leave untouched here the question as to what extent this movement, so strongly infused with the influence of Jewish proletarian intellectuals who were ready for any sacrifice, continued after the catastrophe of the Russian revolution (in 1906).

In Western Europe, ever since the seventeenth century, the viewpoints of Enlightenment religions produced, in both Anglo-Saxon and Gallic culture areas, unitarian and deistic communities and even communities of a syncretistic, atheistic, or free-church variety. Buddhistic conceptions, or what passed for such, also played some part in this development. In Germany, Enlightenment religious views found a hearing among the same groups that were interested in Freemasonry, namely those devoid of economic power, especially university professors but also declassed ideologists and educated groups partly or wholly belonging to the proletariat. In India, on the other hand, both the Hindu Enlightenment (*Brahma-Samaj*) and the Persian Enlightenment were products of contact with European culture.

The practical importance of such movements for the sphere of culture was greater in the past than now. Many elements conspire to render unlikely any serious possibility of a new communal religion borne by intellectuals. This constellation of factors includes the interest of the privileged classes in maintaining the existing religion as an instrument for controlling the masses, their need for social distance, their abhorrence of educational activities among the masses (as tending to destroy the prestige of elite groups), and their deliberate rejection of any faith in the possibility that some new creedal formulation acceptable to large segments of the population could supplant the traditional creeds (from the texts of which everyone interprets something away, orthodoxy ten percent and liberals ninety percent). Finally, and above all, there is the scornful indifference of the privileged classes to religious problems and to the church. Performance of some irksome formalities does not constitute much of a sacrifice, inasmuch as everyone knows they are just that—formalities performed by the official guardians of orthodoxy and the social conventions, and enacted because the state requires them performed in the interest of a successful career.

The need of literary, academic, or café-society intellectuals to include religious feelings in the inventory of their sources of impressions and sensations, and among their topics for discussion, has never yet given rise to a new religion. Nor can a religious renascence be generated by the need of authors to compose books, or by the far more effective need of clever publishers to sell such books. No matter how much the appearance of a widespread religious interest may be simulated, no new religion has ever resulted from the needs of intellectuals or from their chatter. The whirligig of fashion will presently remove this subject of conversation and journalism, which fashion has made popular.

IX. Theodicy, Salvation, and Rebirth

Only Judaism and Islam are strictly monotheistic in principle, and even in the latter there are some deviations from monotheism in the later cult of saints. Christian trinitarianism appears to have a monotheistic trend when contrasted with the tritheistic forms of Hinduism, late Buddhism, and Taoism. Yet in practice, the Roman Catholic cult of masses and saints actually comes fairly close to polytheism. It is by no means the case that every ethical god is necessarily endowed with absolute unchangeableness, omnipotence, and omniscience—that is to say, with an absolutely transcendental character. What provides him with this quality is the speculation and the ethical dynamic of passionate prophets. Only the God of the Jewish prophets attained this trait in an absolute and consistent form, and he became also the God of the Christians and Muslims. Not every ethical conception of god produced this result, nor did it lead to ethical monotheism as such. Hence, not every approximation to monotheism is based on an increase in the ethical content of the god-concept. It is certainly true that not every religious ethic has crystallized a god of transcendental quality who created the universe out of nothing and directed it himself.

Yet the legitimation of every distinctively ethical prophecy has always required the notion of a god characterized by attributes that set him sublimely above the world, and has normally been based on the rationalization of the god-idea along such lines. Of course the manifestation and the significance of this sublimity may be quite different, depending in part on fixed metaphysical conceptions and in part on the expression of the concrete ethical interests of the prophets. But the more the development tends toward the conception of a transcendental unitary god who is universal, the more there arises the problem of how the extraordinary power of

138

such a god may be reconciled with the imperfection of the world that he has created and rules over.

The resultant problem of theodicy is found in ancient Egyptian literature as well as in Job and in Aeschylus, but in very different forms. All Hindu religion was influenced by it in the distinctive way necessitated by its fundamental presuppositions; even a meaningful world order that is impersonal and supertheistic must face the problem of the world's imperfections. In one form or another, this problem belongs everywhere among the factors determining religious evolution and the need for salvation. Indeed, a recent* questionnaire submitted to thousands of German workers disclosed the fact that their rejection of the god-idea was motivated, not by scientific arguments, but by their difficulty in reconciling the idea of providence with the injustice and imperfection of the social order.

Now the problem of theodicy has been solved in various ways. These solutions stand in the closest relationship both to the forms assumed by the god-concept and to the conceptions of sin and salvation crystallized in particular social groups. Let us separate out the various theoretically pure types.

One solution is to assure a just equalization by pointing, through messianic eschatologies, to a future revolution in this world. In this way the eschatological process becomes a political and social transformation of this world. This solution held that sooner or later there would arise some tremendous hero or god who would place his followers in the positions they truly deserved in the world. The suffering of the present generation, it was believed, was the consequence of the sins of the ancestors, for which god holds the descendants responsible, just as someone carrying out blood revenge may hold an entire tribe accountable, and as Pope Gregory VII excommunicated descendants down to the seventh generation. Conversely, it was held that only the descendants of the pious could behold the messianic kingdom, as a consequence of their ancestors' piety. If it perhaps appeared necessary to postpone one's own experience of salvation, there was nothing strange in this. Concern about one's children was everywhere a definite fact of organic social life, pointing beyond the personal

* [Before World War I. Translator's note.]

interest of an individual and in the direction of another world, at least a world beyond one's own death. For those who were alive, the exemplary and strict fulfillment of the positive divine commandments remained obligatory, in order to obtain for the individual himself the optimum opportunity for success in life by virtue of god's favor, and in order to obtain for his descendants a share in the realm of salvation. Sin is a breach of fidelity toward god and an impious rejection of god's promises. Moreover, the desire to participate personally in the messianic kingdom leads to further consequences: a tremendous religious excitation is generated when the establishment of the Kingdom of God here on earth appears imminent. Prophets repeatedly arose to proclaim the coming of the kingdom, but when such supervention of the messianic kingdom appeared to be unduly delayed, it was inevitable that consolation should be sought in genuine otherworldly hopes.

The germ of the conception of a world beyond the present one is already present in the development of magic into a belief in spirits. But it by no means follows that the existence of a belief in the souls of the dead always develops into a conception of a special realm of the dead. Thus, a very widespread view is that the souls of the dead may be incorporated into animals and plants, depending on the souls' different manners of life and death, and influenced by their clan and caste connections. This is the source of all conceptions regarding the transmigration of the soul. Where there exists a belief in a domain of the deceased—at first in some geographically remote place, and later above or beneath the earth—it by no means follows that the existence of the souls there is conceived as eternal. For the souls may be destroyed by violence, may perish as the result of the cessation of sacrifices, or may simply die, which is apparently the ancient Chinese view.

In keeping with the law of marginal utility, a certain concern for one's own destiny after death generally arises when the most essential earthly needs have been met, and thus this concern is limited primarily to the circles of the elite and to the wealthy classes. Only these groups and occasionally the chieftains and priests, but never the poor and only seldom women, can secure for themselves life in the next world. They do not spare great expenditures in doing so. It is primarily the example of these wealthy classes that serves as a strong stimulus for preoccupation with otherworldly expectations.

At this point there is as yet no question of retribution in the world to come. Where a doctrine of retributions arises, errors in ritual are deemed to be the principal causes of such unfortunate consequences. This is seen most extensively in the sacred law of the Hindus: whosoever violates a caste taboo may be certain of punishment in hell. Only after the god-concept has been ethicized does the god employ moral considerations in deciding the fate of human beings in the world to come. The differentiation of a paradise and a hell does not necessarily arise concomitantly with this development, but is a relatively late product of evolution. As otherworldly expectations become increasingly important, the problem of the theoretical relationship of god to the world and the problem of the world's imperfections press into the foreground of thought. The more life here on earth comes to be regarded as a merely provisional form of existence, when compared to that beyond, the more the world comes to be viewed as something created by god *ex nihilo,* and therefore subject to decline. Consequently, to the extent that god himself is conceived as subject to transcendental goals and values, a person's behavior in this world becomes oriented to his fate in the next. At times, the hope for continued existence in the world beyond produces a direct inversion—in accordance with the formula, "the last shall be first"—of the primordial view in which it had held this to be a matter of concern only to the elite and the wealthy.

But this view has seldom been worked out consistently, even in the religious conceptions of pariah peoples. It did play a great role, however, in the ancient Jewish ethic. The assumption that suffering, particularly voluntary suffering, would mollify god and improve one's chances in the world to come is found sprinkled through and developed in many types of expectation regarding continued existence after death. These may arise from very diverse religious motivations, and may arise to some extent from the ordeals of heroic asceticism and the practice of magical mortification. As a rule, and especially in religions under the influence of the ruling classes, the converse view obtained, viz., that terrestrial differentiations of social class would continue into the next world as well, for the reason that they had been divinely ordained. This belief is still apparent in the phrase current in Christian nations, "His late Majesty, the King."

However, the distinctively ethical view was that there would be concrete retribution of justices and injustices on the basis of a trial of the dead, generally conceived in the eschatological process as a universal day of judgment. In this way, sin assumed the character of a *crimen* to be brought into a system of rational casuistry, a *crimen* for which satisfaction must somehow be given in this world or in the next so that one might ultimately stand vindicated before the judge of the dead. Accordingly, rewards and punishments had to be graded into relative degrees of merit and transgression, which was still the case in Dante, with the result that they could not really be eternal. Because of the pale and uncertain character of a person's chances in the next world, the remission of eternal punishments by prophets and priests was practically always regarded as impossible. Severe penalties were deemed to be the only appropriate fulfillments of the demand for vengeance against unbelieving, renegade, and godless sinners, especially those who had gone unpunished on earth.

Heaven, hell, and the judgment of the dead achieved practically universal importance, even in religions such as Buddhism, to the entire nature of which such concepts were completely alien. However, intermediate realms of existence, such as those depicted in the teachings of Zoroaster or in the Roman Catholic conception of purgatory, realms encompassing punishments which would only be undergone for limited durations, could weaken the consistency of conceptions of eternal punishment. There always remained the difficulty of reconciling the punishment of human errors with the conception of an ethical and at the same time all-powerful creator of the world, who is ultimately responsible for these human actions himself. As people continued to reflect about the insoluble problem of the imperfections of the world in the light of god's omnipotence, one result was inevitable: the conception of an unimaginably great ethical chasm between the transcendental god and the human being continuously enmeshed in the toils of new sin. And this conception inevitably led to the ultimate theoretical conclusion, apparently assumed in the Book of Job, that the omnipotent creator God must be envisaged as beyond all the ethical claims of his creatures, his counsels impervious to human comprehension. Another facet of this emerging view was that God's absolute power over his creatures is unlimited, and therefore that the criteria of human justice are utterly inapplicable to his behavior. With the development of this notion, the problem of theodicy simply disappeared altogether.

In Islam, Allah was deemed by his most passionate adherents to possess just such a limitless power over men. In Christianity, the *deus absconditus* was so envisaged, especially by the virtuosi of Christian piety. God's sovereign, completely inexplicable, voluntary, and antecedently established (a consequence of his omniscience) determination has decreed not only human fate on earth but also human destiny after death. The idea of the determinism or predestination from all eternity of both human life on this earth and human fate in the world beyond comes to its strongest possible expression in such views. The damned might well complain that their sinfulness had been imposed by predestination, and animals too might complain because they had not been created human beings, a matter expressly stated in Calvinism.

In such a context, ethical behavior could never bring about the improvement of one's own chances in either this world or the next. Yet it might have another significance, the practical psychological consequences of which could in certain circumstances be of even greater moment; it might be considered as a symptom or index of one's own state of religious grace as established by god's decree. For the absolute sovereignty of an omnipotent god compels a practical religious concern to try, at the very least, to penetrate god's design in individual cases. Above all, the need to ascertain one's own personal destiny in the world beyond becomes of paramount importance. Hence, concomitant with the tendency to regard god as the unlimited sovereign over his creatures, there was an inclination to see and interpret god's providence and his personal interposition everywhere in the world's process.

Belief in providence is the consistent rationalization of magical divination, to which it is related, and which for that very reason it seeks to devaluate as completely as possible, as a matter of principle. No other view of the religious relationship could possibly be as radically opposed to all magic, both in theory and in practice, as this belief in providence which was dominant in the great theistic religions of Asia Minor and the Occident. No other so emphatically affirms the nature of the divine to be an essentially dynamic activity manifested in god's personal, providential rule over the world. Moreover, there is no view of the religious relationship which holds such firm views regarding god's freely distributed grace and the human creature's need of it, regarding the tremendous distance between god and all his creatures, and consequently regarding the reprehensibility of any "deification of creatures" as a sacrilege against the sovereign god. For the very reason that this religion provides no rational solution of the problem of theodicy, it conceals the greatest tensions between the world and god, between the actually existent and the ideal.

Besides predestination, there are two other religious outlooks that provide systematically conceptualized treatment of the problem of the world's imperfections. The first is dualism, as expressed more or less consistently in the later form of Zoroastrianism, in the many forms of religion in Asia Minor influenced by Zoroastrianism, above all in the final form of Babylonian religion (containing some Jewish and Christian influences), and in Mandaeism and Gnosticism, down to the great ideas of Manicheism.

At the turn of the third century, Manicheism seemed to stand on the threshold of a struggle for world mastery, even in the Mediterranean area. According to the Manicheans, god is not almighty, nor did he create the world out of nothingness. Injustice, unrighteousness, and sin—in short, all the factors that have generated the problem of theodicy—result from the darkening of the luminous purity of the great and good gods through contact with the opposite autonomous powers of darkness, which are identified with impure matter. The dominance of these forces, which gives dominion over the world to some satanic power, has arisen through some primordial wickedness of men or of angels, or, as in the view of many Gnostics, through the inferiority of some subordinate creator of the world, e.g., Jehovah or the Demiurge. The final victory of the god of light in the ensuing struggle is generally regarded as certain, and this constitutes a deviation from strict dualism. The world process, although full of inevitable suffering, is a continuous purification of the light from the contamination of darkness. This conception of the final struggle naturally produces a very powerful eschatological emotional dynamic.

One general result of such views must be the enhancement of an aristocratic feeling of prestige on the part of the pure and elect. The conception of evil manifests a purely ethical tendency, in view of the presupposition of a definitely omnipotent god, and may assume a strongly spiritual character. This is because man is not to be regarded as a mere creature of an absolutely omnipotent power contraposed to evil, but as a participant in the realm of light. Moreover, the identification of light with what is clearest in man, namely the spiritual, and conversely, the identification of darkness with the material and corporeal which carry in themselves all the coarser temptations, is practically unavoidable. This view, then, connects easily with the doctrine of impurity found in tabooistic ethics. Evil appears as soiling, and sin—in a fashion quite like that of magical misdeeds—appears as a reprehensible and headlong fall to earth, from the realm of purity and clarity into that of darkness and confusion, leading to a state of contamination and deserved ignominy In practically all the religions with an ethical orientation there are unavowed limitations of divine omnipotence in the form of elements of a dualistic mode of thought.

The most complete formal solution of the problem of theodicy is the special achievement of the Indian doctrine of *karma,* the so-called belief in the transmigration of souls. The world is viewed as a completely connected and self-contained cosmos of ethical retribution. Guilt and merit within this world are unfailingly compensated by fate in the successive lives of the soul, which may be reincarnated innumerable times in animal, human, or even divine forms. Ethical merits in this life can make possible rebirth into life in heaven, but that life can last only until one's credit balance of merits has been completely used up. The finiteness of earthly life is the consequence of the finiteness of good or evil deeds in the previous life of a particular soul. What may appear from the viewpoint of a theory of compensation as unjust suffering in the terrestrial life of a person should be regarded as atonement for sin in a previous existence. Each individual forges his own destiny exclusively, and in the strictest sense of the word.

The belief in the transmigration of souls has certain links with widely diffused animistic views regarding the passage of the spirits of the dead into natural objects. It rationalizes these beliefs, and indeed the entire cosmos, by means of purely ethical principles. The naturalistic "causality" of our habits of thought is thus supplanted by a universal mechanism of retribution, for which no act that is ethically relevant can ever be lost. The consequence for dogma is the complete dispensability, and indeed unthinkableness, of an omnipotent god's interference with this mechanism, for the eternal world process provides for ethical obligations through automatic functioning. The mechanism of retribution is, therefore, a consistent deduction from the super-divine character of the eternal order of the world, in contrast to the notion of a god who is set over the world, rules it personally, and imposes predestination upon it. In ancient Buddhism, where this mechanistic notion of the eternal order of the world has been developed with the greatest consistency, even the soul is eliminated. What alone exists is the sum of individual good or evil actions, which are relevant for the mechanisms of *karma* and associated with the illusion of the ego.

But such good or evil actions are products of the eternally helpless struggle of all created life, which by the very fact of its finite creation is doomed to a merely ephemeral existence and destined for annihilation. All questing for the world to come and all surrender to pleasures here on earth arise from the thirst for life. Strictly speaking, there is no sin, but only offenses against one's own clear interest in escaping from this endless wheel, or at least in not exposing oneself to a rebirth under even more painful circumstances. The meaning of ethical behavior may then lie, when modestly conceived, either in improving one's chances in his next incarnation or—if the senseless struggle for mere existence is ever to be ended—in the elimination of rebirth as such.

In the doctrine of metempsychosis there is none of the bifurcation of the world that is found in the ethical dualistic religions of providence. The dualism of a sacred, omnipotent, and majestic god confronting the ethical inadequacy of all his creatures is altogether lacking. Nor is there, as in spiritualistic dualism, the bisection of all creation into light and darkness or into the pure and clear spirit on the one side with dark and sullied matter on the other. Here, rather, is an ontological dualism, one contrasting the world's transitory events and behavior with the serene and perduring being of eternal order—immobile divinity, resting in dreamless sleep. Only Buddhism has deduced from the doctrine of the transmigration of souls its ultimate consequences. This is the most radical solution of the problem of theodicy, and for that very reason it provides as little satisfaction for ethical claims upon god as does the belief in predestination.

Only a few religions of salvation have produced a single pure solution of the problem of the relation of god to the world and to man, from among the various possible pure types we have just sketched. Wherever such a pure type was produced it lasted for only a little while. Most religions of salvation have combined various theories, as a result of mutual interaction with each other, and above all in attempts to satisfy the diverse ethical and intellectual needs of their adherents. Consequently, the differences among various religious theories of god's relation to the world and to man must be measured by their degree of approximation to one or another of these pure types.

Now the various ethical colorations of the doctrines of god and sin stand in the most intimate relationship to the striving for salvation, the content of which will be different depending upon what one wants to be saved from, and what one wants to be saved for. Not every rational religious ethic is necessarily an ethic of salvation. Thus, Confucianism is a religious ethic, but it knows nothing at all of a need for salvation. On the other hand, Buddhism is exclusively a doctrine of salvation, but it has no god. Many other religions know salvation only as a special concern cultivated in narrow conventicles, frequently as a secret cult. Indeed, even in connection with religious activities which are regarded as distinctively sacred and which promise their participants some salvation that may be achieved only through these activities, the crassest utilitarian expectations frequently replace anything we are accustomed to term "salvation." The pantomimic musical mystery festivals of the great chthonic deities, which controlled both the harvest and the realm of the dead, promised to the participant in the Eleusinian mysteries who was ritually pure, first wealth and then improvement in his lot in the next world. But this was proclaimed without any idea of compensation, purely as a consequence of ritualistic devotion.

In the catalog of goods in the *Shih ching,* the highest rewards promised to the Chinese subjects for their correct performances of the official cult and their fulfillment of personal religious obligations are wealth and long life, while there is a complete absence of expectations in regard to another world and any compensation there. Again, it is wealth that Zoroaster, by the grace of his god, principally expects for himself and those faithful to him, apart from rather extensive promises relating to the world beyond. As rewards for the ethical conduct of its laity, Buddhism promises wealth and a long and honorable life, in complete consonance with the doctrines of all inner-worldly ethics of the Hindu religions. Finally, wealth is the blessing bestowed by God upon the pious Jew.

But wealth, when acquired in a systematic and legal fashion, is also one of the indices of the certification of the state of grace among Protestant ascetic groups, e.g., Calvinists, Baptists, Mennonites, Quakers, Reformed Pietists, and Methodists. To be sure, in these cases we are dealing with a conception that decisively rejects wealth (and other mundane goods) as a religious goal. But in practice the transition to this standpoint is gradual and easy. It is difficult to completely separate conceptions of salvation from such promises of redemption from oppression and suffering as those promises held forth by the religions of the pariah peoples, particularly the Jews, and also by the doctrines of Zoroaster and Muhammad. For the faithful, these promises might include world dominion and social prestige, which the true believer in ancient Islam carried in his knapsack, so to speak, as the reward for holy war against all infidels; or the promises might include a distinctive religious prestige, such as that which the Israelites were taught by their tradition that God had promised them as their future. Particularly for the Israelites, therefore, God was in the first instance a redeemer, because he had saved them from the Egyptian house of bondage and would later redeem them from the ghetto.

In addition to such economic and political salvation, there is the very important factor of liberation from fear of noxious spirits and bad magic of any sort, which is held to be responsible for the majority of all the evils in life. That Christ broke the power of the demons by the force of his spirit and redeemed his followers from their control was, in the early period of Christianity, one of the most important and influential of its messages. Moreover, the Kingdom of God proclaimed by Jesus of Nazareth, which had already come or was held to be close at hand, was a realm of blessedness upon this earth, purged of all hate, anxiety, and need; only later did heaven and hell appear in the doctrine. Of course, an eschatology oriented to a future in this world would show a distinct tendency to become a hope for the world beyond, once the Second Coming (*parousia*) was delayed. Henceforth, emphasis had to be shifted to the afterlife: those alive at present would not be able to see salvation during their lifetime, but would see it after death, when the dead would awaken.

The distinctive content of salvation in the world beyond may essentially mean freedom from the physical, psychological, and social sufferings of terrestrial life. On the other hand, it may be more concerned with a liberation from the senseless treadmill and transitoriness of life as such. Finally, it may be focused primarily on the inevitable imperfection of the individual, whether this be regarded more as chronic contamination, acute inclination to sin, or more spiritually, as entanglement in the murky confusion of earthly ignorance.

Our concern is essentially with the quest for salvation, whatever its form, insofar as it produced certain consequences for practical behavior in the world. It is most likely to acquire such a positive orientation to mundane affairs as the result of a pattern of life which is distinctively determined by religion and given coherence by some central meaning or positive goal. In other words, a quest for salvation in any religious group has the strongest chance of exerting practical influences when there has arisen, out of religious motivations, a systematization of practical conduct resulting from an orientation to certain integral values. The goal and significance of such a pattern of life may remain altogether oriented to this world, or it may focus on the world beyond, at least in part. In the various religions, this has taken place in exceedingly diverse fashions and in different degrees, and even within each religion there are corresponding differences among its various adherents. Furthermore, the religious systematization of the conduct of life has, in the nature of the case, certain limits insofar as it seeks to exert influence upon economic behavior. Finally, religious motivations, especially the hope of salvation, need not necessarily exert any influence at all upon the manner of the conduct of life, particularly the manner of economic conduct. Yet they may do so to a very considerable extent.

The hope of salvation may have the most far-reaching consequences for the conduct of life when the salvation itself takes the form of a process that already casts a shadow before it in this life, the form of a completely subjective process taking place in this world, or the form of a life beyond for which the conditions of this life serve as preliminary sanctification. In the latter case this sanctification may occur as either a gradual process of purification or a sudden transformation of the spirit, a rebirth.

The notion of rebirth as such is very ancient, and its most classical development is actually to be found in the spirit belief of magic. The possession of magical charisma always presupposes rebirth. The distinctive education of the magician himself, his specific pattern of life, and his distinctive training of the warrior hero are all oriented to rebirth and the insurance of the possession of distinctive magical power. This process is mediated by removal or detachment in the form of ecstasy, and by the acquisition of a new soul, generally followed by a change of name. A vestige of these notions is still extant in the monastic consecration ceremony. Rebirth is at first relevant only to the professional magician, as a magical precondition for insuring the charisma of the wizard or warrior. But in the most consistent types of salvation religion it becomes a quality of devotion indispensable for religious salvation, which the individual must acquire and which he must make manifest in his pattern of life.

X. The Different Roads to Salvation

The influence any religion exerts on the conduct of life, and especially on the conditions of rebirth, varies in accordance with the particular path to salvation which is desired and striven for, and in accordance with the psychological quality of the salvation in question. We may first note that salvation may be the accomplishment of the individual himself without any assistance on the part of supernatural powers, e.g., in ancient Buddhism.

One path to salvation leads through the purely ritual activities and ceremonies of cults, both within religious worship and in everyday behavior. Pure ritualism as such is not very different from magic in its effect on the conduct of life. Indeed, ritualism may even lag behind magic, inasmuch as magical religion occasionally produced a definite and rather thorough methodology of rebirth, which ritualism did not always succeed in doing. A religion of salvation may systematize the purely formal and specific activities of ritual into a devotion with a distinctive religious mood, in which the rites to be performed are symbols of the divine. In such a case the religious mood is the true instrument of salvation. Once emphasis has been placed on this inward aspect of salvation, the bare and formal magical ritualism becomes superfluous. This happened as a matter of course again and again in the routinization of all devotional religions.

The consequences of a ritualistic religion of devotion may be quite diversified. The comprehensive ritualistic regimentation of life among pious Hindus, which by European standards placed extraordinary daily demands upon the devout, actually rendered virtually impossible any intensive acquisitive economic activity in communities which followed faithfully the religious injunctions for a meritorious life in this world. Such extreme devotional piety is diametrically opposite to Puritanism in one respect: such a program of ritualism could be executed completely only by a man of means, who is free from the burden of hard work. But this circumstance limiting the number of those whose conduct of life can be influenced by ritualism is to some extent avoidable, whereas another inherent limiting circumstance is even more basic to the nature of ritualism.

Ritualistic salvation, especially when it limits the layman to a spectator role, confines his participation to simple or essentially passive manipulations, or sublimates the ritual mood into the most emotional sort of piety, stresses the mood content of the particular devotional factor that appears to bring the salvation. Consequently, the possession of an essentially ephemeral subjective state is striven after, and this subjective state—because of the idiosyncratic irresponsibility characterizing, for example, the hearing of a mass or the witnessing of a mystical play—has only a negligible effect on behavior once the ceremony is over. The meager influence such experiences frequently have upon everyday ethical living may be compared to the insignificant influence of a beautiful and inspiring play upon the theater public which has witnessed it. All salvation deriving from mysteries has such an inconstant character. Mysteries purport to produce their effect *ex opere operato* by means of a pious occasional devotion. They provide no inner motivation for any such requirement as the believer's demonstration in his life pattern of a religious norm, such as a rebirth might entail.

On the other hand, when the occasional devotion induced by ritual is escalated into a continuing piety and the effort is made to incorporate this piety into everyday living, this ritualistic piety most readily takes on a mystical character. This transition is facilitated by the requirement that religious devotion lead to the participant's possession of a subjective state. But the disposition to mysticism is an individual charisma. Hence, it is no accident that the great mystical prophecies of salvation, like the Hindu and others in the Orient, have tended to fall into pure ritualism as they have become routinized. What is of primary concern to us is that in ritualism the psychological condition striven for ultimately leads directly away from rational activity. Virtually all mystery cults have this effect.

Their typical intention is the accomplishment, by the sheer sacredness of their manipulations, of redemption from guilt and the distribution of sacramental grace. Like every form of magic, this process has a tendency to become diverted from everyday life, thereby failing to exert any influence upon it.

But a sacrament might have a very different effect if its distribution and administration were linked to the presupposition that the sacrament could bring salvation only to those who have become ethically purified in the sight of god, and might indeed bring ruin to all others. Even up to the threshold of the present time, large groups of people have felt a terrifying fear of the Lord's Supper (the sacrament of the Eucharist) because of the doctrine that "whoever does not believe and yet eats, eats and drinks himself to judgment." Such factors could exert a strong influence upon everyday behavior wherever, as in ascetic Protestantism, there was no central source for the provision of absolution, and where further participation in the sacramental communion occurred frequently, providing a very important index of piety.

In all Christian denominations, participation in sacramental communion is connected with a prescription of confession as the prelude to partaking of the Lord's Supper. But in assessing the importance of confession, everything depends upon what religious rules are prescribed as determining whether sacramental communion may be taken with profit to the participant. Only ritual purity was required for this purpose by the majority of non-Christian ancient mystery cults, though under certain circumstances the devotee was disqualified by grave blood guilt or other specific sins. Thus, most of these mysteries had nothing resembling a confessional. But wherever the requirement of ritual purity became rationalized in the direction of spiritual freedom from sin, the particular forms of the requirement and of its sanctions became important for the type and degree of its possible influence upon daily life. From the pragmatic point of view, ritual as such was in every case only an instrument for influencing the all-important extra-ritual behavior. So much is this the case that wherever the Eucharist was most completely stripped of its magical character, and where further no control by means of the confessional existed, e.g., in Puritanism, communion nevertheless exerted an ethical effect, in some cases precisely because of the absence of magical and confessional controls.

A ritualistic religion may exert an ethical effect in another and indirect way, by requiring that participants be specially schooled. This happened where, as in ancient Judaism, the fulfillment of ritual commandments required of the laity some active ritual behavior or some ritual avoidance of behavior, and where the formalistic side of the ritual had become so systematized into a comprehensive body of law that adequate understanding of it required special schooling. Philo emphasized that already in ancient times the Jews, in contrast to all other peoples, were trained from their earliest youth (along the lines of our public school system) and received a continuous intellectual training in systematic casuistry. Indeed, the literary character of Jewish law is responsible for the fact that even in modern times many Jews, e.g., those in Eastern Europe, have been the only people in their society to enjoy systematic popular education. Even in antiquity, pious Jews had been led to equate persons unschooled in the law with the godless. Such casuistic training of the intellect naturally exerts an effect on everyday life, especially when it involves not only ritual and cultic obligations, as those of Hindu law, but also a systematic regulation of the ethics of everyday living as well. Then the works of salvation are primarily social achievements, distinctively different from cultic performances.

The social actions which are regarded as conducive to salvation may be of very different types. Thus, gods of war welcome into their paradise only those who have fallen in battle, or at least show them preference. In the Brahmin ethic the king was explicitly enjoined to seek death in battle once he had beheld his grandson. On the other hand, the social achievements in question may be works of "love for one's fellow men." But in either case systematization may ensue, and, as we have already seen, it is generally the function of prophecy to accomplish just this systematization.

A developing systematization of an ethic of "good works" may assume either of two very different forms. In the first major form of systematization of an ethic of good works, the particular actions of an individual in quest of salvation, whether virtuous or wicked actions, can be evaluated singly and credited to or subtracted from the individual's account. Each individual is regarded as the carrier of his own behavior pattern and as possessing ethical standards only tenuously; he may turn out to be a weaker or a stronger creature in the face of temptation, according to the force of the subjective or external situation. Yet it is held that his religious fate depends upon his actual achievements, in their relationship to one another.

This first type of systematization is consistently followed in Zoroastrianism, particularly in the oldest Gathas by the founder himself, which depict the judge of all the dead balancing the guilt and merit of individual actions in a very precise bookkeeping and determining the religious fate of the individual person according to the outcome of this accounting. This notion appears among the Hindus in an even more heightened form, as a consequence of the doctrine of *karma*. It is held that within the ethical mechanism of the world not a single good or evil action can ever be lost. Each action, being ineradicable, must necessarily produce, by an almost automatic process, inevitable consequences in this life or in some future rebirth. This essential principle of life-accounting also remained the basic view of popular Judaism regarding the individual's relationship to God. Finally, Roman Catholicism and the oriental Christian churches held views very close to this, at least in practice. The *intentio*, to which reference must be made for the ethical evaluation of behavior in Catholicism, is more than a simple and uniform quality of personality, of which conduct is the expression. Rather, it is the "significance" (*Meinung*) in the mind of the person (in the sense of the *bona fides, mala fides, culpa,* and *dolus* of the Roman law) which leads him to perform any particular action. This view, when consistently maintained, eschews the yearning for rebirth in the strict sense of an ethic of inwardness. A result is that the conduct of life remains, from the viewpoint of ethics, an unmethodical and miscellaneous succession of discrete actions.

The second major form of systematization of an ethic of good works treats individual actions as symptoms and expressions of an underlying ethical total personality. It is instructive to recall the attitude of some of the more rigorous Spartans toward one of their comrades who had fallen in battle after having sought such a death as a purification measure which would atone for an earlier manifestation of cowardice. They did not regard him as having rehabilitated his ethical status, since he had acted bravely for a specific reason and not "out of the totality of his personality," as we would term it. In the religious sphere too, formal sanctification by the good works shown in external actions is supplanted by the value of the total personality pattern, which in the Spartan example would be an habitual temper of heroism. A similar principle applies to social actions of all sorts. If they demonstrate "love for one's fellow man," then ethical systematization of this kind requires that the actor possess the charisma of "goodness."

It is of ultimate importance that the specific action be really symptomatic of the total character and that no significance be attached to it when it is a result of accident. This ethic of inwardness, in its most highly systematized forms, may make increased demands at the level of the total personality and yet be more tolerant in regard to particular transgressions. But this is not always the case, and the ethic of inwardness is generally the most distinctive form of ethical rigorism. On the one hand, a total personality pattern with positive religious qualifications may be regarded as a divine gift, the presence of which will manifest itself in a general orientation to whatever is demanded by religion, namely a pattern of life integrally and methodically oriented to the values of religion. On the other hand, a religious total personality pattern may be envisaged as something which may in principle be acquired through training in goodness. Of course this training itself will consist of a rationalized, methodical direction of the entire pattern of life, and not an accumulation of single, unrelated actions. Although these two views of the origin of a religious total personality pattern produce very similar practical results, yet one particular result of the methodical training of the total personality pattern is that the social and ethical quality of actions falls into secondary importance, while the religious effort expended upon oneself becomes of primary importance. Consequently, religious good works with a social orientation become mere instruments of *self-perfection.*

Perfecting of the self is of course equivalent to a planned procedure for attaining religious consecration. Now ethical religions are by no means the first to produce such a planned procedure. On the contrary, highly systematized planned procedures frequently played significant roles in those awakenings to charismatic rebirth which promised the acquisition of magical powers. This animistic trend of thinking entailed belief in the incarnation of a new soul within one's own body, the possession of one's soul by a powerful demon, or the removal of one's soul to a realm of spirits. In all cases the possibility of attaining superhuman actions and powers was involved. "Other-worldly" goals were of course completely lacking in all this. What is more, this capacity for ecstasy might be used for the most diverse purposes. Thus, only by acquiring a new soul through rebirth can the warrior achieve superhuman deeds of heroism. The original sense of "rebirth" as producing either a hero or a magician remains present in all vestigial initiation ceremonies, e.g., the reception of youth into the religious brotherhood of the phratry and their equipment with the paraphernalia of war, or the decoration of youth with the insignia of manhood in China and India (where the members of the higher castes are termed the "twice-born"). All these ceremonies were originally associated with activities which produced or symbolized ecstasy, and the only purpose of the associated training regimens is the testing or arousing of the capacity for ecstasy.

Ecstasy as an instrument of salvation or self-deification, our exclusive interest here, may have the essential character of an acute mental aberration or possession, or else the character of a chronically heightened idiosyncratic religious mood, tending either toward greater intensity of life or toward alienation from life. This escalated, intensified religious mood can be of either a more contemplative or a more active type. It should go without saying that a planned methodology of sanctification was not the means used to produce the state of acute ecstasy. The various methods for breaking down organic inhibitions were of primary importance in producing ecstasy. Organic inhibitions were broken down by the production of acute toxic states induced by alcohol, tobacco, or other drugs which have intoxicating effects; by music and dance; by sexuality; or by a combination of all three—in short by orgies. Ecstasy was also produced by the provocation of hysterical or epileptoid seizures among those with predispositions toward such paroxysms, which in turn produced orgiastic states in others. However, these acute ecstasies are transitory in their nature and apt to leave but few positive traces on everyday behavior. Moreover, they lack the meaningful content revealed by prophetic religion.

It would appear that a much more enduring possession of the charismatic condition is promised by those milder forms of euphoria which may be experienced as either a dreamlike mystical illumination or a more active and ethical conversion. Furthermore, they produce a meaningful relationship to the world, and they correspond in quality to evaluations of an eternal order or an ethical god such as are proclaimed by prophecy. We have already seen that magic is acquainted with a systematic procedure of sanctification for the purpose of evoking charismatic qualities, in addition to its last resort to the acute orgy. For professional magicians and warriors need permanent states of charisma as well as acute ecstasies.

Not only do the prophets of ethical salvation not need orgiastic intoxication, but it actually stands in the way of the systematic ethical patterning of life they require. For this reason, the primary target of Zoroaster's indignant ethical rationalism was orgiastic ecstasy, particularly the intoxicating cult of the soma sacrifice, which he deemed unworthy of man and cruel to beasts. For the same reason, Moses directed his rationalized ethical attack against the orgy of the dance, just as many founders or prophets of ethical religion attacked "whoredom," i.e., orgiastic temple prostitution. As the process of rationalization went forward, the goal of methodically planned religious sanctification increasingly transformed the acute intoxication induced by orgy into a milder but more permanent *habitus,* and moreover one that was consciously possessed. This transformation was strongly influenced by, among other things, the particular concept of the divine that was entertained. The ultimate purpose to be served by the planned procedure of sanctification remained everywhere the same purpose which was served in an acute way by the orgy, namely the incarnation within man of a supernatural being, and therefore presently of a god. Stated differently, the goal was self-deification. Only now this incarnation had to become a continuous personality pattern, so far as possible. Thus, the entire planned procedure for achieving consecration was directed to attaining this possession of the god himself here on earth.

But wherever there is belief in a transcendental god, all-powerful in contrast to his creatures, the goal of methodical sanctification can no longer be self-deification (in the sense in which the transcendental god is deified) and must become the acquisition of those religious qualities the god demands in men. The goal of sanctification becomes oriented to the world beyond and to ethics. The aim is no longer to possess god, for this cannot be done, but either to become his instrument or to be spiritually suffused by him. Spiritual suffusion is obviously closer to self-deification than is instrumentality. This difference had important consequences for the planned procedure of sanctification itself, as we shall later explain. But in the beginning of this development there were important points of agreement between the methods directed at instrumentality and those directed at spiritual suffusion. In both cases the average man had to eliminate from his everyday life whatever was not godlike, so that he himself might become more like god. The primary ungodlike factors were actually the average *habitus* of the human body and the everyday world, as those are given by nature.

At this early point in the development of soteriological methodology of sanctification, it was still directly linked with its magical precursor, the methods of which it merely rationalized and accommodated to its new views concerning the nature of the superhuman and the significance of religious sanctification. Experience taught that by the hysteroid "deadening" of the bodies of those with special religious qualifications it was possible to render such bodies anesthetic or cataleptic and to produce in them by suggestion sundry actions that normal neurological functioning could never produce. It had also been learned from experience that all sorts of visionary and spiritual phenomena might easily appear during such states. In different persons, these phenomena might consist in speaking with strange tongues, manifesting hypnotic and other suggestive powers, experiencing impulses toward mystical illumination and ethical conversion, or experiencing profound anguish over one's sins and joyous emotion deriving from suffusion by the spirit of the god. These states might even follow each other in rapid succession. It was a further lesson of experience that all these extraordinary capacities and manifestations would disappear following a surrender to the natural functions and needs of the body, or a surrender to the disturbing interests of everyday life. As the yearning for salvation developed, men everywhere drew inferences from these experiences with magic, inferences about the relationship of mental states to the natural functioning of the body and to the social and economic requirements of everyday life.

The specific soteriological methods and procedures for achieving sanctification are, in their most highly developed forms, practically all of Hindu provenience. In India they were undoubtedly developed in connection with procedures for the magical coercion of spirits. Even in India these procedures increasingly tended to become a methodology of self-deification, and indeed they never lost this tendency. Self-deification was the prevalent goal of sanctification, from the beginnings of the soma cult of intoxication in ancient Vedic times up through the development of sublime methods of intellectualist ecstasy and the elaboration of erotic orgies (whether in coarser or more refined form, and whether actually enacted in behavior or only imaginatively enacted within the cult), which to this day dominate the most popular form of Hindu religion, the cult of Krishna. The sublimated type of intellectualist ecstasy and the method of orgiastic dervishism were introduced into Islam, in milder forms, by Sufism. To this day Hindus are still the typical carriers of sublimated intellectualist ecstasy in that culture complex, even as far afield as Bosnia.

The two greatest powers of religious rationalism in history, the Roman church in the Occident and Confucianism in China, consistently suppressed this type of ecstasy in their domains. But Christianity also sublimated ecstasy into semi-erotic mysticism such as that of Saint Bernard, fervent Mariolatry, the quietism of the Counter Reformation, and the emotional piety of Zinzendorf. The exceptional nature of the experiences characteristic of all orgiastic cults, and certainly of all erotic ones, accounts for their having exerted no influence at all on everyday behavior, or at least no influence in the direction of increased rationalization or systematization —as seen clearly in the fact that the Hindu and dervish religiosities produced no methodology that aimed at the control of everyday living.

Yet the gap between unusual and routine religious experiences tends to be eliminated by evolution towards the systematization and rationalization of the methods for attaining religious sanctification. Out of the unlimited variety of subjective conditions which may be engendered by methodical procedures of sanctification, certain of them may finally emerge as of central importance, not only because they represent psycho-physical states of extraordinary quality, but because they also appear to provide a secure and continuous possession of the distinctive religious acquirement. This is the *assurance of grace* (*certitudo salutis, perseverantia gratia*). This certainly may be characterized by a more mystical or by a more actively ethical coloration, about which more will be said presently. But in either case, it constitutes the conscious possession of a lasting, integrated foundation for the conduct of life. To heighten the conscious awareness of this religious possession, orgiastic ecstasy and irrational, emotional, and merely irritating methods of deadening sensation are replaced, principally by planned reductions of bodily functioning, such as can be achieved by continuous malnutrition, sexual abstinence, regulation of respiration, and the like. In addition, thinking and other psychological processes are trained in a systematic concentration of the soul upon whatever is alone essential in religion. Examples of such psychological training are found in the Hindu techniques of Yoga, the continuous repetition of sacred syllables (e.g., *Om*), meditation focused on circles and other geometrical figures, and various exercises designed to effect a planned evacuation of the consciousness.

But in order to further secure continuity and uniformity in the possession of the religious good, the rationalization of the methodology of sanctification finally evolved even beyond the methods just mentioned to an apparent inversion, a planned limitation of the exercises to those devices which tend to insure continuity of the religious mood. This meant the abandonment of all techniques that are irrational from the viewpoint of hygiene. For just as every sort of intoxication, whether it be the orgiastic ecstasy of heroes in erotic orgies or the ecstasy of terpsichorean frenzies, inevitably culminates in physical collapse, so hysterical suffusion with religious emotionalism leads to psychic collapse, which in religious terminology is termed a state of profound abandonment by god.

In Greece the cultivation of disciplined martial heroism finally attenuated the warrior ecstasy into the perpetual equableness of *Sophrosyne,* tolerating only the purely musical, rhythmically engendered forms of *ekstasis,* and carefully evaluating the ethos of music for political correctness. In the same way, but in a more thorough manner, Confucian rationalism permitted only the pentatonic scale in music. Similarly, the monastic procedural plan for attaining sanctification developed increasingly in the direction of rationalization, culminating in India in the salvation methodology of ancient Buddhism and in the Occident in the Jesuit monastic order which exerted the greatest historical influence. Thus, all these methodologies of sanctification developed a combined physical and psychic regimen and an equally methodical regulation of the manner and scope of all thought and action, thus producing in the individual the most completely alert, voluntary, and anti-instinctual control over his own physical and psychological processes, and insuring the systematic regulation of life in subordination to the religious end. The goals, the specific contents, and the actual results of the planned procedures were very variable.

That people differ widely in their religious capacities was found to be true in every religion based on a systematic procedure of sanctification, regardless of the specific goal of sanctification and the particular manner in which it was implemented. As it had been recognized that not everyone possesses the charisma by which he might evoke in himself the experiences leading to rebirth as a magician, so it was also recognized that not everyone possesses the charisma that makes possible the continuous maintenance in everyday life of the distinctive religious mood which assures the lasting certainty of grace. Therefore, rebirth seemed to be accessible only to an aristocracy of those possessing religious qualifications. Just as magicians had been recognized as possessing distinctive magical qualities, so also the religious virtuosi who work methodically at their salvation were now given a distinctive religious status within the community of the faithful, and within this circle they attained a degree of honor appropriate to their status.

In India all the sacred laws concerned themselves with the ascetic in this sense, since most of the Hindu religions of salvation were monastic. The earliest Christian sources represent these religious virtuosi as comprising a particular category, distinguished from their comrades in the community, and they later constituted the monastic orders. In Protestantism they formed the ascetic sects or pietistic conventicles. In Judaism they were the *perushim* (*Pharisaioi*), an aristocracy with respect to salvation which stood in contrast to the *am haarez*. In Islam they were the dervishes, and among the dervishes the particular virtuosi were the authentic Sufis. In the Skoptzi sect they constituted the esoteric community of the castrated. We shall later return to the important sociological consequences of these groups.

When methodical techniques for attaining sanctification stressed ethical conduct based on religious sentiment, one practical result was the transcendence of particular desires and emotions of raw human nature which had not hitherto been controlled by religion. We must determine for each particular religion whether it regarded cowardice, brutality, selfishness, sensuality, or some other natural drive as the one most prone to divert the individual from his charismatic character. This matter belongs among the most important substantive characteristics of any particular religion. But the methodical religious doctrine of sanctification always remains, in this sense of transcending human nature, an ethic of virtuosi. Like magical charisma, it always requires demonstration by the virtuosi. As we have already established, religious virtuosi possess authentic certainty of their sanctification only as long as their own virtuoso religious temper continues to maintain itself in spite of all temptations. This holds true whether the religious adept is a brother in a world-conquering order like that of the Muslims at the time of Umar or whether he is a world-fleeing ascetic like most monks of either the Christian or the less consistent Jainist type. It is equally true of the Buddhist monk, a virtuoso of world-rejecting contemplation, and the ancient Christian, who was sometimes an exponent of passive martyrdom and sometimes, like the ascetic Protestant, a virtuoso of the demonstration of religious merit in one's calling. Finally, this holds true of the formal legalism of the Pharisaic Jew and of the acomistic goodness of such persons as St. Francis. This maintenance of the certainty of sanctification varied in its specific character, depending on the type of religious salvation involved, but it always—both in the case of the Buddhist *arhat* and the case of the pristine Christian

—required the upholding of religious and ethical standards, and hence the avoidance of at least the most venal sins.

Demonstration of the certainty of grace takes very different forms, depending on the concept of religious salvation in the particular religion. In pristine Christianity, a person of positive religious qualification, namely one who had been baptized, was bound never again to fall into any mortal sin. "Mortal sin" designates the type of sin which destroys religious qualification. Therefore, it is unpardonable, or at least capable of remission only at the hands of someone specially qualified by virtue of his possession of charisma to endow the sinner anew with religious charisma (the loss of which constituted mortal sin). When this virtuoso doctrine became untenable in practice within the ancient Christian communities, the Montanist group clung firmly and consistently to one virtuoso requirement, that the sin of cowardice remain unpardonable, quite as the Islamic religion of heroic warriors unfailingly punished apostasy with death. Accordingly, the Montanists segregated themselves from the mass church of the average Christians when the persecutions under Decius and Diocletian made even this virtuoso requirement impractical, in view of the interest of the priests in maintaining the largest possible membership in the community.

As we have already stated at a number of points, the specific character of the certification of salvation and also of the associated practical conduct is completely different in religions which differently represent the character of the promised salvation, the possession of which assures blessedness. Salvation may be viewed as the distinctive gift of active ethical behavior performed in the awareness that god directs this behavior, i.e., that the actor is an instrument of god. We shall designate this type of attitude toward salvation, which is characterized by a methodical procedure for achieving religious salvation, as "ascetic." This designation is for our purposes here, and we do not in any way deny that this term may be and has been used in another and wider sense. The contrast between our usage and the wider usage may become clearer later on in this work.

Religious virtuosity, in addition to subjecting the natural drives to a systematic patterning of life, always leads to the control of relationships within communal life, the conventional virtues of which are inevitably unheroic and utilitarian, and leads further to an altogether radical religious and ethical criticism. Not only do the simple, "natural" virtues within the world not guarantee salvation, but they actually place salvation in hazard by producing illusions as to that which alone is indispensable. The "world" in the religious sense, i.e., the domain of social relationships, is therefore a realm of temptations. The world is full of temptations, not only because it is the site of sensual pleasures which are ethically irrational and completely diverting from things divine, but even more because it fosters in the religiously average person complacent self-sufficiency and self-righteousness in the fulfillment of common obligations, at the expense of the uniquely necessary concentration on active achievements leading to salvation.

XI. Asceticism, Mysticism, and Salvation Religion

Concentration upon the actual pursuit of salvation may entail a formal withdrawal from the "world": from social and psychological ties with the family, from the possession of worldly goods, and from political, economic, artistic, and erotic activities—in short, from all creaturely interests. One with such an attitude may regard any participation in these affairs as an acceptance of the world, leading to alienation from god. This is "world-rejecting asceticism" (*weltablehnende Askese*).

On the other hand, the unique concentration of human behavior on activities leading to salvation may require the participation within the world (or more precisely: within the institutions of the world but in opposition to them) of the religious individual's idiosyncratically sacred religious mood and his qualifications as the elect instrument of god. This is "inner-worldly asceticism" (*innerweltliche Askese*). In this case the world is presented to the religious virtuoso as his responsibility. He may have the obligation to transform the world in accordance with his ascetic ideals, in which case the ascetic will become a rational reformer or revolutionary on the basis of a theory of natural rights. Examples of this were seen in the "Parliament of the Saints" under Cromwell, in the Quaker State of Pennsylvania, and in other types of radically pietistic conventicle communism.

As a result of the different levels of religious qualification, such a congery of ascetics always tends to become an aristocratic, exclusive organization within or definitely outside the world of the average people who surround these ascetics. They operate on the principle of the social class system, in this regard. Such a religiously specialized group might be able to master the world, but it still could not raise the religious endowment of the average person to its own level of virtuosity. Any rational religious associations that ignored this obvious fact were bound sooner or later to experience in their own everyday existence the consequences of differences in religious endowment.

From the point of view of the basic values of asceticism, the world as a whole continues to constitute a *massa perditionis*. The only remaining alternative is a renunciation of the demand that the world conform to religious claims. Consequently, if a demonstration of religious fidelity is still to be made within the institutional structure of the world, then the world, for the very reason that it inevitably remains a natural vessel of sin, becomes a challenge for the demonstration of the ascetic temper and for the strongest possible attacks against the world's sins. The world abides in the lowly state appropriate to its status as a created thing. Therefore, any sensuous surrender to the world's goods may imperil concentration upon and possession of the ultimate good of salvation, and may be a symptom of unholiness of spirit and impossibility of rebirth. Nevertheless, the world as a creation of god, whose power comes to expression in it despite its creatureliness, provides the only medium through which one's unique religious charisma may prove itself by means of rational ethical conduct, so that one may become and remain certain of one's own state of grace.

Hence, as the field provided for this active certification, the order of the world in which the ascetic is situated becomes for him a vocation which he must fulfill rationally. As a consequence, and although the enjoyment of wealth is forbidden to the ascetic, it becomes his vocation to engage in economic activity which is faithful to rationalized ethical requirements and which conforms to strict legality. If success supervenes upon such acquisitive activity, it is regarded as the manifestation of god's blessing upon the labor of the pious man and of god's pleasure with his economic pattern of life.

Certain other manifestations of inner-worldly asceticism must be noted. Any excess of emotional feeling for one's fellow man is prohibited as being a deification of the creaturely, which denies the unique value of the divine gift of grace. Yet it is man's vocation to participate rationally and soberly in the various rational, purposive institutions of the world and in their objective goals as set by god's creation. Similarly, any eroticism that tends to deify the human creature is proscribed. On the other hand, it is a divinely imposed vocation of man "to soberly produce children" (as the Puritans expressed it) within marriage. Then, too, there is a prohibition against the exercise of force by an individual against other human beings for reasons of passion or revenge, and above all for purely personal motives. However, it is divinely enjoined that the rationally ordered state shall suppress and punish sins and rebelliousness. Finally, all personal secular enjoyment of power is forbidden as a deification of the creaturely, though it is held that a rational legal order within society is pleasing to god.

The person who lives as a worldly ascetic is a rationalist, not only in the sense that he rationally systematizes his own personal patterning of life, but also in his rejection of everything that is ethically irrational, esthetic, or dependent upon his own emotional reactions to the world and its institutions. The distinctive goal always remains the alert, methodical control of one's own pattern of life and behavior. This type of inner-worldly asceticism included, above all, ascetic Protestantism, which taught the principle of loyal fulfillment of obligations within the framework of the world as the sole method of proving religious merit, though its several branches demonstrated this tenet with varying degrees of consistency.

But the distinctive content of salvation may not be an active quality of conduct, that is, an awareness of having executed the divine will; it may instead be a subjective condition of a distinctive kind, the most notable form of which is mystic illumination. This too is confined to a minority who have particular religious qualifications, and among them only as the end product of the systematic execution of a distinctive type of activity, namely contemplation. For the activity of contemplation to succeed in achieving its goal of mystic illumination, the extrusion of all everyday mundane interests is always required. According to the experience of the Quakers, God can speak within one's soul only when the creaturely element in man is altogether silent. In agreement with this notion, if not with these very words, is all contemplative mysticism from Lao Tzu and the Buddha up to Tauler.

These subjective and mystical beliefs may result in absolute flight from the world. Such a contemplative flight from the world, characteristic of ancient Buddhism and to some degree characteristic of all Asiatic and Near Eastern forms of salvation, seems to resemble the ascetic world view—but it is necessary to make a very clear distinction between the two. In the sense employed here, "world-rejecting asceticism" is primarily oriented to activity within the world. Only activity within the world helps the ascetic to attain that for which he strives, a capacity for action by god's grace. The ascetic derives renewed assurances of his state of grace from his awareness that his possession of the central religious salvation gives him the power to act and his awareness that through his actions he serves god. He feels himself to be a warrior in behalf of god, regardless of who the enemy is and what the means of doing battle are. Furthermore, his opposition to the world is psychologically felt, not as a flight, but as a repeated victory over ever new temptations which he is bound to combat actively, time and again. The ascetic who rejects the world sustains at least the negative inner psychological relationship with it which is presupposed in the struggle against it. It is therefore more appropriate in his case to speak of a "rejection of the world" than of a "flight from the world." Flight is much more characteristic of the contemplative mystic.

In contrast to asceticism, contemplation is primarily the quest to achieve rest in god and in him alone. It entails inactivity, and in its most consistent form it entails the cessation of thought, the nemesis of everything that in any way reminds one of the world, and of course the absolute minimization of all outer and inner activity. By these paths the mystic achieves that subjective condition which may be enjoyed as the possession of, or mystical union with, the divine. This is a distinctive organization of the emotions which seems to promise a certain type of knowledge. To be sure, the subjective emphasis may be more upon the distinctive and extraordinary content of this knowledge or more upon the emotional coloration of the possession of this knowledge; objectively, the latter is decisive.

The unique character of mystical knowledge consists in the fact that, although it becomes more incommunicable the more strongly it is characterized by idiosyncratic content, it is nevertheless recognized as knowledge. For mystical knowledge is not new knowledge of any facts or doctrines, but rather the perception of an overall meaning in the world. This usage of "knowledge" is intended wherever the term occurs in the numerous formulations of mystics; it denotes a practical form of knowledge. Such *gnosis* is basically a "possession" of something from which there may be derived a new practical orientation to the world, and under certain circumstances even new and communicable items of knowledge. But even these items will constitute knowledge of values and non-values within the world. We are not interested here in the details of this general problem, but only in the negative effect upon behavior which is distinctive of all contemplation, an effect so opposed to the effect upon behavior of asceticism, in our sense of the latter term.

The contrast in effects upon behavior is self-explanatory, and pending a more thorough exposition, we may strongly emphasize here that the distinction between world-rejecting asceticism and world-fleeing contemplation is fluid. For world-fleeing contemplation must originally be associated with a considerable degree of systematically rationalized patterning of life. Only this, indeed, leads to concentration upon the boon of salvation. Yet, rationalization is only an instrument for attaining the goal of contemplation and is of an essentially negative type, consisting in the avoidance of interruptions caused by nature and the social milieu. Contemplation does not necessarily become a passive abandonment to dreams or a simple self-hypnosis, though it may approach these states in practice. On the contrary, the distinctive road to contemplation is a very energetic concentration upon certain truths. The decisive aspect of this process is not the content of these truths, which frequently seems very simple to non-mystics, but rather the type of emphasis placed upon the truths. The mystical truths come to assume a central position within, and to exert an integrating influence upon, the total view of the world. In Buddhism, no one becomes one of the illuminated by explicitly affirming the obviously highly trivial formulations of the central Buddhist dogma, or even by achieving a penetrating understanding of the central dogma. The only way to become illuminated is the aforementioned concentration of thought, together with the various other procedures for winning salvation. The illumination consists essentially in a unique quality of feeling or, more concretely, in the felt emotional unity of knowledge and volitional mood which provides the mystic with decisive assurance of his religious state of grace.

For the ascetic too, the perception of the divine through emotion and intellect is of central importance, only in his case it is of a "motor" type, so to speak. The ascetic's assurance of grace is achieved when he is conscious that he has succeeded in becoming a tool of his god, through rationalized ethical action completely oriented to god. But for the contemplative mystic, who neither desires to be nor can be the god's "instrument," but desires only to become the god's "vessel," the ascetic's ethical struggle, whether of a positive or a negative type, appears to be a perpetual externalization of the divine in the direction of some peripheral function. For this reason, ancient Buddhism recommended inaction as the precondition for the maintenance of the state of grace, and in any case Buddhism enjoined the avoidance of every type of rational, purposive activity, which it regarded as the most dangerous form of secularization. On the other hand, the contemplation of the mystic appears to the ascetic as indolent, religiously sterile, and ascetically reprehensible self-indulgence—a wallowing in self-created emotions prompted by the deification of the creaturely.

From the standpoint of a contemplative mystic, the ascetic appears, by virtue of his transcendental self-maceration and struggles, and especially by virtue of his ascetically rationalized conduct within the world, to be forever involved in all the burdens of created things, confronting insoluble tensions between violence and generosity, between empirical reality and love. The ascetic is therefore regarded as permanently alienated from unity with god, and as forced into contradictions and compromises that are alien to salvation. But from the converse standpoint of the ascetic, the contemplative mystic appears not to be thinking of god, the enhancement of his kingdom and glory, or the fulfillment of his will, but rather to be thinking exclusively about himself. Therefore the mystic lives in everlasting inconsistency, since by reason of the very fact that he is alive he must inevitably provide for the maintenance of his own life. This is particularly true when the contemplative mystic lives within the world and its institutions. There is a sense in which the mystic who flees the world is more dependent upon the world than is the ascetic. The ascetic can maintain himself as an anchorite, winning the certainty of his state of grace through the labors he expends in the effort to maintain himself as an anchorite. Not so the contemplative mystic. If he is to live consistently according to his theory, he must maintain his life only by means of what nature or men voluntarily donate to him. This requires that he live on berries in the woods, which are not always available, or on alms. This was actually the case among the most consistent Hindu *shramanas,* and it accounts for the very strict prohibition in all Hindu *bhikshu* regulations (and found also among the Buddhists) against receiving anything that has not been given freely.

In any case, the contemplative mystic lives on whatever gifts the world may present to him, and he would be unable to stay alive if the world were not constantly engaged in that very labor which the mystic brands as sinful and leading to alienation from god. For the Buddhist monk, agriculture is the most reprehensible of all occupations, because it causes violent injury to various forms of life in the soil. Yet the alms he collects consist principally of agricultural products. In circumstances like these, the mystic's inevitable feeling that he is an aristocrat with respect to salvation reaches striking expression, culminating in the mystic's abandonment of the world, the unilluminated, and those incapable of complete illumination, to their inevitable and ineluctable fate. It will be recalled that the central and almost sole lay virtue among the Buddhists was originally the veneration of the monks, who alone belonged to the religious community, and whom it was incumbent upon the laity to support with alms. However, it is a general rule that every human being acts in some fashion, and even the mystic perforce acts. Yet he minimizes activity just because it can never give him certainty of his state of grace, and what is more, because it may divert him from union with the divine. The ascetic, on the other hand, finds the certification of his state of grace precisely in his behavior in the world.

The contrast between the ascetic and mystical modes of behavior is clearest when the full implications of world-rejection and world-flight are not drawn. The ascetic, when he wishes to act within the world, that is, to practice inner-worldly asceticism, must become afflicted with a sort of happy stupidity regarding any question about the meaning of the world, for he must not worry about such questions. Hence, it is no accident that inner-worldly asceticism reached its most consistent development on the foundation of the Calvinist god's absolute inexplicability, utter remoteness from every human criterion, and unsearchableness as to his motives. Thus, the inner-worldly ascetic is the recognized "man of a vocation," who neither inquires about nor finds it necessary to inquire about the meaning of his actual practice of a vocation within the world, the total framework of which is not his responsibility but his god's. For him it suffices that through his rational actions in this world he is personally executing the will of god, which is unsearchable in its ultimate significance.

On the other hand, the contemplative mystic is not in a position to realize his primary aim of perceiving the essential meaning of the world and then comprehending it in a rational form, for the very reason that he has already conceived of the essential meaning of the world as a unity beyond all empirical reality. Mystical contemplation has not always resulted in a flight from the world in the sense of an avoidance of every contact with the social milieu. On the contrary, the mystic may also require of himself the maintenance of his state of grace against every pressure of the mundane order, as an index of the enduring character of that very state of grace. In that case, even the mystic's position within the institutional framework of the world becomes a vocation, but one leading in an altogether different direction from any vocation produced by inner-worldly asceticism.

Neither asceticism nor contemplation affirms the world as such. The ascetic rejects the world's empirical character of creatureliness and ethical irrationality, and rejects its ethical temptations to sensual indulgence, to epicurean satisfaction, and to reliance upon natural joys and gifts. But at the same time he affirms individual rational activity within the institutional framework of the world, affirming it to be his responsibility as well as his means for securing certification of his state of grace. On the other hand, the contemplative mystic living within the world regards action, particularly action performed within the world's institutional framework, as in its very nature a temptation against which he must maintain his state of grace.

The contemplative mystic minimizes his activity by resigning himself to the order of the world as it is, and lives incognito, so to speak, as humble people have always done, since god has ordained once and for all that man must live in the world. The activity of the contemplative mystic within the world is characterized by a distinctive brokenness, colored by humility. He is constantly striving to escape from activity in the world back to the quietness and inwardness of his god. Conversely, the ascetic, whenever he acts in conformity with his type, is certain to become god's instrument. For this reason the ascetic's humility, which he considers a necessary obligation incumbent upon a creature of god, is always of dubious genuineness. Therefore the success of the ascetic's action is a success of the god himself, who has contributed to the action's success, or at the very least the success is a special sign of divine blessing upon the ascetic and his activity. But for the genuine mystic, no success which may crown his activity within the world can have any significance with respect to salvation. For him, his maintenance of true humility within the world is his sole warranty for the conclusion that his soul has not fallen prey to the snares of the world. As a rule, the more the genuine mystic remains within the world, the more broken his attitude toward it becomes, in contrast to the proud aristocratic feeling with respect to salvation entertained by the contemplative mystic who lives apart from the world.

For the ascetic, the certainty of salvation always demonstrates itself in rational action, integrated as to meaning, end, and means, and governed by principles and rules. Conversely, for the mystic who actually possesses a subjectively appropriated state of salvation the result of this subjective condition may be antinomianism. His salvation manifests itself not in any sort of activity but in a subjective condition and its idiosyncratic quality. He feels himself no longer bound by any rule of conduct; regardless of his behavior, he is certain of salvation. Paul had to struggle with this consequence, among others, of mystical contemplation (*panta moi eksestin*); and in numerous other contexts the abandonment of rules for conduct has been an occasional result of the mystical quest for salvation.

For the ascetic, moreover, the divine imperative may require of human creatures an unconditional subjection of the world to the norms of religious virtue, and indeed a revolutionary transformation of the world for this purpose. In that event, the ascetic will emerge from his remote and cloistered cell to take his place in the world as a prophet in opposition to the world. But he will always demand of the world an ethically rational order and discipline, corresponding to his own methodical self-discipline. Now a mystic may arrive at a similar position in relation to the world. His sense of divine inwardness, the chronic and quiet euphoria of his solitary contemplative possession of substantively divine salvation, may become transformed into an acute feeling of sacred possession by or possession of the god who is speaking in and through him. He will then wish to bring eternal salvation to men as soon as they have prepared, as the mystic himself has done, a place for god upon earth, i.e., in their souls. But in this case the result will be the emergence of the mystic as a magician who causes his power to be felt among gods and demons; and this may have the practical consequence of the mystic's becoming a mystagogue, something which has actually happened very often.

If the mystic does not follow this path towards becoming a mystagogue, for a variety of reasons which we hope to discuss later, he may bear witness to his god by doctrine alone. In that case his revolutionary preaching to the world will be chiliastically irrational, scorning every thought of a rational order in the world. He will regard the absoluteness of his own universal acosmistic feeling of love as completely adequate for himself, and indeed regard this feeling as the only one acceptable to his god as the foundation for a mystically renewed community among men, because this feeling alone derives from a divine source. The transformation of a mysticism remote from the world into one characterized by chiliastic and revolutionary tendencies took place frequently, most impressively in the revolutionary mysticism of the sixteenth-century Baptists. The contrary transformation has also occurred, as in the conversion of John Lilburne to Quakerism.

To the extent that an inner-worldly religion of salvation is determined by contemplative features, the usual result is the acceptance of the secular social structure which happens to be at hand, an acceptance that is relatively indifferent to the world but at least humble before it. A mystic of the type of Tauler completes his day's work and then seeks contemplative union with his god in the evening, going forth to his usual work the next morning, as Tauler movingly suggests, in the correct inner state. Similarly, Lao Tzu taught that one recognizes the man who has achieved union with the Tao by his humility and by his self-depreciation before other men. The mystic component in Lutheranism, for which the highest bliss available in this world is the ultimate *unio mystica,* was responsible along with other factors for the indifference of the Lutheran church towards the external organization of the preaching of the gospel, and also for that church's anti-ascetic and traditional-istic character.

In any case, the typical mystic is never a man of conspicuous social activity, nor is he at all prone to accomplish any rational transformation of the mundane order on the basis of a methodical pattern of life directed toward external success. Wherever genuine mysticism did give rise to communal action, such action was characterized by the acosmism of the mystical feeling of love. Mysticism may exert this kind of psychological effect, thus tending—despite the apparent demands of logic—to favor the creation of communities (*gemeinschaftsbildend*).

The core of the mystical concept of the oriental Christian church was a firm conviction that Christian brotherly love, when sufficiently strong and pure, must necessarily lead to unity in all things, even in dogmatic beliefs. In other words, men who sufficiently love one another, in the Johannine sense of love, will also think alike and, because of the very irrationality of their common feeling, act in a solidary fashion which is pleasing to God. Because of this concept, the Eastern church could dispense with an infallibly rational authority in matters of doctrine. The same view is basic to the Slavophile conception of the community, both within and beyond the church. Some forms of this notion were also common in ancient Christianity. The same conception is at the basis of Muhammad's belief that formal doctrinal authorities can be dispensed with. Finally, this conception along with other factors accounts for the minimization of organization in the monastic communities of early Buddhism.

Conversely, to the extent that an inner-worldly religion of salvation is determined by distinctively ascetical tendencies, the usual result is practical rationalism, in the sense of the maximization of rational action as such, the maximization of a methodical systematization of the external conduct of life, and the maximization of the rational organization and institutionalization of mundane social systems, whether monastic communities or theocracies.

The decisive historical difference between the predominantly oriental and Asiatic types of salvation religion and those found primarily in the Occident is that the former usually culminate in contemplation and the latter in asceticism. The great importance of this distinction, even for our purely empirical consideration of religions, is in no way diminished by the fact that the distinction is a fluid one, recurrent combinations of mystical and ascetic characteristics demonstrating that these heterogeneous elements may combine, as in the monastic religiosity of the Occident.

In India, even so ascetical a planned procedure for achieving salvation as that of the Jain monks culminated in a purely contemplative and mystical ultimate goal; and in Eastern Asia, Buddhism became the characteristic religion of salvation. In the Occident, on the other hand, apart from a few representatives of a distinctive quietism found only in modern times, even religions of an explicitly mystical type regularly became transformed into an active pursuit of virtue, which was naturally ascetical in the main. Stated more precisely, there occurred along the way an inner selection of motivations which placed the primary preference upon some type of active conduct, generally a type pointing toward asceticism, and which implemented this motivational preference. Neither the mystical contemplativeness of St. Bernard and his followers, nor Franciscan spirituality, nor the contemplative trends among the Baptists and the Jesuits, nor even the emotional suffusions of Zinzendorf were able to prevent either the community or the individual mystic from attributing superior importance to conduct and to the demonstration of grace through conduct, though this was conceptualized very differently in each case. The stress upon conduct might be purely ascetic or it might be intersected by certain contemplative emphases. It will be recalled that Meister Eckhart finally placed Martha above Mary, notwithstanding the pronouncements of Jesus.

But to some extent this emphasis upon conduct was characteristic of Christianity from the very outset. Even in the earliest period, when all sorts of irrational charismatic gifts of the spirit were regarded as the decisive hallmark of sanctity, Christian apologetics had already given a distinctive answer to the question of how one might distinguish the divine origin of the pneumatic achievements of Christ and the Christians from comparable phenomena that were of Satanic or demonic origin: this answer was that the manifest effect of Christianity upon the morality of its adherents certified its divine origin. No Hindu could make this kind of statement.

There are a number of reasons for this basic distinction between mysticism and asceticism, but at this point it is only necessary to stress the following aspects of the distinction.

First to be considered is the fact that the concept of a transcendental, absolutely omnipotent god, implying the utterly subordinate and creaturely character of the world created by him out of nothing, arose in Asia Minor and was imposed upon the Occident. One result of this for the Occident was that any planned procedure for achieving salvation faced a road that was permanently closed to any self-deification and to any genuinely mystical subjective possession of god, at least in the unique mystical sense of "possession of god," because this appeared to be a blasphemous deification of a mere created thing. The path to the ultimate pantheistic consequences of the mystical position was blocked, this path being always regarded as heterodox. On the contrary, salvation was always regarded as having the character of an ethical justification before god, which ultimately could be accomplished and maintained only by some sort of active conduct within the world. This certification of the really divine quality of the mystical possession of salvation (certification before the ultimate judgment of the mystic himself) could be arrived at through the path of activity alone. Activity in turn introduced into mysticism paradoxes, tensions, and the loss of the mystic's ultimate distance from god. All this was spared to Hindu mysticism. For the Asiatic the world is something simply presented to man, something which has been in the nature of things from all eternity; while for the occidental, even for the occidental mystic, the world is a work which has been created or performed, and not even the ordinances of the world are eternal. Consequently, in the Occident mystical salvation could not be found simply in the consciousness of an absolute union with a supreme and wise order of things as the only true being. Nor, on the other hand, could a work of divine origin even be regarded in the Occident as a possible object of absolute rejection, as it was in the flight from the world characteristic of the Orient.

However, this decisive contrast between oriental and occidental religions is closely related to the character of Asiatic salvation religions as pure religions of intellectuals who never abandoned the concept of the empirical world. For the Hindu, there was actually a way leading directly from insight into the ultimate consequences of the *karma* chain of causality, to illumination, and thence to a unity of knowledge and action. This way remained forever closed to every religion that faced the absolute paradox of a perfect god's creation of a permanently imperfect world. Indeed, in this latter type of religion, the intellectual mastery of the world leads away from god, not toward him. From the practical point of view, those instances of occidental mysticism which have a purely philosophical foundation stand closest to the Asiatic type.

Further to be considered in accounting for the basic distinction between occidental and oriental religion are various practical factors. Particular emphasis must be placed on the fact that occidental Rome alone developed and maintained a rational law, for various reasons yet to be explained. In the Occident the relationship of man to god became, in a distinctive fashion, a sort of legally definable relationship of subjection. Indeed, the question of salvation can be settled by a sort of legal process, a method which was later distinctively developed by Anselm of Canterbury. Such a legalistic planned procedure of achieving salvation could never be adopted by the oriental religions which posited an impersonal divine power or which posited, instead of a god standing above the world, a god standing within a world which is self-regulated by the causal chains of *karma*. Nor could the legalistic direction be taken by religions teaching concepts of Tao, belief in the celestial ancestor gods of the Chinese emperor, or, above all, belief in the Asiatic popular gods. In all these cases the highest form of piety took a pantheistic form, and one which turned practical motivations towards contemplation.

Another aspect of the rational character of a methodical procedure for achieving salvation was in origin partly Roman, partly Jewish. The Greeks, despite all the misgivings of the urban patriciate in regard to the Dionysiac cult of intoxication, set a positive value upon ecstasy, both the acute orgiastic type of divine intoxication and the milder form of euphoria induced primarily by rhythm and music, as engendering an awareness of the uniquely divine. Indeed, among the Greeks the ruling classes especially lived with this mild form of ecstasy from their very childhood. Since the time when the discipline of the hoplites had become dominant, Greece had lacked a social class possessing the prestige of the official nobility in Rome. Social relationships in Greece were in all respects simpler and less feudal. In Rome the nobles, who constituted a rational nobility of office of increasing range, and who possessed whole cities and provinces as client holdings of single families, completely rejected ecstasy, like the dance, as utterly unseemly and unworthy of a nobleman's sense of honor. This is obvious even in the terminology employed by the Romans to render the Greek word for ecstasy (*ekstasis*) into Latin: *superstitio.* Cultic dances were performed only among the most ancient colleges of priests, and in the specific sense of a round of dances, only among the *fratres arvales,* and then only behind closed doors, after the departure of the congregation. Most Romans regarded dancing and music as unseemly, and so Rome remained absolutely uncreative in these arts. The Romans experienced the same distaste towards exercises in the *gymnasium,* which the Spartans had created as an arena for planned exercise. The Senate proscribed the Dionysiac cult of intoxication. The rejection by Rome's world-conquering military-official nobility of every type of ecstasy and of all preoccupation with individually planned procedures for attaining salvation (which corresponds closely to the equally strong antipathy of the Confucian bureaucracy towards all methodologies of salvation) was therefore one of the sources of a strictly empirical rationalism with a thoroughly practical political orientation.

As Christian communities developed in the Occident, they found this contempt for ecstatic procedures to be characteristic of all the various religions that flourished on essentially Roman territory. The Christian community of Rome in particular adopted this attitude against ecstasy quite consciously and consistently. In no instance did this community accept on its own initiative any irrational element, from charismatic prophecy to the greatest innovations in church music, into the religion or the culture. Early Christianity was infinitely poorer than the Hellenistic Orient and the community of Corinth, not only in theological thinkers but also, as the sources seem to suggest, in every sort of manifestation of the spirit (*pneuma*). Whether despite this lack of theology and *pneuma* or because of it, the soberly practical rationalism of Christianity, the most important legacy of Rome to the Christian church, almost everywhere set the tone of a dogmatic and ethical systematization of the faith, as is well known. The subsequent development of the planned procedures of salvation in the Occident continued along similar lines. The ascetic requirements of the old Benedictine regulations and the reforms at Cluny are, when measured by Hindu or oriental standards, extremely modest and obviously adapted to novices recruited from the higher social classes. Yet, it is precisely in the Occident that *labor* emerges as the distinctive mark of Christian monasticism, and as an instrument of both hygiene and asceticism. This emphasis came to the strongest expression in the starkly simple, methodical regulations of the Cistercians. Even the mendicant monks, in contrast to their monastic counterparts in India, were forced into the service of the hierarchy and compelled to serve rational purposes, shortly after their appearance in the Occident. These rational purposes included preaching, the supervision of heretics, and systematic charity, which in the Occident was developed into an actual enterprise (*Betrieb*). Finally, the Jesuit order expelled all the unhygienic elements of the older asceticism, becoming the most completely rational discipline for the purposes of the church. This development is obviously connected with the next point we are to consider.

The occidental church is a uniformly rational organization with a monarchical head and a centralized control of piety. That is, it is headed not only by a personal transcendental god, but also by a terrestrial ruler of enormous power, who actively controls the lives of his subjects. Such a figure is lacking in the religions of Eastern Asia, partly for historical reasons, partly because of the nature of the religions in question. Even Lamaism, which has a strong organization, does not have the rigidity of a bureaucracy.

The Asiatic hierarchs in Taoism and the other hereditary patriarchs of Chinese and Hindu sects were always partly mystagogues, partly the objects of anthropolatric veneration, and partly—as in the cases of the Dalai Lama and Taschi Lama—the chiefs of a completely monastic religion of magical character. Only in the Occident, where the monks became the disciplined army of a rational bureaucracy of office, did asceticism directed toward the outer world become increasingly systematized into a methodology of active, rational conduct of life.

Moreover, only in the Occident was the additional step taken—by ascetic Protestantism—of translating rational asceticism into the life of the world. The inner-worldly order of dervishes in Islam cultivated a planned procedure for achieving salvation, but this procedure, for all its variations, was oriented ultimately to the mystical quest for salvation of the Sufis. This search of the dervishes for salvation, deriving from Hindu and Persian sources, might have orgiastic, spiritualistic, or contemplative characteristics in different instances, but in no case did it constitute "asceticism" in the special sense of that term which we have employed. Hindus have played a leading role in dervish orgies as far afield as Bosnia. The asceticism of the dervishes is not, like that of ascetic Protestants, a religious ethic of vocation, for the religious actions of the dervishes have very little relationship to their secular occupations, and in their scheme secular vocations have at best a purely external relationship to the planned procedure of salvation. Even so, the procedure of salvation might exert direct effects on one's occupational behavior. The simple, pious dervish is, other things being equal, more reliable than a non-religious man, in the same way that the pious Parsee is prosperous as a businessman because of his strict adherence to the rigid injunction to be honest.

But an unbroken unity integrating in systematic fashion an ethic of vocation in the world with assurance of religious salvation was the unique creation of ascetic Protestantism alone. Furthermore, only in the Protestant ethic of vocation does the world, despite all its creaturely imperfections, possess unique and religious significance as the object through which one fulfills his duties by rational behavior according to the will of an absolutely transcendental god. When success crowns rational, sober, purposive behavior of the sort not oriented exclusively to worldly acquisition, such success is construed as a sign that god's blessing rests upon such behavior. This inner-worldly asceticism had a number of distinctive consequences not found in any other religion. This religion demanded of the believer, not celibacy, as in the case of the monk, but the avoidance of all erotic pleasure; not poverty, but the elimination of all idle and exploitative enjoyment of unearned wealth and income, and the avoidance of all feudalistic, sensuous ostentation of wealth; not the ascetic death-in-life of the cloister, but an alert, rationally controlled patterning of life, and the avoidance of all surrender to the beauty of the world, to art, or to one's own moods and emotions. The clear and uniform goal of this asceticism was the disciplining and methodical organization of the whole pattern of life. Its typical representative was the "man of a vocation," and its unique result was the rational organization and institutionalization of social relationships.

Another major theory regarding the attainment of salvation rejects the individual's own labors as completely inadequate for the purpose of salvation. From this point of view, salvation is accessible only as a consequence of the achievement of some greatly endowed hero, or even the achievement of a god who has become incarnate for this very purpose and whose grace will redound to the credit of his devotees, *ex opere operato*. Grace might also become available as a direct effect of magical activities, or it might be distributed to men out of the excess of grace which had accumulated as a result of the human or divine savior's achievements.

XII. Soteriology and
Types of Salvation

Beliefs in salvation through the abundant grace accumulated by a hero's or incarnate god's achievement was aided by the evolution of soteriological myths, above all myths of the struggling or suffering god, who in his various possible manifestations had become incarnate and descended upon earth or even traveled into the realm of the dead. Instead of a god of nature, particularly a sun god who struggles with other powers of nature, especially with darkness and cold, and having won a victory over them ushers in the spring, there now arises on the basis of the salvation myths a savior who, like Christ, liberates men from the power of the demons. The savior type is further exemplified in the Gnostics' seven archons, who save men from enslavement to the astrological determinism of fate; and in Gnosticism's Demiurge and Jehovah, who at the command of the concealed and gracious god rescue the world from the corruption brought upon it by an inferior creator god. The savior, as in the case of Jesus, may save men from the hard-hearted hypocrisy and petrifaction of the world. Or again, the salvation may be from the oppressive consciousness of sin, arising from man's awareness of the impossibility of filling certain requirements of the law, as was the case with Paul and, somewhat differently, with Augustine and Luther. Finally, the salvation may be from the abysmal corruption of the individual's own sinful nature, as in Augustine. On all these cases the savior led man upward toward a secure haven in the grace and love of a good god.

To accomplish these purposes the savior must fight with dragons or evil demons, depending on the character of the salvation in question. In some cases he is not able to engage in such battle—

he is often a child completely pure of sin—and so he must grow up in concealment or must be slaughtered by his enemies and journey to the realm of the dead in order to rise again and return victorious. From this particular belief may develop the view that the death of the savior is a tributary atonement for the power achieved over the souls of men by the devil as a result of men's sins. This is the view of earliest Christianity. Or the death of the savior may be viewed as a means of mollifying the wrath of god, before whom the savior appears as an intercessor for men, as in the cases of Christ, Muhammad, and other prophets and saviors. Again, the savior may, like the ancient bearers of salvation in magical religions, bring man forbidden knowledge of fire, technical arts, writing, or possibly the lore requisite for subjugating demons in this world or on the way toward heaven, as in Gnosticism. Finally, the decisive achievement of the savior may be contained, not in his concrete struggles and sufferings, but in the ultimate metaphysical root of the entire process. This ultimate metaphysical basis would of course be the incarnation of a god as the only device for bridging the gap between god and his creatures. This metaphysical conception constituted the culmination of Greek speculation about salvation, in Athanasius. The incarnation of god presented men with the opportunity to participate significantly in god, or as Irenaeus had already phrased it, "enabled men to become gods." The post-Athanasian philosophical formula for this was that god, by becoming incarnate, had assumed the essence (in the Platonic sense) of humanity. This formula points up the metaphysical significance of the concept of *homoousios* (human nature).

According to another view, the god might not be content with one single act of incarnation, but as a result of the continuing misery of the world, which is practically axiomatic in Asiatic thought, he might become incarnate at various intervals or even continuously. Belief in continuous incarnation is the principal force of the *Mahayana* Buddhist idea of the *Bodhisattva,* though this idea is related to occasional utterances of the Buddha himself, in which he apparently expressed a belief in the limited duration of his doctrine on earth. Furthermore, the Bodhisattva was occasionally represented as a higher ideal than the Buddha, because the Bodhisattva forgoes his own entrance into *Nirvana,* which has only exemplary significance, to prolong his universal function in the service of mankind. Here again, the savior "sacrifices" himself. But just as Jesus was superior in his own time to the saviors of other competing soteriological cults, by virtue of the fact that he had been an actual person whose resurrection had been observed by his apostles, so the continuously corporeal and living incarnation of god in the Dalai Lama is the logical conclusion of every incarnation soteriology. But even when the divine distributor of grace lives on as an incarnation, and especially when he does not linger continuously on earth, certain more tangible means are required to maintain the adherence of the mass of the faithful, who wish to participate personally in the gifts of grace made available by their god. It is these more tangible instruments of grace, exhibiting a wide variety, which exert a decisive influence on the character of the religion.

Of an essentially magical nature is the view that one may incorporate divine power into himself by the physical ingestion of some divine substance, some sacred totemic animal in which a mighty spirit is incarnated, or some host that has been magically transformed into the body of a god. Equally magical is the notion that through participation in certain mysteries one may directly share the nature of the god and therefore be protected against evil powers (sacramental grace).

Now the means of acquiring these divine blessings may take either a magical or a ritualistic form, and in either case they entail, not only belief in the savior of the incarnate living god, but also the existence of human priests or mystagogues. Moreover, the manner in which this divine grace is distributed depends in considerable measure on whether certifying proofs of the personal possession of charismatic gifts of grace are required of these earthly intermediaries between man and the savior. If certifying proofs are required, a religious functionary who no longer shares in such a state of grace, as for example a priest living in mortal sin, cannot legitimately mediate this grace by officiating at the sacraments. Such a strict consistency in the principle of charismatic distribution of grace was maintained by the Montanists, Donatists, and in general all who took the position that the leadership echelon of the church required prophetic and charismatic gifts, e.g., the religious communities of antiquity which remained outside the church. The outcome of this view was that not every bishop who occupied an office or possessed other credentials, but only those bishops who manifested the verification of prophecy or other witnesses of the spirit, could effectively distribute divine grace. This was at least the case when what was required was the distribution of grace to a penitent who had fallen into mortal sin.

When we leave this requirement, we are dealing with an altogether different notion of the distribution of grace. Now salvation supervenes by virtue of the grace which is distributed on a continuous basis by some communal organization that has either divine or prophetic credentials for its establishment. For this type of operation we shall reserve the appellation of "institutional grace" (*Anstaltsgnade*). The official community or congregation may exert its power directly through purely magical sacraments or through its control over the accumulation of supernumerary achievements performed by congregational officials or devotees, achievements which produce divine blessing or grace.

Wherever institutional grace operates consistently, three basic principles are involved. The first is *extra ecclesiam nulla salus:* salvation cannot be obtained apart from membership in a particular institution or church vested with the control of grace. The second principle is that it is not the personal charismatic qualification of the priest which determines the effectiveness of his distribution of divine grace. Third, the personal religious qualification of the individual in need of salvation is altogether a matter of indifference to the institution which has the power to distribute religious grace. That is, salvation is universal; it is accessible to other than the religious virtuosi. Indeed, virtuosi may be regarded as suspect with regard to the genuineness of their religious profession and the certainty of their salvation. Religious virtuosi are bound to be met with suspicion if instead of relying on the capacity of the institutionalized church to distribute grace they seek to attain grace by their own unaided power, treading their own pathway to god. In this theory, all human beings are capable of finding salvation if they but obey god's requirements enough for the accession of grace distributed by the church to suffice for their attainment of salvation. The level of personal ethical accomplishment must therefore be made compatible with average human qualifications, and this in practice means that it will be set quite low. Whoever can achieve more in the ethical sphere, i.e., the religious virtuoso, may thereby, in addition to insuring his own salvation, accumulate good works for the credit of the institution, which will then distribute them to those in need of good works.

The viewpoint we have just described is the characteristic attitude of the Catholic church and determines its idiosyncratic character as an institution of grace, which developed throughout many centuries but has been fixed since the time of Gregory the Great. In practice, however, the viewpoint of the Catholic church has oscillated between a relatively magical and a relatively ethical and soteriological orientation.

The actual conduct of life will be influenced in varying degrees by charismatic individuals' and institutions' distributions of grace, depending upon the conditions which are attached to the vouch-safing of the means of grace. The circumstances play a role here similar to that in ritual, to which indeed both sacramental and institutional grace show strong affinities. Yet another factor occasionally has considerable significance: every authentic distribution of grace by a person, regardless of whether his authority derives from personal charismatic gifts or his official status within an institution, has the net effect of weakening the demands of morality upon the individual, even though the distribution of grace ostensibly works in a moral direction. The vouchsafing of grace always entails the subjective release of the person in need of salvation; it consequently facilitates his capacity to bear guilt and, other things being equal, it largely spares him the necessity of developing an individual planned pattern of life based on ethical foundations. The sinner knows that he may always receive absolution by engaging in some occasional religious practice or by performing some religious rite. It is particularly important that sins remain discrete actions against which other discrete deeds may be set up as compensations or penances. Hence, value is attached to concrete individual acts rather than to the total personality pattern which has been produced by asceticism, contemplation, or eternally vigilant self-control and demonstration of religious fidelity, a pattern that may constantly be determined anew. A further consequence is that no need is felt to attain the *certitudo salutis* by one's own powers, and so this category of the *certitudo salutis*, which may in other circumstances have such significant ethical consequences, entirely recedes in importance.

For the reasons just discussed, the perpetual control of an individual's life pattern by the official, whether father confessor or spiritual director, empowered to distribute grace, a control that in certain respects is very effective, is in practice very often cancelled by the circumstance that there is always grace remaining to be distributed anew. Certainly the institution of the confessional, especially when associated with penances, is ambivalent in its effects, depending upon the manner in which it is implemented. The poorly developed and rather general method of confession which was particularly characteristic of the Russian church, frequently taking the form of a collective admission of iniquity, was certainly no way to effect any permanent influence over the conduct of life. Also, the confessional practice of the early Lutheran church was undoubtedly ineffective. The catalog of sins and penances in the Hindu sacred scriptures makes no distinction between ritual and ethical sins, and enjoins ritual obedience—possibly in deference to the class interests of the Brahmins—as virtually the sole method of atonement. As a consequence, the pattern of everyday life could be influenced by these religions only in the direction of traditionalism. Indeed, the sacramental grace of the Hindu *gurus* even further weakened any possibility of ethical influence.

The Catholic church in the Occident carried through the Christianization of Western Europe with unparalleled force, by virtue of an unexampled system of confessionals and penances, which combined the techniques of Roman law with the Teutonic conception of fiscal expiation (*Wergeld*). But the effectiveness of this system in developing a rational plan of life was quite limited, even apart from the inevitable hazards of a loose system of dispensations. Even so, the influence of the confessional upon conduct is apparent "statistically," as one might say, in the impressive maintenance of the two-children-per-family system among pious Catholics, though the limitations upon the power of the Catholic church in France are evident even in this respect.

A tremendous historical influence was actually exerted by the absence in Judaism and ascetic Protestantism of anything like the confessional, the dispensation of grace by a human being, or magical sacramental grace. This historical influence favored the evolution of an ethically rationalized pattern of life (*ethisch rationalen Lebensgestaltung*) in both Judaism and ascetic Protestantism, despite their differences in other respects. These religions provide no opportunity, such as the confessional or the purveyance of institutional grace, for obtaining release from sins. Only the Methodists maintained at certain of their meetings, the so-called "assemblages of the dozens," a system of confessions which had even comparable effects, and in that case the effects were in an altogether different direction. From such public confessions of sinfulness there developed the semi-orgiastic conversion practices of the Salvation Army.

Institutional grace, by its very nature, ultimately and notably tends to make obedience a cardinal virtue and a decisive precondition of salvation. This of course entails subjection to authority, either of the institution or of the charismatic personality who distributes grace. In India, for example, the *guru* may on occasion exercise unlimited authority. In such cases the resulting pattern of conduct is not a systematization from within, radiating out from a center which the individual himself has achieved, but rather is nurtured from some center outside the self. The content of the pattern of life is not apt to be pushed in the direction of ethical systematization, but rather in the reverse direction.

Such external authority, however, increases the elasticity of concrete sacred commandments and thus makes it easier to adjust them in practice to changed external circumstances, though in a direction different from that of an ethic based on a religious mood. An example of this elasticity is provided by the Catholic church of the nineteenth century in its non-enforcement (in practice) of the prohibition against usury, despite the prohibition's ostensibly eternal validity on the basis of biblical authority and papal decretals. To be sure, this was not accomplished openly by outright invalidation, which would have been impossible, but by an invisible internal directive from the Vatican office to the confessional priests that thenceforth they should refrain from inquiring during confession concerning infractions of the prohibition against usury, and that they should grant absolution for this infraction. This procedure took for granted that if the Holy See should ever return to the older position the confessants would obediently accept such a reversal. There was a period in France when the clergy agitated for a similar treatment of the problem presented by families having only two children. Thus, the ultimate religious value is pure obedience to the institution, which is regarded as inherently meritorious, and not concrete, substantive ethical obligation, nor even the qualification of superior moral capacity achieved through one's own methodical ethical actions. Wherever the pattern of institutional grace is carried through consistently, the sole principle integrating the life pattern is a formal humility of obedience, which like mysticism produces a characteristic quality of brokenness or humility in the pious. In this respect, the remark of Mallinckrodt that the freedom of the Catholic consists in the necessity of his obeying the Pope appears to have universal validity for systems of institutional grace.

Salvation, however, may be linked with belief. Insofar as this concept is not defined as identical with subjection to practical norms, it always presupposes some attribution of truth to certain metaphysical data and some development of dogmas, the acceptance of which becomes the distinctive hallmark of membership in the particular faith. We have already seen that dogmas develop in very different degrees within the various religions. However, some measure of doctrine is the distinctive differential of prophecy and priestly religion, in contrast to pure magic. Of course even pure magic presupposes faith in the magical power of the magician, and, for that matter, the magician's own faith in himself and his ability. This holds true of every religion, including early Christianity. Thus, Jesus taught his disciples that if they doubted their own power they would be unable to cure victims of demonic possession, and that whosoever was completely persuaded of his own powers possessed a faith that could move mountains. On the other hand, the faith of those who demand magical miracles exercises a compulsive influence upon magic, to this very day. So Jesus found himself unable to perform miracles in his birthplace and occasionally in other cities, and "wondered at their disbelief." He repeatedly declared that he was able to heal the crippled and those possessed by demons only through their belief in him and his power. To some degree this faith was sublimated in an ethical direction. Thus, because the adulterous woman believed in his power to pardon sins, Jesus was able to forgive her iniquities.

On the other hand, religious faith developed into an assertion of intellectual propositions which were products of ratiocination, and this is what primarily concerns us here. Accordingly, Confucianism, which knows nothing of dogma, is not an ethic of salvation. In ancient Islam and ancient Judaism, religion made no real demands with respect to dogma, requiring only, as primeval religion does everywhere, belief in the power (and hence also in the existence) of its own god, now regarded by it as the only god, and in the mission of this god's prophets. But since both these religions were scriptural (in Islam the Qur'an was believed to have been divinely created), they also insisted upon belief in the substantive truth of the scriptures. Yet, apart from their cosmogonic, mythologic, and historical narratives, the biblical books of the law and the prophets and the Qur'an contain primarily practical commandments and do not inherently require intellectual views of a definite kind.

Only in the non-prophetic religions is belief equivalent to sacred lore. In these religions the priests are still, like the magicians, guardians of mythological and cosmogonic knowledge; and as sacred bards they are also custodians of the heroic sagas. The Vedic and Confucian ethics attributed full moral efficacy to the traditional literary educations obtained through schooling which, by and large, was identical with mere *memoriter* knowledge. In religions that maintain the requirement of intellectual understanding there is an easy transition to the philosophical, gnostic form of salvation. This transition tends to produce a tremendous gap between the fully qualified intellectuals and the masses. But even at this point there is still no real, official dogmatics—only philosophical opinions regarded as more or less orthodox, e.g., the orthodox *Vedanta* or the heterodox *Sankhya* in Hinduism.

But the Christian churches, as a consequence of the increasing intrusion of intellectualism and the growing opposition to it, produced an unexampled mass of official and binding rational dogmas, as well as a theological faith. In practice it is impossible to require both belief in dogma and the universal understanding of it. It is difficult for us today to imagine that a religious community composed principally of lower-middle-class folk could have thoroughly mastered and really assimilated the complicated contents of the Epistle to the Romans, for example, yet apparently this must have been the case. This type of faith embodied certain dominant soteriological views current among the group of urban proselytes who were accustomed to meditating on the conditions of salvation and who were to some degree conversant with Jewish and Greek casuistry. Similarly, it is well known that in the sixteenth and seventeenth centuries extensive groups of lower-middle-class people achieved intellectual mastery over the dogmas of the Synods of Dort and Westminster, and over the many complicated compromise formulae of the Reformation churches. Still, under normal conditions it would be impossible for such intellectual penetration to take place in congregational religions without producing one of the following results for all those not belonging to the class of the philosophically knowledgeable (Gnostics). These less knowledgeable people, including the "hylics" and the mystically illuminated "psychics," would either be excluded from salvation or limited to a lesser-order salvation reserved for the non-intellectual pious (*pistikoi*). These results occurred in Gnosticism and in the intellectual religions of India.

A controversy raged in early Christianity throughout its first centuries, sometimes openly and sometimes beneath the surface, as to whether theological *gnosis* or simple faith is the higher religious quality, explicitly or implicitly providing the sole guarantee of religious salvation. In Islam, the Mutazilites held that a person who is "religious" in the average sense, and not schooled in dogma, is not actually a member of the real community of the faithful. A decisive influence was everywhere exerted on the character of religion by the relationships between the theological intellectuals, who were the virtuosi of religious knowledge, and the pious non-intellectuals, especially the virtuosi of religious asceticism and the virtuosi of religious contemplation, who equally regarded "dead knowledge" as of negligible value in the quest for salvation.

Even in the Gospels themselves, the parabolic form of Jesus' message is represented as being purposefully esoteric. To avoid the appearance of an esotericism propagated by an intellectualist aristocracy, religious faith must base itself upon something other than a real understanding and affirmation of a theological system of dogma. As a matter of fact, every prophetic religion has based religious faith upon something other than real understanding of theology, either at the very outset or at a later stage when it has become a congregational religion and has generated dogmas. Of course the acceptance of dogmas is always relevant to religious faith, except in the views of ascetics and more especially mystical virtuosi. But the explicit, personal recognition of dogmas, for which the technical term in Christianity is *fides explicita,* was required only with reference to those articles of faith which were regarded as absolutely essential, greater latitude being permitted in regard to other dogmas. Protestantism made particularly strict demands upon belief in dogma, because of its doctrine of justification by faith. This was especially, though not exclusively, true of ascetic Protestantism, which regarded the Bible as a codification of divine law. This religious requirement was largely responsible for the intensive training of the youth of the Protestant sects and for the establishment of universal public schools like those of the Jewish tradition. This same religious requirement was the underlying reason for the familiarity with the Bible on the part of the Dutch and Anglo-Saxon Pietists and Methodists (in contrast to the conditions prevalent in the English public schools, for example), which aroused the amazement of travelers as late as the middle of the nineteenth century. Here too, the people's conviction about the unequivocally dogmatic character of the Bible was responsible for the far-reaching demand that each man know the tenets of his own faith. In a church rich in dogmas, all that may be legitimately required in respect to the mass of dogmas is *fides implicita,* viz., a general readiness to subject one's own convictions to religious authority. The Catholic church has required this to the greatest possible degree, and indeed continues to do so. But no *fides implicita* is any longer an actual personal acceptance of dogmas; rather, it is a declaration of confidence in and dedication to a prophet or to the authority of a structured institution. In this way, faith loses its intellectual character.

Religion retains only a secondary interest in intellectual matters, once religious ethics has become predominantly rational. This happens because the mere assertion of intellectual propositions falls to the lowest level of faith whenever an ethic is based on a religious mood (*Gesinnungsethik*) and is oriented to ultimate ends, as Augustine among others maintained. Faith must also take on a quality of inwardness. Personal attachment to a particular god is more than knowledge and is therefore designated as "faith." This is the case in both the Old and New Testaments. The faith which was "accounted to Abraham to righteousness" was no intellectual assertion of dogmas, but a reliance upon the promises of God. For both Jesus and Paul, faith continued to hold the same central significance. Knowledge and familiarity with dogmas receded far into the background.

In a church organized as an institution, it works out in practice that the requirement of *fides explicita* is limited to priests, preachers, and theologians, all of whom have been trained in dogmatics. Such an aristocracy of those trained and knowledgeable in dogmatics arises within every religion that has been systematized into a theology. These persons presently claim, in different degrees and with varying measures of success, that they are the real carriers of the religion. The view that the priest must demonstrate his capacity to understand more and believe more than is possible for the average human mind is still widely diffused today, particularly among the peasantry. This is only one of the forms in which there comes to expression in religion the class qualification resulting from special education that is found in every type of bureaucracy, be it political, military, ecclesiastical, or commercial. But even more fundamental is the aforementioned doctrine, found also in the New Testament, of faith as the specific charisma of an extraordinary and purely personal reliance upon god's providence, such as the shepherds of souls and the heroes of faith must possess. By virtue of this charismatic confidence in god's support, the spiritual representative and leader of the congregation, as a virtuoso of faith, may act differently from the layman in practical situations and bring about different results, far surpassing normal human capacity. In the context of practical action, faith can provide a substitute for magical powers.

This anti-rational inner attitude characteristic of religions of unlimited trust in god may occasionally produce an acosmistic indifference to obvious practical and rational considerations. It frequently produces an unconditional reliance on god's providence, attributing to god alone the consequences of one's own actions, which are interpreted as pleasing to god. In Christianity and in Islam, as well as elsewhere, this anti-rational attitude is sharply opposed to knowledge and particularly to theological knowledge. Anti-rationality may be manifested in a proud virtuosity of faith, or, when it avoids this danger of arrogant deification of the creaturely, it may be manifested in an unconditional religious surrender and a spiritual humility that requires, above all else, the death of intellectual pride. This attitude of unconditional trust played a major role in ancient Christianity, particularly in the case of Jesus and Paul and in the struggles against Greek philosophy, and in modern Christianity, particularly in the antipathies to theology on the part of the mystical spiritualist sects of the seventeenth century in Western Europe and of the eighteenth and nineteenth centuries in Eastern Europe.

At some point in its development, every genuinely devout religious faith brings about, directly or indirectly, that "sacrifice of the intellect" in the interests of a trans-intellectual, distinctive religious quality of absolute surrender and utter trust which is expressed in the formula *credo non quod sed quia absurdum est.* The salvation religions teaching belief in a transcendental god stress, here as everywhere, the inadequacy of the individual's intellectual powers when he confronts the exalted state of the divinity. Such a turning away from knowledge, based on faith in a transcendental god's power to save, is altogether different from the Buddhist's renunciation of knowledge concerning the world beyond, which is grounded simply in his belief that such knowledge cannot advance contemplation that alone brings salvation. It is also altogether different in essence from skeptical renunciation of the possibility of understanding the meaning of the world, which indeed it is inclined to combat much more harshly than it combats the Buddhist form of renunciation of knowledge. The skeptical point of view has been common to the intellectual classes of every period. It is evident in the Greek epitaphs and in the highest artistic productions of the Renaissance, such as the works of Shakespeare; it has found expression in the philosophies of Europe, China, and India, as well as in modern intellectualism.

Deliberate belief in the absurd, as well as the triumphant joy expressed in the sermons of Jesus over the fact that the charisma of faith has been granted by God to children rather than to scholars, typifies the great tension between this type of salvation religion and intellectualism. Nevertheless, this type of religion constantly seeks to adapt intellectualism to its own purposes. As Christianity became increasingly penetrated by Greek forms of thought, even in antiquity but far more strongly after the rise of universities in the Middle Ages, it came to foster intellectualism. The medieval universities were actually centers for the cultivation of dialectics, created to counterbalance the achievements of the Roman jurists on behalf of the competing power of the Empire.

Every religion of belief assumes the existence of a personal god, as well as his intermediaries and prophets, in whose favor there must be a renunciation of self-righteousness and individual knowledge at some point or other. Consequently, religiosity based on this form of faith is characteristically absent in the Asiatic religions. We have already seen that faith may assume very different forms, depending on the direction in which it develops. To be sure, despite all diversities, a striking similarity to contemplative mysticism characterizes all religions of faith oriented to salvation which are found among peaceful groups, though it does not characterize ancient Islam and the religion of Yahweh, in both of which the primordial trust of the warrior in the tremendous power of his own god was still dominant. This similarity to contemplative mysticism derives from the fact that when the substantive content of salvation is envisaged and striven after as redemption, there is always at least a tendency for salvation to evolve into a primarily emotional relationship to the divine, a *unio mystica*. Indeed, the more systematically the practical psychological character of the faith is developed, the more easily may outright antinomian results ensue, as occurs in every type of mysticism.

The great difficulty of establishing an unequivocal relationship between ethical demands and a religion based on faith, i.e., a genuine salvation religion based on an attitude of utter trust, was already demonstrated by the Pauline Epistles, and even by certain contradictions in the utterances of Jesus, as those utterances are recorded in the tradition. Paul struggled continually with the immediate consequences of his own views, and with their very complicated implications. The consistent development of the Pauline doctrine of salvation by faith achieved in the Marcionite doctrines definitively demonstrated the antinomian consequences of Paul's teaching. As increasing stress was placed upon salvation by faith, there was generally but little tendency for an active ethical rationalization of the pattern of life to take place within everyday religion, although the opposite was the case for the prophet of such a religion. Under certain circumstances, salvation by faith can have directly anti-rational effects in concrete cases as well as in principle. A minor illustration of this is found in the resistance of many religious Lutherans to entering into insurance contracts, on the ground that such action would manifest an irreligious distrust of God's providence. The wider importance of this problem lies in the fact that every rational and planned procedure for achieving salvation, every reliance on good works, and above all every effort to surpass normal ethical behavior by ascetic achievement, is regarded by religion based on faith as a wicked preoccupation with purely human powers.

Wherever the conception of salvation by faith has been developed consistently, as in ancient Islam, trans-worldly asceticism and especially monasticism have been rejected. As a result, the development of belief in salvation by faith may directly augment the religious emphasis placed upon vocational activity within the world, as actually happened in the case of Lutheran Protestantism. Moreover, religion based on faith may also strengthen the motivations for a religiously positive evaluation of vocations within the world, particularly when such religion also devalues the priestly grace of penance and sacrament in favor of the exclusive importance of the personal religious relationship to god. Lutheranism took this stand in principle from its very outset, and strengthened the stand subsequently, after the complete elimination of the confessional. The same effect of the belief in faith upon vocational motivations was particularly evident in the various forms of Pietism, which were given an ascetic cast by Spener and Francke, but which had also been exposed to Quaker and other influences of which they themselves were not too well aware.

Moreover, the German word for "vocation" (*Beruf*) is derived from the Lutheran translation of the Bible. The positive evaluation of ethical conduct within one's worldly calling, as the only mode of life acceptable to god, was central in Lutheranism from the very beginning. But in Lutheranism, good works did not enter into consideration as the real basis for the salvation of the soul, as in Catholicism, nor did good works provide the intellectual basis for the recognition that one had been reborn, as in ascetic Protestantism. Instead, certainty of salvation was derived in Lutheranism from the habitual feeling of having found refuge in God's goodness and grace. Hence, Lutheranism taught, as its attitude toward the world, a patient resignation toward the world's institutional structures. In this teaching of resignation, Lutheranism presents a striking contrast to those religions, especially those forms of Protestantism, which required for the assurance of one's salvation either a distinctive methodical pattern of life or a demonstration of good works, which was known as *fides efficax* among the Pietists and known as *amal* among the Muslim Kharijis, and presents an equally striking contrast to the virtuosi religions of ascetic sects.

Lutheranism lacked any motivation toward revolutionary attitudes in social or political relationships and any inclination toward rational reformist activity. Its teaching required one to maintain, both within the world and against it, the substance of the salvation promised by one's faith, but did not require one to attempt a transformation of the world in any rationalized ethical direction. The Lutheran Christian has all that is needful for him, if only the word of God is proclaimed pure and clear; the remaking of the eternal order of the world and even the remaking of the church is a matter of indifference, an *adiaphoron*. To be sure, this accommodating emotional mood of a faith relatively indifferent to the world, in contrast to the concern for the world found in asceticism, is a somewhat later stage of development.

It is not easy for authentic religions of faith to generate antitraditionalist, rational trends of the patterning of life. In the nature of the case these religions lack any drive toward the rational control and transformation of the world. Faith, in the form known to the martial religions of ancient Islam and of Yahwism, took the form of simple fidelity to god or to the prophets, along the lines that originally characterize all relationships to anthropomorphic gods. Faithfulness is rewarded and disloyalty punished by the god. This personal relationship to the god takes on other qualities when the carriers of salvation religion become peaceful groups, and more particularly when they become members of the middle classes. Only then can faith as an instrument of salvation take on the emotionally tinged character and assume the lineaments of love for the god or the savior. This transformation is already apparent in exilic and postexilic Judaism, and is even more strongly apparent in early Christianity, especially in the teachings of Jesus and John. God now appears as a gracious master or father of a household. But it is of course a vulgar error to see in the paternal quality of the God proclaimed by Jesus an intrusion of non-Semitic religion, since the gods of the Semites and other desert peoples actually "created" man, whereas the Greek deities merely "generated" men; the Christian God never thought of "generating" men. It may be noted here that the phrase "begotten not made" is the distinctive predicate of the triune deified Christ, in contrast to men. Moreover, although this God surrounds men with superhuman love, he is anything but a tender, modern "papa"; rather, he is primarily a benevolent royal patriarch, who is at times strict and indignant, like the Jewish God.

In any case, the emotional content of religions of faith may be deepened whenever the followers of these religions substitute the view that they are children of god for the ascetic view that they are merely his instruments. The result may be a strong tendency to seek the integration of one's pattern of life in subjective states and in an inner reliance upon god, rather than in the certifying consciousness of one's continued religious loyalty. This tendency may even further weaken the rational character of the religion. Such an emotional emphasis is suggested by the "language of Canaan" which came to expression with the renaissance of Pietism, that whining cadence of typical Lutheran sermons in Germany which has so often driven strong men out of the church.

A completely anti-rational effect upon the conduct of life is generally exerted by religions of faith when the relationship to the god or the savior exhibits the trait of passionate devotion, and consequently whenever the religion has a latent or manifest tinge of eroticism. This is apparent in the many varieties of love of god in Sufism, in the Canticles type of mysticism of St. Bernard and his followers, in the cult of Mary and the Sacred Heart of Jesus, in other comparable forms of devotionalism, and finally in the characteristic manifestations of emotionally suffused Pietism within Lutheranism, such as the movement of Zinzendorf. However, its most striking manifestation occurs in the characteristically Hindu religiosity of love (*bhakti*) which from the fifth and sixth centuries on supplanted the proud and elite intellectualistic religion of Buddhism, becoming the popular form of salvation religion among the masses of India, particularly in the soteriological forms of Vishnuism. In this Hindu religiosity of love, devotion to Krishna, who had been apotheosized from the *Mahabharata* to the status of a savior, and more especially devotion to the Krishna child, is raised to a state of erotically tinged devotion. This process takes place through the four levels of contemplation: servant love, friendship love, filial or parental love, and, at the highest level, a piety tinged with definite eroticism, after the fashion of the love of the *gopis* (the love of Krishna's mistresses for him). Since the procedure enjoined by this religion as necessary for salvation is essentially hostile to the concerns of everyday life, it has always presupposed some degree of sacramental intermediation in the achievement of grace, by priests, *gurus,* or *gosains.* In its practical effects, this religion is a sublimated counterpart of the Shakti religion, which is popular among the lowest social classes in India. The religion of Shakti is a worship of goddesses, always very close to the orgiastic type of religion and not infrequently involving a cult of erotic orgies, which of course makes it utterly remote from a religion of pure faith, such as Christianity, with its continuous and unshakeable trust in God's providence. The erotic element in the personal relationship to the savior in Hindu salvation religion may be regarded as largely the technical result of the practices of devotion; whereas, in marked contrast, the Christian belief in providence is a charisma that must be maintained by the exercise of the will of the believer.

Finally, salvation may be regarded as a completely free, inexplicable gift of grace from a god absolutely unsearchable as to his decisions, who is necessarily unchanging because of his omniscience, and utterly beyond the influence of any human behavior. This is the grace of predestination. This conception unconditionally presupposes a transcendental creator god, and is therefore lacking in all ancient Asiatic religions. It is also lacking in warrior and heroic religions, since they posit a super-divine fate, whereas the doctrine of predestination posits a world order or regime which is rational from god's point of view even though it may appear irrational to human beings. On the other hand, a religion of predestination obliterates the goodness of god, for he becomes a hard, majestic king. Yet it shares with religions of faith the capacity for inducing dedication and rigor in its devotees. It has this effect of inducing dedication in spite of the fact, or rather because of the fact, that only in respect to this kind of god is the complete devaluation of all the powers of an individual a prerequisite for his salvation by free grace alone.

Dispassionate and sober ethical men like Pelagius might believe in the adequacy of their own good works. But among the prophets and founders of religions, predestination has been the belief of men animated by a drive to establish rationally organized religious power, as in the case of Calvin and Muhammad, each of whom felt that the certainty of his own mission in the world derived less from any personal perfection than from his situation in the world and from god's will. In other cases, e.g., Augustine and also Muhammad, the belief in predestination may arise as a result of recognizing the necessity for controlling tremendous passions and feeling that this can be accomplished only, if at all, through a power acting upon the individual from without and above. Luther, too, knew this feeling during the terribly excited period after his difficult struggle with sin, but it receded in importance for him after he had achieved a better adjustment to the world.

Predestination provides the individual who has found religious grace with the highest possible degree of certainty of salvation, once he has attained assurance that he belongs to the very limited aristocracy of salvation who are the elect. But the individual must find certain indices (*Symptome*) by which he may determine whether he possesses this incomparable charisma, inasmuch as it is impossible for him to live on in absolute uncertainty regarding his salvation. Since god has deigned to reveal at least some positive injunctions for the type of conduct pleasing to him, the aforementioned indices must reside, in this instance as in the case of every religiously active charisma, in the decisive demonstration of the capacity to serve as one of god's instruments in fulfilling his injunctions, and that in a persevering and methodical fashion, for either one possesses predestined grace or one does not. Moreover, the assurance of this grace is not affected by any particular transgressions of the individual in question. The ultimate certainty of one's salvation and one's continuance in a state of grace, notwithstanding disparate transgressions which the man predestined to salvation commits in the same way that all other sinful creatures commit transgressions, is provided by one's knowledge that, despite these particular errors, one's behavior is acceptable to god and flows out of an inner relationship based on the mysterious quality of grace—in short, salvation is based on a central and constant quality of personality.

The belief in predestination, although it might logically be expected to result in fatalism, produced in its most consistent followers the strongest possible motives for acting in accordance with god's pattern. Of course this action assumed different forms, depending upon the primary content of the religious prophecy. In the case of the Muslim warriors of the first generation of Islam, the belief in predestination often produced a complete obliviousness to self, in the interest of faith in and fulfillment of the religious commandment of a holy war for the conquest of the world. In the case of the Puritans governed by the Christian ethic, the same belief in predestination often produced ethical rigorism, legalism, and rationally planned procedures for the patterning of life. Discipline acquired during wars of religion was the source of the unconquerableness of both the Islamic and Cromwellian cavalries. Similarly, inner-worldly asceticism and the disciplined quest for salvation in a vocation pleasing to God were the sources of the virtuosity in acquisitiveness characteristic of the Puritans. Every consistent doctrine of predestined grace inevitably implied a radical and ultimate devaluation of all magical, sacramental, and institutional distributions of grace, in view of god's sovereign will, a devaluation that actually occurred wherever the doctrine of predestination appeared in its full purity and maintained its strength. By far the strongest such devaluation of magical and institutional grace occurred in Puritanism.

Islamic predestination knew nothing of the "double decree"; it did not dare attribute to Allah the predestination of some people to hell, but only attributed to him the withdrawal of his grace from some people, a belief which admitted man's inadequacy and inevitable transgression. Moreover, as a warrior religion, Islam had some of the characteristics of the Greek *moira,* hardly developing the specifically rational elements of a world order and the specific determination of individual fates in the world beyond. The ruling conception was that predestination determined, not the fate of the individual in the world beyond, but rather the uncommon events of this world, and above all such questions as whether or not the warrior for the faith would fall in battle. The religious fate of the individual in the next world was held, at least according to the older view, to be adequately secured by the individual's belief in Allah and the prophets, so that no demonstration of salvation in the conduct of life is needed. Any rational system of ascetic control of everyday life was alien to this warrior religion from the outset, so that in Islam the doctrine of predestination manifested its power especially during the wars of faith and the wars of the Mahdi. The doctrine of predestination tended to lose its importance as Islam became more urbanized, because the doctrine produced no planned procedure for the control of the workaday world, as did the Puritan doctrine of predestination.

In Puritanism, predestination definitely did affect the fate of the individual in the world beyond, and therefore his assurance of salvation was determined primarily by his maintenance of ethical integrity in the affairs of everyday life. For this reason, the belief in predestination assumed greater importance in Calvinism as this religion became urbanized than it had possessed at the outset. It is significant that the Puritan belief in predestination was regarded by authorities everywhere as dangerous to the state and as hostile to authority, because it made Puritans skeptical of the legitimacy of all secular power. It is interesting to note by way of contrast that in Islam the family and following of Umar, who were denounced for their alleged secularism, were followers of the belief in predestination, since they hoped to see their dominion, which had been established by illegitimate means, legitimized by the predestined will of Allah.

Clearly, every use of predestination to determine concrete events in history, rather than to secure one's orientation to one's place in the world beyond, immediately causes predestination to lose its ethical, rational character. The belief in predestination practically always had an ascetic effect among the simple warriors of the early Islamic faith, which in the realm of ethics exerted largely external and ritual demands, but the ascetic effects of the Islamic belief in predestination were not rational, and for this reason they were repressed in everyday life. The Islamic belief in predestination easily assumed fatalistic characteristics in the beliefs of the masses, viz., *kismet,* and for this reason predestination did not eliminate magic from the popular religion.

Finally, the Chinese patrimonial bureaucracy, in keeping with the character of its Confucian ethic, considered knowledge concerning destiny or fate to be indissolubly associated with the elite mentality. On the other hand, Confucianism permitted destiny to assume certain fatalistic attributes in the magical religion of the masses, though in the religion of the educated classes it assumed approximately a middle position between providence and *moira.* For just as the latter concept, together with the courage to endure it, nurtured the heroic pride of warriors, so also did predestination feed the "pharisaical" pride of the heroes of middle-class asceticism.

But in no other religion was the pride of the predestined aristocracy of salvation so closely associated with the man of a vocation and with the idea that success in rationalized activity demonstrates god's blessing as in Puritanism (and hence in no other religion was the influence of ascetic motivation upon the attitude toward economic activity so strong). Religious virtuosi also believed in predestined grace, which alone rendered tolerable the thought of the everlasting "double decree." But as this doctrine continued to flow into the routine of everyday living and into the religion of the masses, its dour bleakness became more and more intolerable. Finally, all that remained of it in occidental ascetic Protestantism was a vestige, a *caput mortuum:* the contribution which this doctrine of grace made to the rationalized capitalistic temperament, the idea of the methodical demonstration of vocation in one's economic behavior.

The neo-Calvinism of Kuyper no longer dared to maintain the pure doctrine of predestined grace. Nevertheless, the doctrine was never completely eliminated from Calvinism; it only altered its form. Under all circumstances, the determinism of predestination remained an instrument for the greatest possible systematization and centralization of an ethic based on an inner religious mood and oriented to ultimate ends. The "total personality," as we would say today, has been provided with the accent of eternal value by "God's election," and not by any individual action of the person in question.

There is a non-religious counterpart of this religious evaluation, one based on a mundane determinism. It is that distinctive type of guilt and, so to speak, godless feeling of sin which characterizes modern man precisely as a consequence of his organization of ethics in the direction of a system based on an inner religious state, regardless of the metaphysical basis upon which the system was originally erected. It is not that he is guilty of having done any particular act, but that by virtue of his unalterable idiosyncracy he "is" as he is, so that he is compelled to perform the act in spite of himself, as it were—this is the secret anguish that modern man bears. Another source of modern man's *malaise* is the deterministically oriented "Pharisaism" of others as expressed in their rejection of him. He feels that both he and the others are inhuman, because there is no significant possibility of "forgiveness," "contrition," or "restitution"—in much the same way that these human qualities were impossible under the religious belief in predestination, with its picture of a mysterious divine plan.

XIII. Religious Ethics, the World Order, and Culture

The more a religion of salvation has been systematized and internalized in the direction of an ethic based on an inner religious state, the greater becomes its tension with an opposition to the world. This tension between religion and the world appears in a less consistent fashion and less as a matter of principle, so long as the religion has a ritualistic or legalistic form. In these earlier stages, religions of salvation generally assume the same forms and exert the same effects as those of magical ethics. That is to say, a salvation religion generally begins by assigning inviolable sanctity to its traditional religious conventions, since all the followers of a particular god are interested in avoiding the wrath of the deity, and hence in punishing any transgression of the norms enjoined by him. Consequently, once an injunction has achieved the status of a divine commandment, it rises out of the circle of alterable conventions into the rank of sanctity. The regulations enjoined by the religion are therefore regarded, like the arrangements of the cosmos as a whole, as eternally valid—susceptible of interpretation, but not of alteration, unless the god himself reveals a new commandment.

In this stage, the religion exercises a stereotyping effect on the entire realm of legal institutions and social conventions, in the same way that symbolism stereotypes certain substantive elements of a culture and prescription of magical taboos stereotypes concrete types of relationships to human beings and to goods. The sacred books of the Hindus, Muslims, Parsees and Jews, and the classical books of the Chinese treat legal prescriptions in exactly the same manner that they treat ceremonial and ritual norms. All law is sacred law. The dominance of law that has been stereotyped by religion constitutes one of the most significant limitations on the rationalization of the legal order and hence also on the rationalization of the economy.

Conversely, when ethical prophecies have broken through the stereotyped magical or ritual norms, a sudden or a gradual revolution may take place, even in the daily order of human living, and particularly in the realm of economics. It must be admitted, of course, that there are limits to the power of religion in both spheres. It is by no means true that religion is always the decisive element when it appears in connection with the aforementioned transformation. Furthermore, religion nowhere eliminates certain economic conditions unless there are also present in the existing relationships and constellations of interests certain possibilities of, or even powerful drives toward, such an economic transformation. It is not possible to enunciate any general formula that will summarize the comparative substantive powers of the various factors involved in such a transformation or will summarize the manner of their accommodation to one another.

The needs of economic life make themselves manifest either through a reinterpretation of the sacred commandments or through a by-passing of the sacred commandments, either procedure being motivated by casuistry. Occasionally we also come upon a simple, practical elimination of religious injunctions, similar to the actual practice in the ecclesiastical dispensation of penance and grace. One example of this is the elimination within the Catholic church of so important a provision as the prohibition against usury even *in foro conscientiae* (concerning which we shall have more to say presently), but without any express abrogation, which would have been impossible. Probably the same process took place in the case of another forbidden practice, viz., the limitation of offspring to two children per family.

The frequent ambivalence or silence of religious norms with respect to new problems and practices like the aforementioned results in the unmediated juxtaposition of the stereotypes' absolute unalterableness with the extraordinary capriciousness and utter unpredictability of the same stereotypes' validity in any particular application. Thus, in dealing with the Islamic *shariah* it is virtually impossible to assert what is the practice today in regard to any particular matter. The same confusion obtains with regard to all sacred laws and ethical injunctions that have a formal ritualistic and casuistical character, above all the Jewish law.

But the systematization of religious obligations in the direction of an ethic based on inner religious faith produces a situation that is fundamentally different in essence. Such systematization breaks through the stereotypization of individual norms in order to bring about a meaningful total relationship of the pattern of life to the goal of religious salvation. Moreover, an inner religious faith does not recognize any sacred law, but only a "sacred inner religious state" that may sanction different maxims of conduct in different situations, and which is thus elastic and susceptible of accommodation. It may, depending on the pattern of life it engenders, produce revolutionary consequences from within, instead of exerting a stereotyping effect. But it acquires this ability to revolutionize at the price of also acquiring a whole complex of problems which becomes greatly intensified and internalized. The inherent conflict between the religious postulate and the reality of the world does not diminish, but rather increases. With the increasing systematization and rationalization of communal relationships and of their substantive contents, the external compensations provided by the teachings of theodicy are replaced by the struggles of particular autonomous spheres of life against the requirements of religion. The more intense the religious need is, the more the world presents a problem. Let us now clarify this matter by analyzing some of the principal conflicts.

Religious ethics penetrate into social institutions in very different ways. The decisive aspect of the religious ethic is not the intensity of its attachment to magic and ritual or the distinctive character of the religion generally, but is rather its theoretical attitude toward the world. To the extent that a religious ethic organizes the world from a religious perspective into a systematic, rational order and a cosmos, its ethical tensions with the social institutions of the world are likely to become sharper and more principled. A religious ethic evolves that is oriented to the rejection of the world, and which by its very nature completely lacks any of that stereotyping character which has been associated with sacred laws. Indeed, the very tension which this religious ethic introduces into the human relationships toward the world becomes a strongly dynamic factor in social evolution.

Those cases in which a religious ethic simply appropriates the general virtues of life within the world require no exposition here. These general virtues naturally include relationships within the family, truthfulness, reliability, and respect for another person's life and property, including his wife. But the accentuation of the various virtues is characteristically different in different religions. Confucianism placed a tremendous stress on familial piety, a stress which was motivated by belief in magic, in view of the importance of the family spirit. This familial piety was cultivated in practice by a bureaucratic political organization of domination having a patriarchal base. Confucius, according to a dictum attributed to him, regarded "insubordination as more reprehensible than a nasty spirit," which indicates that he expressly interpreted obedience to family authorities very literally as the distinctive mark of all social and political qualities. The directly opposite accentuation of general virtues of life is found in those more radical types of congregational religion which advocate the dissolution of all family ties. "Whosoever cannot hate his father cannot become a disciple of Jesus."

Another example of the different accentuations of virtues is the stress placed on truthfulness in the Hindu and Zoroastrian ethics, whereas the Decalogue of the Judeo-Christian tradition confines this virtue to judicial testimony. Even further from the Hindu and Zoroastrian requirements of truthfulness is the complete recession of the obligation of veracity in favor of the varied injunctions of ceremonious propriety found in the class ethic of the Confucian Chinese bureaucracy. Still another area of difference is found in the prescribed virtues regulating cruelty to animals. Zoroastrianism forbids the torture of animals, as a consequence of the founder's campaign against orgiastic religion. Hindu religion goes far beyond any other in absolutely prohibiting the slaying of any living thing, a position that is based on conceptions of animism and metempsychosis.

The content of every religious ethic which goes beyond particular magical prescriptions and familial piety is primarily determined by two simple motives that condition all everyday behavior beyond the limits of the family, namely, just retaliation against offenders and fraternal assistance to friendly neighbors. Both are in a sense compensations: the offender deserves punishment, the execution of which mollifies anger; and conversely, the neighbor is entitled to assistance. There could be no question in Chinese, Vedic, or Zoroastrian ethics, or in that of the Jews until postexile times, but that an enemy must be compensated with evil for the evil he has done. Indeed, the entire social order of these societies appears to have rested on just compensation. For this reason and because of its tendency to reach accommodation with the world, the Confucian ethic rejected the idea of love for one's enemy, which in China was partly mystical and partly based on notions of social utility, as being contrary to the interests of the state. The notion of love for one's enemy was accepted by the Jews in their postexile ethic, according to the interpretation of Meinhold, but only in the particular sense of causing their enemies all the greater humiliation by the benevolent attitude exhibited by the Jews. The postexile Jews added another proviso, which Christianity retained, that vengeance is the proper prerogative of God, who will the more certainly execute it the more man refrains from doing so himself.

Congregational religion added the fellow worshipper and the comrade in faith to the roster of those to whom the religiously founded obligation of assistance applied, which already included the blood-brother and the fellow member of clan or tribe. Stated more correctly, congregational religion set the co-religionist in the place of the fellow clansman. "Whoever does not leave his own father and mother cannot become a follower of Jesus." This is also the general sense and context of Jesus' remark that he came not to bring peace, but the sword. Out of all this grows the injunction of brotherly love, which is especially characteristic of congregational religion, in most cases because it contributes very effectively to the emancipation from political organization. Even in early Christianity, for example in the doctrines of Clement of Alexandria, brotherly love in its fullest extent was enjoined only within the circle of fellow believers, and not beyond.

The obligation to bring assistance to one's fellow, or brotherly love, was derived—as we have already seen*—from the primordial

* Cf. *Wirtschaft und Gesellschaft*, 4th ed., p. 216. German editor's note.

organization of the neighborhood group. The nearest person helps the neighbor because he may one day require the neighbor's help in turn. The emergence of the notion of universal love is possible only after political and ethnic communities have become considerably intermingled, and after the gods have been liberated from connection with political organizations to become universal powers. The extension of the sentiment of love to include the followers of alien religions is more difficult when the other religious communities have become competitors, each proclaiming the uniqueness of its own god. Thus, Buddhist tradition relates that the Jainist monks expressed amazement that the Buddha had commanded his disciples to give food to them as well as to Buddhist monks.

As social differentiation proceeded, customs of mutual neighborly assistance in work and in meeting immediate needs were transformed into customs of mutual aid among various social classes. This process is reflected in religious ethics at a very early time. Sacred bards and magicians, the professional groups which first lost their contact with the soil, lived from the bounty of the rich. Consequently, the wealthy who share their plenty with religious functionaries receive the praises of the latter at all times, while the greedy and miserly have curses hurled at them. Under the economic conditions of early, natural agricultural economies, noble status is conferred, not just by wealthy, but also by a hospitable and charitable manner of living, as we shall see later on.** Hence, the giving of alms is a universal and primary component of every ethical religion, though new motivations for such giving may come to the fore. Jesus occasionally made use of the aforementioned principle of compensation as a source of motivation for giving to the poor. The gist of this notion was that god would all the more certainly render compensation to the giver of alms in the world beyond, since it was impossible for the poor to return the generosity. To this notion was added the principle of the solidarity of the brothers in the faith, which under certain circumstances might approximate a universal communism of love.

In Islam, the giving of alms was one of the five commandments incumbent upon members of the faith. Giving of alms was the

** [Cf. *Wirtschaft und Gesellschaft*, 4th ed., pp. 538, 544, 687. German editor's note.]

"good work" enjoined in ancient Hinduism, in Confucianism, and in early Judaism. In ancient Buddhism, the giving of alms was originally the only activity of the pious layman that really mattered. Finally, in ancient Christianity, the giving of alms attained almost the dignity of a sacrament, and even in the time of Augustine faith without alms was not regarded as genuine.

The impecunious Muslim warrior for the faith, the Buddhist monk, and the impoverished fellow believers of ancient Christianity, especially those of the Christian community in Jerusalem, were all dependent on alms, as were the prophets, apostles, and frequently even the priests of salvation religions. In ancient Christianity, and among Christian sects as late as the Quaker community, charitable assistance was regarded as a sort of religious insurance, and was one of the most important factors in the maintenance of the religious community and in missionary enterprises. Hence, when congregational religion lost its initial sectarian drive, charity lost its significance to a greater or lesser degree and assumed the character of a mechanical ritual. Still, charity continued to survive in principle. In Christianity, even after its expansion, the giving of alms remained so unconditionally necessary for the achievement of salvation by the wealthy that the poor were actually regarded as a distinctive and indispensable class within the church. The rendering of assistance naturally developed far beyond the giving of alms, and so the sick, widows, and orphans were again and again described as possessing particular religious value.

The relationships among brothers in the faith came to be characterized by the same expectations which were felt between friends and neighbors, such as the expectations that credit would be extended without interest and that one's children would be taken care of in time of need without any compensation. Many of the secularized organizations which have replaced the sects in the United States still make such claims upon their members. Above all, the poor brother in the faith expects this kind of assistance and generosity from the powerful and from his own master. Indeed, within certain limitations, the powerful personage's own rational interests dictated that he protect his own subordinates and show them generosity, since the security of his own income depended ultimately on the goodwill and cooperation of his underlings, apart from which no rational methods of control existed. On the other hand, the possibility of obtaining help or protection from powerful individuals provided every pauper, and notably the sacred bards, with a motive to seek out such individuals and praise them for their generosity. Wherever patriarchal relationships of power and coercion determined the social stratification, but especially in the Orient, the prophetic religions were able, in connection with the aforementioned purely practical situation, to create a protectorate of the weak, i.e., women, children, slaves, etc. The Mosaic and Islamic prophetic religions even extended protection to relationships between classes.

However, it was still regarded as acceptable conduct to exploit one's particular class position in relation to less powerful neighbors with no scruples whatsoever, which is altogether typical of precapitalistic times. This naturally resulted in the merciless enslavement of debtors and the aggrandizement of land holdings, processes which are practically identical. Further, this implied the maximum utilization of one's own purchasing power in acquiring customer goods for the speculative exploitation of the critical condition of those in less favorable positions. Such activities were met with considerable social condemnation and religious censure, as being an offense against group solidarity.

The members of the ancient warrior nobility tended to regard as a parvenu any person who had risen in the social scale as a result of the acquisition of money. Therefore, the kind of avarice just described was everywhere regarded as abominable from the religious point of view. It was so regarded in the Hindu legal books, as well as in ancient Christianity and in Islam. In Judaism, the reaction against such avarice led to the creation of the characteristic institution of a jubilee year in which debts were cancelled and slaves liberated, to ameliorate the conditions of one's fellow believers. This institution led subsequently to the creation of the sabbatical year, a result of theological casuistry and of a misunderstanding on the part of those pious people whose provenience was purely urban. Every systematization in the direction of an ethic based on an inner religious state crystallized from all these particular demands the distinctive religious mood or state known as "charity" (*caritas*).

The rejection of usury appears constantly in the economic sphere as an emanation of the central religious mood, in practically all ethical systems purporting to regulate life. Such a prohibition against usury is completely lacking, outside of Protestantism, only in the religious ethics which have become a mere accommodation to the world, e.g., Confucianism; and in the religious ethics of societies (e.g., ancient Babylonia and the Mediterranean littoral societies of antiquity) in which the urban dwellers (more particularly the nobility residing in the cities and maintaining economic interests in trade) hindered the development of a consistent caritative ethics. The Hindu books of canonical law prohibit the taking of usury, at least for the two highest castes. Among the Jews, collecting usury from one's fellow believers was prohibited. In Islam and in ancient Christianity, the prohibition against usury at first applied only to fellow believers, but subsequently became unconditional. It seems probable that the proscription of usury in Christianity is not original in that religion. Jesus justified the biblical injunction to lend to the impecunious on the ground that God will not reward the lender for transactions which present no risk. This verse was then misread and mistranslated in a fashion that resulted in the prohibition of usury. (μηδένα ἀπελπίζοντες was mistranslated as μηδὲν, which in the Vulgate became *nihil inde sperantes*.)

The original basis for the thoroughgoing rejection of usury was generally the primitive custom of economic assistance to one's fellows, in accordance with which the taking of usury among brothers was undoubtedly regarded as a serious breach against the communal obligation to provide assistance. The fact that the prohibition against usury became increasingly severe in Christianity, under quite different conditions, was due in part to various other motives and factors. The prohibition of usury was not, as the materialist conception of history would represent it, a reflection of the absence of interest on capital under the general conditions of a natural economy. On the contrary, the Christian church and its servants, including the Pope, accepted usury with complete toleration and without any scruple even in the early Middle Ages, i.e., in the very period of a natural economy. It is striking that the ecclesiastical persecution of usurious lending arose and became ever more intense at the time and virtually as a concomitant of the incipient development of actual capitalist forms of communication, and particularly as a concomitant of the development of acquisitive capital in transoceanic commerce. What is involved, therefore, is a struggle in principle between ethical rationalization and the process of rationalization in the domain of economics. As we have seen, only in the nineteenth century was the church obliged, under the pressure of certain unalterable facts, to remove the prohibition in the manner we have described previously.

The real reason for religious hostility toward usury lies deeper and is connected with the attitude of religious ethics toward the legality of the rational acquisitive enterprise as such. In early religions, even those which otherwise placed a high positive value on the possession of wealth, purely business enterprises were practically always the objects of adverse judgment. Nor is this attitude confined to predominantly agrarian economies under the influence of warrior nobilities. This negative criticism of purely commercial acquisitiveness is usually found in relatively well-developed commercial economies, and indeed it arose in conscious protest against such economies.

We may first note that every economic rationalization of a barter economy has a weakening effect on the traditions which support the authority of the sacred law. For this reason alone the pursuit of money, the typical goal of the rational acquisitive quest, is religiously suspect. Consequently, the priesthood favored the maintenance of a natural economy wherever, as was apparently the case in Egypt, the particular economic interests of the temple as a bank for deposit and loans under divine protection did not militate against a natural economy.

But it is above all the impersonal and economically rationalized (but for this very reason ethically irrational) character of purely commercial relationships that evokes the suspicion, never clearly expressed but all the more strongly felt, of ethical religions. For every purely personal relationship of man to man, of whatever sort and even including complete enslavement, may be subjected to ethical requirements and ethically regulated. This is true because the structures of these relationships depend upon the individual wills of the participants, leaving room in such relationships for manifestations of the virtue of charity. But this is not the situation in the realm of economically rationalized relationships, where personal control is exercised in inverse ratio to the degree of rational differentiation of the economic structure. There is no possibility, in practice or even in principle, of any caritative regulation of relationships arising between the holder of a savings and loan bank mortgage and the mortgagee who has obtained a loan from the bank, or between a holder of a federal bond and a citizen taxpayer. Nor can any caritative regulation arise in the relationships between stockholders and factory workers, between tobacco importers and foreign plantation workers, or between industrialists and the miners who have dug from the earth the raw materials used in the plants owned by the industrialists. The material development of an economy on the basis of social associations flowing from market relationships generally follows its own objective rules, disobedience to which entails economic failure and, in the long run, economic ruin.

The rationalization of the structure of an economy always brings about a process of materialization, in the sense just discussed, and it is impossible to control a universe of objective rational business activities by charitable appeals to particular individuals. The functionalized material world of capitalism certainly offers no support whatever for any such charitable orientation. In this rationalized economic world of capitalism, not only do the requirements of religious charity founder against the refractoriness and unreliability of particular individuals, which happens in all systems, but they actually lose their meaning altogether. Religious ethics is confronted by a world of depersonalized relationships which for fundamental reasons cannot submit to even the primary norms of religious ethics. Consequently, priesthoods have always, in an interesting shift of roles and also in the interests of traditionalism, protected patriarchalism against impersonal relationships of dependence, whereas prophetic religion on the contrary breaks through patriarchal social structures. The more a religion is aware of its opposition in principle to economic rationalization as such, the more apt are the religion's virtuosi to reject the world, especially its economic activities.

Systems of religious ethics, because they were forced to make inevitable compromises in the world of facts, experienced very diverse fates. From of old, systems of religious ethics were directly employed for rational economic purposes, especially the purposes of creditors. This was especially true wherever the state of indebtedness legally involved the very person of the debtor, so that the creditor might appeal to the filial piety of the heirs. An example of this practice is the prohibition against pawning the mummy of the deceased in Egypt. Another example is the belief in many Asiatic religions that whoever fails to keep a promise, including a promise to repay a loan and especially a promise guaranteed by an oath, will be tortured in the next world and consequently will disturb the quiet of his descendants by evil magic. In the Middle Ages, as Schulte has pointed out, the credit standing of bishops was particularly high because any breach of obligation on their part, especially of an obligation assumed under oath, might result in their excommunication, which would have ruined a bishop's whole life. This reminds one of the equally high credit ratings of our lieutenants and fraternity students.

By a unique paradox, asceticism actually resulted in the contradictory situation already mentioned on several previous occasions, namely that it was precisely its rationally ascetic character that led to the accumulation of wealth. The cheap labor of ascetic bachelors, who underbid the indispensable minimum wage required by married male workers, was primarily responsible for the expansion of middle-class business in the late Middle Ages. The reaction of the middle classes against the monasteries during this period was based on the "coolie" economic competition offered by the monasteries. In the same way, the secular education offered by the cloister was able to underbid the education offered by married teachers.

The attitudes of a religion can often be explained on grounds of economic interest. The Byzantine monks were economically involved in the worship of icons, and the Chinese monks had an economic interest in the products of their workshops and printing establishments. An extreme example of this kind is provided by the manufacture of alcoholic liquors in modern monasteries, which defies the religious campaign against alcohol. Factors such as these have tended to work against any consistent religious opposition to worldly economic activities. Every organization, and particularly every institutional religion, requires sources of economic power. Indeed, scarcely any doctrine has been belabored with such terrible papal curses, especially at the hands of the greatest financial organizer of the church, John XXII, as the doctrine that Christ requires poverty of his true followers, a doctrine which enjoys scriptural authority and was consistently espoused by the Franciscan faithful. From the time of Arnold of Brescia and down through the centuries, a whole train of martyrs died for this doctrine.

It is difficult to estimate the practical effect of Christianity's prohibition of usury, and even more difficult to estimate the practical effect of Christianity's doctrine with respect to economic acquisitiveness in business, viz., *deo placare non potest*. The prohibitions against usury generated legalistic circumventions of all sorts. Ultimately, after a hard struggle, the church itself was virtually compelled to permit undisguised usury in the charitable establishments of the *montes pietatis* when the loans were in the interests of the poor; this became definitively established after Leo X. Furthermore, emergency loans for businesses at fixed rates of interest were provided during the Middle Ages by allocating this function to the Jews.

We must note, however, that in the Middle Ages fixed interest charges were rare in the entrepreneurial contracts extending business credit to enterprises subject to great risk, especially transoceanic commerce, just as fixed interest charges were rare in connection with the property of wards in Italy. The more usual procedure was actual participation in the risk and profit of an enterprise (*commenda dare ad proficuum de mari*), with various limitations and occasionally with a graduated scale such as that provided in the Pisan *Constitum Usus*. Yet the great guilds of merchants nevertheless protected themselves against the imputation of *usuraria pravitas* by expulsion from the guild, boycott, or blacklist, punitive measures comparable to those taken under our stock exchange regulations against fraudulent practices. The guilds also watched over the personal salvation of the souls of their members by providing them with indulgences (as in the *Arte de Calimala*) and by innumerable testamentary gifts of conscience money or endowments.

The wide chasm separating the inevitabilities of economic life from the Christian ideal was still frequently felt deeply. In any case this ethical separation kept the most devout groups and all those with the most consistently developed ethics far from the life of trade. Above all, it increasingly tended to attach an ethical stigma to the business spirit, and to impede its growth. The rise of a closed, systematic, and ethically regulated mode of life in the economic domain was completely prevented by the medieval institutional church's expedient of grading religious obligations according to religious charisma and ethical vocation and by the church's other expedient of granting dispensations. The fact that people with rigorous ethical standards simply could not take up a business career was not altered by the dispensation of indulgences, nor by the extremely lax principles of the Jesuit probabilistic ethics after the Counter Reformation. A business career was only possible for those who were lax in their ethical thinking.

The inner-worldly asceticism of Protestantism first produced a capitalistic state, although unintentionally, for it opened the way to a career in business, especially for the most devout and ethically rigorous people. Above all, Protestantism interpreted success in business as the fruit of a rational mode of life. Indeed, Protestantism, and especially ascetic Protestantism, confined the prohibition against usury to clear cases of complete selfishness. But by this principle it now denounced interest as hateful usury in situations which the Roman church itself had, as a matter of practice, tolerated, e.g., in the *montes pietatis,* the extension of credit to the poor. It is worthy of note that Christian business men and the Jews had long since felt to be irksome the competition of these institutions which lent to the poor. Very different was the Protestant justification of interest as a legitimate form of participation by the provider of capital in the business profits accruing from the money he had lent, especially wherever credit had been extended to the wealthy and powerful people, e.g., to the nobility, for political purposes. This interpretation was presumably the achievement of Salmasius.

One of the most notable economic effects of Calvinism was its destruction of the traditional forms of charity. First it eliminated miscellaneous almsgiving. To be sure, the first steps toward the systematization of charity had been taken with the introduction

Religious Ethics, World Order, and Culture 221

of fixed rules for the distribution of the bishop's fund in the later medieval church, and with the institution of the medieval hospital—in the same way that the poor tax in Islam had rationalized and centralized almsgiving. Yet miscellaneous almsgiving had still retained its importance in Christianity as a good work. The innumerable charitable institutions of ethical religions have always led in practice to the creation and direct cultivation of mendicancy, and in any case charitable institutions tended to make of charity a purely ritual gesture, as the fixed number of daily meals in the Byzantine monastic establishment or the official soup days of the Chinese. Calvinism put an end to all this, and especially to any benevolent attitude toward the beggar. For Calvinism held that the unsearchable God possessed good reasons for having distributed the gifts of fortune unequally. It never ceased to stress the notion that a man proved himself exclusively in his vocational work. Consequently, begging was explicitly stigmatized as a violation of the injunction to love one's neighbor, in this case the person from whom the beggar solicits.

What is more, all Puritan preachers proceeded from the assumption that the idleness of a person capable of work was inevitably his own fault. But it was felt necessary to organize charity systematically for those incapable of work, such as orphans and cripples, for the greater glory of God. This notion often resulted in such striking phenomena as dressing institutionalized orphans in uniforms reminiscent of fool's attire and parading them through the streets of Amsterdam to divine services with the greatest possible fanfare. Care for the poor was oriented to the goal of discouraging the slothful. This goal was quite apparent in the social welfare program of the English Puritans, in contrast to the program found in Anglicanism, a fact so well described by H. Levy. In any case, charity itself became a rationalized "enterprise," and its religious significance was therefore eliminated or even transformed into the opposite significance. This was the situation in consistent ascetic and rationalized religions.

Mystical religions had necessarily to take a diametrically opposite path with regard to the rationalization of economics. The foundering of the postulate of brotherly love in its collision with the loveless realities of the economic domain once it became rationalized led to the expansion of love for one's fellow man until it came to require a completely unselective generosity. Such unselective generosity did not inquire into the reason and outcome of absolute self-surrender, into the worth of the person soliciting help, or into his capacity to help himself. It asked no questions, and quickly gave a shirt when a cloak had been asked for. In mystical religions, the individual for whom the sacrifice is made is regarded in the final analysis as unimportant and fungible; his individual value is negated. One's fellow man is simply a person whom one happens to encounter along the way; he has significance only because of his need and his solicitation. This results in a distinctively mystical flight from the world which takes the form of a non-specific and loving self-surrender, not for the sake of the man but for the sake of the surrender itself—what Baudelaire has termed "the sacred prostitution of the soul."

XIV. The Relationship of Religion to Politics, Economics, Sexuality, and Art

Every religiously grounded unworldly love and indeed every ethical religion must, in similar measure and for similar reasons, experience tensions with the sphere of political behavior. This tension appears as soon as religion has progressed to anything like a status of equality with the sphere of political associations. To be sure, the ancient political god of the locality, even where he was an ethical and universally powerful god, existed merely for the protection of the political interests of his followers' associations.

Even the Christian God is still invoked as a god of war and as a god of our fathers, in much the same way that local gods were invoked in the ancient *polis*. One is reminded of the fact that for centuries Christian ministers have prayed along the beaches of the North Sea for a "blessing upon the strand," in reaction to the numerous shipwrecks there. On its part the priesthood generally depended upon the political association, either directly or indirectly. This dependence is especially strong in those contemporary churches which derive support from governmental subvention. It was particularly noteworthy where the priests were court or patrimonial officials of rulers or landed magnates, e.g., the *purohita* of India or the Byzantine court bishops of Constantine. The same dependence also arose wherever the priests themselves were either enfeoffed feudal lords exercising secular power, or scions of noble priestly families, e.g., as during the medieval period in the Occident. Among the Chinese and Hindus as well as the Jews, the sacred bards, whose compositions were practically everywhere incorporated into the scriptures, sang the praises of heroic death. According to the canonical books of the Brahmins, a heroic death was as much an ideal obligation of the Kshatriya caste member at the age when he had "seen the son of his son" as withdrawal from the world into the forests for meditation was an obligation of members of the Brahmin caste. Of course, magical religion had no conception of religious wars. But for magical religion, and even for the ancient religion of Yahweh, political victory and especially vengeance against the enemy constituted the real reward granted by god.

The more the priesthood attempted to organize itself as a power independent of the political authorities, and the more rationalized its ethic became, the more this position shifted. The contradiction within the priestly preaching, between brotherliness toward fellow religionists and the glorification of war against outsiders, did not as a general rule decisively stigmatize martial virtues and heroic qualities. This was so because a distinction could be drawn between just and unjust wars. However, this distinction was a product of pharisaical thought, which was unknown to the old and genuine warrior ethics.

Of far greater importance was the rise of congregational religions among politically demilitarized peoples under the control of priests, such as the Jews, and also the rise of large and increasingly important groups of people who, though comparatively unwarlike, became increasingly important for the priests' maintenance of their power position wherever they had developed into an independent organization. The priesthood unquestioningly welcomed the characteristic virtues of these classes, viz., simplicity, patient resignation to trouble, humble acceptance of existing authority, and friendly forgiveness and passivity in the face of injustice, especially since these virtues were useful in establishing the ascendancy of an ethical god and of the priests themselves. These virtues were also complementary to the special religious virtue of the powerful, namely magnanimous charity (*caritas*), since the patriarchal donors desired these virtues of resignation and humble acceptance in those who benefited from their assistance.

The more a religion acquired the aspects of a "communal religion" (*Gemeinde-Religiosität*), the more political circumstances co-operated to lend a religious transfiguration to the ethic of the subjugated. Thus, Jewish prophecy, in a realistic recognition of the external political situation, preached resignation to the dominion of the great powers, as a fate apparently desired by God. As this type of religion spread, several factors continued to lend distinctive religious value to the aforementioned feminine virtues of the subjugated. One such social factor was the assignment to the priests of control over the masses, which was first practiced systematically by foreign rulers like the Persians and later by native Jewish rulers. Other social factors were the distinctively unwarlike activities of the priests themselves and their universal experience of the particularly intense effect of religious stimuli upon women. But there tended in this direction much more than the "slave revolt" in the realm of morality under the leadership of the priests. In addition, every ascetic, and especially mystical and personal quest for salvation which emerged among those individuals who had left tradition behind took this line. This occurred because of the very nature of the autonomous laws of religion, which we have examined. Certain typical external situations also contributed to this development, e.g., the apparently senseless changes of limited and ephemeral small political power structures in contrast to universalistic religions and relatively unitary social cultures such as that of India. Two other historical processes operating in the opposite direction also contributed to the same development: universal pacification and the elimination of all struggles for power in the great world empires, and particularly the bureaucratization of all political dominion, as in the Roman Empire.

All these factors removed the ground from under the political and social interests involved in a warlike struggle for power and involved in a social class conflict, thus tending to generate an antipolitical rejection of the world and to favor the development of a religious ethic of brotherly love that renounced all violence. The power of the apolitical Christian religion of love was not derived from interests in social reform, nor from any such thing as "proletarian instincts," but rather from the complete loss of such concerns. The same motivation accounts for the increasing importance of all salvation religions and congregational religions since the first and second centuries of the Roman period. This transformation was carried out, not only or even primarily by the subjugated classes who in their slave revolts had become the carriers of special anti-political religions, but principally by those who had lost interest in politics, who were without influence in politics, or who had become disgusted by politics.

The altogether universal experience that violence breeds violence, that social or economic power interests may combine with idealistic reforms and even with revolutionary movements, and that the employment of violence against some particular injustice produces as its ultimate result the victory, not of the greater justice, but of the greater power or cleverness, did not remain concealed, at least not from the intellectuals who lacked political interests. This recognition continued to evoke the most radical demands for the ethic of brotherly love, i.e., that evil should not be resisted by force, an injunction that is common to Buddhism and to the preaching of Jesus. But the ethic of brotherly love is also characteristic of mystical religions, because their peculiar quest for salvation fosters an attitude of humility and self-surrender as a result of its minimization of activity in the world and its affirmation of the necessity of passing through the world incognito, so to speak, as the only proven method for demonstrating salvation. Indeed, from the purely psychological point of view, mystical religion must necessarily come to this conclusion by virtue of its characteristically acosmistic and non-specific experience of love. Yet every pure intellectualism bears within itself the possibility of such a mystical development.

On the other hand, inner-worldly asceticism can compromise with the facts of the political power structures by interpreting them as instruments for the rationalized ethical transformation of the world and for the control of sin. It must be noted, however, that the coexistence is by no means as easy in this case as in the case where economic acquisitive interests are concerned. For public political activity leads to a far greater surrender of rigorous ethical requirements than is produced by private economic acquisitiveness, since political activity is oriented to average human qualities, to compromises, to craft, and to the employment of other ethically suspect devices and people, and thereby oriented to the relativization of all goals. Thus, it is very striking that under the glorious regime of the Maccabees, after the first intoxication of the war of liberation had been dissipated, there arose among the most pious

Jews a party which preferred alien hegemony to rule by the national kingdom. This may be compared to the preference found among many Puritan denominations for the subjection of the churches to the dominion of unbelievers, because genuineness of religion can be regarded as proven in such churches. In both these cases two distinct motives were operative. One was that a genuine commitment in religion could be truly demonstrated only in martyrdom; the other was the theoretical insight that the political apparatus of force could not possibly provide a place for purely religious virtues, whether uncompromising rational ethics or acosmistic fraternalism. This is one source of the affinity between inner-worldly asceticism and the advocacy of the minimization of state control such as was represented by the doctrine of the "Manchester school."

The conflict of ascetic ethics, as well as of the mystically oriented temper of brotherly love, with the apparatus of domination which is basic to all political institutions produced the most varied types of tension and compromise. Naturally, the polarity between religion and politics is least wherever, as in Confucianism, religion is equivalent to a belief in spirits or simply a belief in magic, and ethics is no more than a clever accommodation to the world on the part of the educated man. Nor does any conflict at all between religion and politics exist wherever, as in Islam, religion makes obligatory the violent propagandizing of a true prophecy which consciously eschews universal conversion and enjoins the subjugation of unbelievers under the dominion of a ruling class dedicated to the religious war as one of the basic postulates of its faith, without however recognizing the salvation of the subjugated. The practice of coercion poses no problem, since god is pleased by the forcible dominion of the faithful over the infidels, who are tolerated once they have been subjugated.

Inner-worldly asceticism reached a similar solution to the problem of the relation between religion and politics wherever, as in radical Calvinism, it represented as God's will the domination over the sinful world, for the purpose of controlling it, of religious virtuosi belonging to the "pure" church. This view was fundamental in the theocracy of New England, in practice if not explicitly, though naturally it became involved with compromises of various kinds. Another instance of the absence of any conflict between religion and politics is to be found in the intellectualistic salvation doctrines of India, such as Buddhism and Jainism, in which every relationship to the world and to action within the world is broken off, and in which the personal exercise of violence as well as resistance to violence is absolutely prohibited and is indeed without any object. Actual conflicts between concrete demands of a state and concrete religious injunctions arise only when a religion is the pariah faith of a group that is excluded from political equality but still believes in the religious prophecies of a divinely appointed restoration of its social level. This was the case in Judaism, which never in theory rejected the state and its coercion but, on the contrary, expected in the Messiah their own masterful political ruler, an expectation that was sustained at least until the time of the destruction of the Temple by Hadrian.

Wherever communal religions have rejected all employment of force as an abomination to god and have sought to require their members' avoidance of all contact with violence, without however reaching the consistent conclusion of absolute flight from the world, the conflict between religion and politics has led either to martyrdom or to passive anti-political sufferance of the coercive regime. History shows that religious anarchism has hitherto been only a short-lived phenomenon, because the intensity of faith which makes it possible is in only an ephemeral charisma. Yet there have been independent political organizations which were based, not on a purely anarchistic foundation, but on a foundation of consistent pacifism. The most important of these was the Quaker community in Pennsylvania, which for two generations actually succeeded, in contrast to all the neighboring colonies, in existing side by side with the Indians, and indeed prospering, without recourse to violence. Such situations continued until the conflicts of the great colonial powers made a fiction of pacifism. Finally, the American War of Independence, which was waged in the name of the basic principles of Quakerism though the orthodox Quakers did not participate because of their principle of non-resistance, led to the discrediting of this principle, even inwardly. Moreover, the corresponding policy of the tolerant admission of religious dissidents into Pennsylvania brought even the Quakers there to a policy of gerrymandering political wards, which caused them increasing uneasiness and ultimately led them to withdraw from political participation in and co-responsibility for the government.

Typical examples of completely passive indifference to the political dimension of society, from a variety of motives, are found in such groups as the genuine Mennonites, in most Baptist communities, and especially in the numerous Russian sects in various places. The absolute renunciation of the use of force by these groups led them into acute conflicts with the political authorities only where military service was demanded of the individuals concerned. Indeed, attitudes toward war, even of religious denominations that did not teach an absolutely anti-political attitude, have varied in particular cases, depending upon whether the wars in question were fought to protect the religion's freedom of worship from attack by political authority or fought for purely political purposes. For these two types of warlike employment of violence, two diametrically opposite slogans prevailed. On the one hand, there was the purely passive sufferance of alien power and the withdrawal from any personal participation in the exercise of violence, culminating ultimately in personal martyrdom. This was of course the position of mystical apoliticism, with its absolute indifference to the world, as well as the position of those types of inner-worldly asceticism which were pacifistic in principle. But even a purely personal religion of faith frequently generated political indifference and religious martyrdom, inasmuch as it recognized neither a rational order of the outer world pleasing to God, nor a rational domination of the world desired by God. Thus, Luther completely rejected religious revolutions as well as religious wars.

The other possible standpoint was that of violent resistance to the employment of force against religion. The concept of a religious revolution was not consistent with a rationalism oriented to an ascetic mastery of mundane affairs, which taught that sacred institutions and institutions pleasing to God exist within this world. This was the case in Christianity, and particularly in Calvinism, which made it a religious obligation to defend the faith against tyranny by the use of force. It should be added, however, that Calvin taught that this defense might be undertaken only at the initiative of the proper authorities, in keeping with the character of an institutional church. The obligation to bring about a revolution in behalf of the faith was naturally taught by the religions that engaged in wars of missionary enterprise and by their derivative sects, like the Mahdists and other sects in Islam, including the Sikhs—a Hindu sect that was originally pacifist but passed under the influence of Islam and became eclectic.

The representatives of the two opposed viewpoints just described sometimes took virtually contradictory positions toward wars that had no religious motivation. Religions that applied ethically rationalized demands to the political realm had necessarily to take a more fundamentally negative attitude toward purely political wars than those religions that accepted the institutions of the world as "given" and relatively indifferent in value. The unconquered army of Cromwell petitioned Parliament for the abolition of forcible conscription, on the ground that a Christian should participate only in those wars the justice of which could be affirmed by his own conscience. From this standpoint, the mercenary army might be regarded as a relatively ethical institution, inasmuch as the mercenary would have to settle with God and his conscience as to whether he would take up this calling. The employment of force by the state can have moral sanction only when the force is used for the control of sins, for the glory of God, and for combating religious evils—in short, only for religious purposes. On the other hand, the view of Luther, who absolutely rejected religious wars and revolutions as well as any active resistance, was that only the secular authority, whose domain is untouched by the rational postulates of religion, has the responsibility of determining whether political wars are just or unjust. Hence, the individual subject has no reason to burden his own conscience with this matter if only he gives active obedience to the political authority in this and in all other matters which do not destroy his relationship to God.

The position of ancient and medieval Christianity in relation to the state as a whole oscillated or, more correctly, shifted its center of gravity from one to another of several distinct points of view. At first there was a complete abomination of the existing Roman empire, whose existence until the very end of time was taken for granted in antiquity by everyone, even Christians. The empire was regarded as the dominion of Anti-Christ. A second view was complete indifference to the state, and hence passive sufferance of the use of force, which was deemed to be unrighteous in every case. This entailed active compliance with all the coercive obligations imposed by the state, e.g., the payment of taxes which did not directly imperil religious salvation. For the true intent of the New Testament verse about "rendering unto Caesar the things which are Caesar's" is not the meaning deduced by modern harmonizing interpretations, namely a positive recognition of the obligation to pay taxes, but rather the reverse: an absolute indifference to all the affairs of the mundane world.

Two other viewpoints were possible. One entailed withdrawal from concrete activities of the political community, such as the cult of the emperors, because and insofar as such participation necessarily led to sin. Nevertheless, the state's authority was accorded positive recognition as being somehow desired by God, even when exercised by unbelievers and even though inherently sinful. It was taught that the state's authority, like all the institutions of this world, is an ordained punishment for the sin brought upon man by Adam's fall, which the Christian must obediently take upon himself. Finally, the authority of the state, even when exercised by unbelievers, might be evaluated positively, due to our condition of sin, as an indispensable instrument, based upon the divinely implanted natural knowledge of religiously unilluminated heathen, for the social control of reprehensible sins and as a general condition for all mundane existence pleasing to God.

Of these four points of view, the first two mentioned belong primarily to the period of eschatological expectation, but occasionally they come to the fore even in a later period. As far as the last of the four is concerned, ancient Christianity did not really go beyond it in principle, even after it had been recognized as the state religion. Rather, the great change in the attitude of Christianity toward the state took place in the medieval church, as the investigations of Troeltsch have brilliantly demonstrated. But the problem in which Christianity found itself involved as a result, while not limited to this religion, nevertheless generated a whole complex of difficulties peculiar to Christianity alone, partly from internal religious causes and partly from the operation of non-religious factors. This critical complex of difficulties concerned the relationship of the so-called "law of nature" to religious revelation on the one hand, and to positive political institutions and their activities on the other.

We shall have to go into this matter at somewhat greater length, both in connection with our exposition of the forms of religious communities and in our analysis of the forms of domination. But the following point may be made here regarding the theoretical solution of these problems as it affects personal ethics: the general schema according to which religion customarily solves the problem of the tension between religious ethics and the non-ethical or unethical requirements of life in the political and economic structures of power within the world is to relativize and differentiate ethics into an organic ethic of vocation and a contrasting ascetic ethic. This holds true whenever a religion is dominant within a political organization or occupies a privileged status, and particularly when it is a religion of institutional grace.

Christian doctrine, as formulated by Aquinas for example, to some degree assumed the view, already common in animistic beliefs regarding souls and the world beyond, that there are purely natural differences among men, completely independent of any effects of sin, and that these natural differences determine the diversity of destinies in this world and beyond. Troeltsch has correctly stressed the point that this formulation of Christian doctrine differs from the view found in Stoicism and earliest Christianity of an original golden age and a blissful state of generalized anarchistic equality of all human beings.

At the same time, however, Christianity interpreted the power relationships of the mundane world in a metaphysical way. Human beings are condemned—whether as a result of original sin, of an individual causality of *karma,* or of the corruption of the world deriving from a basic dualism—to suffer violence, toil, pain, hate, and above all differences in class and caste position within the world. The various callings or castes have been providentially ordained, and each of them has been assigned some specific, indispensable function desired by god or determined by the impersonal world order, so that different ethical obligations devolve upon each status. The diverse occupations and castes are compared to the constituent portions of an organism, in this type of theory. The various relationships of power which emerge in such a social system must therefore be regarded as divinely ordained relationships of authority. Accordingly, any revolt or rebellion against them, or even the raising of vital claims other than those corresponding to one's status in society, is reprehensible to god because they are expressions of creaturely self-aggrandizement and pride, which are destructive of sacred tradition. The virtuosi of religion, be they of an ascetic or contemplative type, are also assigned their specific responsibility within such an organic order, just as specific functions have been allocated to princes, warriors, judges, artisans, and peasants. This allocation of responsibilities to religious virtuosi is intended to produce a treasure of supernumerary good works which the institution of grace may thereupon distribute. By subjecting himself to the revealed truth and to the correct sentiment of love, the individual will achieve, and that within the established institutions of the world, happiness in this world and reward in the life to come.

For Islam, this organic conception and its entire complex of related problems was much more remote, since Islam rejected universalism, regarding the ideal social stratification as consisting of believers and unbelievers or pariah peoples, with the former dominating the latter. Accordingly, Islam left the pariah peoples entirely to themselves in all matters which were of indifference to religion. It is true that the mystical quest for salvation and ascetic virtuoso religion did conflict with institutional orthodoxy in the Muslim religion. It is also true that Islam did experience conflicts between sacred and profane law, which always arise when positive sacred norms of the law have developed. Finally, Islam did have to face certain questions of orthodoxy in the theocratic constitution. But Islam did not confront the ultimate problem of the relationship between religious ethics and secular institutions, which is the fundamental problem of the relation between law and religion.

On the other hand, the Hindu books of law promulgated an organic, traditionalistic ethic of vocation, similar in structure to medieval Catholicism, only more consistent, and certainly more consistent than the rather thin Lutheran doctrine regarding the *status ecclesiasticus, politicus,* and *economicus.* As we have already seen, the status system in India actually combined a caste ethic with a distinctive doctrine of salvation. That is, it held that an individual's chances of an ever higher ascent in future incarnations upon earth depend on his having fulfilled the obligations of his own caste, be they ever so disesteemed socially. This belief had the effect of inducing a radical acceptance of the social order, especially among the very lowest classes, the classes which would have most to gain in any transmigration of souls.

On the other hand, the Hindu theodicy would have regarded as absurd the medieval Christian doctrine, as set forth for example by Beatrice in the *Paradiso* of Dante, that the class differences which obtain during one's brief span of life upon earth will be perpetuated into some permanent "existence" in the world beyond. Indeed, such a view would have deprived the strict traditionalism of the Hindu organic ethic of vocation of all the infinite hopes for the future entertained by the pious Hindu who believed in the transmigration of souls and the possibility of an ever more elevated form of life upon this earth. Hence, even from the purely religious point of view, the Christian doctrine of the perpetuation of class distinctions into the next world had the effect of providing a much less secure foundation for the traditional stratification of vocations than did the steel-like anchorage of caste to the altogether different religious promises contained in the doctrine of metempsychosis.

The medieval and the Lutheran traditionalistic ethics of vocation actually rested on a general presupposition, one that is increasingly rare, which both share with the Confucian ethic: that power relationships in both the economic and political spheres have a purely personal character. In these spheres of the execution of justice and particularly in political administration, a whole organized structure of personal relations of subordination exists which is dominated by caprice and grace, indignation and love, and most of all by the mutual piety and devotion of masters and subalterns, after the fashion of the family. Thus, these relationships of domination have a character to which one may apply ethical requirements in the same way that one applies them to every other purely personal relationship.

Yet as we shall see later, it is quite certain that the "masterless slavery" (Wagner) of the modern proletariat and above all the whole realm of the rationalized institution of the state—the so-called "rascally state" (*Rackers von Staat*) so abominated by romanticism—no longer possess this personalistic character. In a personalistic order of status it is quite clear that one must act differently toward persons of different statuses. The only problem that may arise on occasion, even for Thomas Aquinas, is how this is to be construed. Today, however, the *homo politicus,* as well as the *homo economicus,* performs his duty best when he acts without regard to the person in question, *sine ira et studio,* without hate and without love, without personal predilection and therefore without grace, but sheerly in accordance with the factual, material responsibility imposed by his calling, and not as a result of any concrete personal relationship. In short, modern man discharges his responsibility best when he acts as closely as possible in accordance with the rational regulations of the modern power system. Modern procedures of justice impose capital punishment upon the malefactor, not out of personal indignation or the need for vengeance, but with complete detachment and for the sake of objective norms and ends, simply for the working out of the rational autonomous lawfulness inherent in justice. This is comparable to the impersonal retribution of *karma,* in contrast to Yahweh's fervent quest for vengeance.

The use of force within the political community increasingly assumes the form of a material and social order founded on a lawful state. But from the point of view of religion, this is merely an effective mimicry of brutality. All politics is oriented to the material facts of the dominant interest of the state, to realism, and to the autonomous end of maintaining the external and internal distribution of power. These goals, again, must necessarily seem completely senseless from the religious point of view. Yet only in this way does the realm of politics acquire a uniquely rational dynamic of its own, once brilliantly formulated by Napoleon, which appears as thoroughly alien to every ethic of brotherliness as do the rationalized economic institutions. The accommodation that contemporary ecclesiastical ethics is making to this situation cannot be discussed in detail here. In general the compromise takes form through reaction to each concrete situation as it arises. Certainly, the goal of the Catholic church is to salvage its ecclesiastical power interests, which have increasingly become objectified into a doctrine of the fundamental interests of the church, by the employment of the same modern instruments of power employed by secular institutions.

The objectification of the power structure, with the complex of problems produced by its rationalized ethical provisos, has but one psychological equivalent: the vocational ethic taught by an asceticism that is oriented to the control of the terrestrial world. An increased tendency toward flight into the irrationalities of apolitical emotionalism, in different degrees and even forms, is one of the actual consequences of the rationalization of coercion, manifesting itself wherever the exercise of power has developed away from the personalistic orientation of individual heroes and wherever the entire society in question has developed in the direction of a national "state." Such apolitical emotionalism may take the form of a flight into mysticism and an acosmistic ethic of absolute goodness or into the irrationalities of non-religious emotionalism, above all eroticism. Indeed, the power of the sphere of eroticism enters into particular tensions with religions of salvation. This is particularly true of one of the most powerful components of eroticism, namely sexual love. For sexual love, along with the "true" or economic interest, and the social drives toward power and prestige, is among the most fundamental and universal components of the actual course of interpersonal behavior.

The relationship of religion to sexuality is extraordinarily intimate, though it is partly conscious and partly unconscious, and though it may be indirect as well as direct. We shall give our undivided attention to a few traits of this relationship that have sociological relevance, leaving out of account as being rather unimportant for our purposes the innumerable relationships of sexuality to magical notions, animistic notions, and symbols. In the first place, sexual intoxication is a typical component of the orgy, which is the communal religious behavior of the laity at a primitive level. The function of sexual intoxication is even retained in relatively systematized religions, in some cases quite directly and by calculation. This is the case in the Shakti religion of India, after the pattern of the ancient phallic cults and rites of the various functional gods who control reproduction, whether of man, beast, cattle, or grains of seed. More frequently, however, the erotic orgy appears in religion as an undesired consequence of ecstasy basically produced by other orgiastic means, namely the dance. Among modern sects, this was still the case in the terpsichorean orgy of the Chlysti. This provided the stimulus for the formation of the Skoptzi sect, which, as we have seen, then sought to eliminate this erotic by-product so inimical to asceticism. Various institutions which have been misunderstood, as for example temple prostitution, are related to orgiastic cults. In practice, temple prostitution frequently fulfilled the function of a brothel for traveling traders who enjoyed the protection of the sanctuary. (In the nature of the case, the typical client of brothels to this very day remains the traveling salesman.) To attribute extraordinary sexual orgies to a primordial and endogamous promiscuity obtaining in the everyday life of the clan or tribe as a generic primitive institution is simply nonsense.

The intoxication of the sexual orgy can, as we have seen, be sublimated explicitly or implicitly into erotic love for a god or savior. But there may also emerge from the sexual orgy, from temple prostitution, or from other magical practices the notion that sexual surrender has a religious meritoriousness. This aspect of the matter need not interest us here. Yet there can be no doubt that a considerable portion of the specifically anti-erotic religions, both mystical and ascetic, represent substitute satisfactions of sexually conditioned psychological needs. What concerns us in this religious hostility to sexuality is not the psychological relationships, important aspects of which are still controversial, but rather the relationships which have significance for our sociological approach. For the religious antipathy to sex may produce quite diverse results in actual conduct, according to the significance which is attributed to sex. Even these consequences for action are of only partial interest here. The most limited manifestation of the religiously grounded antipathy to sexuality is cultic chastity, a temporary abstinence from sexual activity by the priests or participants in the cult prior to the administration of sacraments. A primary reason for such temporary abstinence is usually regard for the norms of taboo which for various magical and spiritualistic reasons control the sexual sphere. The details of this matter do not concern us at this point.

On the other hand, the permanent abstinence of charismatic asceticism and the chastity of priests and religious virtuosi derives primarily from the view that chastity, as a highly extraordinary type of behavior, is a symptom of charismatic qualities and a source of valuable ecstatic abilities, which qualities and abilities are necessary instruments for the magical control of the god. Later on, especially in occidental Christianity, the decisive reason for priestly celibacy was the necessity that the ethical achievement of the priestly incumbents of ecclesiastical office not lag behind that of the ascetic virtuosi, the monks. Another decisive reason for the emphasis upon the celibacy of the clergy was the church's interest in preventing the inheritance of its benefices by the heirs of priests.

At the level of ethical religion, two other significant attitudes of antipathy to sexuality developed in place of the various types of magical motivation. One was the conception of mystical flight from the world, which interpreted sexual abstinence as the central and indispensable instrument of the mystical quest for salvation through contemplative withdrawal from the world. From this view, sexuality, the drive that most firmly binds man to the animal level, furnishes the most powerful temptations to withdrawal from the mystical quest. The other basic position was that of asceticism. Rational ascetic alertness, self-control, and methodical planning of life are seriously threatened by the peculiar irrationality of the sexual act, which is ultimately and uniquely unsusceptible to rational organization. These two motivations have frequently operated together to produce hostility toward sexuality in particular religions. All genuine religious prophecies and all non-prophetic priestly systematizations of religion without exception concern themselves with sexuality, from such motives as we have just discussed, generally terminating in hostility toward sexuality.

Religion primarily desires to eliminate the sexual orgy (the "whoredom" denounced by the Jewish priests), in keeping with prophetic religion's general attitude toward orgies, which we have described already. But an additional effort is made by religion to eliminate all free sexual relationships in the interest of the religious regulation and legitimation of marriage. Such an effort was even made by Muhammad, although in his personal life and in his religious preachments regarding the world beyond he permitted unlimited sexual freedom to the warrior of the faith. It will be recalled that in one of his *suras* he ordained a special dispensation regarding the maximum number of wives permitted for himself. The various forms of extra-marital love and prostitution, which were legal before the establishment of orthodox Islam, have been proscribed in that religion with a success scarcely duplicated elsewhere.

World-fleeing asceticism of the Christian and Hindu types would obviously have been expected to evince an antipathetic attitude toward sex. The mystical Hindu prophecies of absolute and contemplative world-flight naturally made the rejection of all sexual relations a prerequisite for complete salvation. But even the Confucian ethic of absolute accommodation to the world viewed irregular sexual expression as an inferior irrationality, since irregular behavior in this sphere disturbed the inner equilibrium of a gentleman and since woman was viewed as an irrational creature difficult to control. Adultery was prohibited in the Mosaic Decalogue, in the Hindu sacred law, and even in the relativistic lay ethics of the Hindu monastic prophecies. The religious preaching of Jesus, with its demand of absolute and indissoluble monogamy, went beyond all other religions in the limitations imposed upon permissible and legitimate sexuality. In the earliest period of Christianity, adultery and whoredom were regarded as the only absolute mortal sins. The *univira* was regarded as the hallmark of the Christian community in the Mediterranean littoral area, which had been educated by the Greeks and the Romans to accept monogamy, but with free divorce.

The various prophets differed widely in their personal attitudes toward and their religious teachings about woman, her place in the community, and her distinctive feeling tone. The fact that a prophet such as the Buddha was glad to see clever women sitting at his feet and the fact that he employed them as propagandists and missionaries, as did Pythagoras, did not necessarily carry over into an evaluation of the whole female sex. A particular woman might be regarded as sacred, yet the entire female sex would still be considered vessels of sin. Yet practically all orgiastic and mystagogic religious propagandizing, including that of the cult of Dionysos, called for at least a temporary and relative emancipation of women, unless such preachment was blocked by other religious tendencies or by specific resistance to hysterical preaching by women, as occurred among the disciples of the Buddha and in ancient Christianity as early as Paul. The admission of women to an equality of religious status was also resisted due to monastic misogyny, which assumed extreme forms in such sexual neurasthenics as Alfons of Liguori. Women are accorded the greatest importance in sectarian spiritualist cults, be they hysterical or sacramental, of which there are numerous instances in China. Where women played no role in the missionary expansion of a religion, as was the case in Zoroastrianism and Judaism, the situation was different from the very start.

Legally regulated marriage itself was regarded by both prophetic and priestly ethics, not as an erotic value, but in keeping with the sober view of the so-called "primitive peoples," simply as an economic institution for the production and rearing of children as a labor force and subsequently as carriers of the cult of the dead. This was also the view of the Greek and Roman ethical systems, and indeed of all ethical systems the world over which have given thought to the matter. The view expressed in the ancient Hebrew scriptures that the young bridegroom was to be free of political and military obligations for a while so that he might have the joy of his young love was a very rare view. Indeed, not even Judaism made any concessions to sophisticated erotic expression divorced from sexuality's natural consequence of reproduction, as we see in the Old Testament curse upon the sin of Onan (*coitus interruptus*). Roman Catholicism expressed the same rigorous attitude toward sexuality by rejecting birth control as a mortal sin. Of course every type of religious asceticism which is oriented toward the control of this world, and above all Puritanism, limits the legitimation of sexual expression to the aforementioned rational goal of reproduction. The animistic and semi-orgiastic types of mysticism were led by their universalistic feeling of love into only occasional deviations from the central hostility of religion toward sexuality.

Finally, the positive evaluation of normal and legitimate sexual intercourse, and thus of an ultimate relationship between religion and biological phenomena, which is often characteristic of rational prophetic ethics and even of ecclesiastical religious ethics, is still not uniform. Ancient Judaism and Confucianism generally taught that offspring were important. This view, also found in Vedic and Hindu ethics, was based in part on animistic notions and in part on later ideas. All such notions culminated in the direct religious obligation to beget children. In Talmudic Judaism and in Islam, on the other hand, the motivation of the comparable injunction to marry seems to have been based, in part at least, like the exclusion of unmarried ordained clergy from the lower ecclesiastical benefices in the oriental churches, on the conception that sexual expression is absolutely inevitable for the average man, for whom it is better that a legally regulated channel of expression be made available.

These beliefs in the inevitability of sexual expression correspond to the attitude of Paul and to the relativity of lay ethics in the Hindu contemplative religions of salvation, which proscribe adultery for the *upasakas*. Paul, from mystical motivations which we need not describe here, esteemed absolute abstinence as the purely personal charisma of religious virtuosi. The lay ethic of Catholicism also followed this point of view. Further, this was the attitude of Luther, who regarded sexual expression within marriage simply as a lesser evil enjoined for the avoidance of whoredom. Luther construed marriage as a legitimate sin which God was constrained not to notice, so to speak, and which of sourse was a consequence of the ineluctable concupiscence resulting from original sin. This notion, similar to Muhammad's notion, partly accounts for Luther's relatively weak opposition to monasticism at first. There was to be no sexuality in Jesus' kingdom to come, that is in some future terrestrial regime, and all official Christian theory strongly rejected the inner emotional side of sexuality as constituting concupiscence, the result of original sin.

Despite the widespread belief that hostility toward sexuality is an idiosyncracy of Christianity, it must be emphasized that no authentic religion of salvation had in principle any other point of view. There are a number of reasons for this. The first is based on the nature of the evolution that sexuality itself increasingly underwent in actual life, as a result of the rationalization of the conditions of life. At the level of the peasant, the sexual act is an everyday occurrence; primitive people do not regard this act as containing anything unusual, and they may indeed enact it before the eyes of onlooking travelers without the slightest feeling of shame. They do not regard this act as having any significance beyond the routine of living. The decisive development, from the point of view of the sociological problems which concern us, is the sublimation of sexual expression into an eroticism that becomes the basis of idiosyncratic sensations and generates its own unique values of an extraordinary kind. The impediments to sexual intercourse that are increasingly produced by the economic interests of clans and by class conventions are the most important factors favoring this sublimation of sexuality into eroticism. To be sure, sexual relations were never free of religious or economic regulations at any known point in the evolutionary sequence, but originally they were far less surrounded by bonds of convention, which gradually attach themselves to the original economic restrictions until they subsequently become the decisive restrictions on sexuality.

The influence of modern ethical limitations upon sexual relations, which is alleged to be the source of prostitution, is almost always interpreted erroneously. Professional prostitution of both the heterosexual and homosexual types (note the training of tribades) is found even at the most primitive levels of culture, and everywhere there is some religious, military, or economic limitation upon prostitution. However, the absolute proscription of prostitution dates only from the end of the fifteenth century. As culture becomes more complex there is a constant growth in the requirements imposed by the clan in regard to providing security for the children of the girls, and also in the life standards of young married couples. Thereby another evolutionary factor becomes necessarily important. In the formation of ethical attitudes the emergence of a new and progressively rationalized total life pattern, changing from the organic cycle of simple peasant existence, has a far stronger influence but one less likely to be noticed.

Just as ethical religion, especially if it preaches brotherly love, enters into the deepest inner tensions with the strongest irrational power of personal life, namely sexuality, so also does ethical religion enter into a strong polarity with the sphere of art. Religion and art are intimately related in the beginning. That religion has been an inexhaustible spring of artistic expressions is evident from the existence of idols and icons of every variety, and from the existence of music as a device for arousing ecstasy or for accompanying exorcism and apotropaic cultic actions. Religion has stimulated the artistic activities of magicians and sacred bards, as well as stimulating the creation of temples and churches (the greatest of artistic productions), together with the creation of religious artifacts and church vessels of all sorts, the chief objects of the arts and crafts. But the more art becomes an autonomous sphere, which happens as a result of lay education, the more art tends to acquire its own set of constitutive values, which are quite different from those obtaining in the religious and ethical domain.

Every uninhibited, receptive attitude toward art springs from the significance of the content, which may lead to the formation of a community. But the conscious discovery of uniquely esthetic values is reserved for an intellectualist civilization. This development causes the disappearance of those elements in art which are conducive to community formation and conducive to the compatibility of art with the religious will to salvation. Indeed, religion violently rejects as sinful the type of salvation within the world which art *qua* art claims to provide. Ethical religions as well as true mysticisms regard with hostility any such salvation from the ethical irrationalities of the world. The climax of this conflict between art and religion is reached in authentic asceticism, which views any surrender to esthetic values as a serious breach in the rational systematization of the conduct of life. This tension increases with the advance of intellectualism, which may be described as quasi-esthetic. The rejection of responsibility for ethical judgment and the fear of appearing bound by tradition, which come to the fore in intellectualist periods, shift judgments whose intention was originally ethical into an esthetic key. An example is the shift from the judgment "reprehensible" to the judgment "in poor taste." But the subjectivity of all judgments about human relationships, which is unavoidable and which actually comes to the fore in esthetic cults, may well be regarded by religion as one of the profoundest forms of idiosyncratic lovelessness conjoined with cowardice. Clearly there is a sharp contrast between the esthetic attitude and religio-ethical norms, since even when the individual rejects ethical norms he nevertheless experiences them humanly in his knowledge of his own creatureliness. He assumes some such norm to be basic for his own conduct as well as another's conduct in the particular case which he is judging. Moreover, it is assumed in principle that the justification and consequences of a religio-ethical norm remain subject to discussion. At all events, the esthetic attitude offers no support to a consistent ethic of fraternalism, which in its turn has a clearly anti-esthetic orientation.

The religious devaluation of art, which usually parallels the religious devaluation of magical, orgiastic, ecstatic, and ritualistic elements in favor of ascetic, spiritualistic, and mystical virtues, is intensified by the rational and literary character of both priestly and lay education in scriptural religions. But it is above all authentic prophecy that exerts an influence hostile to art, and that in two directions. First, prophecy obviously rejects orgiastic practices and usually rejects magic in general. Thus, the primal Jewish fear of images and likenesses, which originally had a magical basis, was given a spiritualistic interpretation by Hebrew prophecy and transformed in relation to a concept of an absolute and transcendental god. Second, somewhere along the line there arose the opposition of prophetic faith, which is centrally oriented to ethics and religion, to the work of human hands, which in the view of the prophets could promise only illusory salvation. The more the god proclaimed by the prophets was conceived as transcendental and sacred, the more insoluble and irreconcilable became this opposition between religion and art.

On the other hand, religion is continually brought to recognize the undeniable "divinity" of artistic achievement. Mass religion in particular is frequently and directly dependent on artistic devices for the required potency of its effects, since it is inclined to make concessions to the needs of the masses, which everywhere tend toward magic and idolatry. Apart from this, organized mass religions have frequently had connections with art resulting from economic interests. This must be remembered in seeking to understand the traffic in icons by the Byzantine monks. These monks, opponents of the Caesaropapistic imperial power, were supported by the iconoclastic army recruited from the marginal provinces of Islam, which still had a strongly spiritualistic character at that time. The imperial power, threatened with the loss of its sources of income, sought to eliminate the great threat to its plans for control over the church presented by such iconoclastic monks and armies.

Subjectively too, there is an easy way back to art from every orgiastic or ritualistic religion of emotionalism, as well as from every religion of love that culminates in a transcendence of individ-

uality—despite the heterogeneity of the ultimate meanings involved. Orgiastic religion leads most readily to song and music;
ritualistic religion inclines toward the pictorial arts; religions enjoining love favor the development of poetry and music. This relationship is demonstrated by all our experience of Hindu literature and
art; the joyous lyricism of the Sufis, so utterly receptive to the
world; the canticles of St. Francis; and the immeasurable influences
of religious symbolism, particularly in mystically formed attitudes.
Yet particular empirical religions hold basically different attitudes
toward art, and even within any one religion diverse attitudes toward art are manifested by different classes, carriers, and structural
forms. In their attitudes toward art, prophets differ from mystagogues and priests, monks from pious laymen, and mass religions
from sects of virtuosi. Sects of ascetic virtuosi are naturally more
hostile to art on principle than are sects of mystical virtuosi. But
these matters are not our major concern here. At all events, any
real inner compromise between the religious and the esthetic attitudes in respect to their ultimate and subjectively intended meaning
is rendered increasingly difficult once the stages of magic and pure
ritualism have been left behind.

   In all this, the one important fact for us is the significance of
the marked rejection of all distinctively esthetic devices by those
religions which are rational, in our special sense. These are
Judaism, ancient Christianity, and—later on—ascetic Protestantism. Their rejection of esthetics is either a symptom or an instrument of religion's increasingly rational influence upon the conduct
of life. It is perhaps going too far to assert that the second commandment of the Decalogue is the decisive foundation of actual
Jewish rationalism, as many representatives of influential Jewish
reform movements have assumed. But there can be no question at
all that the systematic prohibition in devout Jewish and Puritan
circles of uninhibited surrender to the distinctive form-producing
values of art has effectively controlled the degree and scope of
artistic productivity in these circles, and has tended to favor the
development of intellectually rational controls over the pattern of
life.

XV. Judaism, Christianity, and the Socio-Economic Order

Judaism, in its postexilic and particularly its Talmudic form, belongs among those religions that are in some sense accommodated to the world. Judaism is at least oriented to the world in the sense that it does not reject the world as such but only rejects the prevailing system of social classes in the world.

We have already made some observations concerning the total sociological structure and attitude of Judaism. Its religious promises, in the customary meaning of the word, apply to this world, and any notions of contemplative or ascetic world-flight are as rare in Judaism as in Chinese religion and in Protestantism. Judaism differs from Puritanism only in the relative (as always) absence of systematic asceticism. The ascetic elements of the early Christian religion did not derive from Judaism, but emerged primarily in the heathen Christian communities of the Pauline mission. There is as little justification for equating the observance of the Jewish law with asceticism as for equating it with the fulfillment of any ritual or tabooistic norms.

Moreover, the relationship of the Jewish religion to both wealth and sexual indulgence is not in the least ascetic, but rather highly naturalistic. For wealth was regarded as a gift of God, and the satisfaction of the sexual impulse—naturally in the prescribed legal form—was thought to be so imperative that the Talmud actually regarded a person who had remained unmarried after a certain age as morally suspect. The interpretation of marriage as an economic institution for the production and rearing of children is universal and has nothing specifically Jewish about it. Judaism's strict prohibition of illegitimate sexual intercourse, a prohibition that was highly effective among the pious, was also found in Islam and all other prophetic religions, as well as in Hinduism. Moreover, the majority of ritualistic religions shared with Judaism the institution of periods of abstention from sexual relations for purposes of purification. For these reasons, it is not possible to speak of an idiosyncratic emphasis upon sexual asceticism in Judaism. The sexual regulations cited by Sombart do not go as far as the Catholic casuistry of the seventeenth century and in any case have analogies in many other casuistical systems of taboo.

Nor did Judaism forbid the uninhibited enjoyment of life or even of luxury as such, provided that the positive prohibitions and taboos of the law were observed. The denunciation of wealth in the prophetic books, the Psalms, the Wisdom Literature, and subsequent writings was evoked by the social injustices which were so frequently perpetrated against fellow Jews in connection with the acquisition of wealth and in violation of the spirit of the Mosaic law. Wealth was also condemned in response to arrogant disregard of the commandments and promises of God and in response to the rise of temptations to laxity in religious observance. To escape the temptations of wealth is not easy, but is for this reason all the more meritorious. "Hail to the man of wealth who has been found to be blameless." Moreover, since Judaism possessed no doctrine of predestination and no comparable idea producing the same ethical effects, incessant labor and success in business life could not be regarded or interpreted in the sense of certification, which appears most strongly among the Calvinist Puritans and which is found to some extent in all ascetic Protestant religions, as shown in John Wesley's remark on this point. Of course a certain tendency to regard success in one's economic activity as a sign of God's gracious direction existed in the religion of the Jews, as in the religions of the Chinese and the lay Buddhists and generally in every religion that has not turned its back upon the world. This view was especially likely to be manifested by a religion like Judaism, which had before it very specific promises of a transcendental God together with very visible signs of this God's indignation against the people he had chosen. It is clear that any success achieved in one's economic activities while keeping the commandments of God could be, and indeed had to be, interpreted as a sign that one was personally acceptable to God. This actually occurred again and again.

But the situation of the pious Jew engaged in business was altogether different from that of the Puritan, and this difference remained of practical significance for the role of Judaism in the history of economics. Let us now consider what this role has been. In the polemic against Sombart's book, one fact could not be seriously questioned, namely that Judaism played a conspicuous role in the evolution of the modern capitalistic system. However, this thesis of Sombart's book needs to be made more precise. What were the *distinctive* economic achievements of Judaism in the Middle Ages and in modern times? We can easily list: moneylending, from pawnbroking to the financing of great states; certain types of commodity business, particularly retailing, peddling, and produce trade of a distinctively rural type; certain branches of wholesale business; and brokerage, above all the brokerage of stocks. To this list of Jewish economic achievements should be added: money-changing; money-forwarding or check-cashing, which normally accompanies money-changing; the financing of state agencies, wars, and the establishment of colonial enterprises; tax-farming, naturally excluding the collection of prohibited taxes such as those directed to the Romans; banking; credit; and the floating of bond issues. But of all these businesses only a few, though very important ones, display the legal and economic forms characteristic of modern occidental capitalism in contrast to the forms characteristic of commerce in ancient times, the Middle Ages, and the earlier period in Eastern Asia. The distinctively modern legal forms include stock corporations and business organizations, but these are not of specifically Jewish provenience. The Jews may have introduced these forms into the Occident, but the forms themselves have a common oriental (probably Babylonian) origin, and their influence on the Occident was mediated through Hellenistic and Byzantine sources. In any event they were common to both the Jews and the Arabs. It is even true that the specifically modern forms of these institutions were in part occidental and medieval creations, with some specifically German infusions of influence. To adduce detailed proof of this here would take us too far afield. However, it can be said by way of example that the exchange, as a "market of tradesmen," was created not by Jews but by Christian merchants. Again, the particular manner in which medieval legal regulations were adapted to make possible rationalized economic enterprises (e.g., limited liability companies; privileged companies of all types —*Kommanditen, Maonen, privilegierte Kompagnien aller Art;* and stock companies) was not at all dependent on specifically Jewish influences, no matter how large a part Jews played in the formation of such rationalized economic enterprises. Finally, it must be noted that the characteristically modern principles of public and private financing first arose *in nuce* on the soil of the medieval city. Only later were the medieval legal forms of finance, which were quite un-Jewish in certain respects, adapted to the economic needs of modern states and other modern recipients of credit.

Above all, one element particularly characteristic of modern capitalism was strikingly—and perhaps completely—missing from the extensive list of Jewish economic activities. This was the organization of industrial production (*gewerbliche Arbeit*) or manufacturing in domestic industry and in the factory system. How does one explain the fact that no pious Jew succeeded in establishing an industry employing pious Jewish workers of the ghetto (as so many pious Puritan entrepreneurs had done with devout Christian workers and artisans) at times when numerous proletarians were present in the ghettos, princely patents and privileges for the establishment of any sort of industry were available for a financial remuneration, and areas of industrial activity uncontrolled by guild monopoly were open? Again, how does one explain the fact that no modern and distinctively industrial bourgeoisie of any significance emerged among the Jews to employ the Jewish workers available for home industry, despite the presence of numerous impecunious artisan groups at almost the threshold of the modern period?

All over the world, for several millennia, the characteristic forms of the capitalist employment of wealth have been state-provisioning, the financing of states, tax-farming, the financing of military colonies, the establishment of great plantations, trade, and moneylending. One finds these again and again. One finds Jews involved in just these activities, found at all times and places but especially characteristic of antiquity, as well as involved in those specifically modern legal and organizational forms of economic activity which were evolved by the Middle Ages and not by the Jews. On the other hand, the Jews were relatively or altogether absent from the new and distinctive forms of modern capitalism, the rational organization of labor, especially production in an industrial enterprise of the factory type. The Jews evinced the ancient and medieval business temper which had been and remained typical of all primitive traders, whether small businessmen or large-scale moneylenders, in antiquity, the Far East, India, the Mediterranean littoral area, and the Occident of the Middle Ages: the will and the wit to employ mercilessly every chance of profit, "for the sake of profit to ride through Hell even if it singes the sails." But this temper is far from distinctive of modern capitalism, as distinguished from the capitalism of other eras. Precisely the reverse is true. Hence, neither that which is new in the modern economic *system* nor that which is distinctive of the modern economic *temper* is specifically Jewish in origin.

The ultimate theoretical reasons for this fact, that the distinctive elements of modern capitalism originated and developed quite apart from the Jews, are to be found in the peculiar character of the Jews as a pariah people and in the idiosyncracy of their religion. Their pariah status presented purely external difficulties impeding their participation in the organization of industrial labor. The legally and factually precarious position of the Jews hardly permitted continuous, systematic, and rationalized industrial enterprise with fixed capital, but only trade and above all dealing in money. Also of fundamental importance was the subjective ethical situation of the Jews. As a pariah people, they retained the double standard of morals which is characteristic of primordial economic practice in all communities: what is prohibited in relation to one's brothers is permitted in relation to strangers. It is unquestionable that the Jewish ethic was thoroughly traditionalistic in demanding of Jews an attitude of sustenance toward fellow Jews. As Sombart correctly notes, the rabbis made concessions in these matters, even in regard to business associations with fellow Jews, but these remained nothing more than concessions to laxity, with those who resorted to the employment of these concessions remaining far behind the highest requirements of Jewish business ethics. In any case, it is certain that economic behavior was not the realm in which a Jew could demonstrate his religious merit.

However, for the Jews the realm of economic relations with strangers, particularly economic relations prohibited in regard to fellow Jews, was an area of ethical indifference. This is of course the primordial economic ethics of all peoples everywhere. That this should have remained the Jewish economic ethic was a foregone conclusion, for even in antiquity the Jews almost always regarded strangers as enemies. All the well-known admonitions of the rabbis enjoining honor and faithfulness toward Gentiles could not change the impression that the religious law prohibited taking usury from fellow Jews but permitted it in transactions with non-Jews. Nor could the rabbinical counsels enjoining honesty and reliability in dealing with Gentiles alter the fact, which again Sombart has rightly stressed, that a lesser degree of legality was required by the law in dealing with a stranger, i.e., an enemy, than in dealing with another Jew, in such a matter as taking advantage of an error made by the other party. In fine, no proof is required to establish that the pariah condition of the Jews, which we have seen resulted from the promises of Yahweh, and the resulting incessant humiliation of the Jews by Gentiles necessarily led to the Jewish people's retaining different economic moralities for its relations with strangers and with fellow Jews.

Let us summarize the respective situations in which Catholics, Jews, and Protestants found themselves in regard to economic enterprises. The devout Catholic, as he went about his economic affairs, found himself continually behaving—or on the verge of behaving—in a manner that transgressed papal injunctions. His economic behavior could be ignored in the confessional only on the principle of *rebus sic stantibus,* and it could be permissible only on the basis of a lax, probabilistic morality. To a certain extent, therefore, the life of business itself had to be regarded as reprehensible or, at best, as not positively favorable to God. The inevitable result of this Catholic situation was that pious Jews were encouraged to perform economic activities among Christians which if performed among Jews would have been regarded by the Jewish community as unequivocally contrary to the law or at least as suspect from the point of view of Jewish tradition. At best these transactions were permissible on the basis of a lax interpretation of the Judaic religious code, and then only in economic relations with strangers. Never were they infused with positive ethical value. Thus, the Jew's economic conduct appeared to be permitted by God, in the absence of any formal contradiction with the religious law of the Jews, but ethically indifferent, in view of such conduct's correspondence with the average evils in the society's economy. This is the basis of whatever factual truth there was in the observations concerning the inferior standard of economic legality among Jews. That God crowned such economic activity with success could be a sign to the Jewish businessman that he had done nothing clearly objectionable or prohibited in this area and that indeed he had held fast to God's commandments in other areas. But it would still have been difficult for the Jew to demonstrate his ethical merit by means of characteristically modern business behavior.

But this was precisely the case with the pious Puritan. He could demonstrate his religious merit through his economic activity because he did nothing ethically reprehensible, he did not resort to any lax interpretations of religious codes or to systems of double moralities, and he did not act in a manner that could be indifferent or even reprehensible in the general realm of ethical validity. On the contrary, the Puritan could demonstrate his religious merit precisely in his economic activity. He acted in business with the best possible conscience, since through his rationalistic and legal behavior in his business activity he was factually objectifying the rational methodology of his total life pattern. He legitimated his ethical pattern in his own eyes, and indeed within the circle of his community, by the extent to which the absolute—not relativized—unassailability of his economic conduct remained beyond question. No really pious Puritan—and this is the crucial point—could have regarded as pleasing to God any profit derived from usury, exploitation of another's mistake (which was permissible to the Jew), haggling and sharp dealing, or participation in political or colonial exploitation. Quakers and Baptists believed their religious merit to be certified before all mankind by such practices as their fixed prices and their absolutely reliable business relationships with everyone, unconditionally legal and devoid of cupidity. Precisely such practices promoted the irreligious to trade with them rather than with their own kind, and to entrust their money to the trust companies or limited liability enterprises of the religious sectarians rather than those of their own people—all of which made the religious sectarians wealthy, even as their business practices certified them before their God.

By contrast, the Jewish law applying to strangers, which in practice was the pariah law of the Jews, enabled them, notwithstanding innumerable reservations, to engage in dealings with non-Jews which the Puritans rejected violently as showing the cupidity of the trader. Yet the pious Jew could combine such an attitude with strict legality, with complete fulfillment of the law, with all the inwardness of his religion, with the most sacrificial love for his family and community, and indeed with pity and mercy toward all God's creatures. For in view of the operation of the laws regarding strangers, Jewish piety never in actual practice regarded the realm of permitted economic behavior as one in which the genuineness of a person's obedience to God's commandments could be demonstrated. The pious Jew never gauged his inner ethical standards by what he regarded as permissible in the economic context. Just as the Confucian's authentic ideal of life was the gentleman who had undergone a comprehensive education in ceremonial esthetics and literature and who devoted lifelong study to the classics, so the Jew set up as his ethical ideal the scholar learned in law and casuistry, the intellectual who continuously immersed himself in the sacred writings and commentaries at the expense of his business, which he very frequently left to the management of his wife.

It was this intellectualist trait of authentic late Judaism, with its preoccupation with literary scholarship, that Jesus criticized. His criticism was not motivated by the proletarian instincts which some have attributed to him, but rather by his type of piety and his type of obedience to the law, both of which were appropriate to the rural artisan or the inhabitant of a small town, and constituted his basic opposition to the virtuosi of legalistic lore who had grown up on the soil of the *polis* of Jerusalem. Members of such urban legalistic circles asked "What good can come out of Nazareth?"—the kind of question that might have been posed by any dweller of a metropolis in the classical world. Jesus' knowledge of the law and his observance of it was representative of that average lawfulness which was actually demonstrated by men engaged in practical work, who could not afford to let their sheep lie in wells, even on the Sabbath. On the other hand, the knowledge of the law obligatory for the really pious Jews, as well as their legalistic education of the young, surpassed both quantitatively and qualitatively the preoccupation with the Bible characteristic of the Puritans. The scope of religious law of which knowledge was obligatory for the pious Jew may be compared only with the scope of ritual laws among the Hindus and Persians, but the Jewish law far exceeded these in its inclusion of ethical prescriptions as well as merely ritual and tabooistic norms.

The economic behavior of the Jews simply moved in the direction of least resistance which was permitted them by these legalistic ethical norms. This meant in practice that the acquisitive drive, which is found in varying degrees in all groups and nations, was here directed primarily to trade with strangers, who were usually regarded as enemies. Even at the time of Josiah and certainly in the exilic period, the pious Jew was an urban dweller, and the entire Jewish law was oriented to this urban status. Since the orthodox Jew required the services of a ritual slaughterer, he had necessarily to live in a community rather than in isolation. Even today, urban residence is characteristic of orthodox Jews when they are contrasted with Jews of the Reform group, as for example in the United States. Similarly, the Sabbatical year, which in its present form is certainly a product of postexilic urban scholars learned in the law, made it impossible for Jews to carry on systematic intensive cultivation of the land. Even at the present time,* German rabbis endeavor to apply the prescription of the Sabbatical year to Zionist colonization in Palestine, which would be ruined thereby. In the age of the Pharisees a rustic Jew was of second rank, since he did not and could not observe the law strictly. Jewish law also prohibited the participation of Jews in the procedures of the guilds, particularly participation in commensality with non-Jews, although in antiquity as well as in the Middle Ages commensality was the indispensable foundation for any kind of integration or

* [Before World War I. Translator's note.]

naturalization (*Einbürgerung*) in the surrounding world. But the Jewish institution of the dowry, common to the Orient and based originally on the exclusion of daughters from inheritance, favored the establishing of the Jewish groom at marriage as a small merchant; and indeed, the custom still tends toward this result. Traces of this phenomenon are still apparent in the relatively undeveloped class consciousness of Jewish apprentices.

In all his other dealings, as well as those we have just discussed, the Jew—like the pious Hindu—was controlled by scruples concerning his law. As Guttmann has correctly emphasized, genuine study of the law could be combined most easily with the occupation of moneylending, which requires relatively little continuous labor. The outcome of Jewish legalism and intellectualist education was the Jew's methodical patterning of life and his rationalism. It is a prescription of the Talmud that "A man must never change a practice." Only in the realm of economic relationships with strangers, and in no other area of life, did tradition leave a sphere of behavior that was relatively indifferent ethically. Indeed, the entire domain of things relevant before God was determined by tradition and the systematic casuistry concerned with its interpretation, rather than determined by rational purposes derived from laws of nature and oriented without further presupposition to methodical plans of individual action (*nicht ein rational voraussetsungslos, aus einem "Naturrecht" heraus, selbstorientiertes methodisches Zweckhandeln*). The tendency of scrupulosity before the law to develop rationalization is thoroughly pervasive but entirely indirect.

Self-control—usually accompanied by alertness, equableness, and serenity—was found among Confucians, Puritans, Buddhists and other types of monks, Arab sheiks, and Roman senators, as well as among Jews. But the basis and significance of self-control were different in each case. The alert self-control of the Puritan flowed from the necessity of his subjugating all creaturely impulses to a rational and methodical plan of conduct, so that he might secure his certainty of his own salvation. Self-control appeared to the Confucian as a personal necessity which followed from his disesteem for plebeian irrationality, the disesteem of an educated gentleman who had received classical training and had been bred along lines of honor and dignity. On the other hand, the self-control

of the devout Jew of ancient times was a consequence of the preoccupation with the law in which his mind had been trained, and of
the necessity of his continuous concern with the law's precise fulfillment. The pious Jew's self-control received a characteristic
coloring and effect from the situation of being piously engaged
in fulfilling the law. The Jew felt that only he and his people
possessed this law, for which reason the world persecuted them
and imposed degradation upon them. Yet this law was binding;
and one day, by an act that might come suddenly at any time but
that no one could accelerate, God would transform the social
structure of the world, creating a messianic realm for those who
had remained faithful to his law. The pious Jew knew that innumerable generations had awaited this messianic event, despite all mockery, and were continuing to await it. This produced in the pious
Jew an excessive feeling of alertness. But since it remained necessary for him to continue waiting in vain, he nurtured his feelings of
self-esteem by a meticulous observance of the law for its own sake.
Last but not least, the pious Jew had always to stay on guard,
never permitting himself the free expression of his passions against
powerful and merciless enemies. This repression was inevitably
combined with the aforementioned feeling of *ressentiment* which
resulted from Yahweh's promises and the unparalleled history of
his people who had sinned against him.

   These circumstances basically determined the rationalism of
Judaism, but this is not "asceticism" in our sense. To be sure,
there are ascetic traits in Judaism, but they are not central. Rather,
they are by-products of the law, which have arisen in part from
the peculiar problem-complex of Jewish piety. In any case, ascetic
traits are of secondary importance in Judaism, as are any mystical
traits developed within this religion. We need say nothing more
here about Jewish mysticism, since neither cabalism, Chassidism nor
any of its other forms—whatever symtomatic importance they held
for Jews—produced any significant motivations toward practical
behavior in the economic sphere.

   The ascetic aversion of pious Jews toward everything esthetic
was originally based on the second commandment of the Decalogue,
which actually prevented the once well-developed angelology of
the Jews from assuming artistic form. But another important cause

of aversion to things esthetic is the purely pedagogic and jussive character of the divine service in the synagogue, even as it was practiced in the Diaspora, long before the disruption of the Temple cult. Even at that time, Hebrew prophecy had virtually removed plastic elements from the cult, effectively extirpating orgiastic, orchestral, and terpsichorean activities. It is of interest that Roman religion and Puritanism pursued similar paths in regard to esthetic elements, though for reasons quite different from the Jewish reasons. Thus, among the Jews the plastic arts, painting, and drama lacked those points of contact with religion which were elsewhere quite normal. This is the reason for the marked diminution of secular lyricism and especially of the erotic sublimation of sexuality, when contrasted with the marked sensuality of the earlier Song of Solomon. The basis of all this is to be found in the naturalism of the Jewish ethical treatment of sexuality.

All these traits of Judaism are characterized by one overall theme: that the mute, faithful, and questioning expectation of a redemption from the hellish character of the life enforced upon the people who had been chosen by God (and definitely chosen, despite their present status) was ultimately refocused upon the ancient promises and laws of the religion. Conversely, it was held—although there are no corresponding utterances of the rabbis on this point— that any uninhibited surrender to the artistic or poetic glorification of this world is completely vain and apt to divert the Jews from the ways and purposes of God. Even the purpose of the creation of this world had already on occasion been problematic to the Jews of the later Maccabean period.

Above all, what was lacking in Judaism was the decisive hallmark of that inner-worldly type of asceticism which is directed toward the control of this world: an integrated relationship to the world from the point of view of the individual's proof of salvation (*certitudo salutis*), which proof in conduct nurtures all else. Again in this important matter, what was ultimately decisive for Judaism was the pariah character of the religion and the promises of Yahweh. An ascetic management of this world, such as that characteristic of Calvinism, was the very last thing of which a traditionally pious Jew would have thought. He could not think of methodically controlling the present world, which was so topsy-

258 THE SOCIOLOGY OF RELIGION

turvy because of Israel's sins, and which could not be set right
by any human action but only by some free miracle of God that
could not be hastened. He could not take as his "mission," as the
sphere of his religious "vocation," the bringing of this world and
its very sins under the rational norms of the revealed divine will,
for the glory of God and as an identifying mark of his own salvation. The pious Jew had a far more difficult inner destiny to overcome than did the Puritan, who could be certain of his election
to the world beyond. It was incumbent upon the individual Jew
to make peace with the fact that the world would remain recalcitrant
to the promises of God as long as God permitted the world to stand
as it is. The Jew's responsibility was to make peace with this
recalcitrancy of the world, while finding contentment if God sent
him grace and success in his dealings with the enemies of his people,
toward whom he must act soberly and legalistically, in fulfillment
of the injunctions of the rabbis. This meant acting toward non-Jews
in an objective or impersonal manner, without love and without
hate, solely in accordance with what was permissible.

The frequent assertion that Judaism required only an external
observance of the law is incorrect. Naturally, this is the average
tendency; but the requirements for real religious piety stood on a
much higher plane. In any case, Judaic law fostered in its adherents
a tendency to compare individual actions with each other and to
compute the net result of them all. This conception of man's relationship to God as a bookkeeping operation of single good and evil
acts with an uncertain total (a conception which may occasionally
be found among the Puritans as well) may not have been the
dominant official view of Judaism. Yet it was sufficient, together
with the double-standard morality of Judaism, to prevent the
development within Judaism of a methodical and ascetic orientation to the conduct of life on the scale that such an orientation
developed in Puritanism. It is also important that in Judaism, as
in Catholicism, the individual's activities in fulfilling particular religious injunctions were tantamount to his assuring his own chances
of salvation. However, in both Judaism and Catholicism, God's
grace was needed to supplement human inadequacy, although this
dependence upon God's grace was not as universally recognized in
Judaism as in Catholicism.

The ecclesiastical provision of grace was much less developed in Judaism, after the decline of the older Palestinian confessional, than in Catholicism. In practice, this resulted in the Jew's having a greater religious responsibility for himself. This responsibility for oneself and the absence of any mediating religious personality necessarily made the Jewish pattern of life more systematic and personally responsible than the corresponding Catholic pattern of life. Still, the methodical control of life was limited in Judaism by the absence of the distinctively ascetic motivation characteristic of Puritans and by the continued presence of Jewish internal morality's traditionalism, which in principle remained unbroken. To be sure, there were present in Judaism numerous single stimuli toward practices that might be called ascetic, but the unifying force of a basically ascetic religious motivation was lacking. The highest form of Jewish piety is found in the religious mood (*Stimmung*) and not in active behavior. How could it be possible for the Jew to feel that by imposing a new rational order upon the world he would become the human executor of God's will, when for the Jew this world was thoroughly contradictory, hostile, and—as he had known since the time of Hadrian—impossible to change by human action? This might have been possible for the Jewish freethinker, but not for the pious Jew.

Puritanism always felt its inner similarity to Judaism, but also felt the limits of this similarity. The similarity in principle between Christianity and Judaism, despite all their differences, remained the same for the Puritans as it had been for the Christian followers of Paul. Both the Puritans and the pristine Christians saw the Jews as the people who had once and for all been chosen by God. But the unexampled activities of Paul had the following significant effects for early Christianity. On the one hand, Paul made the sacred book of the Jews into one of the sacred books of the Christians, and at the beginning the only one. He thereby erected a stout fence against all intrusions of Greek, especially Gnostic, intellectualism, as Wernle in particular has pointed out. But on the other hand, by the aid of a dialectic that only a rabbi could possess, Paul here and there broke through what was most distinctive and effective in the Jewish law, namely the tabooistic norms and the unique messianic promises. Since these taboos and promises linked the whole religious worth of the Jews to their pariah position, Paul's break-through was fateful in its effect. Paul accomplished this break-through by interpreting these promises as having been partly fulfilled and partly abrogated by the birth of Christ. He triumphantly employed the highly impressive proof that the patriarchs of Israel had lived in accordance with God's will long before the issuance of the Jewish taboos and messianic promises, showing that they found blessedness through faith, which was the surety of God's election.

The dynamic power behind the incomparable missionary labors of Paul was his offer to the Jews of a tremendous release, the release provided by the consciousness of having escaped the fate of pariah status. A Jew could henceforth be a Greek among Greeks as well as a Jew among Jews, and could achieve this within the paradox of faith rather than through an enlightened hostility to religion. This was the passionate feeling of liberation brought by Paul. The Jew could actually free himself from the ancient promises of his God, by placing his faith in the new savior who had believed himself abandoned upon the cross by that very God.

Various consequences flowed from this rending of the sturdy chains that had bound the Jews firmly to their pariah position. One was the intense hatred of this one man Paul by the Jews of the Diaspora, sufficiently authenticated as fact. Among the other con-sequences may be mentioned the oscillations and utter uncertainty of the pristine Christian community; the attempt of James and the "pillar apostles" to establish an ethical minimum of law which would be valid and binding for all, in harmony with Jesus' own layman's understanding of the law; and finally, the open hos-tility of the Jewish Christians toward Judaism. In every line that Paul wrote we can feel his overpowering joy at having emerged from the hopeless "slave law" into freedom, through the blood of the Messiah. The overall consequence was the possibility of a Christian world mission.

The Puritans, like Paul, rejected the Talmudic law and even the characteristic ritual laws of the Old Testament, while taking over and considering as binding—for all their elasticity—various other expressions of God's will witnessed in the Old Testament. As the Puritans took these over, they always conjoined norms derived from the New Testament, even in matters of detail. The Jews who were actually welcomed by Puritan nations, especially the Americans, were not pious orthodox Jews but rather Reformed Jews who had abandoned orthodoxy, Jews such as those of the present time who have been trained in the Educational Alliance, and finally baptized Jews. These groups of Jews were at first welcomed without any ado whatsoever and are even now welcomed fairly readily, so that they have been absorbed to the point of the absolute loss of any trace of difference. This situation in Puritan countries contrasts with the situation in Germany, where the Jews remain—even after long generations—"assimilated Jews." These phenomena clearly manifest the actual kinship of Puritanism to Judaism. Yet precisely the non-Jewish element in Puritanism enabled Puritanism to play its special role in the creation of the modern economic temper, and also to carry through the aforementioned absorption of Jewish proselytes, which was not accomplished by nations with other than Puritan orientations.

XVI. The Attitude of the Other World Religions to the Social and Economic Order

Islam, a comparatively late product of Near Eastern monotheism, in which Old Testament and Jewish-Christian elements played a very important role, "accommodated" itself to the world in a very unique sense. In the first Meccan period of Islam, the eschatological religion of Muhammad developed in pietistic urban conventicles which displayed a tendency to withdraw from the world. But in the subsequent developments in Medina and in the evolution of the early Islamic communities, the religion was transformed from its pristine form into a national Arabic warrior religion, and even later into a religion with very strong class emphases. Those followers whose conversion to Islam made possible the decisive success of the prophets were consistently members of powerful families.

The religious commandments of the holy law were not directed in the first instance to the purpose of conversion. Rather, the primary purpose was war "until they (the followers of alien religions of the book) will humbly pay the tribute (*jizyah*)," i.e., until Islam should rise to the top of this world's social scale, by exacting tribute from other religions. This is not the only factor that stamps Islam as the religion of a warrior class. Military booty is important in the ordinances, in the promises, and above all in the expectations characterizing even the most ancient period of the religion. Even the ultimate elements of its economic ethic were purely feudal. The most pious adherents of the religion in its first generation became the wealthiest, or more correctly, enriched themselves with military booty—in the widest sense—more than did other members of the faith.

The role played by wealth accruing from spoils of war and from political aggrandizement in Islam is diametrically opposed to the role played by wealth in the Puritan religion. The Muslim tradition depicts with pleasure the luxurious raiment, perfume, and meticulous beard-coiffure of the pious. The saying that "when god blesses a man with prosperity he likes to see the signs thereof visible upon him"—made by Muhammad, according to tradition, to well-circumstanced people who appeared before him in ragged attire—stands in extreme opposition to any Puritan economic ethic and thoroughly corresponds with feudal conceptions of status. This saying would mean, in our language, that a wealthy man is obligated "to live in keeping with his status." In the Quran, Muhammad is represented as completely rejecting every type of monasticism, though not all asceticism, for he did accord respect to fasting, begging, and penitential mortification. Muhammad's attitude in opposition to chastity sprang from personal motivations similar to those which are apparent in Luther's famous remarks so expressive of his strongly sensual nature. A comparable attitude comes to light in the Talmud's expression of the conviction that whoever has not married by a certain age must be a sinner. But we must regard as unique in the hagiology of ethical religions of salvation Muhammad's dictum expressing doubt about the ethical character of a person who has abstained from eating flesh for forty days; as well as the reply of a renowned pillar of ancient Islam, celebrated by some as a Mahdi, to the question why he, unlike his father Ali, had used cosmetics for his hair: "In order to be more successful with women."

But Islam was never really a religion of salvation; the ethical concept of salvation was actually alien to Islam. The god it taught was a lord of unlimited power, although merciful, the fulfillment of whose commandments was not beyond human power. An essentially political character marked all the chief ordinances of Islam: the elimination of private feuds in the interest of increasing the group's striking power against external foes; the proscription of illegitimate forms of sexual behavior and the regulation of legitimate sexual relations along strongly patriarchal lines (actually creating sexual privileges only for the wealthy, in view of the facility of divorce and the maintenance of concubinage with female slaves); the prohibition of usury; the prescription of taxes for war; and the injunction to support the poor. Equally political in character is the distinctive religious obligation in Islam, its only required dogma: the recognition of Allah as the one god and of Muhammad as his prophet. In addition, there were the obligations to journey to Mecca once during a lifetime, to fast by day during the month of fasting, to attend services once a week, and to observe the obligation of daily prayers. Finally, Islam imposed such requirements for everyday living as the wearing of distinctive clothing (a requirement that even today has important economic consequences whenever savage tribes are converted to Islam) and the avoidance of certain unclean foods, of wine, and of gambling. The restriction against gambling obviously had important consequences for the religion's attitude toward speculative business enterprises.

There was nothing in ancient Islam like an individual quest for salvation, nor was there any mysticism. The religious promises in the earliest period of Islam pertained to this world. Wealth, power, and glory were all martial promises, and even the world beyond is pictured in Islam as a soldier's sensual paradise. Moreover, the original Islamic conception of sin has a similar feudal orientation. The depiction of the prophet of Islam as devoid of sin is a late theological construction, scarcely consistent with the actual nature of Muhammad's strong sensual passions and his explosions of wrath over very small provocations. Indeed, such a picture is strange even to the Quran, for even after Muhammad's transfer to Medina he lacked any sort of tragic sense of sin. The original feudal conception of sin remained dominant in orthodox Islam, for which sin is a composite of ritual impurity, ritual sacrilege (*shirk*, i.e., polytheism), disobedience to the positive injunctions of the prophet; and the dishonoring of a noble class by infractions of convention or etiquette. Islam displays other characteristics of a distinctively feudal spirit: the obviously unquestioned acceptance of slavery, serfdom, and polygamy; the disesteem for and subjection of women; the essentially ritualistic character of religious obligations; and finally, the great simplicity of religious requirements and the even greater simplicity of the modest ethical requirements.

Islam was not brought any closer to Judaism and to Christianity in decisive matters by such Islamic developments as the achievement of great scope through the rise of theological and juristic casuistry, the appearance of both pietistic and enlightenment schools of philosophy (following the intrusion of Persian Sufism, derived from India), and the formation of the order of dervishes (which shows strong traces of Hindu influence). Judaism and Christianity were specifically civic and urban religions, but the city had only political importance for Islam. To be sure, a certain sobriety in the conduct of life might be produced by the nature of the official cult in Islam and by its sexual and ritual commandments. But the lower middle class was largely the carrier of the dervish religion, which was disseminated practically everywhere and gradually grew in power, finally surpassing the official ecclesiastical religion. This type of religion, with its orgiastic and mystical elements, with its essentially irrational and extraordinary character, and with its official and thoroughly traditionalistic ethic of everyday life, became influential in Islam's missionary enterprise because of its great simplicity. It directed the conduct of life into paths whose effect was plainly opposite to the methodical control of life found among Puritans, and indeed, found in every type of asceticism oriented toward the control of the world.

Islam, in contrast to Judaism, lacked the requirement of a comprehensive knowledge of the law and lacked that intellectual training in casuistry which nurtured the rationalism of Judaism. The ideal personality type in the religion of Islam was not the scholarly scribe (*Literat*), but the warrior. Moreover, Islam lacked all those promises of a messianic realm upon earth which in Israel were linked with meticulous fidelity to the law, and which—together with election, sin, the priestly doctrine of history, and the dispersion of the Jews—determined the pariah character of the Jewish religion, so fraught with consequences.

To be sure, there were ascetic sects among the Muslims. Large groups of ancient Islamic warriors were characterized by a trend toward simplicity; this prompted them from the outset to oppose the rule of the Umayyads. The latter's merry enjoyment of the world presented the strongest contrast to the rigid discipline of the encampment fortresses in which Umar had concentrated Islamic warriors in the conquered domains; in their stead there now arose a very different feudal aristocracy. But this was the asceticism of a military caste, of a martial order of knights, not of monks. Certainly it was not a middle-class ascetic systematization of the conduct of life. Moreover, it was effective only periodically, and even then it tended to merge into fatalism. We have already spoken of the quite different effect which is engendered in such circumstances by a belief in providence. Islam was diverted completely from any really methodical control of life by the advent of the cult of saints, and finally by magic.

At the opposite extreme from systems of religious ethics preoccupied with the control of economic affairs within the world stands the ultimate ethic of world-rejection, the mystical illuminative concentration of authentic ancient Buddhism (naturally not the completely altered manifestations Buddhism assumed in Tibetan, Chinese, and Japanese popular religions). Even this most world-rejecting ethic is "rational," in the sense that it produces a constantly alert control of all natural instinctive drives, though for purposes entirely different from those of inner-worldly asceticism. Salvation is sought, not from sin and suffering alone, but also from ephemeralness as such; escape from the wheel of *karma* causality and arrival into eternal rest are sought. This search is, and can only be, the highly individualized task of a particular person. There is no predestination, but neither is there any divine grace, any prayer, or any religious service. Rewards and punishments for every good and every evil deed are automatically established by the *karma* causality of the cosmic mechanism of compensation. This retribution is always proportional, and hence always limited in time. So long as the individual is driven to action by the thirst for life, he must experience in full measure the fruits of his behavior in ever-new human existences. Whether his momentary human situation is animal, heavenly, or hellish, he necessarily creates new chances for himself in the future. The most noble enthusiasm and the most sordid sensuality lead equally into new existence in this chain of individuation (it is quite incorrect to term this process transmigration of souls, since Buddhist metaphysics knows nothing of a soul). This process of individuation continues on as long as the thirst for life, in this world or in the world beyond, is not absolutely extinguished. The process is but perpetuated by the individual's impotent struggle for his personal existence with all its illusions, above all the illusion of a distinctive soul or personality.

All rational purposive activity is regarded as leading away from salvation, except of course the subjective activity of concentrated contemplation, which empties the soul of the passion for life and every connection with worldly interests. The achievement of salvation is possible for only a few, even of those who have resolved to live in poverty, chastity, and unemployment (for labor is purposive action), and hence in mendicancy. These chosen few are required to wander ceaselessly—except at the time of the heavy rains—freed from all personal ties to family and world, pursuing the goal of mystical illumination by fulfilling the injunctions relating to the correct path (*dharma*). When such salvation is gained, the deep joy and tender, undifferentiated love characterizing such illumination provides the highest blessing possible in this existence, short of absorption into the eternal dreamless sleep of *Nirvana,* the only state in which no change occurs. All other human beings may improve their situations in future existences by approximating the prescriptions of the rule of life and by avoiding major sins in this existence. Such future existences are inevitable, according to the *karma* doctrine of causality, because the ethical account has not been straightened out, the thirst for life has not been "abreacted," so to speak. For most people, therefore, some new individuation is inevitable when the present life has ended, and truly eternal salvation remains inaccessible.

There is no path leading from this only really consistent position of world-flight to any economic ethic or to any rational social ethic. The universal mood of pity, extending to all creatures, cannot be the carrier of any rational behavior and in fact leads away from it. This mood of pity is the logical consequence of contemplative mysticism's position regarding the solidarity of all living, and hence transitory, beings, This solidarity follows from the common *karma* causality which overarches all living beings. In Buddhism, the psychological basis for this universal pity is the religion's mystical, euphoric, universal, and acosmistic love.

Buddhism is the most systematic of the doctrines of salvation produced in large numbers at many periods by the elite intellectual classes of Hinduism. Its cool and proud emancipation of the individual from life as such, which in effect stood the individual on his own feet, could never become a popular salvation faith. Buddhism's influence beyond the circle of the educated was due to the tremendous prestige traditionally enjoyed by the *shramana,* i.e., ascetics, who possessed magical traits of anthropolatry. As soon as Buddhism became a missionizing popular religion, it duly transformed itself into a savior religion based on *karma* compensation, with hopes for the world beyond guaranteed by devotional techniques, cultic and sacramental grace, and deeds of mercy. Naturally, Buddhism also tended to welcome purely magical notions.

In India itself, Buddhism met competition among the upper classes from a renascent philosophy of salvation based on the Vedas; and met competition among the masses from Hinduistic salvation religions, especially the various forms of Vishnuism, from Tantristic magic, and from orgiastic mystery religions, notably the *bhakti* piety (love of god). In Lamaism, Buddhism became the purely monastic religion of a theocracy which controlled the laity by ecclesiastical powers of a thoroughly magical nature. Wherever Buddhism was diffused in the Orient, its idiosyncratic character underwent striking transformation as it competed and entered into diverse combinations with Chinese Taoism, thus becoming the region's typical mass religion, which pointed beyond this world and the ancestral cult and which distributed grace and salvation.

At all events, no motivation toward a rational system for the methodical control of life flowed from Buddhist, Taoist, or Hindu piety. Hindu piety in particular, as we have already suggested, maintained the strongest possible power of tradition, since the presuppositions of Hinduism constituted the most consistent religious expression of the organic view of society. The existing order of the world was provided absolutely unconditional justification, in terms of the mechanical operation of a proportional retribution in the distribution of power and happiness to individuals on the basis of their merits and failures in their earlier existences.

All these popular religions of Asia left room for the acquisitive drive of the tradesman, the interest of the artisan in sustenance (*Nahrungs-Interesse*), and the traditionalism of the peasant. These popular religions also left undisturbed both philosophical speculation and the conventional class-oriented life patterns of privileged groups. These class-oriented patterns of the privileged evinced feudal characteristics in Japan; patrimonial, bureaucratic, and hence strongly utilitarian features in China; and a mixture of knightly, patrimonial, and intellectualistic traits in India. None of these mass religions of Asia, however, provided the motives or orientations for a rationalized ethical patterning of the creaturely world in accordance with divine commandments. Rather, they all accepted this world as eternally given, and so the best of all possible worlds. The only choice open to the sages, who possessed the highest type of piety, was whether to accommodate themselves to the Tao, the impersonal order of the world and the only thing specifically divine, or to save themselves from the inexorable chain of causality by passing into the only eternal being, the dreamless sleep of *Nirvana*.

"Capitalism" existed among all these religions, even those religions of the type known in occidental antiquity and the medieval period. But there was no development toward modern capitalism, nor even any stirrings in that direction, in these religions. Above all, there evolved no "capitalist spirit," in the sense that is distinctive of ascetic Protestantism. But to assume that the Hindu, Chinese, or Muslim merchant, trader, artisan, or coolie was animated by a weaker "acquisitive drive" than the ascetic Protestant is to fly in the face of the facts. Indeed, the reverse would seem to be true, for what is distinctive of Puritanism is the rational and ethical limitation of the quest for profit. There is no proof whatever that a weaker natural potentiality for technical and economic rationalism was responsible for the actual differences in this respect. At the present time, all these peoples import economic rationalism as the most important product of the Occident, and their capitalistic development is impeded only by the presence among them of rigid traditions, such as existed among us in the Middle Ages, not by any lack of ability or will. The impediments to the development of capitalism must be sought primarily in the domain of religion, although certain purely political factors, such as the inner structural forms of domination (which we shall discuss later on), also played important roles.

Only ascetic Protestantism completely eliminated magic and the supernatural quest for salvation, of which the highest form was intellectualist, contemplative illumination. It alone created the religious motivations for seeking salvation primarily through immersion in one's worldly vocation (*Beruf*). This Protestant stress upon the methodically rationalized fulfillment of one's vocational responsibility was diametrically opposite to Hinduism's strongly traditionalistic concept of vocations. For the various popular religions of Asia, in contrast to ascetic Protestantism, the world remained a great enchanted garden, in which the practical way to orient oneself, or to find security in this world or the next, was to revere or coerce the spirits and seek salvation through ritualistic, idolatrous, or sacramental procedures. No path led from the magical religiosity of the non-intellectual classes of Asia to a rational, methodical control of life. Nor did any path lead to that methodical control from the world accommodation of Confucianism, from the world-rejection of Buddhism, from the world-conquest of Islam, or from the messianic expectations and economic pariah law of Judaism.

The second great religion of world-rejection, in our special sense of the term, was early Christianity, at the cradle of which magic and belief in demons were also present. Its savior was primarily a magician whose magical charisma was an ineluctable source of his unique feeling of individuality. But the absolutely unique religious promises of Judaism contributed to the determination of the distinctive character of early Christianity. It will be recalled that Jesus appeared during the period of the most intensive messianic expectations. Still another factor contributing to the distinctive message of Christianity was the unique concern for erudition in the law characteristic of Jewish piety. The Christian evangel arose in opposition to this legalistic erudition, as a non-intellectual's proclamation directed to non-intellectuals, to the "poor in spirit." Jesus understood and interpreted the "law," from which he desired to remove not even a letter, in a fashion common to the lowly and the unlearned, the pious folk of the countryside and the small towns, who understood the law in their own way and in accordance with the needs of their own occupations. This handling of the law presented a striking contrast to the treatments of the law by the Hellenized, wealthy and upper-class people and by the erudite scholars and Pharisees trained in casuistry. Jesus' interpretation of the Jewish law was milder than theirs in regard to ritual prescriptions, particularly in regard to the keeping of the Sabbath, but stricter than theirs in other respects, e.g., in regard to the grounds for divorce. There already appears to have been an anticipation of the Pauline view that the requirements of the Mosaic law were conditioned by the sinfulness of the superficially pious. There were, in any case, instances in which Jesus squarely opposed specific injunctions of the ancient tradition.

Jesus' distinctive feeling of self-esteem did not come from anything like a "proletarian instinct" and did not come from knowledge that the way to God necessarily led through him, because of his identity with the divine patriarch. The basis of Jesus' distinctive self-esteem was his knowledge that he, a non-scholar, possessed both the charisma requisite for the control of demons and a tremendous preaching ability, far surpassing that of any scholar or Pharisee. Another basis of his self-esteem was his power to exorcise demons, but this power was only operative with respect to people who believed in him. His power to exorcise demons was inoperative with respect to heathens, his own family, the natives of his own town, the wealthy and high-born of the land, the scholars, and the legalistic virtuosi—among none of these did he find the faith that gave him his magical power to work miracles. He did find such a faith among the poor, the oppressed, publicans and sinners, and even Roman soldiers. These various charismatic powers were the absolutely decisive components in Jesus' feelings concerning his messiahship. It should never be forgotten that these powers of his own were the fundamental issue in his denunciation of the Galilean cities and in his angry curse upon the recalcitrant fig tree. His feeling about his own powers also explains why the election of Israel became ever more problematical to him and the importance of the Temple ever more dubious, while the rejection of the Pharisees and the scholars became increasingly certain to him.

Jesus recognized two absolutely mortal sins. One was the "sin against the spirit" committed by the scriptural scholar who disesteemed charisma and its bearers. The other was unbrotherly arrogance, such as the arrogance of the intellectual toward the poor in spirit, when the intellectual hurls at his brother the exclamation "Thou fool!" This anti-intellectualist rejection of scholarly arrogance and of Hellenic and rabbinic wisdom is the only "class element" of Jesus' message, though it is very distinctive. In general, Jesus' message is far from being a simple proclamation for every Tom, Dick, and Harry, for all the weak of the world. True, the yoke is light, but only for those who can once again become as little children. In truth, Jesus set up the most tremendous requirements for salvation; his doctrine has real aristocratic qualities.

Nothing was further from Jesus' mind than the notion of the universalism of divine grace. On the contrary, he directed his whole preaching against this notion. Few are chosen to pass through the narrow gate, to repent and to believe in Jesus. God himself impedes the salvation of the others and hardens their hearts, and naturally it is the proud and the rich who are most overtaken by this fate. Of course this element is not new, since it can be found in the older prophecies. The older Jewish prophets had taught that, in view of the arrogant behavior of the highly placed, the Messiah would be a king who would enter Jerusalem upon the beast of burden used by the poor. This general orientation implies no "social equality." Jesus lodged with the wealthy, which was ritually reprehensible in the eyes of the virtuosi of the law, but when he bade the rich young man give away his wealth, Jesus expressly enjoined this act only if the young man wished to be "perfect," i.e., a disciple. Complete emancipation from all ties of the world, from family as well as possessions, such as we find in the teachings of the Buddha and similar prophets, was required only of disciples. Yet, although all things are possible for God, continued attachment to Mammon constitutes one of the most difficult impediments to salvation into the Kingdom of God—for attachment to Mammon diverts the individual from religious salvation, the most important thing in the world.

Jesus nowhere explicitly states that preoccupation with wealth leads to unbrotherliness, but this notion is at the heart of the matter, for the prescribed injunctions definitely contain the primordial ethic of mutual help which is characteristic of neighborhood associations of poorer people. The chief difference is that in Jesus' message acts of mutual help have been systematized into an ethic with a religious mood and a fraternalistic sentiment of love. The injunction of mutual help was also construed universalistically, extended to everyone. The "neighbor" is the one nearest at hand. Indeed, the notion of mutual help was enlarged into an acosmistic paradox, based on the axiom that God alone can and will reward. Unconditional forgiveness, unconditional charity, unconditional love even of enemies, unconditional suffering of injustice without requiting evil by force—these products of a mystically conditioned acosmism of love indeed constituted demands for religious heroism. But it must not be overlooked, as it so often has been, that Jesus combined acosmistic love with the Jewish notion of retribution. Man must not boast of his virtue in having performed any of the aforementioned deeds of love, since his boasting would presuppose his subsequent reward, while it is believed that God alone will one day compensate, avenge, and reward. To amass treasures in heaven one must in this world lend money to those from whom no repayment can be expected; otherwise, there is no merit in the deed. A strong emphasis upon the just equalization of destinies was expressed by Jesus in the legend of Lazarus and elsewhere. From this perspective alone, wealth is already a dangerous gift.

But Jesus held in general that what is most decisive for salvation is an absolute indifference to the world and its concerns. The kingdom of heaven, a realm of joy upon earth, utterly without suffering and sin, is at hand; indeed, this generation will not die before seeing it. It will come like a thief at night; it is already in the process of appearing among mankind. Let man be free with the wealth of Mammon, instead of clutching it fast; let man give to Caesar that which is Caesar's own—for what profit is there in such matters? Let man pray to God for daily bread and remain unconcerned for the morrow. No human action can accelerate the coming of the kingdom, but man should prepare himself for its coming. Although this message did not formally abrogate law, it did place the emphasis throughout upon religious sentiment. The entire content of the law and the prophets was condensed into the simple commandment to love God and one's fellow man, to which was added the one far-reaching conception that the true religious mood is to be judged by its fruits, by its faithful demonstration (*Bewährung*).

The visions of the resurrection, doubtless under the influence of the widely diffused soteriological myths, generated a tremendous growth in pneumatic manifestations of charisma; in the formation of communities, beginning with Jesus' own family, which originally had not shared Jesus' faith; and in missionary activity among the heathens. Though nascent Christianity maintained continuity with the older Jewish prophecies even after the fateful conversion of Paul had resulted in a breaking away from the pariah religion, still two new attitudes toward the world became decisive in the Christian missionary communities. One was the expectation of the Second Coming, and the other was the recognition of the tremendous importance of charismatic gifts of the spirit. The world would remain as it was until the master would come again. The individual was required to abide in his position and in his calling (Kinois), subordinated to the ruling authority, save where it commanded him to perpetrate a sinful deed.*

* [According to notes in the manuscript, this section was to have been expanded further. German editor's note.]

Appendix I. Chronological Summary
of Max Weber's Life

1864   Born (April 21) in Erfurt. Father subsequently member of
        Berlin Municipal Council and representative in the Reich-
        stag of the National-Liberal Party.
1882   Finishes the *Gymnasium* at Berlin-Charlottenburg.
1882-6 University study including Heidelberg, Strassburg, Berlin,
        Göttingen, with special interest in law, history, and the-
        ology.
1886-9 Post-graduate study at Berlin, participates in the Seminar of
        Professor Ludwig Goldschmidt in commercial law, and in
        the Seminar of August Meitzen in agrarian history.
1889   Ph.D. at the University of Berlin, Dissertation on "The
        Medieval Commercial Associations" (Zur Geschichte der
        Handelsgesellschaften im Mittelalter). Begins to teach at
        the University of Berlin in the faculty of law. His "Habilita-
        tion" thesis concerns itself with the agrarian history of
        Rome, and its implications for public and private law.
1891-2 Conducts an investigation on "The Condition of Agrarian
        Workers in the East Elbe Area" for the Society for Social
        Policy (*Verein für Sozialpolitik*), an organization of the
        so-called "Socialists of the Chair." This research was the
        first of a series of studies on German agrarian problems
        produced by Weber during the next lustrum.
1893   Professor of Law at Berlin.
1892-7 Practices law in Berlin. Acts as legal expert in an official na-
        tional investigation of the German stock market, out of
        which came several essays on the theme of *Die Börse*,
        including an article on "Borsengesetz" for the *Handwörter-
        buch für Sozialwissenschaften* (supplementary volume to
        the first edition, 1897). Undertakes a new and more com-
        prehensive survey on the condition of agricultural workers

275

in Eastern Germany, 1893-4. Participates actively in various Evangelical-Social Conferences concerned with social policy, and is active in the circle of Friedrich Maumann, the leader of the Christian-Social Party (1892-7).

1893   Professor of Commercial and German Law at the University of Berlin.

1893-4   Conducts a renewed and enlarged survey concerning the conditions of agricultural workers in Eastern Germany for the Evangelical-Social Congress.

1894   Professor of Political Economics at Freiburg University.

1897   Professor of Political Science (*Staatswissenschaften*) at Heidelberg University, as successor to Karl Knies. Beginning of nervous illness.

1899   Withdraws from the Alldeutscher Verband because of their attitude to the agrarian question, specifically their neglect of the national welfare in favor of the selfish economic interests of the large landowners.

1903   Nervous breakdown and protracted illness. Resigns teaching post and becomes honorary professor at Heidelberg.

1904   Recovers and begins intensely active period in scholarly production as private scholar. Takes over the editorship of the *Archiv für Sozialwissenschaft und Sozialpolitik* together with Werner Sombart and Edgar Jaffe. Visits the United States to address the St. Louis Congress of Arts and Science on "The Relations of the Rural Community to Other Branches of the Social Sciences" (the original German title was "Deutsche Agrarprobleme in Vergangenheit und Gegenwart"). Produces for the *Archiv* one of his most important essays on "The Objectivity of Knowledge in the Fields of Social Science and Social Policy" ("Die Objektivität sozialwissenschaftlicher und sozialpolitischer Erkenntnis").

1905   Produces his most famous essay on "The Protestant Ethic and the 'Spirit' of Capitalism" ("Die protestantische Ethik und der 'Geist' des Kapitalismus").

1906   Stimulated by the Russian Revolution, he makes a swift study of Russian (in fourteen days) and produces for the *Archiv* two important studies on Russian political conditions and the emergence of constitutional government. Renews his support for the political activity of Friedrich Naumann. Essays on churches and sects.

1907   Analysis of historical materialism and social science method-
        ology in the essay on Rudolf Stammler's "Überwindung
        der materialistichen Geschichtsauffassung"). Replies to
        critics of the Protestant Ethic thesis.

1908   Returns to his interest in the history of ancient agriculture in
        classical times and produces his erudite historico-sociologi-
        cal essay on "Agrarian Conditions in Antiquity" for the
        Handwörterbuch der Staatswissenschaften, 3rd Edition,
        Volume I, 1909 ("Agrarverhältnisse im Altertum").

1908-9 Continued interest in and activity for the Society for Social
        Policy. Conducts a survey for them on "The Adjustment
        and Selection of Workers in Large Scale Industrial Estab-
        lishments." Conducts other researches on industrial psy-
        chology, the results of which were printed in the *Archiv*
        during 1908 and 1909 ("On the Psycho-Physics of Indus-
        trial Labor," etc.).

1909   Becomes editor of the large-scale encyclopedic project on the
        social sciences, *Foundations of Social Economics* (*Grun-
        dris der Sozialökonomik*), and undertakes to produce for
        this series one volume entitled *Economics and Society*
        (*Wirtschaft und Gesellschaft*). Founds the German So-
        ciological Society.

1910   Writes his final comment (in the *Archiv*) on the controversy
        surrounding the Protestant Ethic. Plays leading role at
        first meeting of the German Sociological Society.

1911   Begins his vast studies in the field of the sociology of religion
        on the economic ethics of the world religions (post-
        humously collected in the three volumes of *Gesammelte
        Aufsätze zur Religionssoziologie*).

1911-13 Produces the original manuscript of his promised contribu-
        tion to the collective work, *Foundations of Social Eco-
        nomics,* entitled "Economics and Society." This constitutes
        the high water mark of his pre-world war activity, and
        contains his "Sociology of Law," his "Systematic Sociology
        of Religion," his "Sociology of Economics" (rewritten and
        enlarged in 1919-20), and "The Sociology of Music," all
        designed as parts of his work on *Economics and Society.*
        Also writes the important methodological essay "Cate-
        gories of Interpretive (*vestehenden*) Sociology." Par-
        ticipates actively in the annual meetings of the German
        Sociological Society.

1914   Participates in a significant discussion of the problem of value judgments under the auspices of The Vienna Society for Social Policy. Participates in war effort and is assigned to direct the Heidelberg Hospital.

1915   Released from war duties. Returns to his elaborate studies of the economic ethics of world religions. Starts political journalism. Criticizes various aspects of the military policy, such as the exacerbated submarine warfare and the bungling policy of the Hohenzollerns.

1916-17   Essays in the *Archiv* on the economic ethics of Confucianism, Hinduism, Buddhism, and the philosophical anthropology of these and other world religions.

1917   Foresees Germany's military defeat and calls anew for parliamentary and governmental reform in Germany. Visiting professor at the University of Vienna during the summer, his first resumption of teaching since 1903. Lectures on "Positive Criticism of the Materialistic Interpretation of History" and "The Sociology of the State." In December, he participates in important deliberations in the Ministry of the Interior in Berlin under the leadership of the great authority on constitutional law, Hugo Preuss. Decisions adopted included popular election of the president of the German Reich.

1918-19   Lectures in behalf of the German Democratic Party, forswears an office in the National Assembly. Continues his researches on the economic ethic of the world religions, with essays on ancient Judaism.

1919   Continues political and publicistic activities. Combats France's claim to the Saar and the imputation of Germany's guilt for the war. Before the students' organization at the University of Munich (*Freistudentischer Bund*), he delivers his greatest addresses: "The Vocation of Science" (Wissenschaft als Beruf") and "The Vocation of Politics" ("Politik als Beruf"). Member of the Committe of Experts of the Peace Delegation to Versailles accompanying the German Foreign Minister, Count Brockdorff-Rantzau. Composes the memorandum protesting the imputation of Germany's war guilt. Appointment to the University of Munich as successor to Lujo Brentano. Delivers as his introductory lecture an address on "The Most General Categories of the Science of Society." In the winter semester he lectures on "Universal Social and Economic History" and "Fundamental Categories of Sociology."

1920   Lectures on the sociology of the State. Completes his editorial revision of the first part of his "Categories of Sociology" ("Soziologische Kategorienlehre"). Reworks the various essays on the sociology of religion destined to be published in Volume I of the *Collected Essays in the Sociology of Religion* (*Gesammelte Aufsätze zur Religionssoziologie*).

1920   Dies June 14, in Munich, of pneumonia.

Appendix II. The Background and Fate of Weber's "Wirtschaft und Gesellschaft"

Weber undertook the writing of his massive (and never completed) *Wirtschaft und Gesellschaft* (*Economics and Society*), of which the present book is a self-contained part,[1] in connection with his planning of and participation in the writing of a great collaborative work in the social sciences, *Grundriss der Sozialökonomik* (*Foundations of Sociological Economics*). When Weber helped stake out the plan of this collaborative project, just before World War I, he had already helped found, or more precisely, reorganize, the important social science periodical *Archiv für Sozialwissenschaft und Sozialpolitik,* and he had been instrumental in organizing the national German sociological society. The new series' somewhat modest title tended to conceal the collaborators' actual intention to produce an all-inclusive work on sociology and sociological economics, which would amount to a virtual encyclopedia of the social sciences.[2]

---

[1] *Religionssoziologie: Typen der religiösen Vergemeinschaftung* (*The Sociology of Religion: Types of Religious Association*), appearing as Book II, Chapter IV, of the first three German editions of *Wirtschaft und Gesellschaft,* which were published in 1921-22, 1925, and 1948. In the fourth edition the material in question appears in Part II, Chapter V, pp. 245-381, and bears the title *Typen der religiösen Vergemeinschaftung* (*Religionssoziologie*), *Types of Religious Association* (*The Sociology of Religion*).

[2] *Grundriss der Sozialökonomik.* The entire series, in the planning and production of which Weber played an important role, comprised nine parts in fourteen volumes:

Part I, Vol. 1: *Wirtschaft und Wirtschaftwissenschaft* (*Economics and the Science of Economics*) by K. Bücher, J. Schumpeter, and E. v. Philippovich, 2nd ed., 1924. Part I, Vol. 2: *Theorie der gesellschaftlichen Wirtschaft* (*The Theory of Economy and Society*) by F. v. Wieser, 2nd ed., 1924.

Part II, Vol. 1: *Wirtschaft und Natur* (*Economy and Nature*) by A. Hettner, P. Mombert, R. Michels, K. Oldenberg, and H. Herkner, 2nd ed., 1923.

The corps of German scholars invited to participate in the multi-volume series, e.g., Karl Bücher, J. Schumpeter, and E. v. Philippovich, were really producing what in the United States has come to be termed "institutional economics."

Weber committed himself to the preparation for the series of a work on economics and sociology, something of a manual of sociologically oriented economics (or of an economic sociology), entitled *Wirtschaft und Gesellschaft*.[3] He immediately started writing this contribution to the series, consisting of many book-length parts and actually setting forth his own basic sociology, and he continued to add to the section from 1913 up to the time of his death in 1920. The work was still unfinished at the time of Weber's untimely death and was published posthumously by his wife, in two massive volumes. This treatise contained Weber's fundamental concepts of sociology, e.g., social ac-

---

Part II, Vol. 2: *Wirtschaft und Technik* (*Economy and Technology*) by F. v. Gottl-Ottilienfeld, 2nd ed., 1923.

Part III: *Wirtschaft und Gesellschaft* (*Economy and Society*) by M. Weber, 1922. 4th ed., 1956.

Part IV: *Spezifische Elemente der modernen kapitalistischen Wirtschaft* (*The Distinctive Elements of the Modern Capitalistic Economy*) by W. Sombart, A. Leist, H. Nipperdey, C. Brinkmann, E. Steinitzer, F. Leitner, A. Salz, F. Eulenburg, E. Lederer, O. v. Zwiedineck-Südenhorst, 1925.

Part V, Vol. 1: *Entwicklung, Wesen, und Bedeutung des Handels* (*The Evolution, Nature, and Importance of Commerce*) by H. Sieveking, 2nd ed., 1925.

Part V., Vol. 2: *Der moderne Handel* (*Modern Commerce*) by J. Hirsch, 2nd ed., 1925.

Part V, Vol. 3: *Transportwesen* (*The Transportation Industry*) by K. Widenfeld, 1930.

Part VI: *Industrie, Bauwesen, Bergwesen* (*Manufacturing, The Building Trades, and Mining*) by H. Sieveking, E. Schwiedland, A. Weber, F. Leitner, M. R. Weyermann, O. v. Zwiedineck-Südenhorst, Ad. Weber, E. Gothein, and T. Vogelstein, 2nd ed., 1923.

Part VII: *Land-und forstwirtschaftliche Produktion, Versicherungswesen* (*Agriculture, Forestry, and Insurance*) by T. Brinkmann, J. B. Esslen, and others, 1922.

Part VIII: *Aussenhandel und Aussenhandelspolitik* (*Foreign Trade and Foreign Trade Policy*) by F. Eulenburg, 1929.

Part IX, Vol. 1: *Die gesellschaftliche Schichtung in Kapitalismus* (*Social Stratification under Capitalism*) by C. Brinkmann, L. Pesl, G. Albrecht, E. Lederer, G. Briefs, R. Michels, G. Neuhaus, and J. Marschak, 1926.

Part IX, Vol. 2: *Die autonome und staatliche soziale Binnenpolitik im Kapitalismus* (*Social Policy under Capitalism*) by K. Schmidt, O. Swart, W. Wygodzinski, V. Totomianz, E. Lederer, J. Marschak, T. Brauer, R. Wilbrandt, and Ad. Weber, 1927.

[3] *Grundriss der Sozialokonomik*, Part III, 2nd ed.

tion, legitimate order, charisma, bureaucracy, etc., and contained descriptive treatments of various areas of social life, e.g., primary groups, political structures, law, religion, and even music. The whole, even though never finished, represents an extraordinary sociological system, equally impressive for the refinement of its conceptualization and the erudition of its historical analyses. It was produced in the spirit of emphasizing the functional importance of economic factors in social life, even though Weber has made his academic reputation by attacking Marxist determinism's economic reductionism and even though Weber throughout his life resisted any reification of the economic factor in social action and social change.

At the time of Weber's death, *Wirtschaft und Gesellschaft* was in an incomplete, unpolished, and presumably preliminary state, except for the initial methodological section which he had completed and revised for publication. Some portions of the systematic sociology projected by Weber were never written, and others were broken off in the midst of the presentation. Throughout the text there are numerous promissory references to subsequent discussions of points to which Weber never returned.

The massive biography[4] by his widow, Marianne, a writer on social welfare problems, especially the woman question, provides a distinguished intellectual chronicle of her eminent husband. Yet this account, a primary source, together with Weber's own letters of information about his life and achievement, sheds no light on Weber's purposes and intentions in this work, or its principle of organization. The text of the early editions is obviously corrupt in numerous places, and Weber's original footnotes have apparently been lost.[5] Moreover, there were no subject headings or outlines; and since Weber left no clear directions as to the arrangement of the work, the material was arranged according to the decisions of the widow and her associates in the publishing venture. It has long been obvious that the organization of the text is imperfect, but it was not clear whether this was due to the unfinished state of the manuscript or to other causes. For instance, it was realized that there are obvious discrepancies between the theoretical formulations of Chapter I of the German text and the treatment in subsequent chapters of concrete areas of social life, such as politics, law, and religion.

Recently these interpretative problems presented by a recalcitrant

---

[4] Marianne Weber, *Max Weber, Ein Lebensbild*, 1926; 2nd ed., 1952.
[5] See Johannes Winckelmann's *Vorwort* to the 4th edition of *Wirtschaft und Gesellschaft*, p. xiv.

text have been solved in part by the researches of the German scholar Johannes Winckelmann, who came to his close studies of Weber's text through his own work on some of the problems fruitfully discussed by Weber in *Wirtschaft und Gesellschaft,* notably the problem of legitimacy.[6] Winckelmann proposed a rearrangement of Weber's text based on a learned and acute analysis of the first three editions of the printed German text, but without access to the original manuscript. In 1948 he published an article[7] cogently demonstrating the errors of arrangement in the edition of 1922 and proposing a new and more satisfactory disposition of the text, using not only all the printed text of the *Wirtschaft und Gesellschaft* but suggesting supplementation by various articles or portions of other books. This article closed with a plea for a new edition of *Wirtschaft und Gesellschaft,* based on his suggestions, so that Weber's original intention in writing this work might become evident despite the apparent fragmentariness of the text—a fragmentariness which Winckelmann demonstrated to be the responsibility of those in charge of the publication of the first three editions, not the responsibility of Weber. In his plea for a new edition, Winckelmann also showed the need for a careful editing of the text and for correction of the numerous misprints, occasionally of a gravely misleading character.

To their great credit, Weber's publishers, J. B. Mohr (Siebeck) at Tübingen, thereupon commissioned a new edition, with Dr. Johannes Winckelmann as editor. This new edition was published in 1956, again in two quarto volumes.[8] Winckelmann's plan for the reorganization and improvement of the text was sketched in his aforementioned article and

---

[6] Johannes Winckelmann, *Legitimät und Legalität in Max Webers Herrschaftssoziologie,* 1952. Subsequently, Winckelmann worked on the application of this approach to constitutional questions, as in his article "De erfassungsrechtliche Unterscheidung vom Legitimät und Legalität," which appeared in *Zeitschrift für die gesamte Staatswissenschaft,* 1956 (112), p. 164-175.

[7] Johannes Winckelmann, "Max Webers Opus Posthumum: Eine literarische Studie," in *Zeitschrift für die gesamte Staatswissenschaft* (105), 1948-49, pp. 368-387.

[8] In the interim Winckelmann had edited a revised edition of Weber's *Gesammelte Aufsätze zur Wissenschaftslehre,* 1951. In 1956, the year of publication of the new edition of *Wirtschaft und Gesellschaft,* Winckelmann also published two useful anthologies of Weber's major works: *Max Weber: Soziologie, Weltgeschichtliche Analysen, Politik* (a pocket anthology of Weber's major works in the *Kroners Taschenausgaben* series) and *Staatssoziologie: Soziologi des rationalen Staates und die modernen politischen Parteien und Parlan ente* (an anthology of Weber's works on the sociology of the state and politics).

is summarized in his preface to the new fourth edition.[9] It is sufficient for us here to note that he places the chapters on economic, ethnic, and religious relations and associations earlier in the text than in previous editions, while placing the material on the sociology of authority and domination last. In the new edition the title is also changed to read *Wirtschaft und Gesellschaft: Grundriss der verstehenden Soziologie* (*Economics and Society: Foundations of Interpretive Sociology*), thus omitting any indication in the title that the treatise was once a part of the great collaborative series *Grundriss der Sozialökonomik*. Winckelmann has also edited the entire text, diligently compiled a complete itemization of errata,[10] and corrected misprints and errors in the text, so that we now have at hand a far more reliable text than was available before. He has also prepared a table showing the comparative placement of the materials in the various editions, and he has made a beginning in the colossal task of supplying notes for this ponderous treatise. Moreover, he has filled in the long section on the sociology of the state (Chaper IX, Section 8) with materials drawn from other of Weber's writings which dealt with the same problems though in a more polemic than systematic fashion, notably *Parliament und Regierung im neugeordneten Deutschland,* the *Wirtschaftsgeschichte,* and the essay *Politik als Beruf.* Finally, he has enlarged and improved the index.[11]

[9] Cf. also his review of an English language translation of that portion of the *Wirtschaft und Gesellschaft* which deals with Weber's sociology of law (*Max Weber: On Law in Economics and Society,* edited by Max Rheinstein) in *Zeitschrift für die gesamte Staatswissenschaft,* 1956 (112), pp. 180-184.

[10] Misprints were noted as early as O. Hintze's review of *Wirtschaft und Gesellschaft,* 2nd ed., which appeared in *Schmollers Jhb.* (50), 1926, pp. 83-95, itemizing a considerable list of errata. For Winckelmann's compilation of errata in earlier editions, see *Wirtschaft und Gesellschaft,* 4th ed., Volume II, pp. 929-948.

[11] Winckelmann has thus far produced the following revised editions of Weber's works or anthologies from them: *Wirtschaftsgeschichte,* 3rd ed., enlarged, 1958. *Gesammelte Aufsatze zur Wissenschaftslehre,* 2nd ed., 1951, (third edition is in preparation). *Wirtschaft und Gesellschaft: Grundriss der verstehenden Soziologie,* 4th and revised edition. *Staatssoziologie: Soziologie des rationalen Staates und der modernen politischen Parteien und Parlamente,* 1956. *Max Weber: Soziologie, Weltgeschichtliche Analysen, Politik,* edited and annotated by J. Winckelmann, with introduction by Eduard Baumgarten (*Kröners Taschenausgeben,* No. 229), 1956; 2nd ed., 1959. *Gesammelte Politische Schriften,* 2nd and enlarged edition with introduction by Theodor Heuss, 1958. *Rechtssoziologie,* from Weber's manuscript with introductions by J. Winckelmann, *Soziologische Texte,* Bd. 2, 1960. *Soziologische Grundbegriffe*: reprint from *Wirtschaft und Gesellschaft,* Part 1, 1960.

Yet the editor of the new edition, after discussing textual emendations and improvements, ends by drawing attention anew to the incompleteness of the work.

Even the improved new fourth edition of the *Wirtschaft und Gesellschaft* presents formidable textual and interpretive difficulties. The typography still does little to ease the burden of reading the rarified theoretical sections at the beginning and the convoluted presentation of great masses of descriptive material in later sections. The proliferation of historical examples and excursive digressions, on massive quarto pages, constitutes a verbal inundation which is interrupted by but few paragraph dikes. Much of the material might have gone into properly organized notes, which the treatise lacks almost completely, in contrast to the richly documented essays on the sociology of religion (now assembled in the *Gesammelte Aufsätze zur Religionssoziologie*). Indeed, *Wirtschaft und Gesellschaft* contains no citations or identifications whatever—either for quotations from religious scriptures or for references to the writings of social scientists.

Moreover, the discrepancies between the earlier methodological sections and the later descriptive sections of the treatise persist in the fourth edition. The descriptive chapters were for the most part composed between 1911 and 1913, either before or concomitantly with the composition of the important methodological essay, which first appeared in 1913.[12] However, the categories that appear in the first few chapters of *Wirtschaft und Gesellschaft* were worked out after 1918, and Weber did not live to rework the descriptive materials, including the section on the sociology of religion, in accordance with the new categories.

It appears from Winckelmann's analysis of the text and of various preliminary versions of portions of it, from Weber's announcements of forthcoming sections, from the outlines of Weber's lectures given at Munich University while he was working on the treatise, and from certain references in Marianne Weber's *Lebensbild* that Weber had intended to divide his treatise into two distinct portions. The first was to have been a typological sociological summary of concepts or categories. The second was to have been a descriptive part analyzing the structural forms of communal or societal actions and interpreting the evolution of concrete social institutions and forces, especially in relation to economics. Yet the actual work focuses upon the empirically acting social person rather than upon a doctrine of social forms. The

[12] Max Weber, "Uber einige Kategorien der verstehenden Soziologie," *Logos* (IV), 1913, p. 253ff, now in *Wissenschaftslehre*, 2nd edition, pp. 427ff.

work reflects Weber's rejection of the view that there can be collective social personalities. It is amply clear in the reorganized new edition that the first part of the treatise is a summary of sociological categories, while the main portion of the treatise is an analysis of economic phenomena and their interrelations with social institutions and forces. The central concern of Weber's sociology, as an "interpretive" study of social actions, is with relationships between economic factors and social institutions. The conceptualization in the later, descriptive portions of the *Wirtschaft und Gesellschaft* corresponds to the positions expressed in Weber's aforementioned methodological essay of 1913. But in these descriptive sections, such as the one dealing with the sociology of religion here translated into English, the terminology was simplified by Weber.

Index

Absolution, lxiii, 153, 188, 190
Acosmism, 136, 163, 175–176, 195, 226–227, 236, 273
Adiaphoron, 199
Adultery, 192, 239–241
Aetolians, 19, 80
Agriculture, 57, 81, 93, 172
Ahimsa, lxvi, 83, 106
Ahura-mazda, 66
Aisymnete, 49–51
Alexander, 69, 122, 127
Alienation, xlviii–xlix, lv, 12, 157, 166, 172
Allah, 143, 203–204, 264
Alms, 212–213, 220–221
Analogy, 9–10
Anarchism, 126, 228, 232
Anglicanism, 64, 221
Animism, 2, 4, 8–9, 32, 40, 56, 58, 67–68, 82, 85, 95, 110, 146, 157, 210, 232, 236, 240
Anselm of Canterbury, 179
Anthropolatry, 102, 268
Anthropology, xxx, xxxvi, xxxvii, xxxviii
Anthropomorphism, 10, 25, 33, 35, 199
Antinomianism, 174, 197–198
Anti-rationality, 196
Apollo, 35, 63, 99
Apologists, 130
Apostasy, 164
Apostles, 48, 60, 62, 66, 186, 213, 260
Aquinas, Thomas, 83, 232, 235
Arabs, 53, 71, 248, 255
Arminians, 92
Art, lxiv, 97–98, 166, 183, 196; imperialistic, 103; in India, 103, 245;

magical, 55; and religion, 8, 242–245, 257; Roman, 180
Arte de Calimala, 92, 219
Artisans, 95–100, 129, 249, 253, 268–269
Ascetic, 225, 268; and divine blessing, 174; and ethical action, 171; as reformer or revolutionary, 166; worldly, 168
Asceticism, lxi, lxvi–lxvii, 2, 44, 64, 89, 105, 111, 115, 122–123, 125, 133, 136, 141, 162, 164, 166–183, 188, 193–194, 199–200, 205, 218, 233, 236–238, 240, 243–247, 256, 258; Benedictine, 181; charismatic, 237; Christian, 239; Hindu, 181, 239; inner-worldly, lxi–lxiii, 114, 166–168, 173, 183, 220, 226–227, 229, 257, 266; and Islam, 263, 265–266; lay, 118; middle-class, 205; other-worldly, lxii, trans-worldly, 198; values of, 167; world-rejecting, 166, 169–170. *See also* Protestantism
Asia, 83, 126, 132, 144, 177, 181, 269
Astrology, 8, 22, 184
Atharva Veda, 27, 77
Atonement, 57, 145, 185, 189
Authoritarianism, 52, 84
Authority, 188, 204, 233; biblical, 190, 219; charismatic, xxiii, 190; divine, 106; doctrinal, 176; of institution, 194; political, lxviii, 64, 87, 118, 224, 229–230; priestly, 73; religious, 194; secular, 230; sociological, 284; of state, 231

Babylonia, 22, 118–119, 123, 215, 248; merchant princes of, 91;